The Evangelical
Tradition in America

edited by
LEONARD I. SWEET

MERCER
UNIVERSITY PRESS

ISBN 0-86554-092-6

The Evangelical Tradition in America
Copyright ©1984 by Mercer University Press
Macon, Georgia 31207
All rights reserved
Produced in the United States of America

Library of Congress Cataloging in Publication Data

Main entry under title:

The Evangelical tradition in America.

   Includes bibliographical references.
   1. Evangelicalism—United States—Addresses, essays,
lectures.   I. Sweet, Leonard I.
BR1642.U5E89   1984   280'.4'0973   84-6723
ISBN 0-876654-092-6

Table of Contents

Preface

On 16-24 October 1981, a "Finney Festival" was held in Rochester, New York, commemorating the sesquicentennial of Charles G. Finney's 1830-1831 Rochester Revival, called by Lyman Beecher "the greatest work of God and the greatest revival of religion the world has ever seen in so short a time." The essays in this volume (except the first one) were delivered at a segment of the Finney Festival, a historical conference on American Evangelicalism, that was held on 16-17 October at Colgate Rochester Divinity School/Bexley Hall/Crozer Theological Seminary.

This volume was conceived in the context of demanding if not almost contradictory intentions. One was to celebrate Rochester's unique heritage as a center of the "burned-over district," as witnessed by Finney's first Rochester Revival, and to educate the Rochester community about the significance of its past. The other was to gather historians working on the evangelical tradition together to stimulate each other's scholarship and report on their own. An astute account of how we fared in our twin objectives can be found in Paul D. Vanas's "Rochester Observes its Finney Sesquicentennial," *Oberlin Alumni Magazine* 78 (Winter 1982): 22-27.

It was not the aim of the historical conference (or the volume projected from it) to cover the whole territory encompassing the evangelical tradition in America. Rather, the end of our efforts was to reflect the emerging scholarship of younger historians writing in the field and to evidence generally the current division of historical labor and the direction of American religious historiography.

Since the audience for the historical conference was composed both of those within and outside the profession, the presenters faced a challenge that they met with grace and good humor. In their public lectures, which were often variant versions of the papers that circulated among the historians, Jon Butler, Albert Raboteau, Nathan Hatch, Carroll Smith-Rosenberg, Nancy Hewitt, Henry Bowden, Garth Rosell, Paul Johnson, Joel Carpenter, and Grant Wacker proved themselves faithful to the seriousness of the discipline while being flexible for the occasion.

Those who served as commentators—Stanley L. Engerman, Robert T. Handy, Judith Wellman, Timothy L. Smith, and George Marsden—and as chairpersons for the various sessions—Joseph W. Barnes, Susan M. Stuard, William H. Siles, and William H. Brackney—deserve our gratitude for the way they enlivened our proceedings and enlightened us all. We are especially thankful for the historians who came from across the country and made this conference part of their continuing education.

The historical conference of the Finney Festival was funded largely with a grant from the Lilly Endowment, although the festival could not have been pulled together without aid from Colgate Rochester Divinity School/Bexley Hall/Crozer Theological Seminary, Auburn Theological Seminary, and the Monroe Foundation. I am especially indebted to Robert Lynn, Leon Pacala, Larry Greenfield, Barbara Wheeler, and Harley Rittenhouse for their advocacy of this project. Another important line of support came from the staff here at the Divinity School. Cynthia Snodgrass helped to impose some sense of consistency on the footnote citations of the various authors, and Mary Beth Curtin pulled together the manuscripts and typed them with the excellence and cheer we have come to take for granted.

Finally, a word of appreciation goes out to the members of the Finney Festival Board who planned and organized the various activities of the festival, including the historical conference. Under the leadership of our president, Alma H. Fewster, and our treasurer, Norman Leenhouts, representatives from the academy as well as a cross section of scholars from various ecclesiastical, theological, and ethnic traditions worked with a diligent and congenial spirit to help this event come to pass. To them— Edward C. Atwater, Robert E. Barr, Jr., Eugene C. Bay, Vincent A. Buzard, James Connolly, James C. Miller, L. Dayton Reynolds, William T.

Showalter, James M. Stewart, John E. Stoller, Susan Stuard, Helen Telfer, Charles Thurman, Thomas H. Troeger, Carroll Turner, Robert M. Wainwright, and the committee's unofficial secretary, Connie Johnston—belongs the honor of this publication.

Chapter 1

The Evangelical Tradition in America

Leonard I. Sweet

There are three indisputable facts about the evangelical tradition in America. First, it is important. Second, it is understudied. Third, it is diverse. William G. McLoughlin's introduction to an anthology on representative Evangelicals argues convincingly that it would be as difficult to unscramble a mixed omelette as to separate Evangelicalism from nineteenth-century American culture. He begins with the famous words: "The story of American Evangelicalism is the story of America itself in the years 1800 to 1900," and ends similarly, "To understand it is to understand the whole temper of American life in the nineteenth century."[1] Donald G. Mathews has arrived at similar conclusions about Southern Evangelicalism. It was "the single most influential strain of religious ac-

---

[1]William G. McLoughlin, ed., *The American Evangelicals, 1800-1900: An Anthology* (New York: Harper Torchbooks, 1968) 1:26. These twenty-six pages are still the best single, short introduction to the subject of Evangelicalism.

tivity in the South during the formative years before 1860."[2] When the importance of the evangelical tradition to American history is coupled with the emergence since the 1940s of the "new Evangelicalism," one is in agreement with Martin E. Marty at the "paucity of good research" through the end of the 1970s and at the absence of "more vitality in historical fields surrounding it."[3] Unlike the Puritan tradition, which as a movement has been the focus of extensive critical debate, our understanding of Evangelicalism has by and large been shaped incidentally, almost as a tangent of historical inquiry.

Fortunately, things are beginning to change. The last couple of years have witnessed numerous worthwhile studies, with many more forthcoming. Thanks to the persistence of Timothy L. Smith, historians are increasingly inclined to see many traditions, movements, and theologies within Evangelicalism. This essay calls attention to some studies published since 1970 that elucidate the evangelical tradition. It also examines the present historiographical scene, its major areas of controversy, and historians' stand on the significance of Evangelicalism in American history. The study of history is all too often the study of the latest historiographical trend, but the historiographical essay is perhaps best suited to introduce the essays in this collection.

The elusive nature of Evangelicalism's origins is perhaps one reason for the lack of sharper definitions and crisp interpretations in the field of evangelical studies. Those who trace Evangelicalism's lineage give prompt attention to the movement's theological origins. Gordon Allport once said that psychologists never solve problems, they only get bored

---

[2]Donald G. Mathews, *Religion in the Old South* (Chicago: University of Chicago Press, 1977) xiv.

[3]Martin E. Marty, "The Editor's Bookshelf: American Religious History," *The Journal of Religion* 62 (January 1982): 102. A surprising omission from Marty's survey of works published between 1974 and 1979, especially since the book appeared in Marty's own excellent series entitled "Chicago History of American Religion," is Mathews's *Religion in the Old South*. For comprehensive bibliographical essays on American religion, see Edwin S. Gaustad, Darlene Miller, and G. Allison Stokes, "Religion in America," *American Quarterly* 31 (Bibliography Issue 1979): 250-83 and Dewey D. Wallace, Jr., "Recent Publications on American Religious History: A Bibliographical Essay and Review," *American Studies International* 19 (Spring-Summer 1981): 15-42. Mark A. Noll has an excellent bibliographical essay on seven books relating to "Protestant Theology and Social Order in Antebellum America" in *Religious Studies Review* 8 (April 1982): 133-42.

with them. The problem of Evangelicalism's origins in America has not been solved, and scholars seem bored with the question. However, this is one problem that will not allow serious historians to remain bored for long.

Some studies begin Evangelicalism with the Second Great Awakening and rapid denominational growth on the frontier.[4] Others begin with Evangelicalism as simply an exuberant and at times exclamatory purveyor of Reformation themes like *sola scriptura*, *sola gratia*, and *sola fide*.[5] The majority stand with Sydney E. Ahlstrom in accenting the Puritan ancestry of Evangelicalism, with various developments within Puritanism claiming distinction as sources of the American evangelical tradition. Philip Greven lobbies for psychological pressures within the family generated by the structures of American Puritanism.[6] William K. B. Stoever isolates covenant theology's dialectic of nature and grace that maintained a "taut harmony" between a "frankly flattering" view of human faculties and a strong insistence on divine sovereignty.[7] Ahlstrom supports the doctrine of election and the problem of assurance.[8]

The two scholars who have analyzed most systematically the development of Evangelicalism (James W. Jones and Richard F. Lovelace) have worked up from Puritanism rather than back from the Second Great Awakening. With considerable analytic vigor Jones reconstructs the seventeenth-century "synthesis" that New England Puritanism sustained between the sovereignty of God and human responsibility. The break-

---

[4]Milton C. Sernett's interest is more in the character of Evangelicalism during the national era than in its roots in the first chapter of *Black Religion and American Evangelicalism: White Protestants, Plantation Missions and the Flowering of Negro Christianity, 1787-1865* (Metuchen NJ: Scarecrow Press, 1975).

[5]John H. Gerstner, "The Theological Boundaries of Evangelical Faith" in *The Evangelicals: What They Believe, Who They Are, Where They Are Changing*, ed. David F. Wells and John D. Woodbridge (Nashville: Abingdon, 1975) 21-37.

[6]Philip J. Greven, *The Protestant Temperament: Patterns of Child-Rearing, Religious Experience, and the Self in Early America* (New York: Knopf, 1977).

[7]William K. B. Stoever, *'A Faire and Easie Way to Heaven': Covenant Theology and Antinomianism in Early Massachusetts* (Middletown CT: Wesleyan University Press, 1978) 184-89.

[8]Sydney E. Ahlstrom, "From Puritanism to Evangelicalism: A Critical Perspective," in *The Evangelicals*, ed. Wells and Woodbridge, 272, 269-89.

down of this tenuous balance, which Jones argues had already led to the splitting of Puritanism into evangelical and liberal wings, was confirmed by the Great Awakening.[9] The Puritan origins of Evangelicalism have been deftly explored in Richard F. Lovelace's study of Cotton Mather. Lovelace stresses the "loading" of the conversion experience in both Puritanism and Evangelicalism, and this leads him into some judicious insights about Evangelicalism's transatlantic dimensions, the "kindred experiential movements" of Puritanism and Pietism, the development of an evangelical spirituality, and Mather's role as the "John the Baptist of the coming revivalism."[10]

Another sizeable segment of scholarship traces the theological roots of Evangelicalism either to "Evangelical Calvinists" like the Tennents and Samuel Davies, who are seen as transitional figures in moving American Christianity from the federal theology of the seventeenth century to the Evangelicalism of the nineteenth, or to New Divinity theologians like Samuel Hopkins, whose theology is viewed as a form of "democratic evangelicalism" and as the "bridge between the still recognizably Puritan outlook of Edwards and nineteenth-century American Protestantism."[11] William G. McLoughlin's student, Joseph A. Conforti, sees New Divinity as an extension of the Great Awakening's evangelical Calvinism, thereby downplaying the Arminian components to early nineteenth-cen-

---

[9]James W. Jones, *The Shattered Synthesis: New England Puritanism Before the Great Awakening* (New Haven: Yale University Press, 1973).

[10]Richard F. Lovelace, *The American Pietism of Cotton Mather: Origins of American Evangelicalism* (Grand Rapids: Christian University Press, 1979). For the recent rediscovery of Cotton Mather by historians, see Lovelace's superb bibliographical essay on 290-304, which is listed as an appendix. For nonsociological, nonpsychological studies of the conversion phenomenon in American religion, see N. Ray Hiner, "Preparing For the Harvest: The Concept of New Birth and the Theory of Religious Education on the Eve of the First Awakening," *Fides et Historia* 9 (Fall 1976): 8-25; Jerald C. Brauer, "Conversion: From Puritanism to Revivalism," *Journal of Religion* 58 (July 1978): 227-43. A pathbreaking study of the process of deconversion can be found in Lewis Perry, *Childhood, Marriage and Reform* (Chicago: University of Chicago Press, 1980).

[11]Glenn T. Miller, "God's Light and Man's Enlightenment: Evangelical Theology of Colonial Presbyterianism," *Journal of Presbyterian History* 51 (Summer 1973): 97-115; Sydney E. Ahlstrom, *A Religious History of the American People* (New Haven: Yale University Press, 1972) 405.

tury Evangelicalism.[12] Whereas Conforti interprets New Divinity as a social (and lay) as much as a theological (and clerical) response to the
emerging social realities of the late colonial, early national period, Stephen E. Berk, a student of Sidney Mead, contends that the evangelical
movement known as the Second Great Awakening arrived irrespective of
the consistent Calvinists, all of whom are interpreted as saboteurs of the
Edwardsean Evangelicalism of the First Great Awakening. For Berk, if
the consistent Calvinists could boast theological rigor, it was the rigor of
mortis. They were out of touch with their times through meaningless content and meanness of spirit. It was Timothy Dwight who sired the true
spirit of Evangelicalism, Berk insists, imposing upon it a characteristic
conservative cast that promptly manifested itself in the ways evangelical
activism was employed to fight Jeffersonian democracy.[13]

Lovelace's de-emphasis of Edwards as the theological progenitor of
American Evangelicalism finds corroboration in other studies. Frank
Shuffleton pushes experiential piety and evangelical ministry back from
Edwards to Thomas Hooker.[14] Norman Fiering, who writes with all the
intimacy of a historian immersed in the sources, relates Edwards's
thoughts on ethics to an international setting and calls Edwards an
"anomaly in the mid-eighteenth century."[15] Mark A. Noll presents a devastating dismissal of Edwardsean Calvinists as "mutants in the evolution
of American theology . . . condemned to the intellectual insignificance of
those who have proven themselves unfit for the American environment
by failing to survive." The theological ancestors of those who endorsed
the Second Great Awakening were those who opposed the First Great

---

[12]Joseph A. Conforti, *Samuel Hopkins and the New Divinity Movement* (Grand Rapids:
Christian University Press, 1981). See also Conforti, "Samuel Hopkins and the New Divinity: Theology, Ethics, and Social Reform in Eighteenth-Century New England," *William and Mary Quarterly* 34 (October 1977): 572-89.

[13]Stephen E. Berk, *Calvinism versus Democracy: Timothy Dwight and the Origins of
American Evangelical Orthodoxy* (Hamden CT: Archon Books, 1974).

[14]Frank Shuffleton, *Thomas Hooker, 1586-1647* (Princeton: Princeton University
Press, 1977).

[15]Norman Fiering, *Jonathan Edwards' Moral Thought and Its British Context* (Chapel
Hill: University of North Carolina Press, 1981). See also Fiering's extensive "Bibliographical Note" (371-79) for recent studies of Edwards.

Awakening, Noll concludes after he proceeds from Puritanism to Evangelicalism via the antirevivalists.[16]

Some scholars object to an exaggerated concern with Puritanism in exploring the roots of Evangelicalism. Jerald C. Brauer, who prefers "revivalism" to "evangelicalism" in describing eighteenth-century religious developments, assents equally to Puritanism and Pietism.[17] McLoughlin finds the origins of the evangelical tradition in pietistic strands within Puritanism.[18] But the Pietist connection is presented most forcefully, though unsystematically, by F. Ernest Stoeffler's collection of essays on *Continental Pietism and Early American Christianity* (1976). A common acknowledgment that American Evangelicalism is primarily indebted to the Pietist tradition, which originated in Europe but flourished in America, ties together the contributions to this anthology. Pietistic themes of experiential religion, hymnody, Biblicism, separation of church and state, evangelizing, and social conscience contributed significantly, it is asserted, to the development of an evangelical pattern in American Protestantism.[19]

With the theological lineage of Evangelicalism so multilateral, perhaps Winthrop S. Hudson was on target when he described Evangelicalism as less a "theological system" than a spirit or temperament that swept through both camps of consistent and moderate Calvinism and that was part of an international movement of experiential religion.[20] "From the

---

[16]Mark A. Noll, "Moses Mather (Old Calvinist) and the Evolution of Edwardeanism," *Church History* 49 (September 1980): 281, 273-85.

[17]Brauer, "Conversion: From Puritanism to Revivalism," 227-43.

[18]William G. McLoughlin, "Pietism and the American Character," *American Quarterly* 17 (Summer 1965): 163-86.

[19]F. Ernest Stoeffler, *Continental Pietism and Early American Christianity* (Grand Rapids: Eerdmans, 1976).

[20]Winthrop S. Hudson, *Religion in America* (Third edition, rev.; New York: Charles Scribner's Sons, 1981) 135-36. Ian Bradley has argued that "Evangelicalism was never really a theological system as much as a way of life" in *The Call to Seriousness* (New York: Macmillan Co., 1976) 22. Evangelicalism as a "mood" is also stressed by Bruce Shelley, *Evangelicalism in America* (Grand Rapids: William B. Eerdmans, 1967) 7, and Robert S. Ellwood, Jr., *One Way: The Jesus Movement and Its Meaning* (Englewood Cliffs NJ: Prentice-Hall, 1973) 25. See also Joe I. Kincheloe, Jr., "European Roots of Evangelical Revivalism: Methodist Transmission of the Pietistic Socio-Religious Tradition," *Methodist History* 18 (July 1980): 262-71.

time of the Puritans until Dwight D. Moody," George Marsden has reminded us, "British and American Evangelicalism was, to some extent,
part of a single transatlantic movement."[21] One reason for the obscurity
of Evangelicalism's origins is that we have not taken the international dimension seriously enough.

The influence of Evangelicalism on politics has been most fully explored in eighteenth-century studies, thanks partly to the steady impact
created by Alan Heimert's *Religion and the American Mind* (1966), a monumental work written with authority and cited by John F. Berens as "one
of the most important and controversial books written in the twentieth
century on the American Revolution."[22] Heimert's thesis connected the
American Revolution with the Great Awakening in general and in particular with Jonathan Edwards's evangelical theology and aesthetics.[23] Heimert has remained strangely silent since the book's publication, and has
even seen the accuracy of his sources doubted by some scholars.[24] But
every historian writing on religion and revolution in colonial America
feels a need to engage many of the same questions as Heimert.

The Great Awakening is a subject about which we know both too
much and too little. A voluminous amount of literature has accumulated
detailing various local and regional features of the Awakening, one of the
most covered areas of American religious historiography, including
throat distemper, an outbreak of ergotism, and a diphtheria epidemic that

---

[21]George M. Marsden, *Fundamentalism and American Culture: The Shaping of Twentieth Century Evangelicalism, 1870-1925* (New York: Oxford University Press, 1980) 222.

[22]Alan Heimert, *Religion and the American Mind: From the Great Awakening to the
American Revolution* (Cambridge: Harvard University Press, 1966); John F. Berens, "Religion and Revolution Reconsidered: Recent Literature on Religion and Nationalism in
Eighteenth-Century America," *Canadian Review of Studies in Nationalism* 6 (Fall 1979):
235, 233-45.

[23]For recent reaffirmations of both these positions, see the slackly argued thesis relating evangelical piety to Aaron Burr's republican ideology by Suzanne Geissler, *Jonathan
Edwards to Aaron Burr, Jr.: From the Great Awakening to Democratic Politics* (New York:
Edwin Mellen, 1981), and the study by Roland A. Delattre, "Beauty and Politics: A Problematic Legacy of Jonathan Edwards" in *American Philosophy: From Edwards to Quine*,
ed. Robert W. Shahan and Kenneth R. Merrill (Norman OK: University of Oklahoma
Press, 1977): 20-49.

[24]James West Davidson, "Searching for the Millennium: Problems for the 1790's and
the 1970's," *New England Quarterly* 45 (June 1972): 241-61.

created what its interpreter calls a "Little Great Awakening."[25] Furthermore, in the immediate aftermath of Heimert's sweeping interpretation
of the continuity of evangelical religion in the formation of revolutionary
ideals in eighteenth-century America, a number of historians have refused to cooperate in approaching the Great Awakening as a genesis for
the Revolution, with all the attendant discussions of incipient nationalism, accelerating Americanization, Jeffersonian republicanism, and the
economic and political dimensions of the relationship between religion
and revolution. Instead, they study the Great Awakening as a religious
phenomenon of significance in and of itself;[26] or they shift their focus from
a New Light center to the Separatist fringes or from a religious center to
examine the Awakening within the context of socioeconomic developments, especially local patterns of education, geography, demography,
ethnic interaction, migration and mobility, the overall "localist impulse"
in shaping the revival, and family and political connections;[27] or they

[25]Mary K. Matossian, "Religious Revivals and Ergotism in America," *Clio Medica* 16
(Spring 1982): 185-92; Michael N. Shute, "A Little Great Awakening: An Episode in the
American Enlightenment," *Journal of the History of Ideas* 37 (October-December 1976):
589-602.

[26]Milton J. Coalter, "The Radical Pietism of Count Nicholas Zinzendorf as a Conservative Influence on the Awakener, Gilbert Tennent," *Church History* 49 (March 1980):
35-46; Charles Berryman, *From Wilderness to Wasteland: The Trial of the Puritan God in
the American Imagination* (Port Washington NY: Kennikat Press, 1979) 39-66; Dale D.
Schmitt, "Preparation for the Great Awakening in Connecticut," *Religion in Life* 47 (Winter 1978): 430-40; Hiner, "Preparing for the Harvest," 8-25. For the Great Awakening as
a "professional crisis" among the clergy, see James W. Schmotter, "The Irony of Clerical
Professionalism: New England's Congregational Ministers and the Great Awakening,"
American Quarterly 31 (Summer 1979): 148-68.

[27]Peter S. Onuf, "New Light in New London: A Group Portrait of the Separatists,"
William and Mary Quarterly 37 (October 1980): 627-43; Harry S. Stout and Peter Onuf,
"James Davenport and the Great Awakening in New London," *Journal of American His-
tory* 71 (December 1983): 556-78; Richard Warch, "The Shepherd's Tent: Education and
Enthusiasm in the Great Awakening," *American Quarterly* 30 (Summer 1978): 177-98;
James Walsh, "The Great Awakening in the First Congregational Church of Woodbury,
Connecticut," *William and Mary Quarterly* 28 (October 1971): 543-62; J. M. Bumsted,
"Religion, Finance, and Democracy in Massachusetts: The Town of Norton as a Case
Study," *Journal of American History* 57 (March 1971): 817-31; Gerald F. Moran, "Con-
ditions of Religious Conversion in the First Society of Norwich, Connecticut, 1718-
1744," *Journal of Social History* 5 (Spring 1972): 331-43; John B. Frantz, "The Awakening of Religion among the German Settlers in the Middle Colonies," ibid., 33 (April
1976): 266-88; Ned Landsman, "Revivalism and Nativism in the Middle Colonies: The

characterize the Awakening as an "emotional firestorm" charged with enough heat to weld together an "intercolonial movement;"[28] or they conduct a psychological analysis of the Awakening, with special attention given to generational conflict and young men's coming of age.[29]

Some of the greatest interpretive advances have been made by scholars adopting a sharper tone of inquiry into the various "sides" of the Awakening. Elizabeth I. Nybakken has provided some well-focused "New Light on the Old Side," evidence that the opponents of the revivals are beginning to receive historians' respect.[30] The Great Awakening also

Great Awakening and the Scots Community in East New Jersey," *American Quarterly* 34 (Summer 1982): 149-64; Martin E. Lodge, "The Crisis of the Churches in the Middle Colonies, 1720-1750," *Pennsylvania Magazine of History and Biography* 95 (April 1971): 195-220; Gerald F. Loren, "Conditions of Religious Conversion in the First Society of Norwich, Connecticut, 1718-1744," *Journal of Social History* 5 (Spring 1972): 331-41; William F. Willingham, "Religious Conversion and the Second Society of Windham, Connecticut, 1723-1743: A Case Study," *Societas* 6 (Spring 1976): 109-19; William F. Willingham, "The Conversion Experience During the Great Awakening in Windham, Connecticut," *Connecticut History* 21 (January 1980): 34-61; Philip J. Greven, Jr., *Four Generations: Population, Land, and Family in Colonial Andover, Massachusetts* (Ithaca NY: Cornell University Press, 1970); Kenneth A. Lockridge, *Settlement and Unsettlement in Early America: The Crisis of Political Legitimacy before the Revolution* (New York: Cambridge University Press, 1981); and John W. Jeffries, "The Separation in the Canterbury Congregational Church: Religion, Family, and Politics in a Connecticut Town," *New England Quarterly* 52 (December 1979): 522-49.

[28]Estelle F. Feinstein, *Stamford from Puritan to Patriot: The Shaping of a Connecticut Community, 1641-1774* (1976); Richard Hofstadter, *America at 1750: A Social Portrait* (New York: Knopf, 1971).

[29]Richard L. Bushman, "Jonathan Edwards as Great Man," *Encounter with Erikson: Historical Interpretation and Religious Biography*, ed. Donald Capps, Walter H. Capps, and M. Gerald Bradford (Missoula MT: Scholars Press, 1977): 217-52; Cushing Strout, "Young People of the Great Awakening: The Dynamics of a Social Movement," ibid., 183-216; and Cushing Strout, "Fathers and Sons: Notes on 'New Light' and 'New Left' Young People as a Historical Comparison," *Psychohistory Review* 6 (Fall/Winter 1977-1978): 25-31. The importance of youth and rites of passage in the Revolution is highlighted by Peter Shaw, *American Patriots and the Rituals of Revolution* (Cambridge: Harvard University Press, 1981).

[30]Elizabeth I. Nybakken, "New Light on the Old Side: Irish Influences on Colonial Presbyterians," *Journal of American History* 68 (March 1982): 813-32. Also see Douglas C. Stenerson, "An Anglican Critique of the Early Phase of the Great Awakening in New England: A Letter by Timothy Cutler," *William and Mary Quarterly* 30 (July 1973): 475-88; Charles H. Lippy, *Seasonable Revolutionary: The Mind of Charles Chauncey* (Chicago: Nelson-Hall, 1981).

gave birth to "Radical Evangelicals" who began to fray the Calvinist tradition from within, a feature Stephen A. Marini has discovered in his comparative look at religious sects in rural New England during the Revolutionary era.[31] The New-Side/Old-Side or Calvinist/Liberal dichotomies and ways of discussing the Awakening seem particularly simplistic to scholars like J. M. Bumsted, John E. Van de Wetering, Milton J. Coalter, David Harlan, Nathan O. Hatch, and especially Catherine L. Albanese, who pushes previous historiography to the side in her dismissal of attempts to define a relationship between religion and the American Revolution and instead delineates the Revolution as "in itself a religious experience" on which Americans built their civil religion.[32]

By far the most animated scholarly discussions, however, have explored the relationship between the Great Awakening and the American Revolution.[33] Heimert both continues to set our agenda, and ends up gen-

---

[31]Stephen A. Marini, *Radical Sects of Revolutionary New England* (Cambridge: Harvard University Press, 1982). Also see Ross W. Beales, Jr., ed., "Solomon Prentice's Narrative of the Great Awakening," *Massachusetts Historical Society Proceedings* 83 (1971): 130-47.

[32]J. M. Bumsted and John E. Van de Wetering, *What Must I Do To Be Saved? The Great Awakening in Colonial America* (Hinsdale IL: Dryden Press, 1976); David Harlan, *The Clergy and the Great Awakening in New England* (Ann Arbor: UMI Research, 1980); and Coalter, "Radical Pietism of Zinzendorf"; Nathan O. Hatch, *The Sacred Cause of Liberty: Republican Thought and the Millennium in Revolutionary New England* (New Haven: Yale University Press, 1977); Catherine L. Albanese, *Sons of the Fathers: The Civil Religion of the American Revolution* (Philadelphia: Temple University Press, 1976) 6. See also Glenn Miller, "The American Revolution as a Religious Event: An Essay in Political Theology," *Foundations* 19 (April-June 1976): 111-20.

[33]One would have expected the nation's bicentennial celebration in 1976 to generate throughout the decade studies on evangelical religion and the American Revolution. There were a few, mostly detailing the role of religion in the Revolution (Thomas O'Brien Hanley, *The American Revolution and Religion: Maryland 1770-1800* [Washington DC: Catholic University of America Press, 1971]; William G. McLoughlin, "The Role of Religion in the Revolution: Liberty of Conscience and Cultural Cohesion in the New Nation," in *Essays on the American Revolution*, ed. Stephen G. Kurtz and James H. Hutson [Chapel Hill: University of North Carolina Press, 1973] 197-255; Page Smith, ed., *Religious Origins of the American Revolution* [Missoula MT: Scholars Press, 1976]); the ways in which clergy made peace with war (Emory Elliott, "The Dove and the Serpent: The Clergy in the American Revolution," *American Quarterly* 31 [Summer 1979]: 187-203, and Durward T. Stokes, "The Baptist and Methodist Clergy in South Carolina and the American Revolution," *South Carolina Historical Magazine* 73 [April 1973]: 87-96); and the major religious reponses to the Revolution (Mark A. Noll, *Christians in the American Revolution* [Washington DC: Christian University Press, 1977], which contains an ex-

erally the winner, with historians finding it convenient to yoke the two events. Martin E. Marty talks of "two revolutions," the first an inward and spiritual one that made American religion evangelical (i.e., the Great Awakening), and the second an outward and political one that made American society republican (i.e., the American Revolution).[34] In highly influential articles by Rhys Isaac and a powerful study by Gary B. Nash, elements of lower-class social protest and radical revolutionary ideas have been uncovered among Evangelicals. Isaac's employment of the techniques of a cultural anthropologist in understanding pre-Revolutionary Baptists reveals that Evangelicals made significant contributions to revolutionary ideology through support for democracy, freedom of conscience, and popular education in the South.[35] The new system of mass communications developed by Evangelicals through their use of extemporaneous preaching and itinerancy squelched traditional forms of community and challenged aristocratic values and authority, argues Harry S. Stout in one of the more creative essays to appear on the origins of Revolutionary social and political egalitarianism.[36] Other historians put the

---

tremely useful bibliographical essay. See also Noll's essay, "The Christian and the Revolution: Historiographical Pitfalls, Problems and Progress," *Fides et Historia* 8 [Fall 1975]: 2-19, and William G. McLoughlin's "Patriotism and Pietism: The Dissenting Dilemma—Massachusetts Revolutionary Baptists and the American Revolution," *Foundations* 19 [April-June 1976]: 121-46).

[34]Martin E. Marty, *Religion, Awakening and Revolution* (Wilmington NC: Consortium Books, 1977).

[35]Rhys Isaac, "Evangelical Revolt: The Nature of the Baptists' Challenge to the Traditional Order in Virginia, 1765-1775," *William and Mary Quarterly* 31 (July 1974): 345-68; Isaac, "Dramatizing the Ideology of the Revolution: Popular Mobilization—Virginia, 1744 to 1776," ibid., 33 (July 1976): 357-85; Isaac, "Preachers and Patriots: Popular Culture and the Revolution in Virginia," in *The American Revolution: Explorations in the History of American Radicalism*, ed. Alfred F. Young (Dekalb IL: Northern Illinois University Press, 1976) 125-56; Isaac, *The Transformation of Virginia, 1740-1790* (Chapel Hill: University of North Carolina Press, 1982). For similar conclusions about revivalism's effect, especially on Boston, of drawing the attention of the laboring classes to their social and economic distress, see Gary B. Nash, *The Urban Crucible: Social Change, Political Consciousness and the Origins of the American Revolution* (Cambridge: Harvard University Press, 1979).

[36]Harry S. Stout, "Religious Communications, and the Ideological Origins of the American Revolution," *William and Mary Quarterly* 34 (October 1977): 519-41. See also Thomas Bender, *Community and Social Change in America* (New Brunswick NJ: Rutgers University Press, 1978). Patrick Henry's successful adoption of an evangelical style and

Awakening on a long fuse. One contends that the forces of the revival were still strong enough during and after the Revolution to provide a dynamic evangelical presence in America at a time when religion was supposedly in a state of stagnation or decline. In other words, what has typically been periodized into the First and Second Great Awakenings may more properly be seen as part of the same phenomenon. Another uses counterfactual premises to argue that "Without the Great Awakening and its successors, there would have been a revolution in 1775, but in all probability, no Civil War in 1861."[37] David Harlan undermines conventional assumptions about who provided the rationale for revolution in his study of the moderates.[38] And various scholars have stressed the way in which revivalism helped steer America towards a new form of social order characterized by individualism, voluntarism, and democracy, even if Evangelicals were themselves not always disruptive of the social order or successful at displacing traditional authority.[39] In short, there has been strong historical

---

the affinity between the evangelical and patriot movements is detailed in Charles L. Cohen, "The 'Liberty or Death' Speech: A Note on Religion and Revolutionary Rhetoric," *William and Mary Quarterly* 38 (October 1981): 702-17 and Rhys Isaac, "Patrick Henry: Patriot and Preacher?" *Virginia Cavalcade* 31 (Winter 1982): 168-75.

[37]Douglas H. Sweet, "Church Vitality and the American Revolution: Historiographical Consensus and Thoughts Towards a New Perspective," *Church History* 45 (September 1976): 341-57 and John M. Murrin, "No Awakening, No Revolution? More Counterfactual Speculations," *Reviews in American History* 11 (June 1983): 161-71, 169. For the vitality of religion in the post-Revolutionary period, even among Episcopalians, see Frederick V. Mills, Sr., "The Protestant Episcopal Churches in the United States 1783-1789: Suspended Animation or Remarkable Recovery?" *Historical Magazine of the Protestant Episcopal Church* 46 (June 1977): 151-70.

[38]Harlan, *Clergy and the Great Awakening.*

[39]Robert D. Rossell, "The Great Awakening: An Historical Analysis," *American Journal of Sociology* 75 (May 1970): 907-25; Cedric B. Cowing, *The Great Awakening and the American Revolution: Colonial Thought in the 18th Century* (Chicago: Rand McNally, 1971); Jerald C. Brauer, "Puritanism, Revivalism, and Revolution" in *Religion and the American Revolution*, ed. Jerald C. Brauer (Philadelphia: Fortress Press, 1976) 1-28; Rhys Isaac, "Religion and Authority: Problems of the Anglican Establishment in Virginia in the Era of the Great Awakening and the Parsons' Cause," *William and Mary Quarterly* 30 (January 1973): 3-36; Richard R. Beeman and Rhys Isaac, "Cultural Conflict and Social Change in the Revolutionary South: Lunenburg County, Virginia," *Journal of Southern History* 46 (November 1980): 525-50; Michael Greenberg, "Revival, Reform, Revolution: Samuel Davies and the Great Awakening in Virginia," *Marxist Perspectives* 3 (Summer 1980): 102-19.

consensus that the Great Awakening was "the key to the American Revolution."[40]

Just when historians were lulled into thinking everything of significance had been said about religion and revolution in the eighteenth century, an article by Jon Butler appeared proving the accuracy of Bacon's belief that "the opinion of plenty is the cause of want." Butler argues that the study of the Great Awakening remains in a curiously unsatisfying state, overburdened with local studies that assume too much about the larger, overarching event, yet lacking "even one comprehensive general history." Decrying most of the scholarship on the Awakening as uncritical and poorly focused, Butler denies even the existence of a "Great Awakening" throughout the American colonies and argues, along with Elizabeth C. Nordbeck, that the cohesiveness, expansiveness, and consequences of America's pre-Revolutionary revivals have been shamelessly exaggerated.[41] Some unexpected support for Butler's general position comes from Norman Fiering, whose work on the scholastic background of seventeenth-century moral philosophy reveals that the "Great Awakening" may have been nothing more than a relatively late if lively skirmish in the long-standing battle between intellectualists and voluntarists.[42] The link between revivalism and revolution, Butler says, is "virtually nonexistent." Revivals "seldom became pro-revolutionary, and they failed to change the timing, causes, or effects of the Revolution in any significant way." Most historians will probably contend that some of Butler's argument is overdrawn. But the complexity of interactions between

---

[40]William G. McLoughlin, "Enthusiasm for Liberty: The Great Awakening as the Key to the Revolution," in *Preachers and Politicians: Two Essays on the Origins of the American Revolution*, ed. Jack P. Greene and William G. McLoughlin (Worcester MA: American Antiquarian Society, 1977) 47-73.

[41]Jon Butler, "Enthusiasm Described and Decried: The Great Awakening as Interpretive Fiction," *Journal of American History* 69 (September 1982): 305-25; Elizabeth C. Nordbeck, "Almost Awakened: The Great Revival in New Hampshire and Maine, 1727-1748," *Historical New Hampshire* 35 (Spring 1980): 23-58. For the Great Awakening as a movement of "nativistic revival" rather than of unification, see Landsman, "Revivalism and Nativism in the Middle Colonies," 150-51.

[42]Norman Fiering, *Moral Philosophy at Seventeenth-Century Harvard: A Discipline in Transition* (Chapel Hill: University of North Carolina Press, 1981).

pre-Revolutionary revivals and political development should impose caution on the careful historian writing about the Great Awakening.

Two forums have dominated discussions of nineteenth-century evangelical religion and politics. First, the dispute over civil religion, which at its best has argued that a form of popular evangelicalism became virtually the established religion of nineteenth-century America and served to integrate American society. John F. Wilson's obituarizing of the term "civil religion" and christening of the concept "public religion" may be the impetus needed to propel the "civil religion debate" in a more positive direction.[43] Second is the analysis of party identification and religious affiliation. Ronald P. Formisano was one of the first of Lee Benson's students to decisively challenge the class conflict thesis. More important than economic status in determining voting behavior and political affiliation were region of birth and religious preference, a discovery subsequently reinforced by studies of ethnocultural conflict and political alliances.[44] It is one thing, for example, to find that the abolitionist Liberty party enjoyed its most generous support in "burned-over" districts, or even to discuss abolitionism as an ideological corollary of revivalism. It is quite another to posit the simple equation that revivalism produced "political abolitionism" as John L. Hammond has done in a book more widely heralded in sociological than in historical circles.[45] The use of quantitative

---

[43]John F. Wilson, *Public Religion in American Culture* (Philadelphia: Temple University Press, 1979). See also Robert T. Handy's excellent review essay of Wilson's book, *Theology Today* 37 (October 1980): 342-50.

[44]Ronald P. Formisano, *The Birth of Mass Political Parties in Michigan, 1827-1861* (Princeton: Princeton University Press, 1971). Richard Jensen claims that "One of the most accurate ways to determine a [Northeast or Midwest but *not* Southern] voter's choices in the late nineteenth century was to ascertain his religious preferences" in "The Religious and Occupational Roots of Party Identification: Illinois and Indiana in the 1870's," *Civil War History* 16 (December 1970): 325, 325-43. See also William A. Gudelunas, Jr. and William G. Shade, *Before the Molly Maguires. The Emergence of the Ethno-Religious Factor in the Politics of the Lower Anthracite Region, 1844-1872* (New York: Arno Press, 1976). For the eighteenth century see Owen S. Ireland, "The Ethnic-Religious Dimension of Pennsylvania Politics, 1778-1779," *William and Mary Quarterly* 30 (July 1973): 423-48. For the way in which an evangelical moral crusade could quickly take on political dimensions, see William P. Vaughn's, *The Antimasonic Party in the United States, 1826-1843* (Lexington: University Press of Kentucky, 1983).

[45]John L. Hammond, *The Politics of Benevolence: Revival Religion and American Voting Behavior* (Norwood NJ: Ablex Publishing Company, 1979).

voting analysis from aggregate data can not uncover the subjective ratio-
nales for voting behavior and can not respectably demonstrate that the
majority of Evangelicals ever became abolitionists, much less voted for
the "Bible politics" of the Liberty party. Charles G. Finney's supposed
creation of a "revivalist political ethos" in communities during the Second Great Awakening is too incompatible with the evidence to survive
dispassionate analysis. In fact, Lawrence J. Friedman has recently
pointed to the existence of a non-Garrisonite, non-Tappanite, *tertium quid*
group of Finneyite abolitionists who were dedicated to cultural voluntarism, localism, and political disengagement on the national and state
level.[46] Clearly politics and religion do mix in American history, though
in complex and surprising ways, and the mixing can sometimes be seen
in the relationship between religious values and voting behavior both in
Peoria and on the Potomac.[47] On the whole, however, neither class differences nor ethnoreligious differences provide a neat enough fit to adequately characterize American politics.[48]

We have already seen how, by fastidiously observing the limits of the
available evidence, Jon Butler has subjected almost everything written on
the First Great Awakening to forceful criticism. He has also done much
the same to historical orthodoxy about America's democratizing effect on
religion. On the basis of unevadable data, Butler argues that pre-Revolutionary colonial revivals did not boost lay authority but had quite the

---

[46]Lawrence J. Friedman, "The Gerritt Smith Circle: Abolitionism in the Burned-
Over District," *Civil War History* 26 (March 1980): 18-38.

[47]See as an example Allan J. Lichtman's conclusion that religion best explains the political alignments of 1928 in *Prejudice and the Old Politics: The Presidential Election of 1928*
(Chapel Hill: University of North Carolina Press, 1979). Recent studies that tend to confirm the relationship between voting and values but deny that "Evangelicals" vote as a
bloc include the report "American Values in the '80s: The Impact of Belief," commissioned by the Connecticut Mutual Life Insurance Company and undertaken by Research
and Forecasts; and the Search Institute of Minneapolis study, *Religion on Capitol Hill*
(New York: Harper and Row, 1982).

[48]This is the argument of John F. Reynolds in "Piety and Politics: Evangelism [sic] in
the Michigan Legislature, 1837-1860," *Michigan History* 61 (Winter 1977): 323-51. Unfortunately, Reynolds's mishandling of Evangelicalism (as first evidenced by the article's
title) and mistaken notion of what constituted "evangelical legislation" (he includes laws
relating to fornication and adultery, dueling, divorce, clergy prayers, etc.) seriously flaw
the study.

opposite effect, entrenching rather than disrupting hierarchical patterns and structures.[49] Some scholars of nineteenth-century Methodism in particular and revivalism in general are beginning to see things Butler's way, and are concluding that it was the role of the preacher and not the involvement of the laity that evangelical worship enhanced.[50] If Douglas Greenberg is correct in asserting that the Middle Colonies are most representative of America's varied culture and denominational life, then other religious historians must follow Butler's turn towards the mid-Atlantic states.[51]

Butler continues to change our conceptual framework in his article on "Enlarging the Bonds of Jesus: Slavery, Evangelism and the Christianization of the White South, 1690-1790." Using late seventeenth-century birth and baptismal records, manuscripts from the Society for the Propagation of the Gospel, and Southern sermons, Butler argues that the impact of slavery on white Christianity was as great as the impact of white Christianity on slavery. Indeed, a predominantly non-Christian white population in the colonial South found itself being converted, sent to church, and instructed in the faith as a by-product of Anglican missions to slaves. The dualism of Butler's title highlights the enlargement of organized Christian groups, but at the cost of binding Christianity to the defense of slavery, not so much in the minds of ministers as in the minds of the laity that had earlier worried about linking the two together. The character and vitality of Southern Christianity that had emerged by 1790, therefore, depended on its association with the growth of slavery. The advancement of Christianity and the advancement of slavery went hand-in-chain. In short, the relationship between the development of Southern white Christianity and black slavery was a symbiotic one.

------

[49]Jon Butler, *Power, Authority, and the Origins of American Denominational Order: The English Churches in the Delaware Valley, 1680-1730* (Philadelphia: The American Philosophical Society, 1978).

[50]Doug Adams, *Meeting House to Camp Meeting: Toward a History of American Free Church Worship from 1620-1835* (Saratoga CA: Modern Liturgy/Resource Publications, 1981).

[51]Douglas Greenberg, "The Middle Colonies in Recent American Historiography," *William and Mary Quarterly* 36 (July 1979): 396-427. For the beginning of this literature, see Frantz, "Awakening of Religion," 266-88.

Butler's article comes at a time when historians have not yet learned to distinguish clearly between Evangelicalism's social and political aspects. Recent studies have emphasized that the alliance of evangelical Christianity and proslavery ideology was not the most suitable of unions, thus stressing religion's support for the antislavery impulse. James D. Essig writes that evangelical spirituality in the late eighteenth century nurtured powerful antislavery sensibilities, and James Brewer Stewart attributes what little antislavery activities that existed in the Upper South during the 1820s to evangelical ideology.[52] Both Essig and Stewart accent the continuity in arguments between Southern Evangelicals and the later Northern abolitionist movement which, Lawrence T. Lesick contends, owed an immense debt to Evangelicalism.[53] Anne C. Loveland, who has explored the theological stresses—especially the doctrine of sin—that led Evangelicals in the South to justify slavery, argues that even after Southern Methodists, Baptists, and Presbyterians became proslavery they did not defend slavery as a "positive good," and she sees in their concern for such things as slaves' religious instruction a veiled critique of the "peculiar institution."[54]

The complexity of Evangelicalism and its ability to generate both slaveholding and antislavery ethics has been most creatively analyzed by Donald G. Mathews, Donald Scott, and Drew Gilpin Faust. While Mathews admits that "Evangelicals' world view and theology created an es-

---

[52]James D. Essig, *The Bonds of Wickedness: American Evangelicals Against Slavery, 1770-1908* (Philadelphia: Temple University Press, 1982); James Brewer Stewart, "Evangelicalism and the Radical Strain in Southern Antislavery Thought During the 1820s," *Journal of Southern History* 39 (August 1973): 379-96.

[53]Lawrence Thomas Lesick, *The Lane Rebels: Evangelicalism and Antislavery in Antebellum America* (Metuchen NJ: Scarecrow Press, 1980). Also see J. F. Maclear, "The Evangelical Alliance and the Antislavery Crusade," *Huntington Library Quarterly* 42 (Spring 1979): 141-64; James Brewer Stewart, "Abolitionists, the Bible, and the Challenge of Slavery," in *Bible and Social Reform*, ed. Ernest R. Sandeen (Philadelphia: Fortress Press, 1982): 31-57; and John R. McKivigan, "The Antislavery 'Comeouter' Sects: A Neglected Dimension of the Abolitionist Movement," *Civil War History* 26 (June 1980): 142-60.

[54]Anne C. Loveland, *Southern Evangelicals and the Social Order, 1800-1860* (Baton Rouge: Louisiana State University Press, 1980). Also see her "Evangelicalism and 'Immediate Emancipation' in American Anti-Slavery Thought," *Journal of Southern History* 32 (May 1966): 172-88.

pecially conducive mental context for antislavery action," he asserts that "it is not at all clear whether abolitionism was evidence of the success of evangelicalism or its failure." Indeed, for many abolitionism may have become an ersatz Evangelicalism, a vehicle of replacement for a religion that by the 1830s had "declined into a 'hollow ritual.' "[55] Scott also reconstructs one form of influence that came out of Evangelicalism wherein abolitionists could be seen as carrying Evangelicalism to a "logical end point," including those for whom abolition became a "sacred vocation" if not a religion in its own right. His study is comprehensive, though, as far as exploring the ways in which Evangelicalism's logic could march some toward abolition and others toward antiabolition.[56] Finally, in some insufficiently appreciated studies, Drew Gilpin Faust shows that the proslavery argument stood only a hairbreadth distance from the antislavery argument. The Evangelicalism that unleashed reform energies in the North also did so in the South, she reveals, but in the latter case it was slavery, not abolition, that Evangelicals defined as a humanitarian exercise in moral stewardship. The theological justification of slavery was not a matter of evangelical truancy since it was based on intellectual and theological assumptions shared throughout America.[57] Indeed, Larry Ed-

---

[55]Donald G. Mathews, "Religion and Slavery—The Case of the American South" in *Anti-Slavery, Religion and Reform: Essays in Memory of Roger Anstey*, ed. Christine Bolt and Seymour Drescher (Hamden CT: Archon Books, 1980) 209-32; Mathews, *Religion in the Old South*.

[56]Donald B. Scott, *From Office to Profession: The New England Ministry, 1750-1850* (Philadelphia: University of Pennsylvania Press, 1978) 76-94; see also Scott's essay "Abolition as a Sacred Vocation" in *Antislavery Reconsidered: New Perspectives on the Abolitionists*, ed. Lewis Perry and Michael Fellman (Baton Rouge: Louisiana State University Press, 1979) 51-74. For the story of a pious young man who found his "calling" in antislavery, see Irving H. Bartlett, *Wendell and Ann Phillips: The Community of Reform, 1840-1880* (New York: W. W. Norton, 1979). For abolition as a religion, see Lewis Perry, "Adin Ballou's Hopedale Community and the Theology of Antislavery," *Church History* 39 (September 1970): 372-89. Lawrence J. Friedman illustrates his dismay that "our knowledge of immediatist abolition is at a fairly primitive level" by noting that "We still do not know what distinguished abolitionists from the other evangelical benevolent reformers with whom they worked in the 1820s," and "To this day, we do not know what made one evangelical reformer stay with the established benevolent reform societies while his colleague embraced immediatist abolitionism." "Abolitionist Historiography 1965-1979: An Assessment," *Reviews in American History* 8 (June 1980): 202, 204.

[57]Drew Gilpin Faust, "Evangelicalism and the Meaning of the Proslavery Argument," *Virginia Magazine of History and Biography* 85 (January 1977): 3-17; Faust "A

ward Tise demonstrates convincingly that the theological framework for slavery "emerged from the mainstream of American thought," making proslavery "essentially an American rather than a Southern phenomenon."[58] As the above studies reveal indirectly, Bertram Wyatt-Brown's 1969 biography of Lewis Tappan has been greeted with such respectful attention that many historians have largely shifted scholarship's focus away from "radical" abolitionism and toward "conservative" abolitionists who originated within Evangelicalism and who resembled missionaries in striking ways.[59]

The attention Butler gives to the South is symptomatic of research shared by many American historians. Much has happened in the decade since Wyatt-Brown remarked, "among the unmapped features of the southern landscape, none is so shrouded as its religion."[60] While there is still no systematic, comprehensive study of Southern religion, two schol-

---

Southern Stewardship: The Intellectual and the Proslavery Argument," *American Quarterly* 31 (Spring 1979): 63-80. See also Stephen J. Stein, "George Whitefield on Slavery: Some New Evidence," *Church History* 42 (June 1973): 243-56. Faust's "The Proslavery Argument in History," provides an illuminating introduction to the proslavery literature. See Faust, ed., *The Ideology of Slavery: Proslavery Thought in the Antebellum South, 1830-1860* (Baton Rouge: Louisiana State University Press, 1981) 1-20.

[58]Larry Edward Tise, "The Interregional Appeal of Proslavery Thought: An Ideological Profile of the Antebellum Clergy," *Plantation Society* 1 (February 1979): 62, 63, 58-72.

[59]Bertram Wyatt-Brown, *Lewis Tappan and the Evangelical War Against Slavery* (Cleveland: Press of Case Western Reserve University, 1969); Robert H. Abzug, *Passionate Liberator: Theodore Dwight Weld and the Dilemma of Reform* (New York: Oxford University Press, 1980). Lawrence J. Friedman, "Confidence and Pertinacity in Evangelical Abolitionism: Lewis Tappan's Circle," *American Quarterly* 31 (Spring 1979): 81-106; Edgar F. Raines, Jr., "The American Missionary Association in Southern Illinois, 1850-1862—A Case History in the Abolition Movement," *Journal of Illinois State Historical Society* 65 (Autumn 1972): 246-68; John R. McKivigan, "The American Baptist Free Mission Society: Abolitionist Reaction to the 1845 Baptist Schism," *Foundations* 21 (October-December 1978): 340-55. For the connection between abolitionists and missionaries, see Bertram Wyatt-Brown, "Conscience and Career: Young Abolitionists and Missionaries," in Bolt and Drescher, *Anti-Slavery, Religion and Reform*, 183-203, and Lawrence J. Friedman, *Gregarious Saints: Self and Community in American Abolitionism, 1830-1870* (Cambridge: Cambridge University Press, 1982).

[60]Bertram Wyatt-Brown, "The Antimission Movement in the Jacksonian South: A Study in Regional Folk Culture," *Journal of Southern History* 36 (November 1970): 501-29. For the degree to which times have changed see John B. Boles, "Religion in the South: A Tradition Recovered," *Maryland Historical Magazine* 77 (Winter 1982): 388-401.

ars have done more than anyone else to make Southern religion one of the more intelligent areas of evangelical historiography: Samuel S. Hill and Donald G. Mathews. In lectures, articles, and books Hill has echoed Kenneth K. Bailey's 1964 claim that "in the sphere of religion . . . Southern identity is best delineated,"[61] arguing that Southern distinctiveness owes as much to religion as to politics and race. C. C. Goen's study of denominational schisms confirms this picture and reinforces the role of "regional religion" in shattering Evangelicalism's unifying impact on the nation and paving the way for Civil War.[62] It may be that the more historians study Southern religion, the less regional or "Southern" it will appear to be, although slavery clearly makes it different.[63] Hill's understanding of the South's uniqueness is framed within comparative studies of Northern and Southern religion, and he is too careful a scholar not to maintain the existence of "Varieties of Southern Evangelicalism," as one collection of essays phrases it. Southern Evangelicalism has many mansions, and Hill has helped his readers and colleagues to see the necessity of identifying in which ones they are living and on which ones they are working.[64]

Mathews's scholarship is always an intellectual feast. His analysis of Evangelicalism as a social phenomenon in *Religion in the Old South* (1977)

---

[61]Kenneth K. Bailey, *Southern White Protestantism in the Twentieth Century* (New York: Harper and Row, 1964) ix.

[62]C. C. Goen, "Broken Churches, Broken Nation: Regional Religion and North-South Alienation in Antebellum America," *Church History* 52 (March 1983): 21-35.

[63]Anne C. Loveland tends to veer in this direction in her *Southern Evangelicals*. See also her account of revivalism's importance to Southern religion in "Presbyterians and Revivalism in the Old South," *Journal of Presbyterian History* 57 (Spring 1979): 36-50. Although Edward Pessen does not examine the religious dimension, his case against overblown differences between North and South is a suggestive one. "How Different from Each Other Were the Antebellum North and South?" *American Historical Review* 85 (December 1980): 1119-49.

[64]Samuel S. Hill, *Religion and the Solid South* (Nashville: Abingdon, 1972); *The South and the North in American Religion* (Athens GA: University of Georgia Press, 1980); "The Shape and Shapes of Popular Southern Piety" in *Varieties of Southern Evangelicalism*, ed. David Edwin Harrell, Jr. (Macon GA: Mercer University Press, 1981) 89-114. Also see the introductory essays in two collections edited by Samuel S. Hill, *Religion in the Southern States: A Historical Survey* (Macon GA: Mercer University Press, 1983) and *On Jordan's Stormy Banks: Religion in the South: A Southern Exposure Profile* (Macon GA: Mercer University Press, 1983).

is a classic. In stressing the communal character of Southern Evangelicalism—its contributions toward a public life for women and the importance of the black religious experience as the context for interpreting
Southern religion—Mathews has become a significant presence in the
historiography on Evangelicalism.[65]

To be sure, studies still crop up perpetuating the old stereotypes of
Southern religion. But they appear with much less frequency, even in the
popular, seemingly scholarship-proof writings on campmeetings, circuit
riders, and revivalists.[66] The intelligence and insight is refreshing in Donald E. Byrne's pioneering study of circuit riders and folk religion, an approach to American religious history that should not be discarded.[67]
Dickson D. Bruce, Jr.'s conclusion about the religious nature of campmeetings, no less persuasive for its predictability, and John B. Boles's extensive treatment of Great Revival theology, notwithstanding its
excessive stress on "individualism," reveal the extent to which revivalism
helped to shape the religious, social, and psychological characteristics of
the Southern Appalachian population down to today.[68] Unfortunately,

---

[65]Mathews, *Religion in the Old South*.

[66]See as an example Lloyd A. Hunter, "Mark Twain and the Southern Evangelical
Mind," *Missouri Historical Society Bulletin* 33 (July 1977): 246-64.

[67]Donald E. Byrne, Jr., *No Foot of Land: Folklore of American Methodist Itinerants* (Metuchen NJ: Scarecrow Press, 1975). For the circuit rider in the late nineteenth century see
Hunter D. Farish, *Circuit Rider Dismounts: A Social History of Southern Methodism 1865-
1900* (New York: De Capo Press, 1969).

[68]Dickson D. Bruce, Jr., *And They All Sang Hallelujah: Plainfolk Camp-Meeting Religion, 1800-1845* (Knoxville: University of Tennessee Press, 1974); John B. Boles, *The
Great Revival, 1787-1805: The Origins of the Southern Evangelical Mind* (Lexington: University of Kentucky Press, 1972); Barbara J. Redman, "The Impact of Great Revival Religion on the Personal Characteristics of the Southern Appalachian People," *Southern
Studies* 20 (Fall 1981): 303-10. Also see James I. Robertson, Jr., "Reveling and Religion
in Frontier Kentucky," *Registrar of the Kentucky Historical Society* 79 (Autumn 1981):
354-68; and Mariam J. Houchens, "The Great Revival of 1800," *Registrar of the Kentucky
Historical Society* 50 (July 1971): 216-34. Recent studies of the camp meeting have focused
on its post-Civil War manifestations. See Clyde W. Lord, "The Mineral Springs Holiness
Camp Meetings," *Louisiana History* 16 (Summer 1975): 257-77; Charles Stansfield, "Pit-
man Grove: A Camp Meeting as Urban Nucleus," *Pioneer America* 7 (January 1975): 36-
44; Sylvia C. Henricks, "A Good and Profitable Occasion: The Story of Acton Camp
Ground," *Indiana Magazine of History* 66 (December 1970): 299-317; and Charles A. Parker, "The Camp Meeting on the Frontier and the Methodist Religious Resort in the
East—Before 1900," *Methodist History* 18 (April 1980): 179-92; and D. Gregory Van Dus-

there has been only a smattering of publications on individual evangelical denominations, the religious ecology in individual Southern states, and individual biographies of Southern evangelical leaders.[69]

Nathan O. Hatch's article on "Millennialism and Popular Religion in the Early Republic" is an important one for many reasons. First, he reveals the importance of the Bible to the study of American history, a topic explored further in a collection of essays Hatch and Mark A. Noll have edited entitled *The Bible in America* (1982).[70] An appeal to biblical authority was a two-edged sword that could cut both for and against evangelical theology. A biblical orientation, Hatch shows, was not unique to Evangelicalism.

Second, Hatch broadens our understanding of millennialism, which he has already done much to build, by emphasizing its dimensions in popular religious history. Millennial fever may have reached its peak in American society not in the 1830s and 1840s, as historians have been wont to believe, but in the early years of the republic, a neglected period (1780-1820) that Hatch is now exploring from various angles.[71]

---

sen, "The Bergen Camp Meeting in the American Holiness Movement," *Methodist History* 21 (January 1983): 69-89. Two provocative attempts at relating camp-meeting rituals to political development and the ordering of reality are Joe L. Kincheloe, Jr., "Similarities in Crowd Control Techniques of the Camp Meeting and Political Rally: The Pioneer Role of Tennessee," *Tennessee Historical Quarterly* 37 (Summer 1978): 155-69, and Catherine L. Albanese, "Savage, Sinner, and Saved: Davy Crockett, Camp Meetings, and the Wild Frontier," *American Quarterly* 33 (Winter 1981): 482-501.

[69]Rufus B. Spain, *At Ease in Zion: Social History of Southern Baptists, 1865-1900* (Nashville: Vanderbilt University Press, 1967); Frederick A. Bode, *Protestantism and the New South: North Carolina Baptists and Methodists in Political Crisis, 1894-1903* (Charlottesville: University Press of Virginia, 1976); John B. Boles, *Religion in Antebellum Kentucky* (Lexington: University Press of Kentucky, 1976); Louis B. Weeks, *Kentucky Presbyterians* (Atlanta: John Knox Press, 1983). Sixteen state histories of Southern religious history can be found in Hill, ed., *Religion in the Southern States.*

[70]Nathan O. Hatch and Mark A. Noll, ed., *The Bible in America: Essays in Cultural History* (New York: Oxford University Press, 1982).

[71]See Hatch's unearthing of a "crisis of authority" within the Second Great Awakening in "The Christian Movement and the Demand for a Theology of the People," *Journal of American History* 67 (December 1980): 545-67, and "Sola Scriptura and Novus Ordo Sedorum" in *Bible in America*, ed. Hatch and Noll, 59-78.

So much has been written on millennialism, a characteristic feature of Evangelicalism[72] that the word millennialism has become almost synonymous in recent years with American religious history. Millennialism "formed what was probably the strongest theme in the one religion of the United States," Catherine L. Albanese writes in the most recent survey textbook published on religion in America.[73] "Millenarianism has been a root symbol of American life," John F. Wilson contends, "in the same way that puritanism has been."[74] William G. McLoughlin sums it up this way: "American history is thus best understood as a millenarian movement."[75] Millennial ideology is decisive in shaping such diverse phenomena as myths of American origin and destiny;[76] eighteenth-century activism and Anglo-American partnership;[77] the appeal of Paine's *Common Sense*;[78] a philosophy of history;[79] a conservative social ethos in the early republic;[80] Victorian sexuality;[81] perfectionist experiments (Shak-

---

[72]Leonard I. Sweet, "Millennialism in America: Recent Studies," *Theological Studies* 40 (September 1979): 510-31. For the general importance of millennialism in antebellum America, see the various articles in Edwin S. Gaustad, ed., *The Rise of Adventism: Religion and Society in Mid-Nineteenth-Century America* (New York: Harper and Row, 1974) esp. Ernest R. Sandeen, "Millennialism," 104-18.

[73]Catherine L. Albanese, *America: Religions and Religion* (Belmont CA: Wadsworth Publishing Company, 1981) 275.

[74]John F. Wilson, *Public Religion in American Culture* (Philadelphia: Temple University Press, 1979) 108.

[75]McLoughlin, *Revivals, Awakenings and Social Reform: An Essay in Religion and Social Change in America, 1607-1977* (Chicago: University of Chicago Press, 1978) xiv.

[76]Sacvan Bercovitch, *The American Jeremiad* (Madison: University of Wisconsin Press, 1978); *The Puritan Origins of the American Self* (New Haven: Yale University Press, 1975).

[77]Joseph A. Conforti, *Samuel Hopkins and the New Divinity Movement*; Bruce Tucker, "The Reinterpretation of Puritan History in Provincial New England," *New England Quarterly* 54 (December 1981): 481-98.

[78]Stephen Newman, "A Note on *Common Sense* and Christian Eschatology," *Political Theory* 6 (February 1978): 101-108.

[79]James West Davidson, *The Logic of Millennial Thought: Eighteenth-Century New England* (New Haven: Yale University Press, 1977).

[80]Stephen E. Berk, *Calvinism versus Democracy*.

[81]Charles E. Rosenberg, "Sexuality, Class and Role in 19th-Century America," *American Quarterly* 25 (May 1973): 131-53.

ers, Mormons, and Oneidans);[82] the Christianization of civilization;[83] antebellum health reform and "Christian physiology";[84] abolition;[85] slave revolts and lack of slave revolts;[86] proslavery ideology;[87] the Civil War;[88] religion and politics (both in terms of the development of a "civil religion"[89] and the emergence of religious liberty[90]); theological Modern-

---

[82]Lawrence Foster, *Religion and Sexuality: Three American Communal Experiments of the Nineteenth Century* (New York: Oxford University Press, 1981); Klaus J. Hansen, *Mormonism and the American Experience* (Chicago: University of Chicago Press, 1981). For the importance of millennialism to early Mormonism, see Grant Underwood, "Seminal versus Sesquicentennial Saints: A Look at Mormon Millennialism," *Dialogue* 14 (Spring 1981): 32-44.

[83]Robert T. Handy, *A Christian America: Protestant Hopes and Historical Realities* (2nd ed., rev. and enl., New York: Oxford University Press, 1984, originally published in 1971).

[84]Ronald L. Numbers, *Prophetess of Health: A Study of Ellen G. White* (New York: Harper and Row, 1976); James C. Whorton, *Crusaders for Fitness: The History of American Health Reformers* (Princeton: Princeton University Press, 1982); John B. Blake, "Health Reform," in *Rise of Adventism*, ed. Gaustad, 30-49; James C. Whorton, " 'Christian Physiology': William Alcott's Prescription for the Millennium," *Bulletin of the History of Medicine* 49 (Winter 1975): 466-81; P. Gerard Damsteegt, "Health Reform and the Bible in Early Sabbatarian Adventism," *Adventist Heritage* 5 (Winter 1978): 13-21. Stephen Nissenbaum's very fine book, *Sex, Diet, and Debility in Jacksonian America: Sylvester Graham and Health Reform* (Westport CT: Greenwood Press, 1980) fails to see the connection between health reform and either millennialism or Evangelicalism.

[85]John W. Kuykendall, *Southern Enterprise: The Work of National Evangelical Societies in the Antebellum South* (Westport CT: Greenwood Press, 1982).

[86]Eugene D. Genovese attributes the lack of a revolutionary political tradition among slaves to the absence of millennialism in slave religion. See *Roll, Jordan, Roll: The World the Slaves Made* (New York: Pantheon Books, 1975) 272-79, 587-97. John Jentz, on the other hand, criticizes Genovese for misunderstanding millennialism and underestimating its existence. See "A Note on Genovese's Account of the Slaves' Religion," *Civil War History* 23 (June 1977): 161-69.

[87]Jack A. Maddex, Jr., "Proslavery Millennialism: Social Eschatology in Antebellum Southern Calvinism," *American Quarterly* 31 (Spring 1979): 46-62.

[88]James H. Moorhead, *American Apocalypse: Yankee Protestants and the Civil War, 1860-1869* (New Haven: Yale University Press, 1978).

[89]Nathan O. Hatch, *The Sacred Cause of Liberty: Republican Thought and the Millennium in Revolutionary New England* (New Haven: Yale University Press, 1977); Gordon S. Wood, "Rhetoric and Reality in the American Revolution," *William and Mary Quarterly* 23 (January 1966): 26.

ism,[91] Pentecostalism, and Fundamentalism;[92] early twentieth-century reformers;[93] the development of a strong black and female consciousness;[94] and relationships to Jews and native Americans.[95] The common theological orientations and structural similarities between revivalism and millennialism are explored by Jerald C. Brauer.[96] Quiet warnings not to push the millennial theme too far are given by Lewis O. Saum, whose exploration of the popular mind and "common man" reveals much greater pessimism about human nature and much less buoyancy about the future than normally portrayed,[97] and by Henry Warner Bowden's essay

---

[90]W. Clark Gilpin, *The Millenarian Piety of Roger Williams* (Chicago: University of Chicago Press, 1979).

[91]William R. Hutchison, *The Modernist Impulse in American Protestantism* (Cambridge: Harvard University Press, 1976).

[92]Robert Mapes Anderson, *Vision of the Disinherited: The Making of American Pentecostalism* (New York: Oxford University Press, 1979); Ernest R. Sandeen, *The Roots of Fundamentalism: British and American Millenarianism 1800-1930* (Chicago: University of Chicago Press, 1970); Marsden, *Fundamentalism and American Culture.*

[93]Jean B. Quandt, "Religion and Social Thought: The Secularity of Postmillennialism," *American Quarterly* 25 (October 1973): 390-409.

[94]Leonard I. Sweet, *Black Images of America, 1790-1870* (New York: W. W. Norton, 1976); *The Minister's Wife: Her Role In Nineteenth-Century American Evangelicalism* (Philadelphia: Temple University Press, 1983).

[95]Timothy P. Weber, *Living in the Shadow of the Second Coming: American Pre-millennialism, 1875-1982* (New York: Oxford University Press, 1983, enl. ed.).

[96]Jerald C. Brauer, "Revivalism and Millenarianism in America," in *In the Great Tradition: In Honor of Winthrop S. Hudson,* ed. Joseph D. Ban and Paul R. Dekar (Valley Forge: Judson Press, 1982) 147-59.

[97]Lewis O. Saum, *The Popular Mood of Pre-Civil War America* (Westport CT: Greenwood Press, 1980). See also Saum's "Providence in the Popular Mind of Pre-Civil War America," *Indiana Magazine of History* 72 (December 1976): 315-46. John B. Boles has also directed our attention to the "deep current of pessimism [which] ran through Jacksonian culture, belying the optimistic egalitarianism usually portrayed" in "John Hersey: Dissenting Theologian of Abolitionism, Perfectionism, and Millennialism," *Methodist History* 14 (July 1976): 215-34. Just how different a picture of Providence emerges when one looks at mass sources as opposed to elites can be seen by comparing Saum's book and John F. Berens's *Providence and Patriotism in Early America, 1640-1815* (Charlottesville: University Press of Virginia, 1978).

in this collection. A millennial rationale is absent from the Oberlin mission to the Objibwas.

What became a rather stale discussion has been enlivened by Timothy L. Smith's claim that millennialism was a source and not merely an expression of Perfectionism, which explains for him what Wesleyan Perfectionism was doing in New England theology in the nineteenth century. In even bolder terms, Smith has challenged historians to reconsider millennial aspirations as less ideological and more religious, and particularly as more international in focus than exclusively American.[98] The study of millennialism has been a varied investigation, yielding important conclusions and fresh discoveries. It is foolish to deny the continued fascination of this undertaking. I have participated in it myself. Nonetheless, perhaps the most important insights issuing from this study lie in the past.

A growing list of scholars, Nathan Hatch among them, are destroying H. L. Mencken's stereotype of revivalists as empty-headed country bumpkins. Whereas historians used to contrast the Puritan Age, when theology was a shaping force, with the Methodist Age, when American Protestants looked away from theology, historians like Ronald Walters now feel compelled to claim that "There were ideas of substance behind antebellum revivalism," pointing specifically to millennialism, Perfectionism, and voluntarism as significant contributions to the life of the mind in America.[99] George Marsden was one of the first to confront the mishandling of Evangelicals as intellectual lightweights by their critics, arguing against the notion that Evangelicals had theologically unfurnished minds. He took on both Richard Hofstadter's equation of Evangelicalism with anti-intellectualism[100] and Winthrop Hudson's contention that Evangelicalism displayed little concern for theological exactness and no real theological creativity, thereby preventing the nine-

---

[98]Timothy L. Smith, "Righteousness and Hope: Christian Holiness and the Millennial Vision in America, 1800-1900," *American Quarterly* 31 (Spring 1979): 21-45. The international cast of Samuel Hopkins' millennialism, which Smith emphasizes, has long been acknowledged but recently forgotten. Mark A. Noll extends the international flavor and force of eighteenth-century millennialism to Bellamy and Edwards in "Moses Mather," 283.

[99]Ronald G. Walters, *American Reformers* (New York: Hill and Wang, 1978) 24.

[100]Richard Hofstadter, *Anti-Intellectualism in American Life* (New York: Alfred A. Knopf, 1964) 55-141.

teenth century's development of much theological vitality.[101] Focusing on the Reformed and Calvinist components of Evangelicalism rather than the pietistic, Arminian strand that most historians had emphasized, Marsden touted the "vigorous intellectual life" of most Evangelicals while ultimately admitting Hudson's accuracy in observing that Evangelicalism had so tied itself to American culture, economics, and politics that it lost "the careful theological discipline that had once been characteristic of its heritage."[102] Nothing fails like success.

The rehabilitation of the evangelical mind, which Marsden started with Northern Presbyterians, has been taken South by E. Brooks Holifield, who begins his book with the opening sentence: "The most noticeable feature of American religious thought in the early nineteenth century was its rationality."[103] Southern Evangelicals were not all heart and little head. Nor were rationalism and urbanity unique to nineteenth-century liberalism. An "age of reason" existed in the middle of an "era of revivalism," and the facile identification of Southern religion with revivalism and rural values must be modified after weighing Holifield's work. Southern religion was intellectually vital and theologically able, though it is not entirely clear whether the one hundred Southern "gentlemen theologians" Holifield located—who were urban, rationalist, and informed by Common Sense philosophy, as well as being the founders of colleges and seminaries[104]—would have called themselves "evangelical."

---

[101]Winthrop S. Hudson, *American Protestantism* (Chicago: University of Chicago Press, 1961) 132; *Religion in America*, 80. See also Sidney E. Mead, *The Lively Experiment: The Shaping of Christianity in America* (New York: Harper and Row, 1963) 15, 169, and James F. Findlay, *Dwight L. Moody: American Evangelist, 1837-1899* (Chicago: University of Chicago Press, 1969) 87.

[102]George M. Marsden, *The Evangelical Mind and the New School Presbyterian Experience: A Case Study of Thought and Theology in the Nineteenth-Century Mind* (New Haven: Yale University Press, 1970) 4-5, 244.

[103]E. Brooks Holifield, *The Gentlemen Theologians: American Theology in Southern Culture, 1795-1860* (Durham NC: Duke University Press, 1978).

[104]For the evangelical roots of many educational institutions, see James Findlay, "Agency, Denominations and the Western Colleges, 1830-1860: Some Connections Between Evangelicalism and American Higher Education," *Church History* 50 (March 1981): 64-80; "Western Colleges, 1830-1890: Educational Institutions in Transition," *History of Higher Education Annual* 2 (1982): 35-64; James Axtell, "Death of the Liberal Arts College," *History of Education Quarterly* 2 (Winter 1971): 345.

Within the past few years books have appeared viewing Scottish Realism as a major intellectual source and defining feature of Evangelicalism—a thesis that is both overdue and overdone. The Scottish connection is especially important to Theodore Dwight Bozeman's challenging reconstruction of the remarkably vigorous mental life of Evangelicals, whose intellectual needs were well served by the Baconian ideal.[105] The chief apologetic weapons used in the evangelical fight against transcendentalists and materialists thus were Enlightenment tools: reason and science. It is time historians cease being surprised there was such a thing as

---

[105]Theodore Dwight Bozeman, *Protestants in an Age of Science: The Baconian Ideal and Antebellum Religious Thought* (Chapel Hill: University of North Carolina Press, 1977); see also Bozeman, "Inductive and Deductive Politics: Science, and Society in Antebellum Protestant Thought," *Journal of American History* 64 (December 1977): 704-22. For the place of Scottish Realism in nineteenth-century religion, see Herbert Hovenkamp, *Science and Religion in America, 1800-1860* (Philadelphia: University of Pennsylvania Press, 1978); George M. Marsden, "Everyone One's Own Interpreter?: The Bible, Science, and Authority in Mid-Nineteenth-Century America," in Hatch and Noll, *The Bible in America*, 79-100 and less directly, J. David Hoeveler, Jr., *James McCosh and the Scottish Intellectual Tradition: from Glasgow to Princeton* (Princeton: Princeton University Press, 1981). For the impact of Common Sense on the holiness tradition in general and on Asa Mahan in particular, see respectively James E. Hamilton, "Epistemology and Theology in American Methodism," *Wesleyan Theological Journal* 10 (Spring 1975): 70-79, and Hamilton, "Nineteenth Century Holiness Theology: A Study of the Thought of Asa Mahan," *Wesleyan Theological Journal* 13 (Spring 1978): 51-64. To gauge the influence of Common Sense philosophy on the Princeton formulation of the doctrine of inerrancy and the emergence of biblical Fundamentalism, see John Vander Stelt, *Philosophy and Scripture: A Study in Old Princeton and Westminster Theology* (Marlton NJ: Mack Publishing Company, 1978); Mark A. Noll, ed., *The Princeton Theology: 1812-1921* (Grand Rapids MI: Baker, 1983); and James H. Moorhead, "Joseph Addison Alexander: Common Sense, Romanticism and Biblical Criticism at Princeton," *Journal of Presbyterian History* 53 (Spring 1975): 51-66. The fraying of the tradition of Common Sense Realism among fundamentalists is scrutinized in Timothy P. Weber, "The Two-Edged Sword: The Fundamentalist Use of the Bible" in *Bible in America*, eds. Hatch and Noll, 101-20. The place of Thomas Reid, the founder of the Scottish School, in the history of psychology is touched on by G. P. Brooks, "The Faculty Psychology of Thomas Reid," *Journal of the History of the Behavioral Sciences* 12 (January 1976): 65-77. Two fine review essays on this topic are H. S. Levinson, "Religious Testimony and Empirical Restraint: Baconianism in Antebellum America," *Reviews in American History* 6 (December 1978): 518-23 and Cynthia E. Russett, "Declaring the Glory of God," *History of Education Quarterly* 20 (Summer 1980): 217-21. George Marsden's review article of much of this literature is "Scotland and Philadelphia: Common Sense Philosophy from Jefferson to Westminster," *Reformed Journal* 29 (March 1979): 8-12.

"an Evangelical mind" or that "the study of natural science was valued even by the evangelical . . . president of Oberlin."[106]

What the above historians have done to elucidate the belief in the rationality of the Christian faith by evangelical elites like theologians, pastors, and evangelists, Hatch now does for popular religion. The Alan Heimert-Sidney Mead dichotomy of Evangelical versus Rationalist or Evangelicalism versus Enlightenment will no longer suffice.[107] It was not nearly as simple as that. Hatch's article convincingly outlines the melding of evangelical religion and Enlightenment rationalism, even to the point that the Enlightenment is emphasized over Puritanism in the "democratizing of millennial ideology." The roots of popular millennialism in both evangelical religion and Enlightenment thought are, according to Hatch, manifest in three areas: a revolt against history, a commonsense rationality, and a commitment to democratic forms of social organization. Hatch's account of how Evangelicalism became rationalist will prove extremely valuable to historians trying to draw together the threads of millennialism and popular religion. Furthermore, as Robert T. Handy noted in his comment to Hatch's piece at the conference, Henry F. May's charting of the "didactic" phase of the Enlightenment, which was dominated by Scottish Common Sense philosophers, may prove to be the precise point of influence on popular religious groups.[108]

It is appropriate that in a collection of essays devoted to the evangelical tradition in America, Charles G. Finney is the single figure that receives a separate article: Garth M. Rosell's "Charles G. Finney: His Place in the Stream of American Evangelism." It is hard not to speak in clichés when talking about Finney: the father of American revivalism, the centerpiece of American Evangelicalism, "among our great men" (Richard Hofstadter), the man who "led America out of the eighteenth century" (Perry

---

[106]Rita S. Saslaw, "Student Societies in Nineteenth Century Ohio: Misconceptions and Realities," *Ohio History* 88 (Summer 1979): 192-210.

[107]Bernard Ramm is also guilty of this simplicity in *The Evangelical Heritage* (Waco TX: Ward Books, 1973).

[108]Henry F. May, *The Enlightenment in America* (New York: Oxford University Press, 1976); Robert T. Handy, "Comment on Papers by Hatch, Smith-Rosenberg, Hewitt and Bowden: Finney Historical Conference," 2.

Miller), and so forth. All these assessments are true, illustrating that there is no simple response to Finney. For some Finney stood loyally within the long-standing tradition of Calvinist revivalism;[109] for others Finney hauled American Evangelicalism into its Arminian stage;[110] for still others Finney effected a "synthesis" of Wesleyan and covenant theology.[111] For some Finney embodied Evangelicalism's social progressivism, even radicalism, and symbolized the unity of evangelism and social reform in the evangelical tradition;[112] for others Finney's reformism moved with countervailing conservatism;[113] for still others Finney exhibited a moderate posture toward reform Evangelicalism in the interest of remaining an American cultural leader.[114] For some Finney marked the culmination of a dynamic evangelical tradition;[115] for others Finney spelled the destruction of evangelical theology;[116] for still others Finney represented

---

[109]Howard Alexander Morrison, "The Finney Takeover of the Second Great Awakening During the Oneida Revivals of 1825-1827," *New York History* 59 (January 1978): 27-53.

[110]Winthrop S. Hudson, *Religion in America*, 140-43, 151; Hudson, "The Methodist Age in America," *Methodist History* 12 (April 1974): 3-15.

[111]Timothy L. Smith, "Charles G. Finney's Synthesis of Wesleyan and Covenant Theology," *Wesleyan Theological Journal* 13 (Spring 1978): 92-113; "How Finney Helped Americans Discover the New Covenant: Righteousness Through Grace," introductory essay to his compiling and editing of Finney's *The Promise of the Spirit* (Minneapolis: Bethany Fellowship, 1980) 9-33; and "The Cross Demands, the Spirit Enables," *Christianity Today* 23 (16 February 1979): 22-26.

[112]Timothy L. Smith, *Revivalism and Social Reform: American Protestantism on the Eve of the Civil War* (New York: Abingdon Press, 1957); reprinted Baltimore: Johns Hopkins University Press, 1980; Lawrence Lesick, *Lane Rebels*, and James David Essig, "The Land's Free Men: Charles G. Finney and His Abolitionism," *Civil War History* 24 (March 1978): 25-45.

[113]Leonard I. Sweet, "Views of Man Inherent in New Measures Revivalism," *Church History* 45 (June 1976): 20-21.

[114]James H. Moorhead, "Social Reform and the Divided Conscience of Antebellum Protestantism," *Church History* 48 (December 1979): 416-30.

[115]James E. Hamilton, "Finney: An Appreciation," *Christianity Today*, August 1975, 13-16.

[116]John Opie, "Finney's Failure of Nerve: The Untimely Demise of Evangelical Theology," *Journal of Presbyterian History* 51 (Summer 1973): 155-73; and John H. Gerstner, "The Theological Boundaries of Evangelical Faith," in *The Evangelicals: What They Be-*

Evangelicalism's replacement of mystery with law as the foundation of theology and its brief partnership with lawyers.[117] For some Finney was a strong-willed, indomitable revivalist and "culture hero";[118] for others Finney could be both firm and vacillating, heavily dependent throughout his life on his three wives, all of whom were engaged in varying degrees in his evangelism—the arc of Finney's reputation sliding downward as that of his second wife Elizabeth's career was moving up.[119]

One of the reasons for the confusion is the astonishing absence of a biography of Finney's life. Garth Rosell and Richard Dupuis are presently completing an annotated, unexpurgated edition of his memoirs, but this is only a belated beginning toward the proper biographical treatment Finney requires.[120] In fact, historiography on American Evangelicalism is embarrassingly bereft of biographies, not to mention biographies that achieve such pinnacles of scholarship and sensitivity as James F. Findlay's *Dwight L. Moody* (1969).[121] George Whitefield may have "put a more permanent mark on the Great Awakening and on American evangelical religion in general than any other single colonial figure,"[122] yet we still do not have a current, worthy biography of him. The same can be said for a host of other relevant figures: Gilbert and William Tennent, Francis Asbury, Hezekiah Smith, Jacob Albright, John Philip Boehm, Jesse Lee, Asahel Nettleton, Jacob Knapp, Jabez Swan, Luther Rice, John Mason Peck, Gerritt Smith, Nathan Bangs, Archibald Alexander, Alexander

---

lieve, Who They Are, Where They Are Changing, eds. David F. Wells and John D. Woodbridge (Nashville: Abingdon Press, 1975) 21-37.

[117]David L. Weddle, "The Law and the Revival: A 'New Divinity' for the Settlements," *Church History* 47 (June 1978): 196-214.

[118]William G. McLoughlin, *Revivals, Awakenings and Reform: An Essay in Religion and Social Change in America, 1607-1977* (Chicago: University of Chicago Press, 1978) 122-31; and McLoughlin, "Charles Grandison Finney: The Revivalist as Culture Hero," *Journal of American Culture* 5 (Summer 1982): 80-90.

[119]Sweet, *The Minister's Wife*.

[120]For the continuing interest in reading Finney's writings, see Donald W. Dayton, comp., *Reflections on Revival by Charles G. Finney* (Minneapolis: Bethany Fellowship, 1979) and Timothy L. Smith, comp. & ed., *The Promise of the Spirit*.

[121]Findlay, *Dwight L. Moody*.

[122]Ahlstrom, *Religious History of American People*, 229.

Campbell, Peter Cartwright, Narcissa Whitman, Abraham Marshall, Harriet Livermore, Charles Petit McIlvaine, Richard Furman, William Miller, Phoebe Palmer, Matthew Simpson, James H. Thornwell, Charles Hodge, Josiah Strong, Frances Willard, Augustus Hopkins Strong, Evangeline Lucy Booth, Ira D. Sankey, Adoniram Judson Gordon, James Gresham Machen, Benjamin Warfield, Harold Ockenga, Carl F. H. Henry, and many others. Historians can be found researching the same few, favored figures—John Cotton, Ezra Stiles, Lyman Beecher, Martin Luther King, Jr., Billy Graham—while names like Jonathan Edwards, Charles G. Finney, Horace Bushnell, Abraham Lincoln, and Walter Rauschenbusch send all but the most dedicated running for cover.

Recent preoccupations with social history and quantitative techniques have resulted in a large outcropping of what might be called stick-figure history: accounts written as if people had no faces, no flesh and blood, no personalities, even no thoughts. In such an academic climate, biography is hardly fashionable. This is not to say that some important biographies of evangelical leaders have not been published in the last dozen years. Two of the most prominent evangelical families of the nineteenth century, the Beechers and the Judsons, have been the subject of two very different but superb collective biographies by Marie Caskey and Joan Jacobs Brumberg, the latter widely acclaimed in the profession but the former sorely neglected. In fact, if there is one historian who is the sleeper of the seventies, it is Caskey.[123] One of Finney's converts, Theodore Dwight Weld, has also received expert treatment by a gifted biographer.[124] There are other biographies of evangelical luminaries of

---

[123]Joan Jacobs Brumberg, *Mission for Life: The Story of the Family of Adoniram Judson, the Dramatic Event of the First American Foreign Mission, and the Course of Evangelical Religion in the Nineteenth Century* (New York: Free Press, 1980); Marie Caskey, *Chariot of Fire: Religion and the Beecher Family* (New Haven: Yale University Press, 1978). Milton Rugoff's *The Beechers: An American Family in the Nineteenth Century* (New York: Harper and Row, 1981) has been widely reviewed and acclaimed, but is much less theologically astute and historically incisive than Caskey. For a collective biography of fundamentalist leaders, see C. Allyn Russell, *Voices of American Fundamentalism: Seven Biographical Studies* (Philadelphia: Westminster, 1976).

[124]Despite its title, Abzug's *Passionate Liberator* is less concerned with Weld's public activities than with his thought and feelings.

varying quality that might also be mentioned.[125] Still, for the most part the best of American religious history has become so dominated by the social sciences that biography is almost the scandal of the discipline. Historians who will make fewer concessions to the fashions of the field are in great demand.

More than any other person, Charles G. Finney helped to make Evangelicalism the dominant pattern of American Protestantism. Garth Rosell in his essay also reveals that it was Finney who helped to make social reform an evangelical obligation and a religious act. During his first Rochester revival (1830-1831) Finney popularized a millennial ideology that swept up already existing benevolent societies into a mass movement that believed the kingdom of God could be taken by activism. No longer did Evangelicals wait for the devil to pick on them before they got aroused; now they went out and picked on the devil. To Finney belongs much of the credit for making nineteenth-century Protestantism so busy. After Finney, antebellum Evangelicalism would hardly ever be dull.

Rosell's invocation of this issue reflects perhaps the most distinguishable trend in American religious historiography during the past generation: the shifting of focus from what Bruce Tucker calls "prominent leaders, institutions, and theology to the social and cultural meaning of religious experience."[126] Gilbert Barnes, Whitney R. Cross, and Alice

---

[125]William G. McLoughlin, *The Meaning of Henry Ward Beecher: An Essay on the Shifting Values of Mid-Victorian America, 1840-1870* (New York: Knopf, 1970); George William Pilcher, *Samuel Davies: Apostle of Dissent in Colonial Virginia* (Knoxville: University of Tennessee Press, 1971); William Graveley, *Gilbert Haven: Methodist Abolitionist* (Nashville: Abingdon, 1972); John S. O'Malley, *Pilgrimage of Faith: The Legacy of the Otterbeins* (Metuchen NJ: Scarecrow Press, 1973); Stuart Clark Henry, *Unvanquished Puritan: A Portrait of Lyman Beecher* (Grand Rapids: Eerdmans, 1973); Ray Holder, *William Winans: Methodist Leader in Antebellum Mississippi* (Jackson: University Press of Mississippi, 1977); Clifford E. Clark, Jr., *Henry Ward Beecher: Spokesman for a Middle-Class America* (Urbana: University of Illinois Press, 1978); C. Howard Hopkins, *John R. Mott, 1865-1955: A Biography* (Grand Rapids: Eerdmans, 1979); Mark K. Bauman, *Warren Akin Candler: The Conservative as Idealist* (Metuchen NJ: Scarecrow Press, 1981); Edward H. Madden and James E. Hamilton, *Freedom and Grace: The Life of Asa Mahan* (Metuchen NJ: Scarecrow Press, 1982). Patricia J. Tracy's *Jonathan Edwards, Pastor: Religion and Society in Eighteenth-Century Northampton* (New York: Hill and Wang, 1979) cannot be classified as "biography" in its truest meaning since it chooses not to examine Edwards as a philosopher and theologian.

[126]Bruce Tucker, "Class and Culture in Recent Anglo-American Religious Historiography: A Review Essay," *Labour/Le Travailleur* 6 (Autumn 1980): 160.

Felt Tyler pioneered the way into the regions where religion meets cultural development and social change.[127] Timothy L. Smith, above these others, has set our agenda ever since his publication of *Revivalism and Social Reform* (1957),[128] which is important both as an historical study of Evangelicalism and as an historic evangelical document. Where previous treatments of revivalism tended to be dismissive, Smith linked revivalism to reformist, not reactionary impulses, and insisted that perfectionist ideology was as social as it was personal. William G. McLouglin's provocative work on Great Awakenings as "revitalization movements" represents the more recent (and sometimes *volte-face*) enrollment of numerous historians into the ranks of those who see social, economic, and political consequences to revivalism.[129] Indeed, some would reason that historians' preoccupation with Evangelicalism as a social phenomenon is because Evangelicalism took as its goal nothing less than the reformation of society. Thus the social dimension was necessary for the integrity of the evangelical vision itself. The "evangelical united front" refers not so much to theology as to actions bent on extricating evil everywhere. Its end was to eliminate moral decay and social retrogression. It was a united front for change, for missions, for the millennium, for making America into what Martin E. Marty has called a "righteous empire."[130] Not surprisingly, Paul Boyer has called Evangelicalism "one of the more dynamic and expansive social forces of the early nineteenth-century era."[131]

---

[127]Gilbert H. Baines, *The Antislavery Impulse, 1830-1844* (New York: D. Appleton-Century Co., 1933); Alice Felt Tyler, *Freedom's Ferment: Phases of American Social History to 1860* (Minneapolis: University of Minnesota Press, 1944); Whitney R. Cross, *The Burned-Over District: The Social and Intellectual History of Enthusiastic Religion in Western New York, 1800-1850* (Ithaca NY: Cornell University Press, 1982).

[128]For Smith's own historiographical assessment of where *Revivalism and Social Reform* stands in the literature, see his "Social Reform" in Gaustad, *The Rise of Adventism*, 18-29. For a historian's evaluation of the same question, see Ralph E. Luker's "Revivalism and Revisionism Revisited," *Fides et Historia* 14 (Spring-Summer 1982): 70-74.

[129]McLoughlin, *Revivals, Awakenings and Reform.* See also Anthony F. C. Wallace, "Revitalization Movements," *American Anthropologist* 58 (April 1956): 264-81.

[130]Martin E. Marty, *Righteous Empire: The Protestant Experience in America* (New York: Dial Press, 1970).

[131]Paul Boyer, *Urban Masses and Moral Order in America, 1820-1920* (Cambridge: Harvard University Press, 1978) 1.

Scholars who initially followed Smith's lead in tracing the roots of antislavery, feminism, sexual purity, and temperance to the "reformist heritage" and "reforming spirit" of evangelical theology include Donald Dayton, Lucille Sider Dayton, and Nancy Hardesty. Although they argue among themselves over various nuances of Wesleyan theology, they all agree that Wesley not Calvin, Oberlin not Princeton, "New School" not "Old School" theology is central to nineteenth-century Evangelicalism.[132] Because of them and others,[133] it has become commonplace for historians to refer to Evangelicalism as providing the ideological underpinnings, rhetorical grammar, organizational structures, and technical skills for antebellum reform crusades.[134] We now even have a collection of essays on the theme entitled *The Bible and Social Reform*

---

[132]Donald W. Dayton, *Discovering an Evangelical Heritage* (New York: Harper and Row, 1976); Lucille Sider Dayton and Donald W. Dayton, " 'Your Daughters Shall Prophesy?': Feminism in the Holiness Movement," *Methodist History* 14 (January 1976): 67-92; Nancy Hardesty, Lucille Sider, and Donald W. Dayton, "Women in the Holiness Movement: Feminism in the Evangelical Tradition," in *Women of Spirit: Female Leadership in the Jewish and Christian Traditions*, eds. Rosemary Ruether and Eleanor McLaughlin (New York: Simon and Schuster, 1979) 226-54. Our understanding of Evangelicalism will be enriched when historians begin exploring who were the antagonists of Evangelicalism and why they stood on the other side. The critique of Evangelicalism by transcendentalists, sacramentalists, "Old School" Calvinists, and liberals may shed important light on the subject.

[133]See, for example, Bertram Wyatt-Brown's reconstruction of the way evangelical sponsorship of the Sabbatarian movement afforded crucial political experience that was later put to use in the antislavery movement in "Prelude to Abolitionism: Sabbatarian Politics and the Rise of the Second Party System," *Journal of American History* 58 (September 1971): 316-41. Also see Lois W. Banner's thesis about reform as the social and political outlet for the ambitions of young male Evangelicals in "Religion and Reform in the Early Republic: The Role of Youth," *American Quarterly* 23 (December 1971): 677-95.

[134]For Donald Scott's hypothesis that abolition itself could become for some a "sacred vocation," see Scott, *From Office to Profession*, 76-94. In a seminal article John L. Thomas observed that the evangelical advance into the public arena went from moral to social reform. "Romantic Reform in America, 1815-1865," *American Quarterly* 17 (Winter 1965). Paul Boyer's work on *Urban Masses and Moral Order in America* confirms that sequence within the context of urban reform. David Reynolds's recent analysis of the literature of evangelical "reformist religion" before 1835, on the other hand, reveals that operant by that time there was a transformation in the concept of sin from physical depravity to social depravity and the equation of sin as bad social behavior. See David S. Reynolds's *Faith in Fiction: The Emergence of Religious Literature in America* (Cambridge: Harvard University Press, 1981) 81-85.

(1982).[135] For the post-Civil War era, a recent examination of social Christianity during Reconstruction reveals that Northern Methodist leaders displayed a strong social ethic, while some historians of Southern religion have professed to turn up evidence that connects evangelical religion and a progressive reform spirit in the postbellum South, which lasted well into the twentieth century.[136]

Yet historians are not of one mind on the social ramifications of evangelical theology, as witnessed by a collection of essays in which one author claims that holiness ideology provoked movements for social justice, while another argues that the doctrine of sanctification was without obvious social consequences.[137] In fact, numerous studies have begun to press for well-hedged hypotheses at best about Evangelicalism's association with social reform. One response raises serious questions about any easy identification of Evangelicalism with social progressivism.[138] Another productive investigation argues that evangelical ideology in antebellum America was a much more spacious haven for social conservatism

[135]Sandeen, ed., *Bible and Social Reform*.

[136]For the North see Donald G. Jones, *The Sectional Crisis and Northern Methodism: A Study in Piety, Political Ethics and Civil Religion* (Metuchen NJ: Scarecrow Press, 1979). For the South see John L. Eighmy, *Churches in Cultural Captivity: A History of the Social Attitudes of Southern Baptists* (Knoxville: University of Tennessee Press, 1972) 61:37-87; Anne Frior Scott, "Women, Religion, and Social Change in the South, 1830-1930," in *Religion and the Solid South*, ed. Hill, 93, 92-116; Harry G. Lefever, "The Involvement of the Men and Religion Forward Movement in the Cause of Labor Justice, Atlanta, Georgia, 1912-1916," *Labor History* 14 (Fall 1973): 521-35; Jacquelyn Dowd Hall, *Revolt Against Chivalry: Jessie Daniel Ames and the Women's Campaign Against Lynching* (New York: Columbia University Press, 1979); Dewey W. Grantham, "The Contours of Southern Progressivism," *American Historical Review* 86 (December 1981): 1039, 1035-59; John Patrick McDowell, *The Social Gospel in the South: The Woman's Home Mission Movement in the Methodist Episcopal Church, South 1886-1939* (Baton Rouge: Louisiana State University Press, 1982).

[137]Compare Timothy L. Smith, "Holiness and Radicalism in Nineteenth-Century America" and John Kent, "Methodism and Social Change in Britain" in *Sanctification and Liberation: Liberation Theologies in Light of the Wesleyan Tradition*, ed. Theodore Runyon (Nashville: Abingdon, 1981) 116-41, 83-101.

[138]Sweet, "Views of Man." That the historian working on the relationship between revivalism and social reform must be prepared to have one's expectations constantly thwarted is made apparent in Glenn C. Altschuler and Jan M. Saltzgaber, *Revivalism, Social Conscience, and Community in the Burned-Over District: The Trial of Rhoda Bement* (Ithaca: Cornell University Press, 1983).

than historians have usually accented.[139] Indeed, revivalism has not yet been proven causally to have led communities to embrace reform, and Perfectionism may have operated, as one historian suggests, more like a "wild card" in reform than anything else.[140] Evangelicals in the south Atlantic states entertained a deep sense of divine Providence and a diminished faith in the Puritan doctrine of means, which worked later in Southern history to block urban development in health, education, and housing for the poor, and to barricade Evangelicalism generally from society and politics under the banner of the "spirituality of the church." Herein lay the major irony of Southern religion, what Samuel S. Hill has felicitously called its "ethos without ethics."[141] James H. Moorhead has perhaps best summarized these conflicting tendencies within Evangelicalism, which worked to simultaneously expand and contract the reform impulse, in an important article detailing "the divided conscience" of antebellum Evangelicalism.[142]

Many fine historians lost some of their scholarly composure by adopting too readily the social control explanation for Evangelicalism's dual energies in the nineteenth century. The social control hypothesis is by now rather obsolete, but is discovered anew by each succeeding genera-

---

[139]Moorhead, *American Apocalypse*.

[140]Paul E. Johnson, *A Shopkeeper's Millennium: Society and Revivals in Rochester, New York, 1815-1837* (New York: Hill and Wang, 1978). For the way in which Perfectionism could lead either to social engagement or escape, see Ralph E. Luker, "Religion and Social Control in the Nineteenth-Century American City," *Journal of Urban History* 2 (May 1976): 363-69.

[141]Loveland, *Southern Evangelicals*, 125-26, 158, 265; David R. Goldfield, "The Urban South: A Regional Framework," *American Historical Review* 86 (December 1981): 1021-25, 1009-34; E. Brooks Holifield, "Thomas Smyth: The Social Ideas of a Southern Evangelist," *Journal of Presbyterian History* 51 (Spring 1973): 24-39; Hill, *South and the North*.

[142]Moorhead, "Social Reform," 416-30. Other scholars who have written about the paradoxical conservative-radical pulls within Evangelicalism are Bertram Wyatt-Brown, "Prelude to Abolitionism," 339, and James L. McElroy, "Social Control and Romantic Reform in Antebellum America: The Case of Rochester, New York," *New York History* 58 (January 1977): 17-46. For the continuation of this ambivalence about social change into the Progressive period, see Don S. Kirschner, "The Ambiguous Legacy: Social Justice and Social Control in the Progressive Era," *Historical Reflections* 2 (Summer 1975): 69-88.

tion of historians, making it one of the more copious areas of American religious historiography. With historians functioning more and more like sociologists, and with order the pivotal problem of sociology, the near fixation on a social control mode of analysis was almost predictable. Revivalism and the values it promoted functioned as a middle-class agency of social control, write James L. McElroy, Paul Johnson, Marion L. Bell, and Fred J. Hood.[143] Movements for temperance, social reform, civic betterment, purity crusades, even Noah Webster's *Dictionary* were supposedly motivated by the needs of middle and upper classes to protect their threatened interests.[144]

The problem with the social control explanation is twofold. John W. Kuykendall has put his finger on the first problem. The social control hypothesis is mistaken, he states, because it "misreads the mood" of Evangelicals.[145] Hope rather than fear motivated them. Second, social control theories make easy pickings of an inherently thorny situation by, as James Findlay puts it, "making too much of a certain narrow self-interest."[146]

---

[143]McElroy, "Social Control and Romantic Reform," 17-23; Johnson, *Shopkeeper's Millennium*; Marion L. Bell, *Crusade in the City: Revivalism in Nineteenth Century Philadelphia* (Lewisburg PA: Bucknell University Press, 1977); Fred J. Hood, *Reformed America: The Middle and Southern States, 1783-1837* (Alabama: University of Alabama Press, 1980).

[144]Joseph R. Gusfield, *Symbolic Crusade: Status Politics and the American Temperance Movement* (Urbana: University of Illinois Press, 1963); Charles I. Foster, *An Errand of Mercy: The Evangelical United Front, 1790-1837* (Chapel Hill: University of North Carolina Press, 1960); Clifford S. Griffin, *Their Brother's Keepers: Moral Stewardship in the United States, 1800-1865* (New Brunswick NJ: Rutgers University Press, 1960); W. David Lewis, "The Reformer as Conservative: Protestant Counter-Subversion in the Early Republic" in *The Development of an American Culture*, eds. Stanley Cohen and Lorman Ratner (Englewood Cliffs NJ: Prentice-Hall, 1970); Berk, *Calvinism versus Democracy*; Raymond A. Mohl, *Poverty in New York, 1783-1825* (New York: Oxford University Press, 1970); David J. Pivar, *Purity Crusade: Sexual Morality and Social Control, 1868-1900* (Westport CT: Greenwood Press, 1973); Richard M. Rollins, "Words as Social Control: Noah Webster and the Creation of *The American Dictionary*," *American Quarterly* 28 (Fall 1976): 415-30. See also Lois Banner, "Religious Benevolence as Social Control: A Critique of an Interpretation," *Journal of American History* 60 (June 1973): 23-41; and Ralph E. Luker, "Religion and Social Control in the Nineteenth-Century American City," *Journal of Urban History* 2 (May 1976): 363-69.

[145]John W. Kuykendall, *Southern Enterprise: The Work of National Evangelical Societies in the Antebellum South* (Westport CT: Greenwood Press, 1982).

[146]James Findlay, "The SPCTEW and Western Colleges: Religion and Higher Education in Mid-Nineteenth-Century America," *History of Education Quarterly* 17:1 (Spring 1977): 35.

Catchall categories like "social control" have been used to cover a multitude of complexities, everything from morals to missions, and ought to be gracefully (or at least gratefully) banished to the place where all blanket explanations eventually end up. Those who continue to use it have forgotten that, according to Edward A. Ross, the theoretician who developed the concept of social control in 1901, there is an inevitable and indeed "needed" aspect of social control if there is to be the building of genuine community. The elite manipulation of the masses through religion or politics, cultural symbols or advertisements is an illegitimate employment of social control techniques. Yet there is a universal human need for order in any social life; and when steps are taken to safeguard and secure social order, whether in the realm of church discipline, temperance or Southern "honor,"[147] social control may not be a bad imposition but a benign, even benevolent expression of the general will responding to genuine personal and social needs.

The basic point, however, is not whether social control is good or bad, but whether someone is being controlled and for what purposes. The social control literature needs to be viewed with consideration for the special needs of various groups caught in the process of reconstructing social institutions and individual character. With attack more than analysis on our minds, American religious historians have not even come close to approaching the social control topic with the sensitivity and objectivity that Eric H. Monkkonen brings to his work on uniformed police departments as social control bureaucracies.[148] As Ralph E. Luker suggests, "Social reform and social control are functions of each other."[149] We are properly

---

[147]Henry S. Stroupe, " 'Cite Them Both to Attend the Next Church Conference': Social Control by North Carolina Baptist Churches, 1772-1908," *North Carolina Historical Review* 52 (April 1975): 156-70; Ross Evans Paulson, *Women's Suffrage and Prohibition: A Comparative Study of Equality and Social Control* (Glenview IL: Scott, Foresman and Company, 1973). In a study of Southern culture that offers a high level of scholarship and insight, Bertram Wyatt-Brown argues that the South's ethic of "honor" provided a needed system of social control. Bertram Wyatt-Brown, *Southern Honor: Ethics and Behavior in the Old South* (New York: Oxford University Press, 1982).

[148]Eric H. Monkkonen, *Police in Urban America, 1860-1920* (Cambridge: Cambridge University Press, 1981) 8-10, 150-56.

[149]Luker, "Revivalism and Revisionism Revisited," 73.

cautioned against the appropriateness of social control explanations by Paul Boyer and Ronald G. Walters in their studies on reformers and by Robert J. Loewenberg and John S. Andrew III in their studies on missionaries.[150] If anything, evangelical theology tended to work, Lewis Perry concludes, against the controlling needs of reformers.[151]

Emerging research is beginning to demonstrate that revivalist religion could temporarily integrate and harmonize communities as much as splinter them along theological or social issues,[152] so much so that James Moorhead arrestingly suggests that Finney be seen as a "broker between classes," establishing social harmony and order among different groups by a process of internalizing religious norms.[153] In an era of exploding entrepreneurship, the center of the moral universe shifted from community life, which had customarily mediated relationships to God, to the auton-

---

[150]This is the position of Paul Boyer, *Urban Masses and Moral Order*; Ronald G. Walters, *American Reformers, 1815-1860* (New York: Hill and Wang, 1978); Robert J. Loewenberg, *Equality on the Oregon Frontier: Jason Lee and the Methodist Missions, 1834-43* (Seattle: University of Washington Press, 1976); and John A. Andrew III, *Rebuilding the Christian Commonwealth: New England Congregationalists and Foreign Missions, 1800-1830* (Lexington: University of Kentucky Press, 1976). For other criticism of social control theories, see Carroll Smith-Rosenberg, *Religion and the Rise of the American City: The New York City Mission Movement, 1812-1870* (Ithaca NY: Cornell University Press, 1970), and especially William A. Muraskin, "The Social Control Theory in American History: A Critique," *Journal of Social History* 9 (Summer 1976): 559-69.

[151]Lewis Perry, " 'We Have Had Conversation in the World': The Abolitionists and Spontaneity," *Canadian Review of American Studies* 6 (Spring 1975): 3-26.

[152]Sweet, " 'A Nation Born in a Day': The Union Prayer Meeting Revival and Cultural Revitalization" in *In The Great Tradition: Essays in Honor of Winthrop S. Hudson*, eds. Joseph Ban and Paul R. Dekar (Valley Forge: Judson Press, 1982) 193-221. See also Sandra S. Sizer's *Gospel Hymns and Social Religion: The Rhetoric of Nineteenth-Century Revivalism* (Philadelphia: Temple University Press, 1978) and "Politics and Apolitical Religion: The Great Urban Revivals of the Late Nineteenth Century," *Church History* 48 (March 1979): 81-98. For recent research on the Union Prayer Meeting Revival, see J. Edwin Orr, *The Fervent Prayer: The Worldwide Impact of the Great Awakening of 1858* (Chicago: Moody Press, 1974), and Howard Fenimore Shipps, "The Revival of 1858 in Mid-America," *Methodist History* 16 (April 1978): 128-51. The cohesive effect of evangelical religion on small towns is evident in *Revivalism, Social Conscience, and Community in the Burned-Over District: The Trial of Rhoda Bement* by Glenn C. Altschuler and Jan M. Saltzgaber (Ithaca NY: Cornell University Press, 1983). John L. Hammond, *The Politics of Benevolence*, on the other hand, rejects the interpretation of revivalism as a font or fulfillment of national consensus and social integration.

[153]Moorhead, *American Apocalypse*, 428.

omous individual. Evangelicalism helped to provide a society in danger of collapsing into moral solipsism with a system of internal authority based on conscience, discipline, and deferred gratification, which many scholars almost at once are calling "the ethic of self-control" (Johnson, Lears, Moorhead, McLoughlin, Scott, and Smith).[154] For Donald M. Scott this "new social grammar"—a new and distinctive way of perceiving how the social order was composed, operated, and maintained—was one of Evangelicalism's most important and enduring contributions during the Second Great Awakening.[155] An evangelical conception of social order, replacing hierarchical, deferential, institutional conceptions of order, emerged to dominate American religion until the present. Indeed, fear of vanishing Victorian social ideals of self-control drives much of what Grant Wacker calls today's "Evangelical Right," clinging desperately to the wreckage of old pieties.

Not all evangelical energies went into revivalism, of course. Voluntary societies and other social experiences were also translations of this new vocabulary of social order into vehicles of self-control. In fact, instead of revivalism giving rise to voluntary societies, Richard D. Shiels states in his thesis that the Second Great Awakening (which Butler implicitly argues is the first) is best interpreted as a folk movement that was sparked, not by Timothy Dwight-trained Federalist clergy at Yale, but by lay voluntary societies.[156] Donald Scott also reverses another traditional sequence in his contention that voluntary societies were a cause, not a consequence, of the diminished social status of evangelical clergy.[157] The importance of voluntarism to the study of American history in general and evangelical ecclesiology in particular is highlighted by C. C. Goen, es-

---

[154]T. J. Jackson Lears, *No Place of Grace: Antimodernism and the Transformation of American Culture, 1880-1920* (New York: Pantheon Books, 1981) 12-14; Moorhead, *American Apocalypse*, 428; Timothy L. Smith, "Righteousness and Hope: Christian Holiness and the Millennial Vision in America, 1800-1900," *American Quarterly* 31 (April 1979): 29-30.

[155]Scott, *From Office to Profession*, 36.

[156]Richard D. Shiels, "The Second Great Awakening in Connecticut: Critique of the Traditional Interpretation," *Church History* 49 (December 1980): 401-15. See also Richard Birdsall, "The Second Great Awakening and the New England Social Order," *Church History* 39 (September 1970): 345-64.

[157]Scott, *From Office to Profession*, 52-67.

pecially in his interpretation of states' rights theory as "the political version of evangelical voluntaryism."[158]

Never before has the temperance movement and its voluntary societies been such a popular subject for historical inquiry. In the past more bad books were written on the temperance crusade than on almost any other reform movement. By contrast, today's research into temperance reform is drawing some of the most able minds, weighty analyses, and sophisticated methodologies in all of American history.

Historians have come a long way since Richard Hofstadter's dismissal of prohibition as a "rural-evangelical virus" and "pseudo-reform."[159] Recent scholarship reveals that standard interpretations of the temperance movement (Sydney Ahlstrom called the Anti-Saloon League "the last great corporate work of legalistic evangelicalism") have been clamped too tightly around Evangelicalism, that early nineteenth-century America really did have a drinking problem (W. J. Rorabaugh calls America a "nation of drunkards"), and that sizeable support for temperance reform came from the more progressive corners of America's urban, business, and religious life. Indeed, the leadership of the prohibition movement was drawn overwhelmingly from the ranks of the social gospel and progressive movements with the liquor trust seen as the largest and worst of all trusts.

The current literature on temperance comes at a time when historians appear increasingly prone to psychohistorical angles, and when any book on American history published without a chart, graph, or statistical appendix is immediately suspect. The fact that the quantitative approach does not solve all our problems is partially demonstrated by the statistical profiling of temperance leaders, which reveals everything from their broad social base, their dominance by a cast of upwardly mobile, evangelical, affluent characters, or the existence of a class struggle between the

---

[158]C. C. Goen, "Broken Churches, Broken Nation," 27.

[159]Richard Hofstadter, *The Age of Reform: From Bryan to F.D.R.* (New York: Knopf, 1955). Useful review essays on temperance historiography include Joseph F. Kett, "Review Essay: Temperance and Intemperance as Historical Problems," *Journal of American History* 67 (March 1981): 878-85; Paul A. Carter, "Temperance, Intemperance, and the American Character: or, Dr. Jekyll and Mr. Hyde," *Journal of Social History* 14 (Spring 1981): 481-84; Jed Dannenbaum, "The Crusade Against Drink," *Reviews in American History* 9 (December 1981): 497-502.

lower and middle classes.[160] The difficulty of psychological categories as interpretive explanations is evident in a comparison of Gusfield's treatment of "drys" and Rorabaugh's treatment of "wets." Gusfield argues that abstainers were motivated by anxieties over social and economic upheaval. In an identical vein, Rorabaugh argues that drinkers were motivated by anxiety over social and economic upheaval.[161] Rorabaugh's notion that antebellum Evangelicalism was stimulated at least in part by an attempt of the children of this "alcoholic republic" to relieve anxieties through religious piety, anxieties that their fathers had drowned in drink, is too reductionist to carry much weight.

One historian who has not allowed the successes of class analysis, social science techniques, and psychohistorical speculations to dwarf the cultural context of temperance reform is Norman H. Clark. Clark's analysis of the emergence of temperance ideology out of the shifting of social authority to the individual from the community appears particularly trenchant.[162] Much more work needs to be done, however, in exploring the degree of legitimacy attained by historians who link temperance's appeal with gender (women), religion (Evangelicalism), politics (Whiggery), class (middle), and occupation (clergy and entrepreneurs). Such exploration needs to be conducted, moreover, by scholars who do not have to admit that they "find it difficult to comprehend nineteenth century revivalism fully" (Rorabaugh), who can analyze the role of music and mass communications in the temperance movement,[163] and who are

---

[160]Robert L. Hampel, *Temperance and Prohibition in Massachusetts, 1813-1852* (Ann Arbor: UMI Research Press, 1982); Jack S. Blocker, Jr., ed., *Alcohol, Reform and Society: The Liquor Issue in Social Context* (Westport CT: Greenwood Press, 1979); Ian R. Tyrrell, *Sobering Up: From Temperance to Prohibition in Antebellum America, 1800-1860* (Westport CT: Greenwood Press, 1979).

[161]W. J. Rorabaugh, *The Alcoholic Republic: An American Tradition* (New York: Oxford University Press, 1979); Joseph R. Gusfield, *Symbolic Crusade Status Politics and the American Temperance Movement* (Urbana: University of Illinois Press, 1963).

[162]Norman H. Clark, *Deliver Us From Evil: An Interpretation of American Prohibition* (New York: W. W. Norton, 1976).

[163]Small beginnings have been made here by Grosvenor Fattic, " 'A Few Sterling Pieces': Nineteenth Century Adventist Temperance Songs," *Adventist Heritage* 2 (Summer 1975): 35-41; and Daniel F. Ring, "The Temperance Movement in Milwaukee: 1872-1884," *Historical Messenger* (Milwaukee County Historical Society) 31 (Winter 1975): 98-105.

equipped with the methodological tools to relate religious and cultural change to social and economic forces.

If Robert V. Hines and Don Harrison Doyle are to be believed, evangelical churches and voluntary associations were two of the few achievements of genuine community in America.[164] The making of America into a community with national, not local consciousness, was facilitated by voluntary societies, which lubricated, according to Gregory H. Singleton, the shift of American society into a corporate social order later in the century.[165] Although there have been excellent studies conducted on individual voluntary societies like the Woman's Christian Temperance Union (WCTU) and Alcoholics Anonymous (AA), as well as on clusters of voluntary societies like those engaged in nineteenth-century urban reform, the stories of many other voluntary societies and their grounding in Evangelicalism are still untold. We still have no adequate account of the voluntary society movement in American history, or of the way in which America itself came to resemble a voluntary society.[166] Further work also needs to be done on the relationship of voluntary societies to denominations,[167] voluntary societies in the South,[168] where historians have most

---

[164]Robert V. Hine, *Community on the American Frontier: Separate but Not Alone* (Norman OK: University of Oklahoma Press, 1980); Don Harrison Doyle, *The Social Order of a Frontier Community: Jacksonville, Illinois, 1825-1870* (Urbana: University of Illinois Press, 1978): 156-68, 178-93.

[165]Gregory H. Singleton, "Protestant Voluntary Organizations and the Shaping of Victorian America," *American Quarterly* 27 (December 1975): 549-60.

[166]Ruth Bordin, *Woman and Temperance: The Quest for Power and Liberty, 1873-1900* (Philadelphia: Temple University Press, 1981); Ernest Kurtz, *Not-God: A History of Alcoholics Anonymous* (Center City MN: Hazelden Educational Services, 1979); John F. Woolverton, "Evangelical Protestantism and Alcoholism 1933-1962: Episcopalian Samuel Shoemaker, The Oxford Group and Alcoholics Anonymous," *Historical Magazine of the Protestant Episcopal Church* 52 (March 1983): 53-65; Smith-Rosenberg, *Rise of the American City*.

[167]Findlay, "SPCTEW and Western College," 44-45.

[168]Kuykendall's study of the "Big Five" missionary societies (the American "Education," "Bible," "Sunday School Union," "Tract" and "Home Missionary" Society) in *Southern Enterprise* is still primarily a survey of Northern efforts below the Mason-Dixon line. The relationship between the power possessed by local and regional auxiliaries at voluntary societies and the loss of an evangelical orientation to abolitionism is probed by John R. McKivigan, "The Gospel will Burst the Bonds of the Slave: The Abolitionists' Bibles for Slaves Campaigns," *Negro History Bulletin* 45 (July-August-September 1982): 62-64, 77.

often (and mistakenly) noted their absence, and on the way in which voluntary societies in America were modeled after and moderated by British examples.[169] In short, someone needs to do for voluntarism what Richard Carwardine did for revivalism—that is, to see it as a transatlantic phenomenon. Better still would be a general treatment of Anglo-American Evangelicalism in the eighteenth and nineteenth centuries that recognized the existence of a single Atlantic evangelical culture. In the words of J. F. Maclear, such a culture would contain an "authentic cosmopolitanism—a sense of mutual accountability for each other's moral performance which pervaded British and American evangelical culture in the early Victorian era."[170]

In the pursuit of evangelical life on the borderlands of religion and society, historians have neglected the heartland of Evangelicalism. What did Evangelicals do when they were not trying to change the world? Milton Sernett thinks that Timothy Smith's classic may have inadvertently "turned our heads"[171]—turned them away from the inner spiritual life and everyday fare of evangelical communities, as though Evangelicalism's social engagements were all that mattered. The history of ministry

---

[169]The literature on European and English history of voluntary societies is unknown to most American historians. Recent studies that supplement the earlier work of F. W. B. Bullock and W. K. Lowther Clarke include Eamon Duffy " 'Correspondence Fraternelle': The SPCK, the SPG, and the Churches of Switzerland in the War of the Spanish Succession" in *Reform and Reformation: England and the Continent, c. 1500-c. 1750*, ed. Derek Baker (Oxford: Oxford University Press, 1979): 251-80. Besides detailing interdenominational cooperation through societies, Duffy demonstrates that voluntary societies have a long history that extends far beyond stereotypical "Evangelical" boundaries.

[170]Richard Carwardine, *Transatlantic Revivalism: Popular Evangelicalism in Britain and America, 1790-1865* (Westport CT: Greenwood Press, 1978). J. F. Maclear, "Evangelical Alliance," 164. For some evidence of how this transatlantic evangelical community operated, see Mark Heathcote Hall's "Bishop McIlvaine, The Reluctant Frontiersman," *Historical Magazine of the Protestant Episcopal Church* 44 (March 1975): 81-96. An early and recent call for such a study can be found respectively in Winthrop S. Hudson, "How American is Religion in America," in *Reinterpretation in American Church History*, ed. Jerald C. Brauer (Chicago: University of Chicago Press, 1968) 153-67; and in Martin E. Marty, "Living with Establishment and Disestablishment in Nineteenth-Century Anglo-America," *Journal of Church and State* 18 (Winter 1976): 61-77 and "On Comparing and Connecting Histories" in Ban and Dekar, *In the Great Tradition*, 19-32.

[171]Milton C. Sernett to author, 18 February 1983, private correspondence. For an exploration of evangelical piety see W. Andrew Hoffecher, "The Devotional Life of Archibald Alexander, Charles Hodge and B. B. Warfield," *Westminster Theological Journal* 42 (Fall 1979): 111-29.

in the evangelical tradition, encompassing both views of the ministry (for example, the pastoral image, office and call) and institutional practices and developments, suffers the same neglect, and for probably the same reason.[172]

A major criticism of traditional American religious historiography has been its inattentiveness to the varied religious experiences of non-whites and nonmales. The essays in this volume by Albert J. Raboteau, Carroll Smith-Rosenberg, Nancy A. Hewitt, and Henry Warner Bowden provide excellent examples of the new attempts to remedy this weakness in the history of American Evangelicalism.

The role of evangelical religion in the slave experience as a liberating force and a weapon against oppression has been one of the most significant historical insights to emerge in the last dozen years. The Marxist historian Eugene D. Genovese surprised more historians than he should have *less* with his view of slavery as a paternalistic institution (not socializing or dehumanizing) than with his positive assessment of the spiritual vitality and maturity of slaves' inner experience and of religion as a creative force in slave life—a thesis he underlined by selecting a slave spiritual ("Roll, Jordan, Roll") as a title for his history of slavery and by introducing each

---

[172]Donald M. Scott's *From Office to Profession*, of course, is a significant exception. Milton C. Sernett's "Behold the American Cleric: The Protestant Minister as 'Pattern Man,' 1850-1900" in *Winterthur: Portfolio 8*, ed. Ian M. G. Quinby (Charlottesville: University Press of Virginia, 1973): 1-8, while of a general cast, covers some of these matters. E. Brooks Holifield's "The Hero and the Minister in American Culture," *Theology Today* 33 (January 1977): 370-79, is enormously suggestive, as is Russell E. Richey's "Evolving Patterns of Methodist Ministry," *Methodist History* 22 (October 1983): 20-37. See also Frederick A. Norwood, "The Shaping of Methodist Ministry," *Religion in Life* 43 (Autumn 1974): 337-51; Bruce M. Stephens, "Watchmen on the Walls of Zion: Samuel Miller and the Christian Ministry," *Journal of Presbyterian History* 56 (Winter 1978): 296-309; Dale A. Johnson, "The Methodist Quest for an Educated Ministry," *Church History* 51 (September 1982): 304-20; Michael G. Nickerson, "Historical Relationships of Itinerancy and Salary," *Methodist History* 21 (October 1982): 43-59; and John B. Weaver, "Charles F. Deems: The Ministry as Profession in Nineteenth-Century America," *Methodist History* 21 (April 1983): 156-68. Two recent studies that resist the predominant historical thrust of exploring Evangelicalism outward and instead look at Evangelicalism inward—its worship patterns, spirituality, and theological character—are Doug Adams's *Meeting House to Camp Meeting: Toward a History of American Free Church Worship From 1620 to 1835* (Saratoga NY: Modern Liturgy-Resource Publication, 1981) and Thomas A. Langford, *Practical Divinity: Theology in the Wesleyan Tradition* (Nashville: Abingdon, 1983).

chapter with a biblical quotation.[173] While Genovese's thesis that Christianity gave slaves meaning, purpose, and self-respect still has currency in the debate over religion and slavery,[174] much controversy still surrounds the relative influence of white Evangelicalism and West African religion in shaping the character of the black religious experience. A common evangelical heritage to both black and white religion is stressed by Milton C. Sernett, Albert J. Raboteau, Winthrop S. Hudson, Timothy L. Smith, and Peter H. Wood, with evangelical religion nevertheless taking on a different cast for blacks because of their slave experiences.[175] Eugene Genovese and Donald Mathews emphasize more of a blend of West African and evangelical religion in shaping black religion; Jon Butler argues for the mutual reinforcement of African and Evangelical religion among slaves; and Gayraud S. Wilmore and Mechal Sobel assert the decisiveness of the African memory.[176] A promising way out of this debate might be an examination of transcultural parallels like the ring shout and the jerks, especially the common social and religious conditions that give rise to them. Needed studies of biracial church life, which have yet to appear in any significant numbers,[177] may also cast significant light on the

---

[173]Genovese, *Roll, Jordan, Roll*.

[174]Despite significant differences between Genovese and Lawrence W. Levine (*Black Culture and Black Consciousness: Afro-American Folk-Thought from Slavery to Freedom* [New York: Oxford University Press, 1977]), both agree on the centrality of religion to the Afro-American experience.

[175]Sernett, *Black Religion and American Evangelicalism*; Raboteau, *Slave Religion*, 86; Winthrop S. Hudson, "The American Context as an Area for Research in Black Church Studies," *Church History* 52 (June 1983): 157-71; Timothy L. Smith, "Slavery and Theology: The Emergence of Black Christian Consciousness in Nineteenth-Century America," *Church History* 41 (December 1972): 497-512; Peter H. Wood, " 'Jesus Christ Has Got Thee at Last': Afro-American Conversion as a Forgotten Chapter in Eighteenth-Century Southern Intellectual History," *Bulletin of the Center for the Study of Southern Culture and Religion* 3 (November 1979): 2-7.

[176]Jon Butler, "The Dark Ages of American Occultism, 1760-1848," *The Occult Experience in America*, eds. Howard Kerr and Charles Crow (Urbana: University of Illinois Press, 1983): 58-78; Gayraud S. Wilmore, *Black Religion and Black Radicalism* (Garden City NY: Doubleday, 1972); Mechal Sobel, *Trabelin' On: The Slave Journey to an Afro-Baptist Faith* (Westport CT: Greenwood Press, 1979).

[177]A small but insightful beginning is made by Erskine Clarke, *Wrestlin' Jacob: A Portrait of Religion in the Old South* (Atlanta: John Knox Press, 1979).

discussion and reveal the exaggerated differences between black and white Evangelicalism. Of most pressing need, however, is a general survey of the black religious experience in America; for it is a gap in American religious historiography that grows more conspicuous as each year passes.

While historians continue to unearth important insights about ethnomusicology and the liberation theme of black spirituals;[178] the rise of white racism in Southern churches;[179] black clerical leadership in the abolitionist and civil rights movement;[180] the response of white churches to the slave and black community;[181] the "visible institution" of indepen-

---

[178]Le Roy Moore, Jr., "The Spiritual: Soul of Black Religion," *American Quarterly* 23 (December 1971): 658-76; James H. Cone, "Black Spirituals: A Theological Interpretation," *Theology Today* 29 (April 1972): 54-69; Dena J. Epstein, *Sinful Tunes and Spirituals: Black Folk Music to the Civil War* (Urbana: University of Illinois Press, 1977); Irene V. Jackson, comp., *Afro-American Religious Music: A Bibliography and a Catalogue of Gospel Music* (Westport CT: Greenwood Press, 1979).

[179]H. Shelton Smith, *In His Image, But . . . Racism in Southern Religion* (Durham NC: Duke University Press, 1972). Also see Michael Harrington's review essay, "Evangelicism [sic] and Racism in the Development of Southern Religion," *Mississippi Quarterly* 27 (Spring 1971): 201-209.

[180]Carol V. R. George, "Widening the Circle: The Black Church and the Abolitionist Crusade, 1830-1860," in Perry and Fellman, *Antislavery Reconsidered*, 75-95; and David M. Tucker, *Black Pastors and Leaders: The Memphis Clergy, 1819-1972* (Memphis TN: Memphis State University Press, 1975).

[181]Lester B. Scherer, *Slavery and the Churches in Early America, 1619-1819* (Grand Rapids MI: Eerdmans, 1975); Inez M. Parker, *The Rise and Decline of the Program of Education for Black Presbyterians of the United Presbyterian Church USA, 1865-1970* (San Antonio: Trinity University Press, 1977); Thomas Virgil Peterson, *Ham and Japeth: The Mythic World of Whites in the Antebellum South* (Metuchen NJ: Scarecrow Press, 1978); Ronald E. Butchart, "Evangelical Christianity and Freedmen's Education," in *Northern Schools, Southern Blacks, and Reconstruction: Freedmen's Education, 1862-1875* (Westport CT: Greenwood Press, 1980) 33-52; A. Knighton Stanley, *The Children Is Crying: Congregationalism Among Black People* (New York: Pilgrim Press, 1979); R. E. Hood, "From a Headstart to a Deadstart: The Historical Basis for Black Indifference Toward the Episcopal Church, 1801-1860," *Historical Magazine of the Protestant Episcopal Church* 51 (September 1982): 269-96; Ann C. Lammers, "The Rev. Absalom Jones and the Episcopal Church: Christian Theology and Black Consciousness in a New Alliance," *Historical Magazine of the Protestant Episcopal Church* 51 (June 1982): 159-84; Sandy Dwayne Martin, "The American Baptist Home Mission Society and Black Higher Education in the South, 1865-1920," *Foundations* 24 (October-December 1981): 310-27; James David Essig, "A Very Wintry Season: Virginia Baptists and Slavery, 1785-1797," *Virginia Magazine of History and Biography* 88 (April 1980): 170-85; Julius E. Del Pino, "Blacks in the

dent and quasi-independent black churches;[182] and black involvement in

United Methodist Church from Its Beginning to 1968," *Methodist History* 19 (October 1980): 3-20; Joe M. Richardson, "The Failure of the American Missionary Association to Expand Congregationalism Among Southern Blacks," *Southern Studies* 18 (Spring 1979): 51-73; Harvey K. Newman, "Piety and Segregation—White Protestant Attitudes Toward Blacks in Atlanta, 1865-1906," *Georgia Historical Quarterly* 63 (Summer 1979): 238-51; Wayne C. Tyner, "Charles Colcock Jones: Mission to Slaves," *Journal of Presbyterian History* 55 (Winter 1977): 363-80; J. Earl Thompson, Jr., "Slavery and Presbyterians in the Revolutionary Era," *Journal of Presbyterian History* 54 (Spring 1976): 121-41; Ena L. Farley, "Methodists and Baptists on the Issue of Black Equality in New York, 1865-1868," *Journal of Negro History* 61 (October 1976): 374-92; Donald G. Mathews, "Charles Colcock Jones and the Southern Evangelical Crusade to Form a Biracial Community," *Journal of Southern History* 41 (August 1975): 299-320; Grant S. Shockley, "Methodism, Society and Black Evangelicalism in America: Retrospect and Prospect," *Methodist History* 12 (July 1974): 145-82 and *A.M.E. Zion Quarterly Review News Bulletin* (July 1974): 145-82; W. Harrison Daniel, "The Methodist Episcopal Church and the Negro in the Early National Period," *Methodist History* 11 (January 1973): 40-53; Daniel, "Southern Presbyterians and the Negro in the Early National Period," *Journal of Negro History* 18 (July 1973): 291-312; Daniel, "Virginia Baptists and the Negro in the Early Republic," *The Virginia Magazine of History and Biography* 80 (January 1972): 60-69; Daniel, "Virginia Baptists and the Negro in the Antebellum Era," *Journal of Negro History* 56 (January 1971): 1-16; David H. Bradley, "Francis Asbury and the Development of African Churches in America," *Methodist History* 10 (October 1971): 3-29; Richard N. Watkins, Jr., "The Baptists of the North and Slavery, 1856-1860," *Foundations* 13 (October-December 1970): 317-34.

[182]Sobel, *Trabelin' On*; Joseph R. Washington, Jr., *Black Cults and Sects* (Garden City NY: Doubleday, 1972); Carol V. R. George, *Segregated Sabbaths: Richard Allen and the Emergence of Independent Black Churches* (New York: Oxford University Press, 1973); William J. Walls, *The A.M.E. Zion Church: Reality of the Black Church* (Charlotte NC: A.M.E. Zion Publishing House, 1974); Clarence E. Walker, *A Rock in a Weary Land: The African Methodist Episcopal Church during the Civil War and Reconstruction* (Baton Rouge: Louisiana State University Press, 1982); Lewis V. Baldwin, "The A.V.M.P. and U.A.M.E. Churches: An Unexplored Area of Black Methodism," *Methodist History* 19 (April 1981): 175-78; David R. Roediger, "And Die in Dixie: Funerals, Death, and Heaven in the Slave Community 1700-1865," *Massachusetts Review* 22 (Spring 1981): 163-83; Dennis C. Dickerson, "The Black Church in Industrializing Western Pennsylvania, 1870-1950," *Western Pennsylvania Historical Magazine* 64 (October 1981): 329-44; William B. Graveley, "The Social, Political and Religious Significance of the Formation of the Colored Methodist Episcopal Church," *Methodist History* 18 (October 1979): 3-25; Michael Patrick Williams, "The Black Evangelical Ministry in the Antebellum Border States," *Foundations* 21 (July-September 1978): 225-41; Michael R. Bradley, "The Role of the Black Church in the Colonial Slave Society," *Louisiana Studies* 16 (Winter 1975): 413-21; George A. Levesque, "Inherent Reformers—Inherited Orthodoxy: Black Baptists in Boston, 1800-1873," *Journal of Negro History* 60 (October 1975): 491-519; Jon Butler, "Congregations and Communities: The Black Church in St. Paul, 1860-1900," *Journal of Negro History* 56 (April 1971): 118-34. A review of much of this literature can

missions,[183] the greatest excitement in recent years has attended Albert Raboteau's treatment of the "invisible institution" in the Southern states.[184] With an essay in this collection on "The Black Experience in American Evangelicalism: The Meaning of Slavery," Raboteau continues his delineation of the differences between black and white Evangelicalism and his probings into Evangelicalism's elevating the self-image of the enslaved, fortifying black resistance, and inspiring political activity. He explores how slavery became the matrix from which blacks fashioned their own distinctive evangelical religion and in turn helped shaped the course of American Evangelicalism. It took immense strength to claim the same evangelical religion as the oppressors—even to exert important leadership in spreading evangelical religion—and yet at the same time to assert that key doctrines in the oppressor's religion were wrong. Having lit their spiritual torches at an altar where the gospel of freedom burned away the darkness, blacks held these torches aloft long after white Evangelicals had doused the fires of freedom. Although the black evangelical creed could also lead to "quietism and political withdrawal," as Stanley L. Engerman reminds us,[185] an important aspect of Evangelicalism not only braced blacks to oppose the evils of slavery, it also provided black leadership with the resources to oppose brutalities that white evangelical faith succored. An especially important feature of Raboteau's article is his discussion of slavery's meaning for both Northern blacks and Southern slaves. Whereas a former study of "Why did slavery happen to us?" accented the black answer of "This is the good that can come out of it,"[186] Raboteau argues that the response to the slavery question boiled down to

---

be found in Gayraud S. Wilmore, "Reinterpretation in Black Church History," *Chicago Theological Seminary Register* 73 (Winter 1983): 25-37.

[183]See the pathbreaking collection of essays edited by Sylvia M. Jacobs (one-third of which are by Jacobs herself) entitled *Black Americans and the Missionary Movement in Africa* (Westport CT: Greenwood Press, 1982).

[184]Albert J. Raboteau, *Slave Religion: The "Invisible Institution" in the Antebellum South* (New York: Oxford University Press, 1978).

[185]Stanley L. Engerman, "A Response to Jon Butler and Albert Raboteau: Finney Historical Conference," unpublished manuscript, 11. For other failures of Evangelicalism, see Lawrence N. Jones, "Black Christianity in Antebellum America: In Quest of the Beloved Community," *Journal of Religious Thought* 38 (Spring-Summer 1981): 12-19.

[186]Sweet, *Black Images of America*.

a "This-is-how-we-end-it" resolve, with the consequent emergence in the last three decades of the nineteenth century of black messianisms either for the redemption and restoration of Africa or America.

Except for histories of women in American religion, the history of evangelical missions has been one of the least favorite inquiries in American religious history during the last twenty years.[187] Henry Warner Bowden's essay in this collection on the Oberlin mission to the Ojibwas of northern Minnesota, a project which lasted from 1842 to 1859, is especially welcome, not only because it appears in a sparse field, but it graphically typifies the route by which many historians are returning to missiological inquiries and reopening the study of cultural interaction between whites and native Americans. Recent historical interest in the study of native Americans and Evangelicalism has been primarily twofold: first, the nineteenth-century involvement of evangelical churches in solving

---

[187]Studies that have, for the purpose of historical analysis, factored out missions from other reform endeavors include John K. Fairbank, ed., *The Missionary Enterprise in China and America* (Cambridge: Harvard University Press, 1974); Andrew, *Rebuilding the Christian Commonwealth*; Valentin H. Rabe, *The Home Base of American China Missions, 1880-1920* (Cambridge: Harvard University Press, 1978); Torben Christensen and William Hutchison, eds., *Missionary Ideologies in the Imperialist Era, 1880-1920* (Arhus, Denmark: Aros, 1982); Adrian A. Bennett, *Missionary Journalist in China: Young J. Allen and His Magazines, 1860-1883* (Athens GA: University of Georgia Press, 1983); Donald E. Thompson and Lorna Lutes Sylvester, eds., "The Autobiography of Isaac Reed, Frontier Missionary," *Indiana Magazine of History* 78 (September 1982): 193-214; William H. Brackney, "Yankee Benevolence in Yorker Lands: Origins of the Baptist Home Missions Movement," *Foundations* 24 (October-December 1981): 293-309; Robert T. Handy, "American Baptist Leadership in Cooperative Home Missions: 1900-1950," *Foundations* 24 (October-December 1981): 343-58; Steven C. Shulte, "Alfred Brunson and the Wisconsin Missionary Frontier," *Methodist History* 19 (July 1981): 231-37; John W. Krummel, "Of Mission Boards and Missionaries: The Organization of an Annual Conference in Japan," *Methodist History* 19 (January 1981): 99-117; Kenton J. Clymer, "Methodist Missionaries and Roman Catholicism in the Philippines, 1899-1916," *Methodist History* 18 (April 1980): 171-78; Michael C. Coleman, "Presbyterian Missionary Attitudes Toward China and the Chinese, 1837-1900," *Journal of Presbyterian History* 56 (Fall 1978): 185-200; Lawrence A. Cardoso, "Protestant Missionaries and the Mexican," *New Scholar* 7 (1978): 223-36; John W. Krummel, "Methodist Missionary Graves in Japan," *Methodist History* 15 (January 1977): 122-30; James P. Alter, "American Presbyterian in North India: Missionary Motives and Social Attitudes under British Colonialism," *Journal of Presbyterian History* 53 (Winter 1975): 291-312. Of limited utility is Charles L. Chaney's *The Birth of Missions in America* (South Pasadena CA: William Carey Library, 1976). James Reed is less interested in missions or missionaries than in a "missionary mind" in his *The Missionary Mind and American East Asia Policy, 1911-1915* (Cambridge: Harvard University Press, 1983).

the "Indian problem," primarily through assimilation and Americanization;[188] and second, the native encounter with white missions, a clash of cultures that is illuminated by the history of Christian missions to American Indians.

The missions movement was a major by-product of American revivalism. Historians have come to associate the revivalist Oberlin College with evangelical movements on behalf of blacks and women.[189] In "Oberlin and Ojibwas: An Evangelical Mission to Native Americans," Henry Warner Bowden reminds us that there was a strong missions component in the school as well, though Oberlin may have stood alone in its missionary enterprises partly because of its association in people's minds even then with radical abolitionist and perfectionist tendencies. With all the new developments Evangelicals could account for, as Bowden reveals, they developed nothing really new in their missions to native Americans. Bowden's essay, as well as his book on *American Indians and Christian Missions* (1981), superbly exemplifies the revisionary techniques and sensitivities of what is called the "new Indian history."[190] There is an emphasis on the strong religious world view before the arrival of Christians;

[188]Francis Paul Prucha, *American Indian Policy in Crisis: Christian Reformers and the Indian, 1865-1900* (Norman OK: University of Oklahoma Press, 1976); Robert W. Murdock, *The Reformers and the American Indian* (Columbia: University of Missouri Press, 1971); Loewenberg, *Equality on the Oregon Frontier*; Frederick A. Norwood, "Serpents and Savages," *Religion in Life* 46 (Autumn 1977): 301-15; Henry G. Woltmann, "John C. Lowrie and Presbyterian Indian Administration, 1870-1882," *Journal of Presbyterian History* 54 (Summer 1976):259-76. For rare looks at Evangelicals who protested America's exploitation of native Americans, see William G. McLoughlin, "Civil Disobedience and Evangelism Among the Missionaries to the Cherokee, 1829-1839," *Journal of Presbyterian History* 51 (Summer 1973): 116-39; Frederick A. Norwood, "Native Americans and Frontier Justice," *Christian Century* 97 (28 May 1980): 614-15; and Francis Paul Prucha, ed., *Cherokee Removal: The "William Penn" Essays and other Writings By Jeremiah Evants* (Knoxville TN: University of Tennessee Press, 1981).

[189]Lori D. Ginzberg, "Women in an Evangelical Community: Oberlin 1835-1850," *Ohio History* 89 (Winter 1980): 78-88.

[190]Bowden, *American Indians and Christian Missions: Studies in Cultural Conflict* (Chicago: University of Chicago Press, 1981). Also see Bowden and James P. Ronda's excellent introductory essay in their editing of John Eliot's *Indian Dialogues: A Study in Cultural Interaction* (Westport CT: Greenwood Press, 1980). A review article by Wilbur R. Jacobs critiques some of the literature in the "new Indian history." See "Native American History: How It Illuminates Our Past," *Journal of American History* 80 (June 1975): 595-609.

the mutuality of misconceptions and judgments by tribes and missionaries; the intelligence and creativity of tribal responses to an intrusive society and ethnocentric attempts at acculturation; and the triumph of native religious systems and communities in the face of cultural chauvinism.

Ever since Robert F. Berkhofer's pioneering *Salvation and the Savage* (1965),[191] historians have especially accented two themes, imposition and failure, in describing Anglo-American contacts with Indians. Generally they have highlighted the political dimension of missions,[192] the cultural

---

[191]Robert F. Berkhofer, *Salvation and the Savage: An Analysis of Protestant Missions and American Indian Response, 1787-1862* (Westport CT: Greenwood Press, 1977; originally published in 1965).

[192]Historians have largely forsaken the image of the missionary as a benevolent, compassionate soul-winner. Those who stress the political goals of missionaries and see mission activities as a revolutionary enterprise include Berkhofer, *Salvation and the Savage*; Francis Jennings, "Goals and Functions of Puritan Missions to the Indians," *Ethnohistory* 18 (Summer 1971): 197-212, and *The Invasion of America: Indians, Colonialism, and the Cost of Conquest* (Chapel Hill: University of North Carolina Press, 1975); Neal Salisbury, "Red Puritans: The 'Praying Indians' of Massachusetts Bay and John Eliot," *William and Mary Quarterly* 31 (January 1974): 27-54; Michael C. Coleman, "Christianizing and Americanizing the Nez Perce: Sue L. McBeth and Her Attitudes to the Indians," *Journal of Presbyterian History* 53 (Winter 1975): 339-61; G. E. Thomas, "Puritans, Indians and the Concept of Race," *New England Quarterly* 48 (March 1975): 3-27; Robert H. Keller, Jr., *American Protestantism and United States Indian Policy, 1869-1882* (Lincoln: University of Nebraska Press, 1983); and James P. Ronda, "The Bible and Early American Indian Missions," in Sandeen, *Bible and Social Reform*, 9-30. A new rash of problems breaks out with such unmeasured criticism of white interaction with American Indian culture as found in Neal Salisbury's *Manitou and Providence: Indians, Europeans and the Making of New England, 1500-1643* (New York: Oxford University Press, 1982). Attempts at a more balanced assessment of the motives of missionaries can be found in James S. Patterson's "Motives in the Development of Foreign Missions Among American Baptists, 1810-1826," *Foundations* 19 (October-December 1970): 298-319; George A. Schultz, *An Indian Canaan: Isaac McCoy and the Vision of an Indian State* (Norman OK: University of Oklahoma Press, 1972); David C. Stineback, "The Status of Puritan-Indian Scholarship," *New England Quarterly* 51 (March 1978): 80-90; and in Mary E. Young, *Friends of the Indians—II: "The Christian Party in Politics"* (N.p; The Carroll Lectures, presented at Mary Baldwin College, 8-9 October 1980): 13-30. For the perceptual problems of white Christians in general, see William S. Simmons, "Cultural Bias in the New England Puritans' Perception of Indians," *William and Mary Quarterly* 38 (January 1981): 56-72; Frank Shuffleton, "Indian Devils and Pilgrim Fathers: Squanto, Hobomok, and the English Conception of Indian Religion," *New England Quarterly* 49 (March 1976): 108-16; John J. Teunissen and Evelyn J. Hinz, "Roger Williams, St. Paul, and American Primitivism," *Canadian Reviews of American Studies* 4 (Fall 1973): 121-36; Alden T. Vaughan, "From White Man to Redskin: Changing Anglo-American Perceptions of the American

violence of evangelical intruders, and the relative imperviousness of American Indian culture to overtures by Christian missionaries. Bowden's rendition of the Oberlin mission as a chronicle of failure parallels similar conclusions in other studies by the best historians of red-white relations.[193] As new materials both from native American sources and from mission board archives are mined,[194] and historians of Christian missions

Indian," *American Historical Review* 87 (October 1982): 917-53; and Frederick A. Norwood, "Two Contrasting Views of the Indians: Methodist Involvement in the Indian Trouble in Oregon and Washington," *Church History* 49 (June 1980): 178-87.

[193]For other failures among the Ojibwas, see Frederick A. Norwood, "Conflict of Cultures: Methodist Efforts with the Ojibway, 1830-1880," *Religion in Life* 8 (Autumn 1979): 360-76; and Sister Claire Lynch, "William Thurston Boutwell and the Chippewas," *Journal of Presbyterian History* 58 (Fall 1980): 239-54. For anti-missionism among the Cherokees and failed Presbyterian missions, see William G. McLoughlin, "Cherokee Anti-Mission Sentiment, 1824-1828," *Ethnohistory* 21 (Fall 1974): 361-70; A. Mark Conrad, "The Cherokee Mission of Virginia Presbyterians," *Journal of Presbyterian History* 58 (Spring 1980): 35-49; William G. McLoughlin, "Parson Blackburn's Whiskey and the Cherokee Indian Schools, 1809-1810," *Journal of Presbyterian History* 57 (Winter 1979): 427-45; and Dorothy C. Bass, "Gideon Blackburn's Mission to the Cherokees: Christianization and Civilization," *Journal of Presbyterian History* 52 (Fall 1974): 203-26. For Anglican missions, see Gerald J. Goodwin, "Christianity, Civilization and the Savage: The Anglican Mission to the American Indian," *Historical Magazine* 42 (June 1973): 93-110. An "inconclusive" mission project, not as dismal as the others but certainly not a success story, is chronicled in Ronald Rayman's "David Lowry and the Winnebago Indian School, 1833-1848," *Journal of Presbyterian History* 56 (Summer 1978): 108-20. Other studies of the failure of white missions to seriously dent native American religious patterns include James Axtell, "The White Indians of Colonial America," *William and Mary Quarterly* 32 (January 1975): 55-88; Axtell, "The European Failure to Convert the Indians: An Autopsy," Proceedings of the Sixth Algonquin Conference, National Museum of Man, *Mercury Series* (Ottawa: National Museum of Canada, 1975); John Hutchins, "The Trial of Reverend Samuel H. Worcester," *Journal of Cherokee Studies* 2 (Winter 1977): 356-74; Mark T. Banker, "Presbyterians and Pueblos: A Protestant Response to the Indian Question, 1872-1892," *Journal of Presbyterian History* 60 (Spring 1982): 23-40; and Axtell's collection of essays, *The European and the Indian: Essays in the Ethnohistory of Colonial North America* (New York: Oxford University Press, 1981). Even when historians scrutinize tribal communities which converted (like the Narragansetts), the emphasis still ends up being the failure of white missionaries. See William S. Simmons and Cheryl L. Simmons, eds., *Old Light on Separate Ways: Narragensetts Diary of Joseph Fish, 1765-1776* (Hanover NH: University Press of New England, 1982). William G. McLoughlin has studied the relationship between evangelical missions and American Indian slaveowners in "Indian Slaveholders and Presbyterian Missionaries, 1837-1861," *Church History* 42 (December 1973): 535-51; "Red Indian, Black Slavery and White Racism: America's Slaveholding Indians," *American Quarterly* 36 (October 1974): 367-85; Cherokee Slaveholders and Baptist Missionaries, 1845-1860," *Historian* 45 (February 1983): 147-66.

begin to study those American Indians who converted to Christianity, they may come to chronicle as well some evangelical successes in organizing Indian churches.[195] Perhaps they also will begin to analyze the role of Evangelicalism in rebuilding tribal institutions and revitalizing individual personalities, processes that occurred both through conversion, as Bowden makes clear, and through the forces of syncretism, which Anthony F. C. Wallace outlines so beautifully in *The Death and Rebirth of the Seneca* (1970).[196] In his study of Indian-Puritan religious contacts, for example, J. William T. Youngs, Jr., has argued against the pigeonholing of native Americans into one of two categories: total repudiation of either red or white culture. The tangled knot of missionization analysis is not fully unraveled, he contends, until historians have taken into account American Indians who did not commit cultural suicide but who "stood between two cultures," converts to Christianity who may have even "converted Christianity," as Mary Young aptly puts it, "to their own special needs."[197]

---

[194]For helpful bibliographies, see Richard N. Ellis, "Published Source Materials on Native Americans," *Western Historical Quarterly* 7 (April 1976): 187-92, and James P. Ronda and James Axtell, *Indian Missions: A Critical Bibliography* (Bloomington IN: Indiana University Press, 1978).

[195]See Margaret Whitehead, "Christianity, a Matter of Choice: The Historical Role of Indian Catechists in Oregon Territory and British Columbia," *Pacific Northwest Quarterly* 72 (July 1981): 98-106 and Paul Stuart, "The Christian Church and Indian Community Life," *Journal of Ethnic Studies* 9 (Fall 1981): 47-55. See also William G. McLoughlin, "The Cherokee Baptist Preacher and the Great Schism of 1844-45," *Foundations* 24 (April-June 1981): 137-47.

[196]Anthony F. C. Wallace, *The Death and Rebirth of the Seneca* (New York: Alfred A. Knopf, 1970). Mary Young has pointed out in private correspondence (31 January 1983) that with so many historians treating evangelism as "yet one more process whereby the intruders did the Indians in," the history of Indian evangelization is "about where the history of black religion was before Genovese."

[197]J. William T. Youngs, Jr., "The Indian Saints of Early New England," *Early American Literature* 16 (1981/82): 241-56 and Mary Young, "The Cherokee Nation: Mirror of the Republic," *American Quarterly* 33 (Winter 1981): 524, 502-24. For a good start down this path, see Elise M. Brenners's critique of the imposed acculturation model as itself "ethnocentric" in "To Pray or to be Prey: That is the Question. Strategies for Cultural Autonomy of Massachusetts Praying Town Indians," *Ethnohistory* 27 (Spring 1980): 135-52, and James P. Ronda, "Generations of Faith: The Christian Indians of Martha's Vineyard," *William and Mary Quarterly* 38 (July 1981): 369-94, which follows an earlier article entitled " 'We Are Well As We Are': An Indian Critique of Seventeenth-Century Mis-

The recent respectability of inquiries into the melding of religion and healing in native American culture has made it easier for historians of American Evangelicalism to give more than a grimacing glance to the history of healing, a submerged subject in American religious historiography. Navajo and Tewa Pueblo healing methods serve as a fulcrum for Catherine L. Albanese's discussion of nineteenth-century healing practices.[198] Another historian has traced the first rumblings of Pentecostalism not to "speaking in tongues" but to the "faith-healing" movement within the mainstream of American Evangelicalism in the 1870s and 1880s.[199] Studies of this kind lay no longer on the outskirts of scholarship as evidenced by David Edwin Harrell's attempt to analyze what one historian has called "the most neglected area of American religious history"—the shabbily produced healing revivals of the 1940s and 1950s, which were transformed into the slickly choreographed and trendy "charismatic" revivals of the 1960s and 1970s.[200] One historian of native American religion has even gone so far as to insist that a major agenda for future research into the relationship between religion and health is the acceptance of native American religion on its own terms and the rejection of the notion that "religion is incapable of affecting the world. Or, to put it more crudely, that the native American gods ain't there."[201]

More than ever before, historians are discovering that women dominated the history of American Evangelicalism and helped to set American culture on an evangelical track. Not surprisingly, therefore, the history of women in the American evangelical tradition is flourishing, entailing

---

sions," *William and Mary Quarterly* 34 (January 1977): 66-82. This latter article tends to fall within Young's criticism.

[198]Catherine L. Albanese, "The Poetics of Healing: Root Metaphors and Rituals in Nineteenth-Century America," *Soundings* 63 (Winter 1980): 381-406.

[199]Raymond J. Cunningham, "From Holiness to Healing: The Faith Cure in America 1872-1892," *Church History* 43 (December 1974): 499-513.

[200]Mary L. Schneider, "Are All Things *Really* Possible?" *Reviews in American History* 5 (March 1977): 118; David Edwin Harrell, Jr., *All Things Are Possible: The Healing and Charismatic Revivals in Modern America* (Bloomington: Indiana University Press, 1976); Jon Butler, "The People's Faith in Europe and America: Four Centuries in Review," *Journal of Social History* 12 (Fall 1978): 159-67.

[201]Sam D. Gill, "Native American Religions," *Bulletin/CSR* 9 (December 1978): 127.

some of the most inquisitive and sophisticated sociohistorical methods in the discipline today.

Barbara Welter first spelled out some possible ramifications for the relationship of Evangelicalism and women's experiences in her widely quoted and reprinted essay "The Cult of True Womanhood," in which evangelical piety is seen within the context of submissiveness, domesticity, and purity.[202] In her historiographical essay on "The Last Fifteen Years," Kathryn Kish Sklar says that Welter's article "did for the historical study of women in American religion and society what [Betty] Friedan's book [*The Feminine Mystique* (1963)] did for the development of feminism."[203] Although it sometimes appeared as if subsequent historians who emphasized Evangelicalism's encouragement of a public role for women were breaking down a door already opened by Welter, much of the scholarship throughout the 1970s was clearly "revisionist," refining and rebutting Welter's interpretations, especially those regarding the lack of affinity between Evangelicalism and feminism.

In trying to understand the appeal of religion to women, historians have emphasized the way Evangelicalism gave women's lives social and psychological enlargement as well as public usefulness by stretching the scope of their mission. Nancy F. Cott, while criticized for soft-pedaling the coercive, restricting features of women's sphere ideology, nevertheless has mounted an impressive argument that sees Evangelicalism's "cult of domesticity" as largely a positive development for middle-class women.[204] It led to a growing self-identity, collective consciousness, and

---

[202]Barbara Welter, "The Cult of True Womanhood: 1820-1860," *American Quarterly* 18 (Summer 1966): 151-74, as reprinted in Barbara Welter, *Dimity Convictions: The American Woman in the Nineteenth Century* (Athens OH: Ohio University Press, 1976): 21-41.

[203]Sklar identifies five stages to historiography on women and American religion in "The Last Fifteen Years" in *Women in New Worlds: Vol. 1*, eds. Hilah F. Thomas and Rosemary Skinner Keller (Nashville: Abingdon, 1981): 48-65. A more traditional but very fine historiographical review of the same subject can be found in Jean McMahon Humez, ed., *Gifts of Power: The Writings of Rebecca Jackson, Black Visionary, Shaker Eldress* (Amherst: University of Massachusetts Press, 1981): 339-47.

[204]Nancy F. Cott, *The Bonds of Womanhood: "Woman's Sphere" in New England, 1780-1835* (New Haven: Yale University Press, 1977). See also Winthrop S. Hudson's "Early Nineteenth-Century Evangelical Religion and Women's Liberation," *Foundations* 23 (April-June 1980): 181-85.

organizational solidarity that manifested itself in female societies like the American Female Moral Reform Society, which Carroll Smith-Rosenberg has studied so brilliantly.[205] Anyone wishing a closer look at the effects of "Evangelical domesticity" on women should read Kathryn Kish Sklar's biography of Catharine Beecher.[206] Keith Melder's work on women's societies[207] and the findings of those working on the doctrine of Christian perfection,[208] reveal the extent to which evangelical religion could help women come alive, break out of accepted patterns, and expand their boundaries in the antebellum period. Late nineteenth- and early twentieth-century women who both decorously and rancorously rejected the denial of their full rights within various denominations[209] often based

[205]Carroll Smith-Rosenberg, "Beauty, the Beast and the Militant Woman: Sex Roles and Social Stress in Jacksonian America," *American Quarterly* 23 (October 1971): 562-84.

[206]Kathryn Kish Sklar, *Catharine Beecher: A Study in American Domesticity* (New Haven: Yale University Press, 1973).

[207]Keith E. Melder, *Beginnings of Sisterhood: The American Woman's Rights Movement, 1800-1850* (New York: Schocken Books, 1977).

[208]Lucille Sider Dayton and Donald W. Dayton, " 'Your Daughters Shall Prophesy': Feminism in the Holiness Movement," *Methodist History* 14 (January 1976): 67-92; Nancy Hardesty, Lucille Sider Dayton, and Donald W. Dayton, "Women in the Holiness Movement: Feminism in the Evangelical Tradition," in *Women of Spirit: Female Leadership in the Jewish and Christian Traditions*, eds. Rosemary Ruether and Eleanor McLaughlin (New York: Simon and Schuster, 1979): 226-54; Nancy A. Hardesty, "The Wesleyan Movement and Women's Liberation" in *Sanctification and Liberation*, ed. Theodore Runyon 164-73; Anne C. Loveland, "Domesticity and Religion in the Antebellum Period: The Career of Phoebe Palmer," *The Historian* 39 (May 1977): 455-71; Ivan Howard, "Wesley versus Phoebe Palmer: An Extended Controversy," *Wesleyan Theological Journal* 6 (Spring 1971):31-40. For the importance of Phoebe Palmer in the development of American Perfectionism, see Charles Edwin Jones, *Perfectionist Persuasion, the Holiness Movement, and American Methodism, 1867-1936* (Metuchen NJ: Scarecrow Press, 1974).

[209]Kenneth E. Rowe, "The Ordination of Women, Round One: Anna Oliver and the General Conference of 1880," *Methodist History* 12 (April 1974): 60-72; William T. Noll, "Women as Clergy and Laity in the 19th-Century Methodist Protestant Church," *Methodist History* 15 (January 1977): 107-21; Lois A. Boyd, "Shall Women Speak? Confrontation in the Church, 1876," *Journal of Presbyterian History* 56 (Winter 1978): 281-94; Janet Harbison Penfield, "Women in the Presbyterian Church—An Historical Overview," *Journal of Presbyterian History* 55 (Summer 1977): 107-24; R. Douglas Breckenridge, "Equality for Women? A Case Study in Presbyterian Polity, 1926-1930," *Journal of Presbyterian History* 58 (Summer 1980): 146-65; Virginia Lieson Brereton and Christa Ressmeyer Klein, "American Women in Ministry: A History of Protestant Beginning

their arguments on positions first formulated by evangelical women. In short, the roots of liberation and feminism can be uncovered in evangelical religion. Or as Lydia Maria Child first put it, "The sects called evangelical were the first agitators of the woman question."[210]

Whereas earlier historians concentrated on the frontier as a liberating force for women and were relatively indifferent to or divided about Evangelicalism, contemporary historians display an almost reverse posture, with revivalism controlling historians' energies and thoughts.[211] The development of political feminism may have been blunted by evangelical religion, Joan Jacobs Brumberg contends, since "religious feminism" or "evangelical feminism" tended to deflect women's attention overseas into the foreign missions movement.[212] Yet it was the sense of moral superiority, which Evangelicalism nurtured, that provided the inspiration

---

Points," in Ruether and McLaughlin, *Women of Spirit*, 302-32; articles by William T. Noll, Donald K. Garrell, Rosemary Skinner Keller, Virginia Shadron, and Jualynne Dodson in the section on "The Status of Women in Institutional Church Life" in *Women in New Worlds: Vol. I*, eds. Hilah F. Thomas and Rosemary Skinner Keller, 219-92; James E. Will, "Ordination of Women: The Issue in the Church of the United Brethren in Christ," *Women in New Worlds: Vol. II*, eds. Rosemary Skinner Keller, Louise L. Queen, and Hilah F. Thomas (Nashville: Abingdon, 1982) 290-99. Also see the important study by Lois A. Boyd and R. Douglas Brackenridge, *Presbyterian Women in America: Two Centuries of a Quest for Status* (Westport CT: Greenwood Press, 1983) and James W. Albers, "Perspectives on the History of Women in the Lutheran Church - Missouri Synod During the Nineteenth Century," *Lutheran Historical Conference* 9 (1982): 137-83.

[210]Quoted in Dorothy C. Bass, " 'Their Prodigious Influence': Women, Religion and Reform in Antebellum America," Ruether and McLaughlin, *Women of Spirit*, 280.

[211]Glenda Riley and Julie Roy Jeffrey's studies of frontier and pioneer women have displayed an agonizing lack of consensus, with Riley concluding that the frontier exerted a beneficial impact on women's elevation, but Jeffrey concluding that in spite of the frontier's challenge to the domestic ideal, it still won out. Compare Glenda Riley, *Frontierswomen: The Iowa Experience* (Ames IA: Iowa State University Press, 1981) and Julie Roy Jeffrey, *Frontier Women: The Trans-Mississippi West, 1840-1880* (New York: Hill and Wang, 1979). The need to study missionary couples in the Pacific Northwest is evident from Clifford M. Drury, "Wilderness Diaries," *American West* 13 (November-December 1976): 4-9, 62. The diversity of historians' interest in revivalism can be seen in such disparate publications as Martha Tomhave Blauvelt, "Women and Revivalism" in *Women and Religion in America, Volume I: The Nineteenth Century*, eds. Rosemary Radford Ruether and Rosemary Skinner Keller (San Francisco: Harper and Row, 1981) 1-9; Joe L. Kincheloe, Jr., "Transcending Role Restrictions: Women at Camp Meetings and Political Rallies," *Tennessee Historical Quarterly* 40 (Summer 1981): 158-69.

[212]Brumberg, *Mission for Life*, 79-106.

for women's reform movements throughout the nineteenth century, including the post-Civil War campaign for the ballot.[213] More work is needed, however, on tracing the specific link of Evangelicalism, reform, and feminism. The emerging work of Nancy Hewitt suggests links between the first two but not necessarily leading to the third.[214] For example, if male ministers did indeed replace husbands as key authority figures in the midst of revivals, Hewitt asks, was it not still a case of men dominating women?

Research into the ways in which women helped to shape the character and function of American religion has had a salutary effect on American historiography in recent years. Some historians have called this phenomenon "feminization," by which Barbara Welter and Richard Shiels mean the growing female audience and softened theology in American religion beginning with the Second Great Awakening, and by which Ann Douglas means the exaltation of emotion over reason in the nineteenth century.[215] The recasting of the church's hymnody to accommodate a gentle, femi-

---

[213]Women's sense of moral superiority stemmed partly from their "passionlessness," Nancy Cott says in her article, "Passionlessness: An Interpretation of Victorian Sexual Ideology, 1790-1850," *Signs* 4 (Winter 1978): 219-36. For the relationship between moral superiority and suffrage, see Ellen Carol DuBois, *Feminism and Suffrage: The Emergence of an Independent Women's Movement in America, 1848-1869* (Ithaca NY: Cornell University Press, 1978). A dissenting voice about the role of women's moral superiority in the suffrage movement can be found in William Leach, *True Love and Perfect Union: The Feminist Reform of Sex and Society* (New York: Basor Books, 1980).

[214]For Nancy Hewitt's thesis that, at least in nineteenth-century Rochester, women's rights advocates came almost exclusively from the most antievangelical ranks of the Hicksite Quakers, see "Yankee Evangelicals and Agrarian Quakers: Gender, Religion, and Class in the Formation of a Feminist Consciousness," *Radical History Review* 28 (forthcoming 1984) and "The Social Origins of Women's Antislavery Politics in Western New York" in *Crusaders and Compromisers: Essays on the Relationship of the Antislavery Struggle to the Antebellum Party System*, ed. Alan M. Kraut (Westport CT: Greenwood Press, 1984) 204-33.

[215]Barbara Welter, "The Feminization of American Religion: 1800-1860" in Welter, *Dimity Convictions*, 83-102; Richard D. Shiels, "The Feminization of American Congregationalism, 1730-1835," *American Quarterly* 33 (Spring 1981): 46-62; and Ann Douglas, *The Feminization of American Culture* (New York: Alfred A. Knopf, 1977). The two best critiques of Douglas's book are by David Schuyler and David S. Reynolds, the former accusing Douglas of "Inventing a Feminine Past," *New England Quarterly* 51 (September 1978): 291-308, and the latter accusing her of exaggerating the existence of one: "The Feminization Controversy: Sexual Stereotypes and the Paradoxes of Piety in Nineteenth-Century America," *New England Quarterly* 53 (March 1980): 96-106.

nine Jesus has been scrutinized by Sandra S. Sizer.[216] Amanda Porterfield has outlined the "domestication of theology" as exemplified in Evangelicalism's growing penchant for illustrations, stories, anecdotes, and sentimentality.[217]

Women's assumption of leadership roles in American Evangelicalism has received the attention of a growing number of historians.[218] "Maternal evangelism" was the centerpiece of revivalism in the Second Great Awakening, Mary Ryan has argued. Her study connecting social, economic, and religious developments to the origins of the middle class reveals that women were so in charge of revivals in Oneida County that they "could do without the assistance of Charles Finney or any other minister."[219] Kathryn Kish Sklar's pioneering study of a female seminary (Mt. Holyoke) breaks ground for further work into Evangelicalism's contribution toward the growth of women's education in the nineteenth century.[220]

---

[216]Sizer, *Gospel Hymns.*

[217]Amanda Porterfield, *Feminine Spirituality in America: From Sarah Edwards to Martha Graham* (Philadelphia: Temple University Press, 1980), esp. 51-82. See also David S. Reynolds, "From Doctrine to Narrative: The Rise of Pulpit Storytelling in America," *American Quarterly* 32 (Winter 1980): 439-98, where the nineteenth-century shifts in homiletic style are traced to developments in Evangelicalism exclusive of the "domestication" of religion.

[218]For leadership issues in general see Earl Kent Brown, "Women in Church History: Stereotypes, Archetypes and Operational Modalities," *Methodist History* 18 (January 1980): 109-32. Barbara Brown Zikmund has explained the pro and con arguments used in women's struggle for leadership in her "Biblical Arguments and Women's Place in the Church" in Sandeen, *Bible and Social Reform,* 85-104.

[219]Mary P. Ryan, "Women's Awakening: Evangelical Religion and the Families of Utica, New York, 1800-1840," in *Women in American Religion,* ed. Janet Wilson James (Philadelphia: University of Pennsylvania Press, 1980) 89-110 and Mary P. Ryan, *Cradle of the Middle Class: The Family in Oneida County, New York, 1790-1865* (Cambridge: Cambridge University Press, 1981) 98.

[220]Kathryn Kish Sklar, "The Founding of Mount Holyoke College," in *Women of America, A History,* eds. Carol Ruth Berkin and Mary Beth Norton (Boston: Houghton Mifflin Company, 1979) 177-201. See also Nancy Green, "Female Education and School Competition: 1820-1850," *History of Education Quarterly* 18 (Summer 1978): 129-42; Lori D. Ginzberg, "Women in an Evangelical Community: Oberlin 1812-1835," *Ohio History* 89 (Winter 1980): 78-88; Catherine Clinton, "Equally Their Due: The Education of the Planter Daughter in the Early Republic," *Journal of the Early Republic* 2 (Spring 1982): 39-60; and William Webb Pusey III, "Lexington's Female Academy," *Virginia Cavalcade* 32 (Summer 1982): 40-47.

The creation of what Smith-Rosenberg calls a "homosocial female culture" was facilitated by Evangelicalism's encouragement of women to get together and form "female networks" and religious associations.[221] In fact, the degree of "female bonding" and sense of sisterly spirit often determined whether women's organizations floundered or flourished.[222] An unforeseen dimension of evangelical women's support for foreign missions, which has been studied quite vigorously in recent years,[223] has

---

[221]Carroll Smith-Rosenberg, "The Female World of Love and Ritual," *Signs* 1 (Autumn 1975): 1-29. For female associations see Nancy F. Cott, "Young Women in the Second Great Awakening in New England," *Feminist Studies* 3 (Fall 1975): 15-29; Mary P. Ryan, "The Power of Women's Networks: A Case Study of Female Moral Reform in Antebellum America," *Feminist Studies* 5 (Spring 1979): 66-86, and Ryan's chapter on "The Era of Associations: Between Family and Society, 1825-1845" in her *Cradle of the Middle Class*, 105-44; Mary F. Kihlstrom, "The Morristown Female Charitable Society," *Journal of Presbyterian History* 58 (Fall 1980): 255-73; Richard A. Meckel, "Educating a Ministry of Mothers: Evangelical Maternal Associations, 1815-1860," *Journal of the Early Republic* 2 (Winter 1982): 403-23; Elizabeth M. Gripe, "Women, Restructuring and Unrest in the 1920's," *Journal of Presbyterian History* 52 (Summer 1974): 188-99; and Norma Taylor Mitchell, "From Social to Radical Feminism: A Survey of Emerging Diversity in Methodist Women's Organizations, 1867-1974," *Methodist History News Bulletin* 4 (April 1975): 21-44 and *A.M.E. Zion Quarterly Review, News Bulletin* (April 1975): 21-44. For home missions see Carolyn L. Stapleton, "Belle Harris Bennett: Model of Holistic Christianity," *Methodist History* 21 (April 1983): 131-42; Patricia V. Horner, "Mary Richardson Walker: The Shattered Dreams of a Missionary Woman," *Montana* 32 (Summer 1982): 20-31.

[222]Catherine M. Prelinger and Rosemary S. Keller, "The Function of Female Bonding" in Keller, Queen, and Thomas, *Women in New Worlds: Volume II*, 318-37. See also Rosemary Skinner Keller, "The Deaconess: 'New Woman' of Late Nineteenth Century Methodism," *Explor* 5 (Spring 1979): 33-41, and Charles W. DeWeese, "Deaconess in Baptist History: A Preliminary Study," *Baptist History and Heritage* 12 (January 1972): 152-57.

[223]See especially Brumberg, *Mission for Life*; Barbara Welter, "She Hath Done What She Could: Protestant Women's Missionary Careers in Nineteenth-Century America," in James, *Women in American Religion*, 111-26; Frederick B. Hoyt, " 'When a field was found too difficult for a Man, a Woman should be Sent': Adele M. Fielde in Asia, 1865-1890," *Historian* 44 (May 1982): 314-34; Rosemary Skinner Keller, "Creating a Sphere for Women in the Church: How Consequential an Accommodation?" *Methodist History* 18 (January 1980): 83-94; Patricia R. Hill, "Heathen Women's Friends: The Role of Methodist Episcopal Women in the Women's Foreign Missions Movement, 1869-1915," *Methodist History* 19 (April 1981): 146-55; Helen Emery Falls, "Baptist Women in Missions Support in the Nineteenth-Century," *Baptist History and Heritage* 12 (January 1977): 27-36; and R. Pierce Beaver, *American Protestant Women in World Missions: History of the First Feminist Movement in North America* (Grand Rapids MI: Eerdmans, 1980, rev. ed., originally published in 1968). See also the section on "Foreign Missions and Cultural

been illuminated by Joan Jacobs Brumberg: evangelical ethnology helped to pave the way for Progressive reforms by its increasing calls for aggressive state involvement in protecting oppressed and abused women.[224]

Ronald W. Hogeland has isolated four distinct life-styles for women available from 1820 to 1860—"Ornamental," "Romanticized," "Radical," and "Evangelical Womanhood"—and attributes to "Evangelical Womanhood" a self-assertive, reform-minded posture. Hogeland points directly to ministers' wives as embodying this ideal. "In almost every way," Hogeland writes, "Lydia Finney as well as Finney's second wife was her husband's equal in the task of remaking America over in the evangelical image."[225] Numerous studies like *The Minister's Wife* (1983) are now exploring the significance of the clergyman's wife for the creation of an evangelical culture in nineteenth-century America.[226]

Imperialism" with articles by Joan Jacobs Brumberg, Adrian A. Bennett, Sylvia M. Jacobs, and Carol A. Page in Keller, Queen, and Thomas, *Women in New Worlds: Volume II*, 234-89.

[224]Joan Jacobs Brumberg, "Zenanas and Girlless Villages: The Ethnology of American Evangelical Women, 1870-1910," *Journal of American History* 69 (September 1982): 347-71.

[225]Ronald W. Hogeland, " 'The Female Appendage': Feminine Life-Styles in America, 1820-1860," *Civil War History* 17 (June 1971): 110, 101-14.

[226]Sweet, *The Minister's Wife*. See also Ronald L. Numbers, *Prophetess of Health: A Study of Ellen G. White* (New York: Harper and Row, 1976); Julie Roy Jeffrey, "Ministry Through Marriage: Methodist Clergy Wives on the Trans-Mississippi Frontier," and Clotilde Falcon Nanez, "Hispanic Clergy Wives: Their Contribution to United Methodism in the Southwest, Later Nineteenth Century to the Present" in Thomas and Keller, *Women in New Worlds*, 143-77; Emora T. Brannan, "A Partnership of Equality: The Marriage and Ministry of John and Mary Goucher," and Rosa Peffly Motes, "The Pacific Northwest: Changing Role of the Pastor's Wife Since 1840," in Keller, Queen, and Thomas, *Women in New Worlds: Volume II*, 132-61; Paul Boyer, "Minister's Wife, Widow, Reluctant Feminist: Catherine Marshall in the 1950's," in James ed., *Women in American Religion*, 253-71; Lois A. Boyd, "Presbyterian Minister's Wives—A Nineteenth Century Portrait," *Journal of Presbyterian History* 59 (Spring 1981): 3-17; and Lois A. Boyd and R. Douglas Brackenridge, "Ministers' Wives: Untitled Professionals" in *Presbyterian Women in America*, 189-204. Although Patricia Grimshaw's discovery that maternal obligations frustrated women's public involvement is not likely to surprise anyone, her study of missionary wives is extremely valuable. See " 'Christian Woman, Pious Wife, Faithful Mother, Devoted Missionary': Conflicts in Roles of American Missionary Women in Nineteenth-Century Hawaii," *Feminist Studies* 9 (Fall 1983): 489-522.

The study of evangelical women's participation in nineteenth-century reform movements is flourishing, with abolition and moral reform eliciting the greatest interest.[227] The evangelical roots of the temperance movement have been explored by Ian R. Tyrrell. Though he sees the evangelical stage (preceding the reform and political campaigns of the 1840s and 1850s) as a conservative and confining one, Evangelicals successfully found a place for women in reform activities, although they limited that role to "charitable and sacrificial qualities." Tyrrell's study is unique since it spotlights women's antebellum temperance activities at a time when most other scholars, such as Barbara Leslie Epstein and Ruth Bordin, concentrate on the post-Civil War temperance movement.[228] Historians have only begun to examine evangelical women's involvement in mission work among blacks, industrial reform, peace reform, and the civil rights of blacks and native Americans.[229] While we are not altogether ignorant of the experiences of black women in the evangelical tradition,

---

[227]For abolition see Alice Rossi, "Introduction: Social Roots of the Women's Movement in America," *The Feminist Papers* (New York: Columbia University Press, 1973): 241-81, and Dorothy C. Bass " 'Their Prodigious Influence,' " 280-300. For the moral reform movement see Smith-Rosenberg, "Beauty, the Beast;" Ryan, "Power of Women's Networks"; Barbara J. Berg, *The Remembered Gate: Origins of American Feminism* (New York: Oxford University Press, 1978); and Smith-Rosenberg, *Rise of the American City*.

[228]Ian R. Tyrrell, "Women and Temperance in Antebellum America, 1830-1860," *Civil War History* 28 (June 1982): 128-52. See also Susan Dye Lee, "Evangelical Domesticity: The Woman's Temperance Crusade of 1873-1874," and Carolyn DeSwarte Gifford, "For God and Home in Native Land: The W.C.T.U's Image of Woman in the Late Nineteenth Century," in Thomas and Keller, *Women in New Worlds*, 293-327; Barbara Leslie Epstein, *The Politics of Domesticity: Women, Evangelicalism, and Temperance in Nineteenth-Century America* (Middletown CT: Wesleyan University Press, 1981) and Bordin, *Woman and Temperance*.

[229]Jacqueline Jones, *Soldiers of Light and Love: Northern Teachers and Georgia Blacks, 1865-1873* (Chapel Hill: University of North Carolina Press, 1980); McDowell, *Social Gospel in the South*; Mary E. Frederickson, "Shaping a New Society: Methodist Women and Industrial Reform in the South, 1880-1940," in Thomas and Keller, *Women in New Worlds*, 345-61; Arnold Shankman, "Dorothy Tilly, Civil Rights, and the Methodist Church," *Methodist History* 18 (January 1980): 95-108; Frederick A. Norwood, "American Indian Women: The Rise of Methodist Women's Work, 1850-1939"; Anastatia Sims, "Sisterhoods of Service: Women's Clubs and Methodist Women's Missionary Societies in North Carolina, 1890-1930"; and Arnold M. Shankman, "Civil Rights, 1920-1970: Three Southern Methodist Women," in Keller, Queen, and Thomas, *Women in New Worlds: Volume II*, 176-233.

this is a subject that deserves more critical attention, as indeed does the whole subject of male piety and masculine religious rituals.[230]

The role of women in American Evangelicalism, which Carroll Smith-Rosenberg and Nancy A. Hewitt present to us in this volume, is a striking one. The task of the historian is no longer one of merely "understanding women's experiences," Smith-Rosenberg argues in her formidable essay; "it now equally concerns the interplay of cultural forms and social structure." Smith-Rosenberg brings together social, economic, intellectual, and religious history into a single reading of women's history. Along with Mary Ryan and others, she has been in the forefront arguing that history should not be exclusive, but should establish links with sociology, economics, psychology, and anthropology. Smith-Rosenberg's essay is one more manifestation of the links being made, for it is representative of the anthropological approach to revivalism characterized by the recent work of Rhys Isaac, Paul Johnson, and William McLoughlin.

Smith-Rosenberg's discussion of the relationship between cosmology and social structure is interesting. She is dealing here with what Judith Wellman terms "perhaps the most conceptually difficult period in American history for understanding American women."[231] Evangelical women's attraction to antistructure and antiritualism is interpreted within the context of revivalism as an initiation rite into an industrial and mercantile economy. Evangelicalism's revolutionary impact on women was only temporary, however, as Smith-Rosenberg traces the route from radical Evangelicalism to bourgeois Evangelicalism. Women who sought to challenge male dominance in religion faced defeat from the start, given Evangelicalism's complicity with the forces of bourgeois capitalism.

---

[230]For an important resource see Marilyn Richardson, "Black Women and Religion: A Bibliography" (Boston: G. K. Hall, 1980). For a strong beginning see the work of Sylvia M. Jacobs, especially "Three Afro-American Women: Missionaries in Africa, 1882-1904," in Keller, Queen, and Thomas, *Women in New Worlds: Volume II*, 268-80, and "Their 'Special Mission': Afro-American Women as Missionaries to the Congo, 1894-1937" in *Black Americans and the Missionary Movement in Africa*, ed. Sylvia M. Jacobs (Westport CT: Greenwood Press, 1982): 155-75. That women have been the staple, if not sole fare in gender research is made amply apparent by such a refreshing study as E. Anthony Rotundo's "Body and Soul: Changing Ideals of American Middle-Class Manhood, 1770-1920," *Journal of Social History* 17 (Summer 1983): 23-38.

[231]Judith Wellman, "Comment on Papers by Hatch, Smith-Rosenberg, Hewitt and Bowden: Finney Historical Conference," unpublished manuscript, 3.

Clergy who initially encouraged enlarged roles for women quickly plotted women's return into a new reigning orthodoxy where little had changed; men once again held the institutional authority.

A conceptual framework holds many traps, not the least of which is the need for historical theories to be held accountable to what often turn out to be recalcitrant but sticky facts. Robert T. Handy has cited a geologist, later president of the University of Wisconsin, who once observed that "the mind lingers with pleasure upon the facts that fall happily into the embrace of the theory, and feels a natural coldness toward those that assume a refractory attitude."[232] Historians must be especially careful to historicize the unhistorical discipline of anthropology with its often rampant antihistorical bias and its utilization of theories as magic wands to wave over a society and organize its data. As E. P. Thompson has warned, the tumescent typologies of anthropology and sociology must be ruthlessly subjected to "the discipline of historical context."

Nancy Hewitt's essay is called "Part II" because it totally immerses Smith-Rosenberg's anthropological theories in the specific historical context of women who participated in Finney's revivals. In demonstrating that Finney's female followers do indeed fit into the separation-liminality-reintegration pattern outlined by Smith-Rosenberg, Hewitt also makes an important discovery that helps describe why some women responded to the revivals differently than others. Her work undergirds a point made by Dorothy Bass and Mary Ryan whose research also yields a compound picture of women's religious experiences. Three groups of women coexisted in Rochester's religious community: "Pre-Finneyite benevolent women," "evangelical perfectionists," and "Progressive Quaker egalitarians." Each group defined and elaborated distinct roles for women in the community as well as within the church.

The relationship of Evangelicals to youth has been explored most fully by students of women's history. If Joan Jacobs Brumberg is right in asserting that "the role of youth is central to an understanding of the workings of antebellum America's distinctly evangelical religious culture,"[233] then our "understanding" is in dire need of repair and refinement. Nu-

---

[232]Quoted by Robert T. Handy, "Finney Festival Papers," 4.

[233]Brumberg, *Mission for Life*, 42. See also Ryan, *Cradle of the Middle Class*, 65-79, 105-44.

merous studies now enable us to claim with confidence that nineteenth-century evangelical women came to reign supreme in the moral and spiritual instruction of children at home, at school, and at church. From this point, however, there is both contention and confusion. Philip Greven's controversial thesis, for example, holds that an "evangelical" personality type was shaped by authoritarian patterns of child-rearing, which from 1600 to 1850 wrestled conversions into existence through breaking the will, suppressing the self, and submerging the rage of children. Unfortunately, Greven's imaginative typologies play fast and loose with historical contexts through an undisciplined exercise in metahistory.[234] The critical attention surrounding his work is not entirely undeserved. If Greven's work forces historians to look at evangelical modes of child-rearing and discipline, the controversy will be as fruitful as it has been fun.[235]

A prime mechanism for studying the relationship between Evangelicalism and youth is the Sunday school. Yet historians have been strangely uninterested in this part of the evangelical apparatus, leading Bertram Wyatt-Brown to properly call the Sunday school "one of the most understudied major undertakings in American education."[236] Robert W. Lynn, author of the only history of the Sunday school, has convincingly demonstrated that the movement must be interpreted within the context of nineteenth-century evangelical Protestantism.[237] Most of what we do know about the Sunday school comes from historians like Anne M. Boylan, Page Putnam Miller, and Joanna Bowen Gillespie working in the

---

[234]Philip Greven, *The Protestant Temperament: Patterns of Child-Rearing, Religious Experience, and the Self in Early America* (New York: Alfred A. Knopf, 1977).

[235]For an unrepresentative sampling of evangelical discipline see William G. McLoughlin, "Evangelical Childrearing in the Age of Jackson: Francis Wayland's Views on When and How to Subdue the Willfulness of Children," *Journal of Social History* 9 (Fall 1975): 21-34.

[236]Bertram Wyatt-Brown, "The Mission and the Masses: The Moral Imperatives of the City Bourgeoisie," *Reviews in American History* 7 (December 1979): 530.

[237]Robert W. Lynn and Elliott Wright, *The Big Little School: 200 Years of the Sunday School* (Nashville: Abingdon, 1980). The Sunday school bicentennial in 1980 unleashed a flood of articles, but almost all of these were popular treatments. For the best of these see Martin E. Marty, "The Sunday School: Battered Survivor," *The Christian Century* 97 (4-11 June 1980): 634-36; D. Campbell Wyckoff, "As American as Crab Grass: The Protestant Sunday School," *Religious Education* 75 (January-February 1980): 27-35.

fields of women's history.[238] Boylan traces the transformation of America's Sunday schools economically (from poor to middle class), philosophically (from secular to religious education), and geographically (from local community to individual congregations) during the formative period of the 1820s, and credits the ecumenical Sunday school movement that grew out of revivals with providing a forum for the elaboration and extension of the ideal of "evangelical womanhood."[239] Miller stresses the expansive opportunities that opened up for Presbyterian women by Sunday school involvement.[240] And Gillespie's analysis of Episcopal and Methodist Sunday school curriculum materials reinforces early impressions about the supremacy of mothers in child development and the power they enjoyed in shaping an ideology of women as redeemer figures.[241] But we still know too little about who went to Sunday schools, who taught in them, how popular they were, what exactly children learned, what reading material they took home with them from Sunday school libraries, and how else people spent their Sundays. The revival of Sabbatarianism in nineteenth-century Evangelicalism, especially its more

---

[238]Exceptions to this generalization include Grover L. Hartman, *A School for God's People: A History of the Sunday School Movement in Indiana* (Indianapolis: Central Publishing Company, 1980); William B. Kennedy, "Neo-Orthodoxy Goes to Sunday School: The Christian Faith and Life Curriculum," *Journal of Presbyterian History* 58 (Winter 1980): 326-70; J. Parker Jameson, "The Sunday School in the National Period," *Historical Magazine of the Protestant Episcopal Church* 51 (April 1982): 285-89; Grover L. Hartman, "The Hoosier Sunday School: A Potent Religious/Cultural Force," *Indiana Magazine of History* 78 (September 1982): 215-41; and the theme issue on the history of Southern Baptist Sunday Schools found in *Baptist History in Heritage* 18 (January 1983) with articles on "The Contribution of the Sunday School to Southern Baptist Churches" by William P. Clemmons, 31-33; "Major Thrust in Sunday School Development Since 1900," by James E. Fitch, 17-30; "The Emerging Role of Sunday Schools in Southern Baptist Life to 1900," by Lynn E. May, Jr., 6-16.

[239]Anne M. Boylan, "Sunday Schools and Changing Evangelical Views of Children in the 1820's," *Church History* 48 (September 1979): 320-33; "Evangelical Womanhood in the Nineteenth Century: The Role of Women in Sunday Schools," *Feminist Studies* 4 (October 1978): 62-80; "Presbyterians and Sunday Schools in Philadelphia, 1800-1824," *Journal of Presbyterian History* 58 (Winter 1980): 299-310.

[240]Page Putnam Miller, "Women in the Vanguard of the Sunday School Movement," *Journal of Presbyterian History* 58 (Winter 1980): 311-25.

[241]Joanna Bowen Gillespie, "The Sun in their Domestic System," Keller, Queen and Thomas, *Women in New Worlds: Volume II*, 45-59; and Gillespie, "Carrie, or the Child in the Rectory: 19th-Century Episcopal Sunday School Prototype," *Historical Magazine of the Protestant Episcopal Church* 51 (December 1982): 359-70.

strident, paranoid, negative form between 1860 and 1890, awaits treatment similar to that given Puritan Sabbatarianism by Winton U. Solberg.[242]

No studies of the Sunday school phenomenon in America exist that even approximate what E. P. Thompson and Thomas Walter Laqueur have done for the English Sunday schools and their role in an industrial society.[243] Certain American historians have leaned in the direction of E. P. Thompson's famous thesis that both bourgeois control and working-class radicalism were outgrowths of English Methodism and that the Sunday school was the place where the upper and middle classes endeavored to place working people under the yoke of bourgeois, counter-Revolutionary ideology. For example, Paul E. Johnson and Anthony F. C. Wallace see evangelical religion as a mechanism of social discipline and capitalist schooling which succeeded by keeping political order and social control over workers. Other American historians like Herbert Gutman and Joan Jacobs Brumberg are more inclined to side with Laqueur. Admitting that Sunday school instruction may have taught bourgeois values of self-discipline, punctuality, cleanliness, sobriety, thrift and order, they go on to show that many workers nevertheless made their Sunday school training serve a different cause, sometimes that of working-class radicalism. Paul S. Boyer believes that nineteenth-century Evangelicals failed to reach working-class culture. Certain research suggests otherwise, as Gutman argues that Sunday school symbols and language, so far from turning laborers into "fodder for factories," actively fortified them in their fight against economic oppression.[244] Additionally, Paul Johnson allows that members of the working class by the late 1830s "found their

---

[242]Winton U. Solberg, *Redeem the Time: The Puritan Sabbath in Early America* (Cambridge: Harvard University Press, 1977). For a preliminary probing of the topic see Louis B. Weeks, "The Scriptures and Sabbath Observance in the South," *Journal of Presbyterian History* 59 (Summer 1981): 267-83.

[243]E. P. Thompson, *The Making of the English Working Class* (New York: Pantheon, 1964); Thomas Walker Laqueur, *Religion and Respectability: Sunday Schools and Working Class Culture, 1780-1850* (New Haven: Yale University Press, 1976).

[244]Boyer, *Urban Masses*, 34-53; Herbert S. Gutman, "Protestantism and the American Labor Movement: The Christian Spirit in the Golden Age," in *Work, Culture, and Society in Industrializing America: Essays in American Working-Class and Social History* (New York: Knopf, 1976): 79-117. See also Kenneth Fones-Wolf, "Revivalism and Craft Unionism in the Progressive Era: The Syracuse and Auburn Labor Forward Movements of 1913," *New York History* 63 (October 1982): 389-416.

own uses for the Protestant tradition."[245] Whereas Boyer contends Evangelicals were backward-looking and nostalgic in their use of Sunday schools' printing presses and other propaganda paraphernalia, Brumberg's attempt to relate religious ideology to social history by showing how Evangelicalism worked demonstrates that "evangelical communications theory" was a modern, skillful, innovative method of socialization that made "literature and the printed page a moral and political problem" through its positing of a direct relationship between reading and behavior. Indeed, the breeding of Evangelicalism among the young was enormously prolific partly because Evangelicals proved to be more "tactically adroit" than liberals and more able "to adapt contemporary cultural forms to their own purpose."[246]

To what extent this utilitarian cast to Evangelicalism helped it to gain an audience among workers as well as youth is still uncertain. Scholarship that opposes Gutman's findings that evangelical ideology aided the development of a trade-union movement includes David Montgomery's research in antebellum Philadelphia, where Evangelicalism appears to have fragmented the working class, and anthropologist Anthony F. C. Wallace's excavation of Rockdale, Pennsylvania, where evangelical religion sabotaged workers' sense of class solidarity and thus prevented class conflict.[247] Evangelicalism's relationship to workers was, to say the least, far from simple. We may despair at such a hodgepodge of contradictory and incoherent research, but no matter how conflicting the studies, they all tend to establish, in the words of Bruce Tucker, "the critical importance of religion in labour history."[248]

In the late nineteenth century the evangelical empire collapsed, and certain Evangelicals did a flip. Something shattering happened to the evangelical consensus, which was strong in 1855 (when seventy percent

[245]Paul Johnson, *Shopkeeper's Millennium*, 116-35.

[246]Brumberg, *Mission for Life*, 70, 66-78, 20-33, 43, 208.

[247]Anthony F. C. Wallace, *Rockdale: The Growth of an American Village in the Early Industrial Revolution* (New York: Alfred A. Knopf, 1978).

[248]David Montgomery, "The Shuttle and the Cross: Weavers and Artisans in the Kensington Riots of 1844," *Journal of Social History* 5 (Summer 1972): 439; Bruce Tucker, "Class and Culture in Recent Anglo-American Religious Historiography," 160.

of Protestants were Methodists and Baptists) but a shambles by 1915 (when it meant very little to be Methodist or Baptist). David O. Moberg has explicated what Timothy Smith calls the "Great Reversal," where those once in the vanguard of social reform now took up the rear.[249] It is perhaps more precisely called the Great Split. But we still do not know adequately why Evangelicalism splintered into competing segments that have been variously styled "Public Christians" versus "Private Christians" (Marty), modernists versus fundamentalists, "evangelical liberals" versus conservatives (Cauthen), or social gospelers versus personal gospelers.[250] The reasons for the fragmentation of the evangelical tradition are poorly understood, partly because so little work has been done on late nineteenth-century Evangelicalism in the last decade. It has something to do with a change in eschatology from post-to premillennialism,[251] but it may also have something to do with the introduction of biblical criticism and transformation of institutions of higher education;[252] the anti-Modernism that attended the transition from entrepreneurial capitalism to corporate capitalism;[253] the impact of lay philanthropy on denominations;[254] a "chastened view of human history" and the lack of historical

---

[249]David O. Moberg, *The Great Reversal: Evangelism Versus Social Concern* (Philadelphia: J. B. Lippincott, 1972). For a cautionary note about this theme see George M. Marsden, "The Gospel of Wealth, The Social Gospel, and the Salvation of Souls in Nineteenth-Century America," *Fides et Historia* 5 (Fall 1972/Spring 1973): 10-21.

[250]Martin E. Marty, *Righteous Empire: The Protestant Experience in America* (New York: Dial Press, 1970) 177-87; W. Kenneth Cauthen, *The Impact of American Religious Liberalism* (Washington: University Press of America, 1983, originally published 1962).

[251]Weber, *Shadow of the Second Coming.*

[252]Glenn T. Miller's provocative analysis of heresy trials taps popular piety and its charges in "Trying the Spirits: the Heresy Trials of the Nineteenth Century as Cultural Events," *Perspectives in Religious Studies* 9 (Spring 1982): 49-63. The whole area of religion and higher education needs further investigation. See James Findlay, "Agency, Denominations and the Western Colleges, 1820-1860: Some Connections between Evangelism and American Higher Education," *Church History* 50 (March 1981): 64-80 and David Riesman, "The Evangelical Colleges: Untouched by the Academic Revolution," *Change* 13 (January/February 1981): 13-20.

[253]Lears, *No Place of Grace.*

[254]Donald B. Marti, "Laymen, Bring Your Money: Lee Claflin, Methodist Philanthropist, 1791-1871," *Methodist History* 14 (April 1976): 165-85.

consciousness;[255] shifting Christologies; and alterations in the under-standing of the relationship between the individual and society.

Clearly, use of the term "Great Reversal" for this period is applicable to only a segment of the evangelical tradition and obscures the evangelical roots of the progressive and social gospel movements, which Timothy Smith first brought to our attention, but since has been inadequately stud-ied. Winthrop S. Hudson has also argued that there was an evangelical wing to the social gospel movement best represented by Walter Raus-chenbusch, Finney's truest heir.[256] In fact, Ronald C. White, Jr. and C. Howard Hopkins begin their survey of the social gospel by scanning its revivalistic pedigree, thereby warning readers against simply equating social activism with theological liberalism.[257] A recent batch of research in late nineteenth-, early twentieth-century American religious history has also demonstrated that opposition to the social gospel movement did not necessarily entail opposition to the social claims of the gospel. Ferenc Morton Szasz's important book, *The Divided Mind of Protestant America, 1880-1930* (1982) argues that from 1901-1917 conservatives and liberals

---

[255]Richard S. Taylor, "Beyond Immediate Emancipation: Jonathan Blanchard, Ab-olitionism, and the Emergence of American Fundamentalism," *Civil War History* 29 (September 1981): 260-74, and Grant Wacker, "The Demise of Biblical Civilization," Hatch and Noll, *Bible in America*, 121-38.

[256]Winthrop S. Hudson, "Walter Rauschenbush and the New Evangelism," *Religion in Life* 30 (Summer 1961): 412-30. For the various types of social gospelers, see Kenneth L. Smith and Leonard I. Sweet, "Shailer Mathews: A Chapter in the Social Gospel Move-ment, Part I," *Foundations* 18 (July-September 1975): 219-37. Robert M. Crunden threat-ens the tidiness of recent historical synthesis with his intensely interesting look at the evangelical origins of progressivism in *Ministers of Reform: The Progressives' Achievement in American Civilization, 1889-1920* (New York: Basic Books, 1982).

[257]Ronald C. White, Jr. and C. Howard Hopkins, *The Social Gospel: Religion and Re-form in Changing America* (Philadelphia: Temple University Press, 1976). For further def-inition of the relationship of revivalism and reform within the context of the social gospel movement, see Ronald C. White, Jr., "Social Reform and the Social Gospel in America," in *Separation Without Hope?*, ed. Julio de Santa Ana (Geneva: World Council of Churches, 1978): 50-59. John R. Mott's concern for social issues has been interpreted by Hopkins as an ancestral burden bequeathed to him by Evangelicalism. See Hopkins, *John R. Mott*, 274. For James Warley Miles as a case study in theological liberalism and social conservatism, see Ralph E. Luker, "Liberal Theology and Social Conservatism: A South-ern Tradition, 1840-1920," *Church History* 50 (June 1981): 193-204.

were equally involved in social reconstruction, though "each in its own way."[258] Revivalistic, holiness groups engaged in urban social work in Northern states; Southern Evangelicals allied themselves with "progressive" capitalism in North Carolina; and premillennial fundamentalists in most places supported the temperance crusade.[259]

In sum, studies in the late Victorian era are our weakest links in reconstructing the evangelical tradition in America.[260] Witness the glaring omission of this period in the enclosed collection. Whereas the evangelical responses to Reconstruction and immigration have been well researched in previous decades, hardly anyone today is working in these areas.[261] Richard J. Mouw has decried the prevalence in treatments of American Evangelicalism of an "Anglo-American" bias that refuses to see that many Evangelicals were not only not anti-immigrationist but were immigrants themselves, thus slighting the histories of evangelical groups like the Christian Reformed Church, Missouri Synod Lutherans, and so forth.[262] George Marsden's volume on Fundamentalism helps to remedy the late Victorian hiatus in our historiography, but only partially.[263] Ironically, it may be the least commented on chapter in Donald M. Scott's

---

[258]Ferenc Morton Szasz, *The Divided Mind of Protestant America, 1880-1930* (Tuscaloosa: University of Alabama Press, 1982): 56.

[259]Norris Magnuson, *Salvation in the Slums: Evangelical Social Work, 1865-1920* (Metuchen NJ: Scarecrow Press, 1977); Bode, *Protestantism in the New South*; Weber, *Second Coming*.

[260]Significant exceptions include Paul A. Carter, *The Spiritual Crisis of the Gilded Age* (De Kalb IL: Northern Illinois University Press, 1971) and Clark, *Henry Ward Beecher*.

[261]For examples of the diminishing focus of the work being conducted in Reconstruction and immigration studies, see Sylvia Krebs, "Funeral Meats and Second Marriages: Alabama Churches in the Presidential Reconstruction Period," *Alabama Historical Quarterly* 37 (Fall 1975): 206-16; and Terry M. Henry, "Immigration as a Factor in the Division of the Evangelical Association," *Methodist History* 19 (October 1980): 41-57. A good study of Evangelicals and Nativism is Lawrence B. Davis's *Immigrants, Baptists, and the Protestant Mind in America* (Urbana: University of Illinois Press, 1973).

[262]See Richard J. Mouw's review essay in *Calvin Theological Journal* 11 (November 1976): 260-64.

[263]Marsden, *Fundamentalism and American Culture*.

widely heralded study, the chapter on Victorian spirituality, which has profound implications for theology in the late nineteenth century.[264]

One reason the period from 1880-1920 is one of the most parched areas in American religious historiography is due to historians' loss of interest in the social gospel movement, a reflection of our general disillusionment with liberal reform movements. But in some ways this has benefited our understanding of the evangelical tradition, for instead of mainly analyzing Evangelicals vis-à-vis disputes with liberals and modernists over evolution, eschatology, Scripture, and social witness, historians have begun to appreciate the ways in which all of American Protestantism succumbed (though in varying degrees) to the same acculturating forces in the late nineteenth, early twentieth centuries. It was not just liberals and modernists who suffered from an erosion of theological identity, Ferenc M. Szasz and Joseph D. Ban have shown. Evangelicals and fundamentalists also acquiesced in cultural norms and intellectual developments.[265] Nor was it just liberal clergy who became lapdogs to the rich, or liberal Bibles that became how-to-be-a-success-in-living handbooks, or liberal churches that accepted the sweets of capitalism and then became hooked on them, as William T. Doherty, Jr. has demonstrated. Evangelicals also became allies and partners to business.[266] In fact, Ben Primer suggests that the most significant development in American Protestantism in the period from 1880-1930 was "the bureaucratization of the Church," the modeling of religious institutions after the hierarchical modes and organizational

---

[264]Scott, *From Office to Profession*, 133-47. See also Sandra Sizer's analysis of the message of Sankey's hymns in *Gospel Hymns*.

[265]Ferenc M. Szasz, "T. DeWitt Talmage: Spiritual Tycoon of the Gilded Age," *Journal of Presbyterian History* 59 (Spring 1981): 18-32; Joseph D. Ban, "Two Views of Our Age: Fosdick and Straton," *Foundations* 14 (April-June 1971): 153-70. Also see Philip D. Jordan, "Immigrants, Methodists and a Conservative Social Gospel, 1865-1908," *Methodist History* 17 (October 1978): 16-43, and David T. Morgan, "The Revivalist as Patriot: Billy Sunday and World War I," *Journal of Presbyterian History* 51 (Summer 1973): 199-215.

[266]William T. Doherty, Jr., "The Nineteenth Century Businessman and Religion," *North Dakota Quarterly* 46 (Spring 1978): 4-18; "The Twentieth Century's Secular Religion," *North Dakota Quarterly* 47 (Autumn 1979): 54-63; Marti, "Laymen, Bring Your Money."

values of corporate capitalism—a change motivated by the frantic desire to be modern by being managerial, to be relevant by being efficient.[267]

The significance of Fundamentalism to an understanding of twentieth-century American religion is one of the most important historiographical developments in the 1970s. In an illuminating review essay on Fundamentalism, William E. Ellis traces the contours of a basically liberal, "progressive" interpretation that dominated the study of Fundamentalism until the 1970s: the lumping of all conservatives together, followed by a robust debunking and an abrupt dismissal of their impact and importance.[268] Of all the historians of this era, George Marsden observed in his remarks at the Finney Festival, "Winthrop S. Hudson should be given the credit . . . for most clearly recognizing that the 'third force' including fundamentalists, holiness-folk and pentecostals, might lead the way to Protestant recovery."[269] Hudson no longer stands alone. Joel Carpenter's essay in this collection on "The Fundamentalist Leaven and the Rise of an Evangelical United Front" is a graphic illustration of Robert Moats Miller's claim that "Today scholarly writing on Protestant fundamentalism in modern America is far more abundant in quantity and superior in quality to that on Protestant liberalism."[270]

Although revisionist scholarship actually began during the 1960s, it was the publication in 1970 of Ernest Sandeen's *The Roots of Fundamentalism* that inaugurated a new era in fundamentalist studies. Downplaying the Southern, rural, and ignorant components of the fundamentalist phenomenon, Sandeen demonstrated the theological integrity of Fundamen-

---

[267]Ben Primer, *Protestants and Americans Business Methods* (Ann Arbor: UMI Research Press, 1979). For a positive slant on the modernization and rationalization of denominational structures, see William McGuire King's "Denominational Modernization and Religious Identity: The Case of the Methodist Episcopal Church," *Methodist History* 20 (January 1982): 75-89.

[268]William E. Ellis, "Evolution, Fundamentalism, and the Historians: An Historiographical Review," *The Historian* 44 (November 1981): 15-35.

[269]George M. Marsden, "Comments on Papers by Joel Carpenter and Grant Wacker: Finney Historical Conference," unpublished manuscript, 1.

[270]Robert Moats Miller, "A Complete (Almost) Guide Through the Forest of Fundamentalism," *Reviews in American History* 9 (September 1981): 393, 392-97.

talism based on dispensationalism and Princeton theology.[271] Other historians immediately were eager to put Sandeen's thesis to the test. Some found Sandeen's emphasis on Princeton's contribution to biblical literalism wobbly.[272] Others approved his emphasis on eschatology over evolution as the matrix out of which Fundamentalism emerged, though that approach was still considered too narrow in scope. Studies of Southern Baptists by James J. Thompson, Jr. and William F. Ellis, as well as biographical sketches of fundamentalist leaders by C. Allyn Russell, for example, pointed to the tremendous mixture of theological, social, and economic emphases that Sandeen had not appreciated. These works highlighted as well the strong intellectual strands in Fundamentalism, especially its respect for reason and science, which Sandeen had partly acknowledged.[273] Theological analyses of Fundamentalism, whether by supporters (Bernard I. Ramm) or detractors (James Barr), demonstrated the powerful intellectualist (some might say scholastic) scaffolding to Fundamentalism and the degree to which fundamentalist thought has been subject to the same cultural process of change, evolution, and mediation that affects other movements.[274] Renewed attention to holiness

---

[271]Sandeen, *Roots of Fundamentalism*.

[272]Bruce Shelley, "A. J. Gordon and Biblical Criticism," *Foundations* 14 (January-March 1971): 69-77.

[273]James J. Thompson, Jr., "Southern Baptist City and Country Churches in the Twenties," *Foundations* 17 (October-December 1974): 351-63; Thompson, "Southern Baptists and the Antievolution Controversy of the 1920s," *Mississippi Quarterly* 29 (Winter 1975-1976): 67-81; Thompson, *"Tried as by Fire": Southern Baptists and the Religious Controversies of the 1920s* (Macon GA: Mercer University Press, 1982); William F. Ellis, "Edgar Young Mullins and the Crisis of Moderate Southern Baptist Leadership," *Foundations* 19 (April-June 1976): 171-85; C. Allyn Russell, *Voices of American Fundamentalism*; Ellis, "Donald Grey Barnhouse: Fundamentalist Who Changed," *Journal of Presbyterian History* 59 (Spring 1981): 33-57; Ellis, "Mark Allison Matthews: Seattle Fundamentalist and Civic Reformer," *Journal of Presbyterian History* 57 (Winter 1979): 446-66. Richard S. Taylor's study of conservative Evangelicals like Jonathan Blanchard who paved the way for Fundamentalism reveals the relative insignificance of eschatology and the importance of social theology in the emergence of the fundamentalist movement. See "Beyond Immediate Emancipation: Jonathan Blanchard, Abolitionism and the Emergence of American Fundamentalism," *Civil War History* 29 (September 1981): 260-74.

[274]Ramm, *Evangelical Heritage*; James Barr, *Fundamentalism* (Philadelphia: Westminster, 1978). For an extended response to Barr's criticisms, see Carl F. H. Henry, "Those Incomprehensible British Fundamentalists: Part I," *Christianity Today* 22 (2

movements—their history, theology, and connection with Pentecostal-ism—provided a needed corrective to Sandeen's orientation, and enabled historians to realize that the Reformed element was as strong in the holiness and Pentecostal movements as in Fundamentalism.[275] Students of fundamentalist social views, especially on race and Jews, revealed much that surprises. It is all not what we had supposed.[276] The fiftieth anniversary of what some have described as "the world's most famous court trial," the Scopes Trial of 1925, helped generate many revisionist looks at the evolutionist controversy, William Jennings Bryan's role in it, and the overall evangelical stance towards science.[277] It also led the National Park

June 1978): 1092-96; "Part II," *Christianity Today* 22 (23 June 1978): 1146-50; and "Part III," *Christianity Today* 22 (21 July 1978): 1205-08.

[275]Melvin E. Dieter, *The Holiness Revival of the Nineteenth Century*, (Metuchen NJ: Scarecrow Press, 1980); Madden and Hamilton, *Freedom and Grace*; Paul M. Bassett, "A Study in the Theology of the Early Holiness Movement," *Methodist History News Bulletin* 4 (April 1975): 61-84 and *A.M.E. Zion Quarterly Review, News Bulletin* (April 1975): 61-84; E. Dale Dunlap, "Tuesday Meetings, Camp Meetings, and Cabinet Meetings: A Perspective On the Holiness Movement in the Methodist Church in the United States in the Nineteenth Century," *Methodist History News Bulletin* 4 (April 1975): 85-106 and *A.M.E. Zion Quarterly Review, News Bulletin* (April 1975): 85-106; Bruce Shelley, "Sources of Pietistic Fundamentalism," *Fides et Historia* 5 (Fall/Spring 1972): 68-78; Synan, *The Holiness-Pentecostal Movement in the United States* (Grand Rapids MI: Eerdmans, 1971); Synan, ed., *Aspects of Pentecostal-Charismatic Origins*, (Plainfield NJ: Logos International, 1975); Donald W. Dayton, "The Doctrine of the Baptism of the Holy Spirit: Its Emergence and Significance," *Wesleyan Theological Journal* 13 (Spring 1978): 114-26; Robert F. Martin, "The Holiness-Pentecostal Revival in the Carolinas, 1896-1940," *Proceedings of the South Carolina Historical Association* (1979): 59-78. For bibliographical aids in this area, see Donald W. Dayton, *The American Holiness Movement: A Bibliographic Introduction* (Wilmore KY: Asbury Theological Seminary, 1971) and David D. Bundy, *Keswick: A Bibliographical Introduction to the Higher Life Movements* (Wilmore KY: Asbury Theological Seminary, 1975).

[276]Henry Y. Warnock, "Prophets of Change: Some Southern Baptist Leaders and the Problem of Race, 1900-1921," *Baptist History and Heritage* 7 (July 1972): 172-83; Kirk Mariner, "The Negro's Place: Virginia Methodists Debate Unification: 1924-1925," *Methodist History* 18 (April 1980): 155-70; David A. Rausch, *Zionism Within Early American Fundamentalism, 1878-1918: A Convergence of Two Traditions* (New York: Edwin Meller Press, 1979); Rausch, "Our Hope: An American Fundamentalist Journal and the Holocaust, 1937-1945," *Fides et Historia* 112 (Spring 1980): 89-103.

[277]Ferenc Szasz, "The Scopes Trial in Perspective," *Tennessee Historical Quarterly* 30 (Fall 1971): 288-98; William James Morison, "Bryan and Darrow at Dayton: Issues or Personalities?" *Mississippi Valley Collection* 5 (Fall 1972): 61-76; Judith V. Graviner and Peter D. Miller, "Effects of the Scopes Trial," *Science* 175 (6 September 1974): 832-37;

Service in 1977 to designate the trial courthouse a National Historic Landmark.

Yet the refiner's fire did not always soften Sandeen's thesis. A hardening of support for the centrality of millennialism in defining Fundamentalism came with Timothy P. Weber's monograph on premillennialism.[278] Moreover, Sandeen's approach to Fundamentalism as not merely a "response" to liberalism and "new theology" but a religious movement stemming from sources deep within American Evangelicalism itself still holds sway. In many ways Sandeen has not so much been proven wrong as not right enough.

The greatest advance in our understanding of Fundamentalism, however, has been made by George M. Marsden, first in his ongoing debate with Sandeen.[279] He accused Sandeen of having an overdeveloped sense of premillennialism and an underdeveloped sense of diversity and complexity within the movement. In his own studies Marsden charted the movement's transatlantic context and theological character, and located its intellectual origins in Common Sense Realism and Baconian philoso-

---

Szasz, "Fundamentalist-Modernist Controversy," 259-78; Robert D. Linder, "Fifty Years After Scopes: Lessons to Learn, A Heritage to Reclaim," *Christianity Today* 19 (18 July 1975): 1009-12; D. Elving Anderson, "Evangelicals and Science: Fifty Years After the Scopes Trial (1925-45)," in Wells and Woodbridge, *The Evangelicals*, 249-68; Bill L. Weaver, "Kentucky Baptists' Reaction to the National Evolution Controversy, 1922-26," *Filson Club History Quarterly* 49 (July 1975): 266-75; William H. Smith, "William Jennings Bryan at Dayton: A View Fifty Years Later," *Proceedings of the Indiana Academy of the Social Sciences* 10 (17 October 1975): 80-88; Willard B. Gatewood, Jr., "Science and Religion: The Controversy Over Evaluation," *The Forum Series* (St. Charles MO: Forum Press, 1975); Ina Turner Gray, "Monkey Trial—Kansas Style," *Methodist History* 14 (July 1976): 235-51; William E. Ellis, "The Fundamentalist-Moderate Schism Over Evolution in the 1920s," *Register of Kentucky Historical Society* 74 (April 1976): 112-23; R. M. Cornelius, "Their Stage Drew All the World: A New Look at the Scopes Evolution Trial," *Tennessee Historical Quarterly* 40 (Summer 1981): 129-43; Hans Schwarz, "The Significance of Evolutionary Thought for American Protestant Theology: Late Nineteenth-Century Resolutions and Twentieth-Century Problems," *Zygon* 16 (September 1981): 261-84; and Leo P. Ribuffo, "Monkey Trials, Past and Present," *Dissent* 28 (Summer 1981): 358-61.

[278]Weber, *Second Coming*.

[279]George Marsden, "Defining Fundamentalism," *Christian Scholar's Review* 2 (Winter 1971): 141-51. For Sandeen's reply, see *Christian Scholar's Review* 1 (Spring 1971): 227-32.

phy, holiness Pietism, and Biblicism.[280] An entire decade of research by Marsden and others culminated in 1980 with Marsden's *Fundamentalism and American Culture*, a work both of great synthesis and great originality. For Marsden a full picture of Fundamentalism makes for a crowded canvas—Baconian science, revivalism (especially Moody), Pietism, conservative theology (Warfield, Hodge, and Machen), holiness movements (especially Keswick), dispensationalism, and so forth—but somehow he manages to draw the threads together in skillful and ingenious ways.

Like other truly seminal works, Marsden's *Fundamentalism and American Culture* illuminates the unexplored areas of American Fundamentalism. The fundamentalist impact on mainline denominations is insufficiently understood.[281] Marsden's conclusion that Fundamentalism was an "American phenomenon" based on the nonseparatist character of British Fundamentalism needs to be tested in light of the vast numbers of American fundamentalists who also were not separatists. Historians may discover, for example, that the strength of the National Association of Evangelicals was within the denominations, not outside. They may also come to appreciate that while American Fundamentalism was not exactly the same as Canadian or English Fundamentalism, one ought not to obscure the closeness of the relationships that were maintained. Roland Robertson and John M. Mulder, among others, have declared that Fundamentalism needs to be interpreted as a worldwide phenomenon that can be found lodged in major religions like Judaism, Islam, Protestantism, and Roman Catholicism.[282]

---

[280]George Marsden, "Fundamentalism as an American Phenomenon, A Comparison with English Evangelicalism," *Church History* 46 (June 1977): 215-32; Marsden, "J. Gresham Machen, History, and Truth," *Westminster Theological Journal* 42 (Fall 1979): 157-75; Marsden, "The New School Heritage and Presbyterian Fundamentalism," *Westminster Theological Journal* 32 (May 1970): 129-47; Marsden, "From Fundamentalism to Evangelicalism: A Historical Analysis," in Wells and Woodbridge, *The Evangelicals*, 122-42.

[281]For a beginning see Winthrop S. Hudson, "The Divergent Careers of Southern and Northern Baptists," *Foundations* 16 (April-June 1973): 171-83.

[282]Roland Robertson is quoted by David Martin, "Back to the Beginning," *Times Literary Supplement*, 18 December 1981, 1461; Mulder's remarks occur in a review of Marsden's book in *Theology Today* 38 (January 1982): 523.

Gregory H. Singleton has uncovered an important topic in his look at "Fundamentalism and Urbanization," though his quantitative attack on "impressionist interpretations" is scarcely advanced by his supposedly more precise classifications of "Definitely Fundamentalist," "Sympathetic," and "Fundamentalist Influence."[283] To what extent Fundamentalism is an expression of anti-Modernism or dying civil religions requires further research. William Ellis has also suggested that the pendulum has swung so far in the direction of fundamentalist intellectualism that the grass roots are virtually forgotten.[284] If Fundamentalism was a popular movement, and a self-conscious one at that after World War I (Marsden), then it needs to be studied as a popular and not just an intellectual and cultural movement.

Joel Carpenter has done much to encourage this line of thinking. His research into the institutional history of Fundamentalism continues to uncover many theories Marsden has done so much to establish for the scholars who follow him. Carpenter has already shown that Fundamentalism was more than a mentality; it was a dynamic, popular movement that withdrew from the mainline denominations in the 1920s, regrouped, and relocated in its own educational and evangelistic organizations in the 1930s, and eventually reappeared confident and aggressive in the 1940s. While the "mainstream" of Protestantism may have been experiencing a "religious depression" during the 1930s, Fundamentalism was creatively improvising new strategies and strengthening its reticular structures for the challenges of the future.[285] The emergence of a revitalized fundamentalist-Evangelicalism, which sought to assume a prominent position of leadership within the American evangelical tradition, is the focus of this essay, as Carpenter looks through the optics of organizational history at the formation of the National Association of Evangelicals in

---

[283]Gregory H. Singleton, "Fundamentalism and Urbanization: A Quantitative Critique of Impressionist Interpretations," in *The New Urban History*, ed. Leo F. Schnore (Princeton: Princeton University Press, 1975) 205-27.

[284]Ellis, "Evolution, Fundamentalism and the Historian," 32.

[285]Joel A. Carpenter, "Fundamentalist Institutions and the Rise of Evangelical Protestantism, 1929-1942," *Church History* 49 (March 1980): 62-75. See also another revisionist history of postwar reaction as outlined by James J. Thompson, Jr., "Southern Baptists and Postwar Disillusionment, 1918-1919," *Foundations* 21 (April-June 1978): 113-22.

1942 and what its establishment says about the "leavening" effect of Fundamentalism on the divergent sectors of Evangelicalism. Fundamentalists sought to ignite a spirit of ecumenism among Evangelicals, and the degree to which their efforts were either unifying or disruptive on an emerging evangelical "coalition" makes fascinating reading.

Various scholars have bemoaned the absence of a "fundamental" definition or description of Fundamentalism. In part, each fundamentalist wore the label in a highly individual way. This problem is multiplied when trying to discuss the myriad forms and segments of the contemporary "Evangelical Renaissance,"[286] which stands as the most significant development in American religious history since the 1970s. The three features of current Evangelicalism receiving the most academic attention are its origins and numerical growth,[287] its familiarity with the satellite and silicon chip,[288] and its political activism.[289] Upon retiring as editor of

---

[286]See Donald G. Bloesch's thoughtful work, *The Evangelical Renaissance* (Grand Rapids MI: Eerdmans, 1973).

[287]Dean Kelley, *Why Conservative Churches are Growing* (New York: Harper and Row, 1972). See also Robert Wuthnow, ed., *The Religious Dimension: New Directions in Quantitative Research* (New York: Academic Press, 1979); Dean R. Hoge and David A. Roozen, eds., *Understanding Church Growth and Decline: 1950-1978* (New York: Pilgrim Press, 1979). Benton Johnson suggested in his 1981 presidential address to the Society for the Scientific Study of Religion that one of the reasons for Evangelicalism's rise was that it adopted much of the liberal program, but placed it within a different system of authority. See "Taking Stock: Reflections on the End of Another Era," *Journal for the Scientific Study of Religion* 21 (September 1982): 189-200. Martin E. Marty places the rise of Evangelicalism within the context of "resurgent antimodern religion" in his very important article, "Religion in America Since Mid-Century," *Daedalus* 111 (Winter 1982): 149-63.

[288]Virginia Stem Owens, *The Total Image: Or Selling Jesus in the Modern Age* (Grand Rapids MI: Eerdmans, 1980); James A. Taylor, "Progeny of Programmers: Evangelical Religion and the Television Age," *Christian Century* 94 (20 April 1977): 379-82; Jeffrey K. Hadden and Charles E. Swann, *Prime Time Preachers: The Rising Power of Televangelism* (Reading ME: Addison-Wesley, 1981); Jeffrey K. Hadden, "Soul Saving via Video," *Christian Century* 97 (28 May 1980): 609-10.

[289]Erling Jorstad has staked his claim on this subject through various books and articles. See especially *The Politics of Doomsday: Fundamentalists of the Far Right* (Nashville: Abingdon Press, 1970); *The Politics of Moralism: The New Christian Right in American Life* (Minneapolis: Augsburg Publishing House, 1981); *Evangelicals in the White House: The Cultural Maturation of Born Again Christianity, 1960-1981* (New York: Edwin Mellen Press, 1981); and "The New Christian Right," *Theology Today* 38 (July 1981): 193-200. Also see Peggy L. Shriver, *The Bible Vote: Religion and the New Right* (New York: Pilgrim Press, 1981) and Robert D. Linder, "The Resurgence of Evangelical Social Concern

Christianity Today, Kenneth Kantzer was asked to enumerate the most important changes in American Evangelicalism. His response: "The single most startling change in evangelicalism is its shift toward political and social involvement," a phenomenon recently chronicled in Robert Booth Fowler's *A New Engagement* (1983).[290]

Anyone who seeks a lively and perceptive assessment of this development can read Grant Wacker's essay in this collection: "Searching for Norman Rockwell: Popular Evangelicalism in Contemporary America." After rehearsing the standard reasons given for the rise of Evangelicalism in the 1970s, Wacker surprises us by stating that what was growing was not so much Evangelicalism as a distinct movement within Evangelicalism that had steadfastly held out for a vision of "Christian Civilization" while the rest of American Evangelicalism had quietly been changed by the historical processes of modernity and secularity. The emergence of this noisy Fundamentalism and its aggressive campaign to return America to Victorian ideals displays all the strength and stamina Evangelicalism had exhibited in the past. In his distinction between "religious fundamentalism" and "cultural fundamentalism," Wacker has made a signal contribution to our understanding of the contemporary religious scene.

Wacker's essay is part of a second wave of scholarship that neither applauds nor attacks[291] the movement for a "Christian America" but instead

---

(1929-75)," in Wells and Woodbridge, *The Evangelicals*, 189-210, and Louise J. Lorentzen, "Evangelical Life Style Concerns Expressed in Political Action," *Sociological Analysis* 41 (Summer 1980): 144-54.

[290]"Reflections: Five Years of Change," *Christianity Today* 26 (26 November 1982): 14; Robert Booth Fowler, *A New Engagement: Evangelical Political Thought, 1966-1976* (Grand Rapids MI: Eerdmans, 1983). Also see Robert Zwier and Richard Smith, "Christian Politics and the 'New Right,' " *Christian Century* 97 (8 October 1980): 937-41; Richard Pierard, *The Unequal Yoke: Evangelical Christianity and Political Conservatism* (Philadelphia: Lippincott, 1970). For the ways in which the feminist movement has influenced even the most conservative corners of Evangelicalism, see Carol Virginia Pohli, "Church Closets and Back Doors: A Feminist View of Moral Majority Women," *Feminist Studies* 9 (Fall 1983): 529-58, though her argument is under considerable strain when detailing the pinched perspectives and parlous state of evangelical women's social and political ignorance.

[291]For attacks on the religious Right as "resurgent McCarthyism," "born-again fascists" and "Holy Terror," see Edward L. Ericson, *American Freedom and the Radical Right* (New York: Ungar, 1982); Daniel C. Maguire, *The New Subversives: Anti-Americanism of the Religious Right* (New York: Continuum, 1982); and Flo Conway and Jim

seeks to understand it. William G. McLoughlin is one of the few brave historians who has ventured out and contrasted the Religious Right of today with nineteenth-century evangelicals and early twentieth-century fundamentalists, an approach as promising as it is perilous.[292] The most balanced assessments of the political involvement of evangelicals can be found in works by Peggy Shriver, Samuel Hill, and Dennis Owen.[293] Martin E. Marty's "Taxonomy of the Born Again" suggests some new departure for analysis, especially if we view Evangelicalism as "less a movement of congregations and more an attraction of clienteles."[294] A theological assessment of the Religious Right is given by Gabriel Fackre, and John L. Kater concludes his historical and theological survey of the movement by demonstrating that "Christians on the Right" are as culturally captivated as the liberals they denounce.[295] One form of evangelical adaptationism is its acquiescence in the forces of subjectivization, which shows up theologically in a "new Evangelical theodicy."[296] No one has systematically analyzed the theological differences between the various shades of contemporary liberals and conservatives to anyone's satisfaction.

In order to bring an ordered discussion of the full scope of contemporary Evangelicalism into focus, historians have tried to distinguish one

---

Siegelman, *Holy Terror: The Fundamentalist War on America's Freedoms in Religion, Politics and Our Private Lives* (New York: Doubleday, 1982).

[292]William G. McLoughlin, "The Illusions and Dangers of the New Christian Right," *Foundations* 25 (April-June 1982): 128-43.

[293]Shriver, *The Bible Vote*; and Samuel Hill and Dennis Owen, *The New Religious/Political Right in America* (Nashville: Abingdon, 1982). See also Robert Zwier, *Born-Again Politics: The New Christian Right in America* (Downers Grove IL: InterVarsity Press, 1982).

[294]Martin E. Marty, "A Taxonomy of the Born-Again," *Christian Century* 95 (October 1978): 924-30.

[295]Gabriel Fackre, *The Religious Right and the Christian Faith* (Grand Rapids MI: Eerdmans, 1982); John L. Kater, *Christians on the Right: The Moral Majority in Perspective* (New York: Seabury, 1982).

[296]James Davison Hunter, "Subjectivization and the New Evangelical Theodicy," *Journal for the Scientific Study of Religion* 21 (March 1982): 39-47.

brand of Evangelicalism from another.[297] The key words scholars employ
to describe Evangelicalism's permeation of American religion across a
wide ecclesiastical spectrum are "diversity," "complexity," "range,"
and "inclusiveness," and the guiding metaphors used include "mosaic,"
"families," and the "big tent." Martin E. Marty's mapping of religion in
America is the simplest. He draws careful distinctions between "Evangelicals" and "Fundamentalists" that are based on behavioral more than
theological differences.[298] Max L. Stackhouse finds three distinct
branches in the evangelical heritage: Puritan Evangelicalism, pietistic
Evangelicalism, and fundamentalist Evangelicalism.[299] Richard Quebedeaux, whose taxonomy of Evangelicalism becomes almost casually ty-
pological, isolates five groups in his *Young Evangelicals* (1974)—
separatist fundamentalists, open fundamentalists, establishment Evangelicals, new Evangelicals, and young Evangelicals—but uses only two
broad categories in his *Worldly Evangelicals* (1978)—"Evangelical Right
and Center" and "Young Evangelical Left."[300] Augustus Cerillo classi-
fies Evangelicals in terms of their social stances as conservative, liberal,
and radical.[301]

While historians are awaiting Timothy L. Smith's promised piecing
together of the evangelical "mosaic," Cullen Murphy finds another met-
aphor more fitting. Under the "vast tent of evangelical faith," he avers,
there is a "12-ring" circus with shows in progress by peace-church conservatives, Arminian conservatives, Wesleyans, Baptists, conservative
Calvinists, immigrant churches, Pietist churches, Adventists, black Pen-

---

[297]Richard V. Pierard's bibliographical essay on some of this literature is helpful. See
"The Quest for the Historical Evangelicalism: A Bibliographical Excursus," *Fides et Historia* 11 (Spring 1979): 60-72.

[298]Martin E. Marty, *A Nation of Behavers* (Chicago: University of Chicago Press,
1976). See also Marty's "Tension Within Contemporary Evangelicalism: A Critical Appraisal," in Wells and Woodbridge, *The Evangelicals*, 170-88.

[299]Max L. Stackhouse, "Religious Right: New? Right?" *Commonweal* 29 (January
1982): 52-6.

[300]Richard Quebedeaux, *The Young Evangelicals* (New York: Harper and Row, 1974);
The Worldly Evangelicals (San Francisco: Harper and Row, 1978).

[301]Augustus Cerillo, Jr., "Survey of Recent Evangelical Social Thought," *Christian
Scholars' Review* 5 (no. 3, 1976): 272-80.

tecostals, white Pentecostals, black Evangelicals, and fundamentalists.[302] Even the spaciousness of the circus tent does not accommodate the
"orthodox Evangelicals," who have reclaimed a sacramental spirituality
that E. Brooks Holifield lifted up as a prominent part of New England
religious life by the beginning of the eighteenth century.[303] Whether neo-
Pentecostals belong within the evangelical canvas at all is still problematic
for some historians.[304]

As the essays in this collection show, the evangelical phenomena is a
complex and challenging one for historians. It looks as if everyone at times
has either been drawn into the loosely twined evangelical camp or claimed
the label, thereby stripping the concept of Evangelicalism of much analytic purchase. Donald W. Dayton has so despaired of talking about
Evangelicalism, given the fact that "the differences within it are as great
as the differences between it and the rest of the church world," that he
recommends historians consider "giving up the word entirely."[305]

The original Evangelicals, the Lutherans, for example, still claim to
be evangelical though few people see them as such.[306] Can there be such a
thing as non-pietistic, liturgical, confessional Evangelicals? Can Roman
Catholics be Evangelicals? What proportion of Evangelicalism is style,

---

[302]Cullen Murphy, "Protestantism and the Evangelicals," *Wilson Quarterly* 5 (Autumn 1981): 105-16.

[303]Robert Webber and Donald Bloesch, *The Orthodox Evangelicals: Who They Are and
What They Are Saying* (New York: Thomas Nelson, 1978). For Holifield's rediscovery of
this strand in colonial religion, see "The Renaissance of Sacramental Piety in Colonial
New England," *William and Mary Quarterly* 29 (January 1972): 33-48, and *The Covenant
Sealed: The Development of Puritan Sacramental Theology in Old and New England, 1570-
1720* (New Haven: Yale University Press, 1974).

[304]Erling Jorstad, for example, calls neo-Pentecostals "an ally, but not an organic
member" of the evangelical family. See *Evangelicals in the White House: The Cultural Maturation of Born Again Christianity, 1960-1981* (New York: Edwin Mellen Press, 1981) 9.

[305]"An Interview with Donald W. Dayton," *Faith and Thought* 1 (Spring 1983): 25,
24-34.

[306]Milton C. Sernett, "Welcoming the 'Evangelicals'—A Call to End One-Upman-
ship," *Currents in Theology and Mission* 6 (June 1979): 154-8. One of the stranger ex-
changes about whether a denomination is "evangelical" can be found in James Leo
Garrett, Jr., E. Glenn Hinson, and James E. Tull, *Are Southern Baptists "Evangelicals"?*
(Macon GA: Mercer University Press, 1983).

theology, spirit, or historical accident? The need for a definition of Evangelicalism, or what sociologist James Davison Hunter calls "operationalizing Evangelicalism,"[307] is to kick the hornet's nest. But we have no choice if we are to move ahead.

If it appears that we have ended up where we began, it is because we need to study the interior life of Evangelicalism as well as the opponents of Evangelicals and non-Evangelicals to gain greater precision of technique and clarity of treatment in understanding the evangelical tradition in America. Until then, Evangelicalism will continue to afford rich scope for unanswered ambiguities and fuzziness of thought. In spite of all the emerging literature, we have only just begun.

---

[307]James Davison Hunter, "Operationalizing Evangelicalism: A Review, Critique & Proposal," *Sociological Analysis* 42 (Winter 1981): 363-72.

Chapter 2

Enlarging the Bonds of Christ: Slavery, Evangelism, and the Christianization of the White South, 1690-1790

Jon Butler

Any reconsideration of Evangelicalism in American history must deal in some significant way with the American South. Historians traditionally have isolated Evangelicalism to the South, and the characterization they have drawn of it there has stamped nearly all of American Evangelicalism with its modern identity, or, at least, with its modern stereotype. Thus, until recently, American historians long tagged the South as the nearly exclusive home of American Evangelicalism and castigated religion and region alike by linking them to the South's "poor white," "plain folk" culture, to anti-intellectualism, slavery, sometimes to violence, and almost always to an allegedly regressive Fundamentalism that presumably kept the region unique and backward until at least the 1950s.[1]

---

[1]A sampling of this opinion might include Paul A. Carter, *Decline and Revival of the Social Gospel: Social and Political Liberalism in American Protestant Churches, 1920-1940* (Ithaca NY: Cornell University Press, 1956), and W. J. Cash, *The Mind of the South* (Garden City NY: Doubleday, 1941).

The power of this traditional characterization is all the more obvious by the way it contrasts with the more recent portrait drawn by historians plying what can be termed a "new evangelical" thesis in American history. Appearing first in the work of historians such as Perry Miller and Timothy L. Smith, and summarized and extended into political history in Alan Heimert's controversial work on the evangelical origins of the American Revolution, this new scholarship has reversed the image of Evangelicalism in American history. Concentrating on the impact of Evangelicalism in the Northern colonies and states (the "real" America), these historians have linked Evangelicalism to the most distinctive values of nineteenth-century American society: individualism, democracy, social reform, public education, abolitionism, and manifest destiny. All but the last of these evokes sympathetic responses from modern historians.[2]

Will historians eventually erase these distinctions between Southern and "Northern" Evangelicalism? Two recent studies reverse their customary images. Paul Johnson's widely read book, *A Shopkeeper's Millennium: Society and Revivals in Rochester, New York, 1815-1837* (New York, 1978), places Northern Evangelicalism in an unfamiliar and unflattering light by emphasizing its social control functions, while Rhys Isaac's book, *The Transformation of Virginia, 1740-1790: Communications, Religion and Authority* (Chapel Hill, 1982) improves the traditional stereotype of Southern Evangelicalism by stressing the eighteenth-century Baptist contribution to popular education and political democracy. Still, contrasts remain. Moreover, they are heuristically useful because they raise important questions about Evangelicalism's role in American history. Did a firm, consistent Christian Evangelicalism successfully mold American society from the mid-eighteenth century into the twentieth century? Did many "Evangelicalisms" exist in the American past, some shifting by time, some by denomination, some perhaps by sex and age? Did their influence accelerate and wane erratically? Or, put in social science vocab-

---

[2]Among the more positive treatments of Evangelicalism are Timothy L. Smith's pioneering *Revivalism and Social Reform in Mid-19th-Century America* (New York and Nashville: Abingdon Press, 1957); Alan Heimert, *Religion and the American Mind from the Great Awakening to the Revolution* (Cambridge MA: Harvard University Press, 1966); Nathan O. Hatch, *The Sacred Cause of Liberty: Republican Thought and the Millennium in Revolutionary New England* (New Haven CT: Yale University Press, 1977); and Donald G. Mathews, *Religion in the Old South* (Chicago: University of Chicago Press, 1977).

ulary, was American Evangelicalism a dependent or independent variable in the making of American society?

This short sketch intends to advance the discussion of some of the important questions about American Evangelicalism by probing the spiritual world Evangelicals inherited in the Southern colonies after about 1750. It outlines changes between 1680 and 1750 that restructured the relationship between organized Christianity and the region's white population. It uncovers a central connection between the evangelical capture of the South after 1750 and an important but otherwise obscure Anglican Christianization program dating from the 1680s. Additionally, it revises our notions about the role organized religion played in the development of American slavery by shifting our attention from the legislation legalizing slavery passed in the mid-seventeenth century to the development of a slavery ideology and ethic in the century after 1680. It further locates one of the foundations of that ideology and ethic in a radical doctrine of total slave obedience laid down by Anglican Christianizers and their Dissenting successors between 1680 and the American Revolution.

The emergence of organized Christianity as a powerful force in the Southern colonies occurred in a distinctive three-stage process. The first stage involved an ignominious failure that closely tied the region's white settlers to the Europe they had only recently left; that is, the region was notoriously indifferent to Christianity before 1690. Historians have long acknowledged this lethargy but never have explained it satisfactorily. They have preferred instead to settle for a simple descriptive contrast between the irreligion of the seventeenth-century Southern colonies and the Puritan piety of New England. In fact, the indifference to organized Christianity in the Southern colonies links them as firmly to seventeenth-century Europe and England as does New England's involvement with Puritanism. This link is found in the brilliant work of several European social historians, among them Jean Delumeau, Keith Thomas, Carlo Ginzburg, Mikhail Bakhtin, Emanuel Le Roy Ladurie, Natalie Zemon Davis, and Gerald Strauss, who have revolutionized our view of Christianity's strengths in the preindustrial West. They have argued that a look at actual religious practice among the Continental and British populace suggests that the formal Christian institutions of society rode uneasily atop an only partially Christianized people. Irrespective of the loyalties of princes and kings, men and women in country and city attached themselves to Christianity and Christian churches in often erratic ways and sometimes ignored the fundamental precepts of Christianity altogether. They consulted astrologers to predict the future, hired magical practitioners to arrange marriages and find lost objects, and sought occult healers to cure diseases. They frequently possessed no accurate knowledge of even the most elemental Christian doctrines, and they often misused what little doctrine they did know by manipulating Christian ritual in quasi-occult ways.[3]

Efforts at popular education did not necessarily improve the situation. Gerald Strauss has argued persuasively that by 1600 the German Reformation had emerged as a monumental popular failure, and Michel Vovelle has argued that progress made in Christianizing France's population between 1500 and 1750 evaporated in the half-century surrounding the French Revolution through a "dechristianization" that stripped the Church of priests and loosened its already tenuous hold on the population. In short, on the eve of the American Revolution and for the next century the leaders of "Christian" Europe presided over a population so thoroughly ignorant of elemental Christian evangelism (meaning the preaching of the gospel and its simplest doctrines) that the "evangelical" problem of a personal commitment to the leading figure of Christianity (usually evidenced in a "new birth") was a matter of almost secondary consideration.[4]

The religious patterns of the seventeenth-century South reveal how thoroughly European cultural patterns shaped New World colonial societies. If New England Puritanism represented the extension of reformed Protestantism to the New World, the condition of organized Christianity in the seventeenth-century Southern colonies revealed that popular European indifference to Christianity could be exported to the New World as well. This did not mean that early Southern colonists were

---

[3]Much of this work is summarized by Marc Venard in "Popular Religion in the Eighteenth Century," in *Church and Society in Catholic Europe of the Eighteenth Century* ed. William J. Callahan and David Higgs (Cambridge, England: Cambridge University Press, 1977) 138-54; and Carlo Ginzburg, *The Cheese and the Worms: The Cosmos of a Sixteenth-Century Miller*, trans., John and Anne Tedeschi (Baltimore MD: Johns Hopkins University Press, 1981) 1-10.

[4]Gerald Strauss, *Luther's House of Learning: Indoctrination of the Young in the German Reformation* (Baltimore MD: Johns Hopkins University Press, 1978); Michel Vovelle, *Piété baroque et déchristianisation en Provence au xviii siècle* (Paris: Plon, 1973).

not religious. Rather, as in England, they still could be religious without being narrowly and fully Christian. Thus, a significant body of evidence suggests that Southern colonists frequently brought beliefs in magic, astrology, and occultism with them when they traveled to the New World and that they and their descendants sustained these beliefs well into the eighteenth century. As Darrett Rutman has described the situation:

> In sound mind and with a clear conscience a Virginian could ascribe his poor hunting to the spell of another (1626), hold that only the horseshoe over his door protected his sick wife from the evil intentions of a neighbor woman who perforce passed under it on her way to saying black prayers at his wife's bedside (1671), could attribute to a witch the death of his pigs and withering of his cotton (1698), and, in court, faced with a suit for slander, insist that "to his thoughts, apprehension or best knowledge" two witches "had rid him along the Seaside & home to his own house" (again 1698).[5]

An incomplete legal establishment weakened the already erratic popular attachment to Christianity in the Southern colonies before 1690. Of course, Virginia was a formally Anglican colony from its formation and after 1649 Maryland officially tolerated Protestant Christianity only. But nowhere did both law and government promote Christian practice effectively. In Virginia, the parish system that emerged in the 1630s and 1640s replicated the traditional English institution that handled local social problems; but before 1680, at least, it failed as an instrument for imposing the Church of England and official Christianity on the Virginia populace. Elsewhere, only the weakest of parish "systems" developed in seventeenth-century Maryland and South Carolina. As a result, the Christian congregations that surfaced and survived in these colonies lacked doctrinal and ecclesiastical cohesion. Puritanism prospered in some places. New England ministers who preached briefly in Virginia's Nansemond County in the 1640s were succeeded by a Virginia layman, William Durand, who preached out of notes taken from sermons Thomas Hooker delivered in London in the 1620s. In the 1660s the Anglican minister in Charles City County apparently restricted communion to persons who

---

[5]Darrett B. Rutman, "The Evolution of Religious Life in Early Virginia," *Lex et Scientia: The International Journal of Law and Science* 14 (1978): 194-95. See also Jon Butler, "Magic, Astrology, and the Early American Religious Heritage, 1600-1760," *American Historical Review* 84 (April 1979): 317-46.

displayed a firm knowledge of Protestant doctrine and exhibited moral if not saintly behavior, much as many New England ministers were doing. But organized Christian activity languished in most places. Some parishes went vacant for years. Other parishes simply supported any minister they could keep. For example, Virginia's Accomack County vestry supported the Reverend Thomas Teackle for over forty years after 1655 despite the fact that Teackle was a drunk and an acquisitive slaveholder. What is more, he sued his vestrymen for his salary and his parishioners for libel while steadily perusing Rosicrucian and Hermetic occultism in books he purchased on a regular basis up to his death in 1697.[6]

This ecclesiastical chaos gave full play to the heterodox religious instincts of British settlers in the early Southern colonies. It sent some colonists scurrying to Dissenters. Ex-Puritans and nominal Anglicans in Maryland, Virginia, and North Carolina flocked to hear George Fox on his first American tour in 1672. Hadn't he actually raised men and women from the dead in England? Later, they provided ready audiences for more obscure Public Friends who traveled through these colonies. Some of these settlers actually became Quakers and were hard to win back. In 1697 the Maryland Anglican minister Nicholas Moreau reported that he had recovered one such family but not without being criticized by the couple's three-year-old daughter who called Moreau a "naughty man" and complained that he hurt her "with cold during the baptismal ceremony." Some statistical evidence demonstrates that other colonists ignored organized religion altogether. Virginia law required Anglican ministers to record births as well as baptisms, and two surviving sets of records from parishes where Dissenters were not active demonstrate that some Virginians eschewed even the elemental rite of baptism. Between 1685 and 1715, nearly 300 of the 1,200 whites born in St. Peter's Parish in New Kent County went unbaptized after birth. The situation was more alarming in Charles Parish in York County. Between 1649 and 1670, 111 of 130 whites born there went unbaptized, and between 1670 and 1680 the figure was 145 of 169 who went unbaptized at birth. Popular interest in organized Christianity appears to have been equally lethargic in Maryland and early

---

[6]Susie M. Ames, *Studies on the Virginia Eastern Shore in the Seventeenth Century* (Richmond VA: The Dietz Press, 1940) 208-42; Jon Butler, ed., "Two 1642 Letters from Virginia Puritans," *Proceedings*, Massachusetts Historical Society 84 (1972): 99-109.

South Carolina. Before 1700 the few Anglican ministers there regularly described each colony as a "Hotch Potch" of the spiritually bankrupt whose settlers knew so little Christian doctrine that they should not be baptized and could not receive communion.[7]

A major attempt in the 1690s to assert the authority of the Church of England in the Southern colonies produced the first major program in popular evangelization and Christianization there and dramatically confronted the popular indifference to organized Christianity rampant in the previous century. This reassertion of Anglican authority and the resulting program in Christianization occurred in most colonies in three steps. First, the Bishop of London appointed commissaries to act as his personal representatives and uphold ecclesiastical discipline among Anglican clergymen in each colony. These included James Blair for Virginia in 1689, Thomas Bray for Maryland in 1696, and Gideon Johnston for South and North Carolina in 1704. Second, the commissaries sought to improve the Anglican legal establishment in each colony. In Virginia this meant strengthening the parish system that descended from the 1640s. In the other colonies it meant securing Anglican establishment for the first time. The effort never was fully successful in North Carolina and took more than a decade elsewhere. But it succeeded in Maryland in 1701 and in South Carolina in 1706, and it had at least partially succeeded in North Carolina by 1705.[8]

---

[7]John L. Nickalls, ed., *The Journal of George Fox* (Cambridge, England: Cambridge University Press, 1952) 641-42; Nicholas Moreau to the Bishop of Lichfield and Coventry, 12 April 1697, in *Historical Collections Relating to the American Colonial Church*, ed. William S. Perry (Hartford CT: Printed for the Subscribers, 1870) 1:29-32; Frank J. Klingberg, ed., *Carolina Chronicle: The Papers of Commissary Gideon Johnston, 1707-1716* (Berkeley CA: University of California Press, 1946); statistics on births and baptisms are taken from C. G. Chamberlayne, ed., *Vestry Book and Register of St. Peter's Parish, New Kent and James City Counties, Virginia, 1684-1786* (Richmond VA: Virginia State Library Board, Division of Purchase and Printing, 1937) and Landon C. Bell, ed., *Charles Parish, York County, Virginia, History and Registers* (Richmond VA: Virginia State Library Board, Division of Purchase and Printing, 1932).

[8]George M. Brydon, *Virginia's Mother Church and the Political Conditions Under Which It Grew . . . 1607-1727* (Richmond VA: Virginia Historical Society, 1947); Nelson W. Rightmyer, *Maryland's Established Church* (Baltimore MD: Church Historical Society for the Diocese of Maryland, 1956) 55-77; Sidney S. Bolton, "The Anglican Church of Colonial South Carolina, 1704-1754: A Study in Americanization," (Ph.D. diss., University of Wisconsin, 1973) 8-54.

The third step in establishing Anglican authority and Christianizing the Southern colonies involved formation of the Society for the Propagation of the Gospel in Foreign Parts (hereafter S. P. G.) in London in 1701. Led by Anglican reformers and "evangelists" including Thomas Bray, a onetime Anglican commissary of Maryland who promoted an often ignored program of spiritual renewal in the 1690s, the S. P. G. initially promoted Christianity only among British colonists and took little interest in other "pagans" such as American Indians and African slaves. In the colonies the S. P. G. consistently supported large numbers of Anglican missionaries in North and South Carolina and at least a few missionaries in Virginia because the colony's legal establishment of the Church of England had been so successful. The influence of the S. P. G. was felt in these regions because it distributed thousands of books to Anglican ministers throughout the Southern colonies, including those in Virginia.[9]

American historians have long maligned the Anglican renaissance in the Southern colonies. Most of them have argued that the real story of religion in the Southern colonies involves the fall of the European state church tradition represented by Anglicanism and the rise of the English Dissenting denominations, the latter occurring after 1740. Certainly the Anglican renaissance was not without its limitations. The Church of England obviously promoted both Christianization and its legal establishment to further its own institutional interests. Thus London authorities had to veto the 1704 South Carolina Church Act because the act stripped South Carolina Dissenters of their political rights, and the S. P. G. secretary in London had to remind an overzealous New York missionary "that our title is not the Society for Propagating the Church, but the Gospel[,] in Foreign Parts." Nor did the Anglican program replicate the Church of England in the Southern colonies or prevent the rise of Dissenters there, although it is true that Dissenters really did not prosper there until after 1740, some sixty years after the Anglican Christianization program had been instituted.[10]

---

[9]Henry Paget Thompson, *Thomas Bray* (London: S. P. C. K., 1954) 43-81; Jon Butler, "Power, Authority, and the Origins of American Denominational Order: The English Churches in the Delaware Valley, 1680-1730," in *Transactions*, American Philosophical Society (1978) 68:2:25-27.

[10]S. P. G. to John Thomas, 7 August 1708, S. P. G. Papers at Lambeth Palace, 16:211; for the traditional negative view of the Anglican endeavor, see Sydney E. Ahlstrom, *A Religious History of the American People* (New Haven: Yale University Press, 1972) ch. 14.

The Anglican Christianization program of the late seventeenth century is central to the history of organized religion in colonial America. It constituted the first major effort at popular evangelization and Christianization in colonies where organized Christianity had been exceptionally weak, and its sometimes paradoxical successes paved the way for later evangelical activity. Through it, literally thousands of Southern colonists observed the systematic performances of Christian rituals for the first time in years, some for the first time in their lives. Colonies that earlier had erected and administered parishes only haphazardly now found themselves possessed with effective parish administrative agencies for the first time. Between 1680 and 1740 most of these parishes constructed church buildings where none had existed before. Their vestrymen conducted parish business, levied taxes, provided for the sick, poor, and elderly, and hired ministers who preached, catechized, performed baptisms, marriages and funerals, and administered communion. The coercive use of the law made the public visibility of Christianity regular and, especially, inevitable. As in New England, if one could not escape church taxes one might not be able to escape church activity either. Admittedly, previous government inactivity in religion had produced no flowering of piety, whether orthodox or unorthodox. And now, this new state support for Christianity, albeit in a Church of England form, reflected government eagerness to advance Protestantism in the aftermath of the Glorious Revolution, which had just exiled the Catholic Stuarts to the European continent.[11]

A survey of Anglican parish reports in Maryland exemplifies much of its success elsewhere. In 1690 the colony possessed no coherent parish system and supported only three Anglican ministers, as well as a few Catholic priests (at least that was the claim of the Anglican clergymen there), several Quaker meetings and, at best, one Presbyterian minister. By 1696 local enforcement of a 1692 Church act (later actually vetoed in London) had created no less than thirty parishes, each governed by six vestrymen, and by 1701 half of these parishes had obtained permanent ministers. If this meant that another half of the new parishes still lacked ministers, it

---

[11]Rightmyer, *Maryland's Established Church*, 55-77; Bolton, "Anglican Church of Colonial South Carolina," ch. 2. Although both authors provide the important facts about the Anglican program, they describe the program in narrow denominational terms only.

also meant that by 1701 the colony contained five times as many clergy-men as it did in 1692.[12]

After a quarter of a century some parishes still presented problems. Anglican reports in 1724 revealed that St. Paul's Parish in Baltimore County seldom drew more than twenty-five communicants from among its 363 white families, although few parish residents were Dissenters or Catholics. The rector of Great Choptank parish in Dorchester County had served there since 1697, but in 1724 he reported that he still lacked a "competent number of communicants" and no "necessaries"—wine chalices and bread plates—to offer communion regularly. In some areas, the laity apparently refused to substitute solemn church ceremonies for secular holiday festivities. The 300 persons who attended Sabbath services at St. Barnabas Parish dropped to "not above 20 on holidays, and often fewer," despite the rector's encouragement. The weather and seasonal agricultural demands also affected church attendance, as it had in England. A Somerset County minister reported in 1724 that "some hundreds attended in summer," as the need for field labor slackened between spring planting and fall harvest, but also noted that winter audiences were small nonetheless "because the ways are very deep, and as the season is very cold."[13]

But the 1724 reports also detailed solid success for the Anglican program in many other parishes. In King and Queen's, All Saints, and Stepney parishes, communicants numbered as many as a third of the total number of white families in the parish. More important, they reflected the larger audiences hearing sermons in the Maryland parishes. Even ministers who reported small numbers of communicants sometimes commented that their weekly audiences for church services were relatively large. The minister at St. James Parish in Ann Arundel County who admitted that he administered communion to fewer than 40 persons also reported that he had 100 "hearers" in the parish, which had 150 white families, and the rector at St. Barnabas Parish in Queen Anne County reported as many as 300 persons at his Sabbath services.[14]

---

[12]For descriptions of the Anglican progress in Maryland, see the reports from 1724 in Perry, *Historical Collections*, 4:190-231.

[13]Ibid.

[14]Ibid.

This Anglican program of evangelization and Christianization would have been important in any society. But it was especially important in the Southern mainland colonies because it paralleled the massive turn to slavery occurring there in the very same years. Although the four decades before 1680 witnessed creation of a necessary legal base for British colonial slavery, it was the half-century after 1680 that produced the first significant use of slavery in the economic and social systems of the mainland colonies. Hence at the same moment that the Anglican Christianization program was reshaping the outward appearance of Christianity in the Southern colonies, the mainland settlers were, for the first time, turning from an earlier, fitful use of slaves to a true slave economy and society. It was after 1680 that they first began importing African captives in massive numbers to replace more costly indentured English servants. This change in turn altered the nature and meaning of slave ownership in the Southern colonies. After 1680 colonial assemblymen produced new baroque slave codes that transcended the simpler, cruder legislation defining ownership passed in earlier decades. Colonists also began developing complex informal mechanisms to govern both master and slave in an increasingly massive slave system. And after 1740, captive Africans themselves began developing distinctive Afro-American cultures in colonies where none had existed before.[15]

The significance of any relationship between the development of colonial slavery and the Anglican Christianization program might be questioned on several levels. Moses Finley has pointed out in *Ancient Slavery and Modern Ideology* (New York, 1980) that most religious systems whether Christian or pagan, ancient or modern, nearly always supported slavery. For this reason, emphasizing Anglican support for slavery may say little that is new about either religion or slavery. In addition, the development by English colonists of a massive slave system in the West Indies by 1660, superbly analyzed in Richard S. Dunn's *Sugar and Slaves: The Rise of the Planter Class in the English West Indies, 1624-1713* (Chapel Hill, 1972), offered mainland settlers a ready model for slavery that reduced the potential significance of a later Anglican contribution to colonial slavery.

---

[15]Ira Berlin, "Time, Space, and the Evolution of Afro-American Society on British Mainland North America," *American Historical Review* 85 (1980): 44-78. This article considers one dimension of a problem still little studied by historians.

Despite our knowledge of these points, the case is not closed. First, historians have slighted slavery's effect on colonial Christianity although the Christian churches and slavery expanded in the Southern colonies in the same decades. Second, although it is not surprising that the leaders of organized religion, especially those of the Church of England, sanctioned and supported colonial slavery, historians have not given sustained attention to the way their words and behavior shaped slavery in the colonies. The conditions of their support and that of missionaries in the field were as important as the support itself. All these men directly helped determine the kind of slavery that emerged in the Southern colonies. Their labor was particularly important because it alleviated the widespread worry of laymen that Christianity and slavery were incompatible—laymen who knew nothing of the long historical record of support for slavery by most Western religions, including Christianity, uncovered by modern historians. Third, although slavery in the English West Indies offered colonists a specific English precedent for owning slaves, mainland colonists nonetheless developed a slave system remarkably different from the West Indies model. Richard Dunn notes that slavery on the islands was more harsh and cruel than its mainland counterpart. West Indian slaves died quickly and did not reproduce. They were soon replaced by newer captives who also died rapidly. They were managed by single white overseers, and both the slaves and the overseers worked for English owners who seldom visited their New World plantations. In contrast, captive Africans in the Southern mainland colonies began reproducing rather quickly, albeit at different rates in different colonies; steadily built family networks; and developed long-term relationships with the large white population among which they lived. In this setting the early Anglican delineation of a slavery ethic for planters became as important to the evolution of slavery as to the evolution of Christianity in America.[16]

The Anglican impact on colonial slavery did not rest on its success in Christianizing Africans, however. In 1711 Bishop William Fleetwood announced a major S. P. G. program for slave Christianization in a sermon delivered before the Society in London. Historians from Marcus Jernegan to Albert Raboteau have long realized that the program failed.

---

[16]Richard S. Dunn, *Sugar and Slaves: The Rise of the Planter Class in the English West Indies, 1624-1713* (Chapel Hill: University of North Carolina Press, 1972) 224-29.

Although ministers could nearly always report some successes among slaves, no massive movement of Africans to Christianity occurred before 1760 in the Southern colonies. Thus Charles Martyn admitted in 1762 that only 500 of South Carolina's 46,000 slaves had been Christianized, and this ratio was only marginally better in the Chesapeake. Yet, paradoxically, the unsuccessful program in slave Christianization shaped the views and behavior of Southern whites who were being introduced to important aspects of both Christianity and slavery for the first time after 1690.[17]

The first major contribution Anglican missionaries made to both white Christianization and the development of a slave system in the mainland colonies was to deflect deep public worry that Englishmen could not hold baptized Africans in captivity. Historians generally have ascribed this doubt to what Winthrop Jordan calls a "vague but persistent fear that no Christian might lawfully hold another Christian as a slave." This may not be quite accurate since fear of conversion and baptism flowered despite weak Christianization among English whites in the Southern colonies. None of the complaints voiced by laymen were theologically informed: colonists cited no scripture verses or formal doctrines of Christian ethics to support their case. Indeed, their occasional allusions to Christian practice reveal their wonder at the new Christianity they were adopting. The South Carolina missionary Francis Le Jau reported that a worried slaveowning woman asked him, "will any of my slaves go to Heaven, and must I see them there?" while another parishioner simply had "resolved never to come to the Holy Table while slaves are received there." In Le Jau's view, these sentiments only measured the distance of his parishioners from Christianity.[18]

In fact, the root of lay objections to slave conversion was secular and political. They worried that Christian conversion, symbolized in baptism, would make slaves irascible, dangerous, uppity, and "saucy." They

---

[17]Charles Martyn to S. P. G., 11 April 1762, Fulham Papers at Lambeth Palace, 10:153-54; Albert J. Raboteau, *Slave Religion: The "Invisible Institution" in the Antebellum South* (New York: Oxford University Press, 1978) 106-107, 115-20, 125-26.

[18]Winthrop D. Jordan, *White Over Black: American Attitudes Toward the Negro, 1550-1812* (Chapel Hill: University of North Carolina Press, 1968) 180-86; Le Jau quoted in Frank J. Klingberg, *Appraisal of the Negro in Colonial South Carolina* (Washington DC: The Associated Publishers, 1941) 23.

believed that baptized persons could not be held as slaves successfully or properly in a society whose formal institutions and laws upheld Christianity. The actual religious practices of individual owners or the minimal Christianization of the larger populace mattered little in this regard.[19]

The Anglican response to these objections has always been well known even if its significance has been slighted. Leading Anglican ministers could have turned contemporary lay anxiety about the slavery-Christianity relationship to different, albeit paradoxical, ends. They could have used their new prestige and position in the Southern colonies to demand that authorities limit the expansion of mainland slavery or to insist that colonial lawmakers give slaves traditional English legal rights. But Anglican leaders in London and ministers in America moved in starkly different directions. They could not justify slavery as a traditional social institution deserving traditional forms of obedience since even West Indian slavery was relatively new and since the large-scale use of slavery was only just beginning in the mainland colonies. Instead, they simply applied the traditional Protestant interpretation of the Pauline epistles—with which, for example, Martin Luther denounced the German Peasants Revolt of 1524-1525—to the new social order emerging in the Southern colonies. In words later used by nearly every eighteenth-century Anglican writer on slavery, Bishop William Fleetwood argued in his 1711 S. P. G. sermon that since the "Liberty of Christianity is entirely Spiritual," baptism did "not exempt [anyone] from continuing in the same State of Life he was before," even when the word "before" referred only to Africans as enslaved laborers rather than as members of their native societies.[20]

Anglicans circulated this English Christian sanction of slavery and their emerging slavery ethic to white colonists in two ways. The most obvious means was the literature circulated to whites to encourage slave

---

[19]For a sampling of white objections to slave baptism, see Frank J. Klingberg, ed., *The Carolina Chronicle of Dr. Francis Le Jau, 1706-1717* (Berkeley and Los Angeles CA: University of California Press, 1956) 7, 11, 50, 52, 55, 60, 78, 81, 86, 97, 102, 116, 121, 124, 129.

[20]Fleetwood's sermon is reprinted in Frank J. Klingberg, *Anglican Humanitarianism in Colonial New York* (Philadelphia: The Church Historical Society, 1940) 195-212. See also Jordan, *White Over Black*, 191-92.

Christianization, such as Bishop Fleetwood's 1711 S. P. G. sermon. More important was the literature Anglicans intended to use directly in Christianizing slaves but which, paradoxically, became a major instrument, perhaps the major instrument, in the Anglican effort to Christianize Southern whites. This literature circulated in enormous numbers among white slave-owners. Although precise figures do not exist, evidence from book orders placed by Anglican ministers and missionaries suggests that Anglicans distributed these tracts more widely among whites in the colonial South than any other literature. They appeared in four forms. These included the S. P. G. sermons by leading Anglicans encouraging planters to Christianize slaves, such as the 1711 Fleetwood sermon, as well as later sermons by Bishops George Berkeley (1731) and Thomas Secker (1741); tracts like Edmund Gibson's *Three Addresses on the Instruction of the Negroes* (London, 1727), which offered general descriptions of ways to instruct slaves; detailed catechetical publications such as Thomas Wilson's *Knowledge and Practice of Christianity Made Easy to the Meanest Capacities* (London, 1741); and sermons preached to slaves by colonial Anglican ministers such as those by Maryland's Thomas Bacon which the S. P. G. published in London several times after Bacon delivered them in Maryland in 1748.[21]

This Anglican literature in slave Christianization offered new slaveholders coherent views about the nature of slavery available in no other popular literature. First, it presented the emerging slaveholder class with a doctrine of absolute slave obedience that underwrote the major social values of the new slave society in the Southern colonies. South Carolina's Francis Le Jau even created a new church ritual that illustrated the doctrine and its sanction by Christian authorities before a printed literature existed on the subject. In 1707 Le Jau forced newly converted slaves to swear an oath before his white parish congregation "that you do not ask for the holy baptism out of any design to free your self from the Duty and Obedience you owe to your Master while you live"; otherwise, Le Jau would not baptize them. If slaves viewed the oath cynically—and Le Jau worried that they did—its real significance rested on its role in shaping

---

[21]Much of this literature, together with information on orders placed by Anglican ministers for copies of these and other books is found in John C. Van Horn, " 'Pious Design': The American Correspondence of the Associates of Dr. Bray, 1731-1775" (Ph.D. diss., University of Virginia, 1979).

white perceptions of both slavery and Christianity. For planters, having slaves baptized provided relief from worry about the political and social significance of the rite. And for whites just learning a new Christian discipline, the rite visually and aurally revealed the ethics of Christianity in a critical period when Southern colonists were simultaneously shaping their economy and their religion.[22]

Doctrines of obedience scarcely were new in early modern Western societies. C. John Sommerville has demonstrated that seventeenth-century Anglicans and Dissenters both argued that obedience was the cement of society and that citizens should obey kings just as wives should obey husbands and servants should obey masters. But the Anglican doctrine of slave obedience differed from traditional English conceptions in two important ways. First, Anglican evangelizers revolutionized the traditional concept of obedience used in the English household setting when they sketched notions of obedience applicable in the rising slavocracies of the colonial South. In England, centuries of custom and court decisions restricted the authority that husbands, fathers, and masters held over wives, children, and servants. The latter possessed legally recoverable rights against their superiors, and household obedience did not require submission to physical mistreatment or psychological abuse. But in America, enslaved Africans remained unprotected by law and custom. Indeed, as A. Leon Higginbotham, Jr.has observed, the colonial law actually became an instrument of oppression for Africans rather than a key to freedom or even a guarantee of humane treatment.[23]

Thus in addition to supporting the concept of slavery as lifetime servitude, the early Anglican evangelizers actively formulated a new ethic for slaveholders. They bypassed traditional limitations on household and servant obedience to emphasize the slave's absolute rather than conditional obligation to obey masters. The Anglican Christianizers provided no legitimate means with which slaves could refuse to obey their owners, and by the 1740s they commonly argued that slaves should obey masters

---

[22]Le Jau to S. P. G., 20 October 1709, in *Carolina Chronicle of Dr. Francis Le Jau*, 60.

[23]C. John Sommerville, *Popular Religion in Restoration England* (Gainesville FL: University Press of Florida, 1977) 123-24, 126; A. Leon Higginbotham, *In the Matter of Color: Race and the American Legal Process: The Colonial Period* (New York: Oxford University Press, 1980).

in all things, not just in most things. Thus in his 1748 Maryland sermons, Thomas Bacon cautioned slaves not to take exception to the "behaviour of your masters and mistresses." Slaves must give owners absolute obedience, even to commands that "may be [for]ward, peevish, and hard." Bacon ignored statutes that formally obligated colonial authorities to investigate cases of owner mistreatment of slaves while informing slaves (and owners) that any moral transgressions committed at the direction of masters would be forgiven by God in the next world. Not surprisingly, Bacon called slaveholders "God's overseers." Slaves ought to "do all service for *them* as if [they] did it for *God* himself"; refusal to obey masters in anything constituted nothing less than "faults done against God himself."[24]

Second, the early Anglican Christianizers spread their advice about unconditional slave obedience through the early eighteenth-century South at a time when Whigs and Tories in England were bitterly debating the high Tory doctrine of nonresistance. After the restoration of the monarchy in 1660, leading Anglicans developed the argument that citizens should refuse to resist a sovereign, an argument they believed would avoid future civil wars and executions of kings. After the Glorious Revolution of 1688, however, many high Tory champions of nonresistance rejected allegiance to William and Mary, left the Church of England, and launched a bitter public criticism of the new monarchy. The threat posed by these challenges finally led the Whig-dominated Parliament to try the notorious Tory, Dr. Henry Sacheverell, in 1710 for advocating nonresistance and for attacking the 1688 Revolution.[25]

The existence of the debate about political obedience in late Stuart England highlights three features of the role the Anglican Christianizers played in shaping mainland slavery in America. First, it demonstrates the willfulness of the Anglican arguments about slave obedience. Anglicans did not stumble into their arguments about unconditional slave obedi-

---

[24]Thomas Bacon, *Four Sermons Preached at the Parish Church of St. Peter, in Talbot County,* . . . (London: J. Oliver, ca., 1753) 30, 31, 34.

[25]J. P. Kenyon, *Revolution Principles: The Politics of Party 1689-1720* (Cambridge: Cambridge University Press, 1977) 64-65, 88-89; G. V. Bennett, *The Tory Crisis in Church and State 1688-1730: The Career of Francis Atterbury, Bishop of Rochester* (Oxford: Oxford University Press, 1975) 103-16; Geoffrey Holmes, *The Trial of Doctor Sacheverell* (London: Eyre Methuen, 1973) 31-34, 138-42, passim.

ence. They developed them at a time of extraordinary public debate over the limits of proper political obedience. Second, the same Anglicans who fashioned a slavery ethic for slaveholders simultaneously rejected high Tory doctrines of nonresistance in English politics. These included Bishop William Fleetwood, author of the S. P. G.'s 1711 pronouncement on slave Christianization, as well as Anglican missionaries working in America, including South Carolina's Francis Le Jau and Robert Maule. Third, these Anglican evangelizers did not apply a high Tory doctrine of nonresistance to slaves in America, however attractive it might have seemed to them in that setting. Rather, they acted in far more perverse and devastating ways. Nonresistance required citizens to make conscious choices in politics and therefore conferred extraordinary moral virtue on its advocates. But Anglican evangelizers required only obedience in slaves, not nonresistance. Nowhere did they even suggest that slaves were capable of nonresistance. Thus lodged within this early Anglican doctrine of unconditional slave obedience was the notion that slaves lacked the capacity for moral judgment. And lodged within the widespread circulation of this Anglican (and later Dissenting) formula were important popular roots of white prejudice against the mental capacities and cultures of the Africans then pouring into the mainland colonies.

Eugene Genovese, in his massive study *Roll, Jordan, Roll*, suggested in passing that the paternalism of antebellum American slavery originated in the "close living of masters and slaves" that separated eighteenth-century mainland slavery from its Caribbean variety. Yet it was the way the Anglican evangelizers shaped that "close living" that turned social circumstance into a cultural imperative. Ministers like Francis Le Jau and Robert Maule extended and rationalized early planter complaints about unruly slave behavior such as lying, refusing to work, or seemingly aberrant sexual practices. They transformed white slaveholder views about slave peculiarities into the powerfully detailed canvas of African depravity upon which white racism and paternalism flourished in the nineteenth-century South. By the 1740s their successors had transformed planter complaints about white "responsibilities" and about the burdens of slaveholding into a powerful pre-Revolutionary ethic of slaveholder paternalism.[26]

---

[26]Eugene Genovese, *Roll, Jordan, Roll: The World the Slaves Made* (New York: Pantheon Books, 1974) 5; for the complaints of Le Jau and Maule, see Klingberg, *Appraisal of the Negro in Colonial South Carolina*, chs. 1 and 2, where Klingberg treats them as Christian humanitarians. See also Bacon, *Four Sermons*, 81-84.

Maryland's Thomas Bacon expressed this slaveholder ethic with special vigor. Bacon asked, "Do not your masters, under God, provide for you?" Indeed, the slaves had "a great advantage over most white people." Slaveholders had to care for themselves as well as for their slaves both today and tomorrow. But slaves, Bacon reasoned, "are quite eased from all these cares, and have nothing but [their] daily labour to look after, and when that is done to take [their] needful rest." They did not even have to worry about old age because slaveholders provided for them.[27]

Finally, Anglican ministers provided slaveowners with an important corollary doctrine of punishment that helped owners discipline Africans with measures that involved violent physical abuse. Of course, the missionaries deplored the owners' use of violence against slaves and, like Francis Le Jau, protested laws that allowed owners to kill disobedient slaves, usually while performing legally sanctioned castrations. Nonetheless, the Anglican clerics advanced the violent punishment of slaves in the colonial period in three specific ways. First, as M. I. Finley notes, Christian criticism of slave mistreatment usually supported slavery by tracing the roots of such abuse to individual owners rather than to the institution itself. Similarly, in the colonial period clerical criticism of individual owners never encouraged ministers to attack slavery itself even in its formative decades.[28]

Second, Anglicans who offered early slaveowners a broad doctrine of obedience never formulated an effective doctrine of limitations that might have prevented slave mistreatment in the way traditional legal customs restrained British husbands, masters, and kings. No one acknowledged the missionaries' failure to provide such restraints better than Thomas Bacon did when he asked masters

> If our servants neglect or refuse to give us that which is just and equal, the law hath given us power to correct and force them to do it. But if we refuse them that which is just and equal, where is their remedy?

Since the remedy lay only with owners, Bacon's question paradoxically

---

[27]Bacon, *Four Sermons*, 31, 38, 83-84.

[28]M. I. Finley, *Ancient Slavery and Modern Ideology* (New York: The Viking Press, 1980) 121.

reminded them better of their power than of the moral responsibilities in which Bacon hoped to instruct them.[29]

Third, the doctrines of paternalism and absolute slave obedience helped slaveowners rationalize violent slave punishment directly. The doctrine of paternalism did so by loading owners with obligations which the forced, exploitative nature of slave labor made difficult to fulfill. This, in turn, stimulated owner resentment of slaves that only encouraged physically abusive punishment even when owners knew (and, perhaps precisely because they knew) that their slaves had not received good care. And in a simpler way, the doctrine of absolute obedience encouraged owners to exercise virtually limitless punishments against slaves who violated their obligations.[30]

These doctrines ravished slaves and transformed English culture in the colonial South. Even white settlers who approved slave Christianization treated African slaves cruelly. Francis Le Jau described the case of one overseer who encouraged a slave to be baptized but later punished him viciously for losing a bundle of rice by starving him and putting him "into a hellish Machine . . . [in] the shape of a Coffin where he could not Stirr." After spending several days in the coffin, the slave committed suicide with a knife his own child furnished him. According to Le Jau, the overseer destroyed four other slaves in the same way in two or three years and was only one example of white slaveowners who seemed to find the Christianity of neither themselves nor their slaves a bar to slave mistreatment.[31]

The law also bore witness to the slavery doctrines elaborated by the Anglican evangelizers. The baroque slave codes adopted in all the Southern colonies after 1690 clearly set eighteenth-century slavery apart from its seventeenth-century predecessor. The kind of easy, albeit erratic freedom allowed to both blacks and whites before 1690 that is described for Virginia in T. H. Breen and Stephen Innes, "*Myne Own Ground*": *Race*

---

[29]Thomas Bacon, *Sermons Addressed to Masters and Servants, and published in the year 1743 [sic]. . .* (Winchester VA: John Heiskell, ca. 1813) 19; Jordan, *White Over Black*, 191-92; Klingberg, *Appraisal of the Negro in Colonial South Carolina*.

[30]Genovese, *Roll, Jordan, Roll*, 147-48, describes the potential for violence on the part of slaves who accepted or submitted to the paternalism of white owners.

[31]Le Jau to S. P. G., 23 February 1713, in *Carolina Chronicle of Dr. Francis Le Jau*, 130.

and Freedom on Virginia's Eastern Shore, 1640-1676 (New York, 1980), disappeared as colonial legislators restricted the latitude of white and black behavior after 1690. The laws they wrote always endorsed the broad authority of slaveowners to punish disobedient slaves on the grounds already suggested by the Anglican evangelizers: that the owners' right to punish slaves derived both from the slaves' absolute obligation to obey and, oddly enough, from the owners' obligations to care for their slaves.[32]

In turn, the rise of slavery profoundly affected Christianity in the Southern colonies. Its principal effect was to introduce into organized Christianity in the Southern colonies a thoroughly pathological, unrealistic interpretation of religious ethics that emphasized love, sentiment, and charity in all social relations while disregarding their implications for slavery. In a collection of sermons published in 1750, Charleston's Anglican minister Samuel Quincy stressed the need for mutual love in society. He insisted that love involved the "fulfilling of the Law," claimed that afflictions were "of the greatest Love and Kindness to sinful Creatures," and argued that the apostle Paul preferred charity to "miraculous gifts." Significantly, he never outlined the consequences of these ideas for the institution of slavery. In a sermon delivered in the same year to Maryland Masons entitled "Freedom and Love," William Brogden played on the presence of slavery in Maryland to reinforce several important points, pointing out that "By Nature, every man is a *Slave* in a spiritual Sense," and that "The Selfish Man is in truth a Slave to a wretched tyrannizing Master." He described the "well ordered *Society*" as "cemented together by mutual Help and Love." It contained members who "lighten each other's Burthen, and constitute one undivided well-compacted Edifice." But he never revealed whether his comments applied to whites, Africans, or masters and slaves together.[33]

Other ministers drew strict limits to the obedience planters might give in politics, although they eschewed such limits for slaves. Independent Josiah Smith wrote in his *Duty of Parents to Instruct their Children* (Boston, 1730) that although children must learn to recognize proper authority, the

---

[32]Higginbotham, *In the Matter of Color*, 193-98, passim.

[33]Samuel Quincy, *Twenty Sermons* (Boston: J. Draper, 1750) 38-54, 235-54, 255-64; William Brogden, *Freedom and Love* (Annapolis MD: 1750).

"doctrine of unlimited Passive Obedience is but a Chimera." As expected, he never applied the aphorism to slavery. In 1746 John Gordon celebrated the defeat of the Stuart pretender and Britain's "Deliverance from Oppression and Slavery"; but he failed to criticize the form of chattel slavery that had emerged in the Southern colonies, although he enjoined readers to "despise and detest the absurd and slavish doctrine of *unlimited Submission, Non-Resistance*, and *hereditary Right*." Even the Quaker Sophia Hume fell victim to this dichotomous moralizing. Her *Exhortation to the Inhabitants of the Province of South Carolina* (Philadelphia, 1750), excoriated the colony for its "Masquerades," "Musickgardens," and "theatrical Entertainments" and criticized adults who instructed children in "Rule and Authority, by teaching and allowing them a Superiority over Servants." But she too never applied the lesson directly to slavery. Indeed, she never mentioned the subject in her three-hundred-page treatise.[34]

Slavery and Christianity continued this interaction in the next several decades even though the Anglican evangelization and Christianization program lagged after 1730. Although the full pattern is not yet clear, the dramatic gains in white Christianization made between 1690 and 1730 waned in the next quarter-century. Anglican endeavor failed to keep pace with the dramatic population expansion that occurred in the Southern colonies between 1730 and 1760. Ministers in older settled areas complained of rising numbers of laymen who neglected communion and sabbath services, while newly settled areas lacked both ministers who could complain and settlers who would worship. Thus Thomas Bacon admitted in 1750 that "religion among us seems to wear the face of the Country; part moderately cultivated, the greater part wild and savage," while the peripatetic Charles Woodmason reported in 1767 that in the Carolina backcountry listeners assembled "out of Curiosity, not Devotion, and seem so pleased with their native Ignorance, as to be offended at any Attempts to rouse them out of it."[35]

---

[34]Josiah Smith, *The Duty of Parents to Instruct Their Children* (Boston: D. Henchman, 1730) 17-18; John Gordon, *A Thanksgiving Sermon on the Defeat of the Rebels* (Annapolis MD: 1746) 1, 18, 20, 27; S[ophia] H[ume], *An Exhortation to the Inhabitants of the Province of South Carolina* . . . (Philadelphia: William Bradford, 1747).

[35]Thomas Bacon to S. P. G., 4 August 1750, in Perry, *Historical Collections*, 4:324-25; Richard James Hooker, ed., *The Carolina Backcountry on the Eve of the Revolution: The Journal and Other Writings of Charles Woodmason, Anglican Itinerant* (Chapel Hill NC:

Still, the Anglican evangelists met with one extremely important cultural success. Although rates of white Christianization rose and fell, Anglican missionaries actually convinced a once-skeptical laity, much of which still avoided Christian churches, that Christianity did not merely sanction slavery but endorsed it enthusiastically. Crucial evidence of this transformation comes from two sources. The first is the increasing numbers of planters who allowed slaves to be baptized. Even as most slaves still rejected Christianity before 1760, enough converted to suggest that a significant proportion of owners then allowed slaves to be instructed in Christianity although most owners had refused to do so before 1720. The second source is documents descending from the campaign to save slavery in Virginia in 1784-1785. Petitions signed by several thousand backcountry Virginia laymen complained that persons "pretending to be moved by Religious Principles" sought to abolish slavery. But the petitioners noted that "slavery was permitted by the Deity himself" and, in eloquent testimony to the work of the early Anglican evangelists, argued that slavery had survived

> through all the Revolutions of the Jewish Government, down to the Advent of our Lord . . . [and] Christ and his Apostles hath in the mean time, come into the World, and past out of it again, leaving behind them the New-Testament, full of all instructions necessary to our Salvation; and hath not forbid it: But left that matter as they found it, giving exortations to Masters and Servants how to conduct themselves to each other.[36]

This Anglican education of the South's laity helps explain the weak antislavery record of all the major Dissenting groups (except the Quakers) that later became active in the Southern colonies. When, after 1750,

----

University of North Carolina Press, 1953) 13. Ahlstrom, *A Religious History of the American People*, ch. 14, describes the conditions of the Anglican Church in the Southern colonies in a thoroughly negative fashion with little knowledge of the earlier Christianization program.

[36]Despite the importance of the subjects, neither the rates of slave baptism nor the rates of owners allowing slave baptism have been studied systematically. For some sense of the rise of the latter, if not of the former, see the registers cited in note 7. For the rhetoric of popular proslavery Christian sentiment, see Fredrike T. Schmidt and Barbara R. Wilhelm, "Early Pro-Slavery Petitions in Virginia," *William and Mary Quarterly*, 3d ser., 30 (January 1973): 133-46.

Southern evangelism turned evangelical, its record on slavery scarcely improved. Of course, historians traditionally have emphasized the evangelical criticism of slavery in the South between 1750 and 1800. In fact, this criticism was as shallow as it was short-lived. The Presbyterian John Thomson alluded only vaguely to slavery in his *Explication of the Shorter Catechism* (Williamsburg VA, 1749); it is not clear whether his suggestion that children "under the Jurisdiction of professing Christians, [who] depend on them for Education, have a right to Baptism" referred to slaves or white apprentices, and nowhere did Thomson mention slavery when he discussed Christian moral values. Evangelicals active in the religious revivals of the eighteenth century, such as George Whitefield and Samuel Davies, criticized the treatment of slaves and sometimes even the institution that bound them but never lent their charismatic authority to a crusade to abolish it. The Baptist record on slavery proved equally dismal. Virginians like John Leland questioned slavery largely as a by-product of their attack on Virginia's aristocratic government, which refused to allow them to preach in Virginia; and by the early 1780s a statewide Baptist body had condemned slavery as antiscriptural. But as James David Essig has argued, this Baptist criticism waned as the movement prospered and government interference ended. Virtually all Virginia Baptist congregations ignored the antislavery resolution, and denominational leaders dropped their antislavery campaign by 1790. They refused to discuss the problem in denominational meetings and described the question as a "political" one. Anglican evangelists had long assured Virginia laymen that slavery was compatible with Christianity, and the brief Baptist antislavery campaign died from a suffocation imposed by its own lay converts. In this context, the better known Methodist acquiescence to slavery after 1790 appears to have been a nearly inevitable outcome of the earlier Anglican success in training lay planters in at least one version of Christian ethics if not in a doctrine of individual salvation.[37]

---

[37]John Thomson, *An Explication of the Shorter Catechism Composed by the Assembly of Divines, Commonly Called, the Westminster Assembly* (Williamsburg VA: W. Parks, 1749) 161; James David Essig, "A Very Wintry Season: Virginia Baptists and Slavery, 1785-1797," *Virginia Magazine of History and Biography* 88 (1980): 170-85. For a more positive evaluation of the contribution of the eighteenth-century religious revivals to antislavery thought, see Jordan, *White Over Black*, 212-14.

What these patterns suggest, of course, is that the origins of much of the South's distinctive antebellum slave culture had been laid down in the early eighteenth century by Anglican evangelizers who plowed and fertilized the spiritual soil later tilled so successfully by Evangelicals. If this is true, then the widely known and much lamented "cultural captivity" of evangelical denominations in the South did not occur because Evangelicals could not effectively challenge an already established slave culture. Rather, it occurred because the Anglicans of the colonial South and the Evangelicals who succeeded them played a powerful role in creating that culture. In the crucial decades between 1690 and 1760 when thousands of Southern whites bought captive Africans for the first time, Anglican evangelizers shaped the emerging system of slavery even as they attempted to Christianize both Southern whites and blacks. In decades when many different kinds of slavery might have emerged in the South, these Anglican ministers provided new slaveowners with crucial doctrines of obedience, paternalism, and punishment that had not previously been used in British slavery. They also encouraged whites to indulge protoromantic notions of love, sentiment, and charity, yet discouraged the application of these notions to slavery or slaves. In turn, Anglican evangelizers shaped the history of the Evangelicalism that later overwhelmed them because they furnished Evangelicals a laity already well instructed in the limits of Christian political activism. All the new denominations became defenders rather than critics of the new, revolutionary slave society of the Southern colonies. They interpreted the "new birth" as an event centered in the individual, and they permitted only the kind of social criticism that left slavery intact, thereby muting much of the tension that sometimes characterized the relationship of Evangelicalism to secular culture in other settings.

If this revised history of the emergence of slavery and Christianity in the eighteenth-century Southern colonies suggests that evangelism and Evangelicalism did not, in themselves, guarantee morality, social reform, or enlightened political principle, we might usefully notice that a different model of evangelical enterprise somewhat surprisingly comes down to us from the otherwise dismal history of twentieth-century Europe. It is detailed in Philip Hallie's remarkable study, *Lest Innocent Blood Be Shed: The Story of the Village of Le Chambon and How Goodness Happened There* (New York, 1979), which describes a French Protestant campaign to save Jews from shipment to German concentration camps between 1941 and

1944. Hallie demonstrates that this campaign succeeded when particular, perhaps unique, historical circumstances combined to infuse the secular setting with an evangelical Protestant vision that produced literally life-transforming results. Why Protestant Evangelicalism should have produced this result in Le Chambon and not in the eighteenth-century Southern colonies, and how frequently similar results emerged in nineteenth-century America, are surely some of the questions that historians can ponder when they reassess the relationship between Evangelicalism and the evolution of American society.

Chapter 3

Millennialism
and Popular Religion
in the Early Republic

Nathan O. Hatch

> *Without the Spirit, I am nothing.*
> —Joanna Southcott
>
> *The Bible was now to me a new book . . . a feast of reason.*
> —William Miller

For all that has been written about millennial movements as outbursts of popular protest, eighteenth-century millennialism in the Anglo-American world remained largely the preserve of gentlemen and scholars. Methodism and the Great Awakening, genuinely popular movements to be sure, produced no offspring comparable to Ranters, Diggers, and Fifth-Monarchy Men. In fact, with the notable exception of Jonathan Edwards, it was men of the Enlightenment—Isaac Newton, Joseph Priestley, Benjamin Rush—who are most notable in this era for their interpretations of prophecy. The study of prophecy offered rational men opportunity to see how God's plan unfolded in history and offered tangible and coherent proof of religious doctrine.[1] By the end of the eigh-

---

[1] The rational bent of eighteenth-century studies of prophecy is discussed in Margaret C. Jacob, *The Newtonians and the English Revolution, 1689-1720* (Ithaca NY: Cornell University Press, 1976); Clarke Garrett, *Respectable Folly: Millenarians and the French Revolution in France and England* (Baltimore: Johns Hopkins University Press, 1975); and Donald J. D'Elia, *Benjamin Rush: Philosopher of the American Revolution* (Philadelphia: American Philosophical Society, 1974).

teenth century, millennialism was on the verge of becoming the inverse of Norman Cohn's sociological stereotype of a millennial movement. Far from mystical prophets whipping up the landless poor, students of the end times turned out to be men like the Universalist Elhanan Winchester, whom Benjamin Rush called "a theological Newton," the scientist and judge James Winthrop of Harvard, and the Loyalist Joseph Galloway of Pennsylvania, who spent the final years of his exile in London at the turn of the century writing a massive commentary on the book of Revelation.[2]

Yet the Age of Democratic Revolutions had the effect of giving awesome reality to what had been polite and respectable "folly." Not since the English Civil War had such swift and unpredictable currents threatened the traditions of Western society. What fired apocalyptic imaginations far more than the mere fact that battles had been won and constitutions written was the realization that the very structures of society were undergoing a drastic democratic winnowing. The atheism of revolutionary France—an "apocalyptic earthquake," said one minister—the crumbling of European monarchies, the separation of church and state, the domination of the Papacy by civil authority, all took on a more awesome moment as the cement of an ordered and hierarchical society seemed to be dissolving. People confronted new kinds of issues: common folk not respecting their betters, organized factions speaking and writing against civil authority, sharp attacks against elite professions, the growth of new and strange religious groups.[3] All of this seemed so far outside the range of ordinary experience that elites and commoners alike rushed to biblical prophecy for help in understanding the troubled times that were upon

---

[2]Winchester's writings include: *A Course of Lectures on Prophecies that Remain to Be Fulfilled*, 4 vols. (London: Philadelphia Society, 1789-1790) and *The Three Woe Trumpets* (London: n.p., 1793); James Winthrop, *A Systematic Arrangement of Several Scripture Prophecies* (Boston: Thomas Hall, 1795); and Joseph Galloway, *Brief Commentaries upon Such Parts of the Revelation and Other Prophecies as Immediately Refer to the Present Times*, 2 vols. (London: n.p., 1802).

[3]On the crisis of authority in the early republic, see Gordon S. Wood, "The Democratization of Mind in the American Revolution," in *Leadership in the American Revolution: Papers Presented at the 3rd Library of Congress Symposium on the American Revolution, May 9 and 10, 1974* (Washington DC: Library of Congress, 1974) 63-89; and Nathan O. Hatch, "The Christian Movement and the Demand for a Theology of the People," *Journal of American History* 67 (1980): 545-67.

them. Beset with such unsettling conditions, the English poet and mystic William Blake confessed to a friend in 1800:

> Terrors appear'd in the heavens above and in Hell beneath, a mighty and awful change threatened the Earth. The American Way began. All its dark horrors passed before my face Across the Atlantic to France. Then the French Revolution commenc'd in thick clouds, and My Angels have told me that seeing such visions I could not subsist on earth.[4]

A dictionary of works on prophecy, published in England in 1835, listed no fewer than 274 publications in England and Scotland between 1775 and 1815; and the list omitted certain popular works such as the 65 different writings of Joanna Southcott. A similar outpouring of eschatology, orthodox and sectarian, issued from the American press. Judged by the number of sermons and books addressing prophetic themes, the first generation of United States citizens may have lived in the shadow of Christ's second coming more intensely than any generation of American Christians. In Ernest Sandeen's words, Americans of this era were "drunk on the millennium."[5]

A central question at the outset of this study is to explain how the millennialism of a Joseph Priestly evolved into that of an Alexander Campbell, a William Miller, or a Joseph Smith. How did the millennialism so evident in certain forms of popular religion in the early republic assume its characteristic form? At first glance, our answer might be that an eschatology of the Enlightenment had little or nothing to do with forms of popular millennialism that boasted strong evangelical and revivalistic pedigrees. Would not the Great Awakening, rather than the Enlightenment, be a more appropriate point of departure for studying the kinds of popular ideas about prophecy that swept through the Burned-Over District? Had not evangelical and rationalist traditions been at odds for much of the eighteenth century? And had not Evangelicals during the 1790s be-

---

[4]Letter to John Flaxman, 12 September 1800, in *Blake: Complete Writings*, ed. Geoffrey Keynes (Oxford: Oxford University Press, 1969) 799. Quoted in James Kirkland Hopkins, "Joanna Southcott—A Study of Popular Religion and Radical Politics, 1789-1814," (Ph.D. diss., University of Texas, 1972).

[5]Joshua Brooks, *A Dictionary of Writers on the Prophecies* (London: Simpkin, Marshall & Co., 1835). Ernest R. Sandeen, *The Roots of Fundamentalism: British and American Millenarianism, 1800-1930* (Chicago: University of Chicago Press, 1930) 42.

come locked in mortal combat with the forces of infidelity and the Enlightenment?[6]

Historical categories too often are drawn around participants in a given debate, in this case the contest between Evangelicals and Rationalists. "Nothing strikes me more when I read the controversies of past ages," C. S. Lewis once noted, "than the fact that both sides thought that they were as completely opposed as two sides could be, but in fact they were all the time secretly united."[7] This essay explores what I believe is a fascinating irony, the ways in which the popular millennialism of the early republic—evangelical to the core—nevertheless underwent a process of becoming "secretly united" with viewpoints of the Enlightenment. Apocalyptic themes, long resonant in American popular culture, reappeared laced with the thought of Jefferson and the Age of Reason. The millennium, in short, became explicitly democratized.

In a preliminary manner, I wish to look at certain themes common to the "Christians," the Disciples, the Millerites, and the Mormons, popular religions all of which flourished in this region of New York 150 years ago. The eschatologies of these movements, placed against a backdrop of popular millennialism in England and France during the same period, offer certain insights into the American evangelical tradition as it emerged from the winnowing of the democratic revolutions.

Elias Smith and William Miller

Two brief episodes will introduce the complexity and irony of this process. The first concerns Elias Smith, who until 1800 filled the pulpit of the respectable Baptist Church in Woburn, Massachusetts, and gave little attention to political and social questions. During the presidential election of that year, he fell under the powerful influence of the radical Jeffersonian publicist Benjamin Austin, Jr., who wrote regularly for the Boston *In-*

---

[6]Two works, among many, that see eighteenth-century religious history turning on the dichotomy between Evangelicals and Rationalists are Sidney E. Mead, *The Lively Experiment: The Shaping of Christianity in America* (New York: Harper & Row, 1963) and Alan Heimert, *Religion and the American Mind from the Great Awakening to the Revolution* (Cambridge: Harvard University Press, 1966).

[7]C. S. Lewis, *God in the Dock: Essays in Theology and Ethics* (Grand Rapids MI: Eerdmans, 1970) 202.

dependent Chronicle.[8] Smith grew increasingly sympathetic to Austin's writing, which made much of popular self-determination and raised serious questions about the authority of elites, of formal education, and of received tradition. Resigning from his church—as a manifesto of his liberty—and denouncing formal religion of all kinds, Smith became a radical publicist *par excellence*, launching the first religious newspaper in the United States in 1808, the *Herald of Gospel Liberty*, and cranking out an avalanche of pamphlets, tracts, and books. In all of these, Smith championed a new view of history, radically discontinuous with the past. In his view, the foundations of Christ's millennial kingdom were laid in the American and French Revolutions. "The time will come," he said, "when there will not be a *crowned head* on earth. Every attempt which is made to keep up a kingly government, and to pull down a Republican one, will serve to destroy monarchy. . . . Every small piece or plan of Monarchy which is a part of the *image* [of Antichrist] will be wholly dissolved, when *the people* are resolved to 'live free or die.' "[9]

Smith's involvement with a group who called themselves merely "Christians" is less significant than the process by which his own evangelical convictions came to resonate with powerful egalitarian themes, creating a rhetoric of civil and religious liberty. Language that had seemed benign when used by respectable clergymen during the Revolution came to have radical connotations for Smith. "For many years," Smith recounted in the *Herald of Gospel Liberty*, "the New England Clergy, particularly the most learned among them have, by their publications, been engaged in describing to the people the words *Anti-Christ, mystery Babylon,* the *Great Whore* that sitteth on many waters, the beast with seven heads and ten horns, the *man of sin* etc."[10] Turning such attacks upon elites of all kinds, Smith inveighed against respectable clergymen as "tyrannical oppressors," "the mystery of iniquity," "friends of monarchy

---

[8]For a more thorough discussion of Smith, see Hatch, "The Christian Movement," and "The Communication Strategy of Elias Smith and the *Herald of Gospel Liberty*," unpublished paper presented to the Conference on Printing and Early American Society, American Antiquarian Society, October, 1980.

[9]Elias Smith, *A Discourse Delivered at Jefferson Hall . . . The Subject, Nebuchadnezzar's Dream* (Portsmouth NH: Manning & Loring, 1803) 30-32.

[10]*Herald of Gospel Liberty*, 20 May 1815, 685.

religion," "Old Tories," "an aristocratical body of uniform nobility," and "hireling priests." People who would submit to their authority Smith labeled as "priest-ridden," "slavishly dependent," "passively obedient." Smith thus exploited the potent language of tyranny, slavery, and Antichrist to topple its very architects.[11]

The youthful experience of the Adventist William Miller provides another example of how ideas that came to the fore in what is referred to as the Enlightenment could serve as practical guides for people far removed from centers of influence. Born in rural Vermont in 1782, the young Miller received little formal education but fulfilled his considerable thirst for learning by frequenting the library of none other than the radical republican Matthew Lyon, a near neighbor. Lyon, who would become congressman and be the first tried and imprisoned under the Sedition Act, launched a relentless crusade, in the name of the rights of man, to awaken common people to the responsibility of thinking for themselves and throwing off the oppressive yoke of traditional elites.[12] In one of his publications *The Scourge of Aristocracy*, Lyon mocked the pretension of Federalist clergymen:

> Our Parish Priest, with as much zeal
> For Politics as Prayer,
> Declared if Jefferson came in,
> 'Twould breed a civil war.

> I listen'd to the Solemn Tale,
> And thought it was no lie, sir;
> But now I find that Priests can err
> As well as you or I sir.

> I'd rather in my Bible trust,
> Than sacerdotal Fiction;
> I'll strive to keep the strongest side,
> And spurn their interdiction.[13]

[11]Elias Smith, *The Life, Conversion, Preaching, Travels and Sufferings of Elias Smith* (Portsmouth NH: Beck & Foster, 1816) 384, 402-403; *Herald of Gospel Liberty*, 30 October 1809, 117.

[12]On Matthew Lyon and William Miller, see Aleine Austin, *Matthew Lyon: "New Man" of the Democratic Revolution, 1749-1822* (University Park PA: Pennsylvania State University Press, 1981) 81.

[13]Matthew Lyon, *The Scourge of Aristocracy* (Fairhaven VT: James Lyon, 1798) 149-50.

Influenced by the "vast array of historical data" in Lyon's "reference center," William Miller became an outspoken advocate of Deism. In step with the rationalism of his age, Miller ridiculed the Bible for its "contradictions and inconsistencies"—"so dark and intricate that no man could understand it;" the church as "a history of blood, tyranny, and oppression; in which the common people were the greatest sufferers;" and the clergy as "designing men whose object was to enslave the mind of man; operate on their hopes and fears, with a view to aggrandize themselves."[14]

When Miller returned to the Christian fold in 1816, he did so as an unrelenting Rationalist. "I felt that to believe in such a Savior without evidence, would be visionary in the extreme." He determined that he would not accept the Bible unless he could "harmonize all the apparent contradictions to my own satisfaction, or I would be a deist still." From 1816 to 1818, Miller devoted himself to intense Bible study, laying aside "all commentaries, former views, and prepossessions, and determined to read and try to understand for myself." At the conclusion of that period Miller emerged as a staunch defender of the Bible's integrity: "The Bible was now to me a new book. It was indeed a feast of reason: all that was dark, mystical or obscure to me in its teaching, had been dissipated before my mind."[15]

Miller was confident that by his inductive investigation a clear and simple system of truth was evident in the Bible. Anything but a mystic or visionary, Miller became a "stickler for literal interpretation." "We are in no case allowed to speculate on the Scriptures, and suppose things which are not clearly expressed." What confirmed beyond question the Bible's authority for Miller was the timeliness of its message. Upon applying mathematical science to scriptural prophecy, thus eliminating theory and speculation, a precise formula emerged that pointed with awesome moment to the year 1843.[16]

---

[14]Joshua V. Himes, *Views of the Prophecies and Prophetic Chronology* (Boston: M. A. Dow, 1841) 9.

[15]William Miller, *Apology and Defense* (Boston: J. V. Himes, 1845) 6, 12-13; Joshua Himes, *View of the Prophecies*, 9, 11.

[16]Joshua Himes, *View of the Prophecies*, 16, 33. Patricia Cline Cohen has an interesting discussion of the growing interest in mathematics in the young republic as a way to approach issues inductively and to eliminate theorizing and speculation. See "Statistics and the State: Changing Social Thought and the Emergence of a Quantitative Mentality in America, 1790-1820," *William and Mary Quarterly*, 3d ser., 38 (January 1981): 35-55.

When William Miller finally began publicizing his views, the Adventist message was not primarily an emotional harangue that the Second Coming would catch people unaware, nor was it a word of consolation for those who had lost hope that they could manage their own affairs. Instead, it was an appeal that common people should assert their own reason, resist deferring to clergymen, and learn to prove everything "by the Bible and nothing but the Bible." "The divinity taught in our schools," Miller protested,

> is always founded on some sectarian creed. It may do to take a blank mind and impress it with this kind, but it will always end in bigotry. A free mind will never be satisfied with the views of others. Were I a teacher of youth in divinity, I would first learn their capacity, and mind. If these were good, I would make them study the Bible for themselves, and send them out free to do the world good. But if they had no mind, I would stamp them with another's mind, write bigot on their forehead, and send them out as slaves.[17]

Both Elias Smith and William Miller had their Christianity refracted through the prism of a democratic enlightenment. Three aspects of this general process are worth exploring: 1) a pervasive revolt against history characteristic of the Enlightenment; 2) a commonsense rationality that rejected the mysterious and complicated and instead appealed to objects of empirical science; and 3) a commitment to democratic forms of social organization that confirmed the United States as a model for the millennial kingdom.

Prophecy and the Revolt Against History

Despite the luxuriant variety of millennial faiths that flowered in the early republic, most seemed to spring from a common conception of history: a pervasive sense that Christian tradition since the time of the Apostles was a tale of sordid corruption in which kingcraft and priestcraft wielded orthodoxy in order to enslave the minds of the people. This severing of ties with both Catholic and Protestant traditions was coupled with a heady sense of anticipation that a new restoration of the primitive church was at hand as an introduction to the millennium.

William Miller, Elias Smith, Alexander Campbell, Barton Stone, and Joseph Smith all believed that since the age of the Apostles, a great falling

---

[17]*Signs of the Times*, 15 May 1840, 26.

away had severed the relationship of God and man, leaving the visible church during the "Dark Ages" in control of the "Whore of Babylon." These persons also agreed that whatever good the Protestant Reformation had done, it had not reopened the heavens, restored authentic Christianity, or destroyed religious tyranny, the primary work of Antichrist. As Alexander Campbell once put it: "Catholic and Protestant Popery are plodding and plotting for supremacy." He also strenuously asserted that "If the mother sect was a tyrant, the daughter will ape her temper; and when of mature age and reason, she will imitate her practice."[18] Each of these leaders was also convinced that they were part of a process by which God was restoring the purity of the ancient gospel or, in other words, "the ancient order of things."

Most strident in this conviction, of course, were the Mormons, who claimed that for the first time in eighteen hundred years, the brazen heavens had reopened. The reconvening of the Quorum of the Twelve Apostles symbolized this restoration, as did the words of a popular Mormon hymn:

The Spirit of God like fire is burning!
The latter-day glory begins to come forth;
The visions and blessings of old are returning,
And angels are coming to visit the earth.[19]

Such a decisive expatriation from the past has few parallels among eighteenth-century Evangelicals, either British or American. It is much closer to Thomas Jefferson's thoughts on breaking the grip of custom and precedent. Similarly, the sense of dramatic, impending change corresponds most closely with the views of history held by one such as Tom Paine: "A situation, similar to the present," he had concluded, "hath not happened since the days of Noah until now. The birthday of a new world is at hand."[20]

---

[18]*Christian Baptist*, 1828, 541; *Millennial Harbinger*, 1833, 469-70.

[19]Quoted in Klaus J. Hansen, *Mormonism and the American Experience* (Chicago: University of Chicago Press, 1981) 28.

[20]On Jefferson, see Edmund S. Morgan, *The Meaning of Independence: John Adams, George Washington, Thomas Jefferson* (Charlottesville VA: University Press of Virginia, 1976) 71-79 and Daniel J. Boorstin, *The Lost World of Thomas Jefferson* (Boston: H. Holt, 1948). On Paine, see James Kirkland Hopkins, "Joanna Southcott," 6.

The most common expression of this revolt against history turned out to be an appeal to the idea "No creed but the Bible." "I have endeavored to read the scriptures as though no one had read them before me," claimed Alexander Campbell, "and I am as much on my guard against reading them to-day, through the medium of my own views yesterday, or a week ago, as I am against being influenced by any foreign name, authority, or system whatever."[21] By mid-century, John W. Nevin claimed, after reading the statements of faith of fifty-three American denominations, that the distinctive feature of American evangelical religion was this attempt to disentangle the pure teachings of Scripture from the corruptions of any human mediation.[22]

Such an appeal to the Bible's exclusive authority, despite its popularity among Evangelicals, actually had its origins among eighteenth-century rationalists who first employed it to undermine evangelical theology. Seeking to make peace with the Enlightenment, English divines such as Samuel Clarke and John Taylor advocated a new method of "free, impartial, and diligent" Scripture study in order to jettison, respectively, the doctrines of the Trinity (Clarke's *The Scripture-Doctrine of the Trinity*, London, 1712) and of original sin (Taylor's *The Scripture-Doctrine of Original Sin*, London, 1740). In the 1750s, in the wake of the Great Awakening, Charles Chauncy spent seven years engaged in the kind of Bible study he had found so appealing in the works of these English divines. The fruits of his labors led Chauncy to draft a manuscript rejecting the idea of eternal punishment and embracing Universalism; the work was finally published in 1784.[23] Unitarians, Universalists, and other rationalist Christians continued to appeal to "the Bible alone" well into the nineteenth century. By 1800, however, this technique was becoming more a hallmark of Evangelicals such as "the humble farmer of Hampton-Low,"

---

[21]*Christian Baptist*, 3 April 1826, 229.

[22]John Williamson Nevin, "Antichrist and the Sect," in *The Mercersburg Theology* ed. James Hastings Nichols (New York: Oxford University Press, 1966) 93-119, 98-99. I discuss this theme extensively in "*Sola Scriptura* and *Novus Ordo Seclorum*," in *The Bible in America: Essays in Cultural History*, eds. Nathan O. Hatch and Mark A. Noll (New York: Oxford University Press, 1982).

[23]Conrad Wright, *The Beginnings of Unitarianism in America* (Boston: Star King Press, 1955) 231-35. Edward M. Griffin, *Old Brick: Charles Chauncy of Boston, 1705-1787* (Minneapolis: University of Minnesota Press, 1980) 109-25.

William Miller, who, like Chauncy, defended the right of private judgment, appealed to the Bible's exclusive authority, and gave himself over to two years of concentrated, inductive Bible study.

Prophecy and Common Sense

If the biblical orientation of millennialism in the early republic revealed a stubborn rejection of history, it also suggested a marked rationality and insistence upon empirical methods—this in stark contrast to prophets and millennialists that flourished simultaneously in England and France. Recent studies of such movements in Europe such as J. F. C. Harrison's *The Second Coming*; W. H. Oliver's *Prophets and Millennialists*; Hillel Schwartz's *The French Prophets*; Clarke Garrett's *Respectable Folly*; and Thomas Kselman's forthcoming book *Miracles and Prophecies: Popular Religion and the Church in Nineteenth-Century France* all emphasize the antirational, mystical, and visionary quality of popular millennialism in Britain and France.[24] Prophets such as Richard Brothers and Joanna Southcott, for instance, based their claims on inspiration and supernatural manifestations. Southcott resolutely exalted the Spirit rather than the Word as the source of her ideas. In 1804, she claimed that she had not studied the Bible for nine years: "I never read any books, at all," she claimed, "but write by the spirit as I am directed. I should not like to read any books to mix my senses with any works but those of the spirit by whom I write."[25] Similarly, the French prophetess Jeane Leroyer (1730-1798), who took the religious name Soeur Nativité, spoke in the 1790s on the basis of visions; and Thomas Martin, a prophet after the restoration of Louis XVIII, was so on the basis of supposed visits with the archangel Raphael.[26]

---

[24]J. F. C. Harrison, *The Second Coming: Popular Millenarianism, 1780-1850* (New Brunswick NJ: Rutgers University Press, 1979); W. H. Oliver, *Prophets and Millennialists: The Uses of Biblical Prophecy in England from the 1790s to the 1840s* (Auckland: Oxford University Press, 1978); Hillel Schwartz, *The French Prophets: The History of a Millenarian Group in Eighteenth-Century England* (Berkeley: University of California Press, 1980); Garrett, *Respectable Folly*; and Thomas Kselman, *Miracles and Prophecies in Nineteenth-Century France* (New Brunswick NJ: Rutgers University Press, 1983).

[25]James Kirkland Hopkins, "Joanna Southcott," 37.

[26]Thomas Kselman, *Miracles and Prophecies*, 60-83.

In sharp contrast, the tenor of popular millennialism in America was decidedly rationalistic, as self-made students of Scripture eschewed speculation and claimed to draw principles inductively from what Alexander Campbell called the "facts of the Bible." William Miller, as we have seen, claimed to avoid speculation entirely: "We have sought to spread the truth, not by fanatical prophecies arising out of our own hearts, but by the light of the scriptures, history, and by sober argument. We appeal only to the Bible, and give you our rules of interpretation." Even more ruthless as a rationalist, Alexander Campbell argued that speculation was the principal source of skepticism, and defined faith simply as "the belief of testimony" as opposed to any mystical gift of the Spirit. Campbell was so intent on making "the principles of the inductive philosophy . . . my rule and guide" that some of his followers believed he was bewitched by the Enlightenment, as Robert Frederick West has suggested in *Alexander Campbell and Natural Religion*.[27]

Self-educated people, surprisingly literate, and manifesting a thirst for knowledge—these were the principle constituencies of Millerites, Disciples, and Mormons alike. Their common appeal was that people take up the Bible and consider the evidence for themselves. "In establishing the foundation of his kingdom," Campbell said, "Jesus establishes the doctrine of personal liberty, of freedom of choice, and of personal responsibility, by commanding every man to judge reason, and act for himself." For Campbell this process of enlightenment was clearly the chief means by which the millennium would be introduced.[28]

But how could Joseph Smith and the Mormons, who appealed to new forms of revelation rather than to the Scripture alone, find their place within the scope of such an interpretation? Were they not more like the tradition of mystical prophets that came to the fore in Europe? I think not. Joseph Smith's instincts were not to reject the ahistorical and rationalistic mood of his day; he simply carried its logic to what he believed was a dead end and then made a rational judgment of what move was next. Joseph

---

[27]*The Midnight Cry*, 17 November 1842, 3; Francis D. Nichol, *The Midnight Cry* (Washington DC: Review and Herald Publishing Association, 1944) 120; Robert Frederick West, *Alexander Campbell and Natural Religion* (New Haven: Yale University Press, 1948).

[28]*Millennial Harbinger*, 445.

Smith's mother, Lucy, had become so disillusioned with sectarian rivalry shortly after 1800 that she concluded that a new biblical form of Christianity should supplant the corrupt versions of Christianity then vying for members. Joseph moved in the same direction, but by 1820 despaired that unity could ever be attained by sending every person off to interpret Scripture for themselves.

> In the midst of this war of words and tumult of opinions, I often said to myself, What is to be done? Who of all these parties are right? Or, are they all wrong together? If one of them is right, which is it, and how shall I know? The teachers of religion of the different sects destroy all confidence in settling the question by an appeal to the Bible. At length I came to the conclusion that I must remain in darkness or confusion, or else I must do as James directs, that is ask of God.

Smith immediately began to seek direct revelation and found his hopes fulfilled in a series of visions.[29]

What reinforced the conviction that new light had to supersede Scripture was Smith's extreme view of history: real Christianity since the Apostles had been totally eclipsed, not just darkened, as Elias Smith, Alexander Campbell, and William Miller would have argued. The glad proclamation that God had removed the barrier of silence between heaven and earth gave Mormonism great appeal for many Campbellites: Orson Hyde, Parley Pratt, Orson Pratt, Lyman Wright, Sidney Rigdon, Edward Partridge, and Frederick G. Williams, to name the most prominent. "One thing has been done by the coming forth of the *Book of Mormon*," one contemporary mused, "It has puked the Campbellites effectively; no emitic could have done half as well." In the case of Sidney Rigdon, at one time Campbell's chief lieutenant, it was clearly a continuing quest for "the ancient order of things" that made him vulnerable to Mormon claims that they embodied "the Gospel in its purity as it was anciently preached by the Apostles." Parley Pratt admitted the same in his autobiography: "After duly weighing the whole matter in my mind, I saw clearly that these things were true; and that myself and the whole world were without baptism, and without the ministry and ordinances of God; and that the whole

---

[29]Lucy Smith, *Biographical Sketches of Joseph Smith the Prophet* (Liverpool: S. W. Richards, 1853; rpt., New York: Arno Press, 1969) 37, 46-49; Joseph Smith, *The Pearl of Great Price: Being a Choice Selection from the Revelations, Translations, and Narrations of Joseph Smith* (Salt Lake City: G. Q. Cannon, 1891) 56-70.

world had been in this condition since the days that inspiration and revelation had ceased."[30]

In his new book *Mormonism and the American Experience*, Klaus J. Hansen also emphasizes the Mormons' commitment to a kind of common-sense rationality. He suggests that in certain ways the Mormons may have been even more rationalistic than most people in a climate of revivalism. "However anti-intellectual Mormonism may appear to a modern citizen of the twentieth century, it had an internal consistency as well as a commonsense rationality that set it very much apart from much of emotionally infused, non-intellectual emphasis of antebellum American revivalism."[31] Many early Mormon converts, such as Brigham Young and Heber Kimball, had been disillusioned by revivals and sought to be able to reason out their relationship to God.[32]

Like Spiritualists of this era, the Mormons appealed not so much to inward illumination and mystical experience as to the observable objects of empirical science.[33] The plain people of Western New York were challenged to examine for themselves the truth of the Book of Mormon—"a New World Bible" claiming to bring Scripture up to date. Brigham Young, for instance, who had earlier rejected the enthusiasm of the revival and had prayed for "a solid judgment and a discreet mind ripened upon a good solid foundation of common sense," withheld judgment when he encountered the *Book of Mormon*. "I examined the matter studiously for two years before I made up my mind to receive that book. . . . I wished time sufficient to prove all things for myself."[34]

---

[30]F. Mark McKiernan, *The Voice of One Crying in the Wilderness: Sidney Rigdon, Religious Reformer, 1793-1876* (Lawrence KS: Coronado Press, 1971) 36, 30; Parley Parker Pratt, *The Autobiography of Parley Parker Pratt. One of the Twelve Apostles of the Church of Jesus Christ of Latter-Day Saints* (New York: Russell Brothers, 1874) 39.

[31]Hansen, *Mormonism*, 41.

[32]Ibid., 39-41. See also Marvin S. Hill, "The Rise of Mormonism in the Burned-Over District: Another View," *New York History* 61 (1980): 411-30.

[33]For the empirical cast of nineteenth-century Spiritualism, see R. Laurence Moore, *In Search of White Crows: Spiritualism, Para-psychology, and American Culture* (New York: Oxford University Press, 1977) 7.

[34]Hansen, *Mormonism*, 40.

The Mormons also had a passion for demonstrating physical evidence—golden plates, spectacles, the papyri of the Book of Abraham—and for collecting witnesses to certify the facts of their faith. One Methodist convert to the Mormons reasoned that "the New Bible" was four times better substantiated than the New Testament because the disciples of Joseph Smith had four living witnesses to sustain the Book of Mormon. As Gordon Wood has noted, the Mormons "brought the folk past and enlightened modernity together . . . forging a new popular amalgam out of traditional folk beliefs and the literary culture of the gentry."[35]

Prophecy and Democracy

The revolutions in America and in France late in the eighteenth century created in America a profound sense that events of truly apocalyptic significance were unfolding before people's eyes. While many Congregationalists and Presbyterians associated democratic advance with the Antichrist of French infidelity, as in the frenzy over the Bavarian Illuminati, many other Americans, particularly those who had not known formal education and high social standing, came to interpret the movement of Providence very differently. To them, a potent dose of liberty and equality seemed just the needed tonic for church and state.[36] In a sermon after the second election of Jefferson, Elias Smith stated that God had raised up Jefferson, like Cyrus, "to dry up the Euphrates of mystery Babylon." Being firmly grounded on the principles of liberty and equality, Jefferson's administration actually foreshadowed the millennium.[37] In the same vein, Alexander Campbell announced in the preface to volume seven of the *Christian Baptist* in 1829:

> The prospects of emancipating myriads from the dominion of prejudice and tradition—of restoring a pure speech to the people of God—of ex-

---

[35]Gordon S. Wood, "Evangelical America and Early Mormonism," *New York History* 61 (1980): 383.

[36]On the Bavarian Illuminati frenzy, see Hatch, *The Sacred Cause of Liberty: Republican Thought and the Millennium in Revolutionary New England* (New Haven: Yale University Press, 1977) 130-32.

[37]Elias Smith, *The Whole World Governed by a Jew: or the Government of the Second Adam, as King and Priest* (Exeter NH: Henry Ranlet, 1805) 74.

pediting their progress from Babylon to Jerusalem—*of contributing efficiently to the arrival of the Millennium—have brightened with every volume
of this work.* . . .

The following year Campbell declared that 4 July 1776 should be remembered as the Jewish Passover because of what it had done in delivering
people "from the melancholy thraldom of relentless systems. . . . This
revolution, taken in all its influences, will make men free indeed."[38]

The Mormons, ironically, who seemed to have rejected American values, actually developed the most Americanized theology of all. Joseph
Smith made the Garden of Eden a New World paradise, with America
becoming the cradle of civilization. In due time, the *Book of Mormon* re-
counts, God prevailed upon Columbus "to venture across the sea to the
Promised Land, to open it for a new race of free men." A variety of Mormon authors suggest that it was the free institutions of America that prepared the way for the new prophet, Joseph Smith. "The chief claim of the
Mormon preachers," W. H. Oliver has written, "was that they had a new
church based upon a new revelation, that this newness was true antiquity,
and that continuity between the new and the old was effected in a way
which escaped contamination for the antiChristian interim. . . . This orientation, the theology of America as a cosmic fact, is the significant in-
novation of the Mormons."[39]

The significance of America assuming such a millennial role did not
lie just in the religious patriotism that followed. Early in the nineteenth
century, as Thomas Kselman suggests, a revival of messianic nationalism
could also be found in England, France, Italy, Poland, and Russia.[40]
What seems distinctive about the American context is the extent to which
the ideals of civil and religious liberty, central planks of the Enlightenment, became the most important prophetic sign of the time. Among
Christians, Disciples, Millerites, and Mormons, it was the flowering of
democracy, releasing common folk to think for themselves, that became
the primary harbinger of the millennium. "How or by what means will
the millennium be introduced?" the radical Christian Abel M. Sargent

---

[38]West, *Alexander Campbell*, 169, 4.

[39]W. H. Oliver, *Prophets and Millennialists*, 235.

[40]Thomas Kselman, *Miracles and Prophecies*, 80-83.

asked in 1807: "First by a revolution in *politics*. There must be an universal suppression and downfall of Monarchy and Aristocracy—the rights of sovereignty—of free thinking and free speaking must be secured to the common people—to the meek of the earth."[41]

That democracy became a sacred cause is all the more significant given simultaneous events in France and England. In those countries after 1789, the polarization of politics conspired against any alliance between prophecy and liberty, between millennialists and democrats. The virulent attacks against Christianity in the name of reason and democracy tainted any quest for the rights of man and turned students of prophecy away from the likes of Thomas Paine. After the publication of Paine's *Age of Reason* in 1794, James K. Hopkins has argued, the words "deist" and "democrat" became virtually synonymous, and popular millennialists and radical liberterians were rent asunder:

> When the millennialists split off from the radical forces, they turned inward on their journey to the Heavenly City, with only the light of the spirit to illuminate the enveloping darkness. They came to rely on their "feelings" and "spiritual guides" for direction.[42]

French prophets early in the nineteenth century had the same tendency to reject the Enlightenment and opt for political or Royalist solutions. In both England and France, then, the continuation both of monarchy and of aristocratic privilege, on the one hand, and of democratic alternatives stigmatized by infidelity, on the other, meant that common folk could never fully align the cause of God with the evolving ideals of the nation.

American popular culture, however, allowed self-educated people to espouse millennial hopes rife with the conviction that a *novus ordo seculorum* was unfolding before them, that common folk could challenge their betters without violating conscience, and that democracy was the cause of God. The collapse of Federalism, the last symbolic refuge of privilege, rekindled these hopes and the conviction that the millennium was to have an intimate relationship with the "land of the free and the home of the brave."

---

[41]Abel M. Sargent, *The Halcyon Itinery and True Millennium Messenger*, August 1807, 9.

[42]James Kirkland Hopkins, "Joanna Southcott," 402.

Thus, popular millennialism in the early republic resisted traditional norms, particularly the hegemony of elites, insisted that freedom of thought be extended to those outside of power structures, and identified aspirations of common folk with the will of God. All of this leaves the impression that popular religion in the "Burned-Over District" could be as much a vehicle for liberation as of control, that it could serve to undermine rather than reinforce the dominance of particular groups. The religion represented by Christians, Disciples, Millerites, and Mormons mirrors the needs not of dominant groups, as Paul Johnson suggests of the Finney Revival in Rochester, but of people unwilling to abide "the beliefs and modes of comportment that suited their employers." However bizarre and extreme their popular theologies came to appear, these were people who refused to be beguiled by the establishment. They insisted on being masters of their own religious destiny.

With this legacy, it is little wonder that popular millennialism, in one form or another, has retained a powerful hold on the imagination of America's people and that such millennial movements as dispensationalism have been characterized by an antidevelopmental or ahistorical strain, as George Marsden has noted in his recent book on Fundamentalism. One is also led to conjecture that one reason religious patriotism has retained a firm hold within the American evangelical tradition is that it has not been the exclusive property of elites, invoked in God's name for the ends of social control. American people outside normal means of power and influence have continued to appeal to America's millennial mission. On these shores, after all, the staid graduates of Harvard, Yale, and Princeton have never really held sway over "God's humble people." In America, even eschatology, that most sophisticated and arcane branch of theology, has been rudely democratized. William Miller deigned to undertake the same kind of rational study of prophetic Scripture that had challenged the talents of an Isaac Newton or a Jonathan Edwards. In our own day, the same spirit moved a converted seaman named Hal Lindsay to take up the books of Daniel and Revelation and interpret them for himself in light of contemporary events. The popularity of *The Late Great Planet Earth*— the best selling paperback in America during the decade of the 1970s—is testimony to the appeal that a democratized and rational eschatology continues to have for the American evangelical tradition.

Chapter 4

Charles G. Finney:
His Place in the Stream
of American Evangelicalism

Garth M. Rosell

Although also a lawyer, pastor, professor and college president, Charles Grandison Finney (1792-1875) is most often remembered as a revivalist—and rightly so, for despite the fascinating diversity of his career, religious revivals clearly remained the organizing center and motivating passion of his life.[1] An "immensely important man in American history by any standard of measure," as Sydney Ahlstrom has phrased it, Finney

---

[1] Finney's preoccupation with religious revivals is clearly reflected in the "Memoirs of Charles G. Finney," a handwritten manuscript in the Oberlin College Archives, Oberlin, Ohio. The printed version, edited by his successor at Oberlin College, President James Harris Fairchild, and first published in 1876, differs substantially from the original. Consequently, citations throughout this paper are from the handwritten MS with parallel citations from the 1908 Fleming H. Revell edition, *Charles G. Finney: An Autobiography*, noted in tandem. The reader may be interested to know that Richard A. G. Dupuis and I are currently collaborating on the *Memoirs of Charles Finney: The Complete, Original, and Unedited Edition*, to be published by the Zondervan Corporation of Grand Rapids, Michigan, in 1984.

introduced literally thousands in his own generation and since to that kind of evangelical Christianity, which united by a common authority (the Bible), shared experience (new birth/conversion), and commitment to the same sense of duty (obedience to Christ through evangelism and benevolence). Finney came to love and sought to practice what the old preachers used to call a religion of heart, head, and hands.[2]

Heart

When Perry Miller suggested, in his *Life of the Mind in America*, that American revivalism reflected a triumph of heart over head, he was merely summarizing what has become a standard interpretation by historians about that period. Revivalists of the post-Revolutionary generation, one is told, aimed their appeals largely at the hearts of their listeners, seeking to stir the passions and excite the emotions. Revivals were, first and foremost, affairs of the heart.[3]

The popularity of such an interpretation is not difficult to understand. Any interested reader can quickly locate, in convenient form, detailed analyses of New York's "burned-over district," picturesque accounts of the excesses of utopian visionaries, or colorful stories of people actually jerking, barking, or laid out stiff at the camp meetings of Kentucky and Tennessee.[4] Such tales have added spice to more than one undergraduate lecture course in American history; and on one level it is only proper that this should be so, for in substantial measure these unusual occurrences can be verified by the kind of good hard evidence that is the stuff of historical research. Less praiseworthy, however, has been the tendency to allow these catchy episodes to represent either the revival tradition in par-

---

[2]Sydney E. Ahlstrom, *A Religious History of The American People* (New Haven: Yale University Press, 1972) 461.

[3]Perry Miller, *The Life of the Mind in America: From the Revolution to the Civil War* (New York: Harcourt, Brace and World, 1965) 3-155, especially 25-26, 120, 133. Compare William Warren Sweet, *Revivalism in America: Its Origin, Growth and Decline* (New York: Charles Scribner's Sons, 1945).

[4]Richard M'Nemar, *The Kentucky Revival* (Cincinnati OH: Art Guild Reprints, 1968) iii-70; Bernard A. Weisberger, *They Gathered at the River: The Story of the Great Revivalists and Their Impact on Religion in America* (Chicago: Quadrangle Books, 1966) 20-50. Compare John B. Boles, *The Great Revival: 1787-1805* (Lexington: University of Kentucky Press, 1972).

ticular or the mainstream of American Evangelicalism in general. Such an approach should be greeted with caution. This is especially true, I would suggest, in the case of Charles G. Finney.

Born in Warren, Connecticut and reared in the "new Connecticut" of western New York State, Finney discovered early in life the Yankee's deep respect for the mind.[5] Sitting in the gallery of the family church, watching his aging Congregationalist pastor, Peter Starr, insert all of his fingers into his big pulpit Bible to mark the texts for his lengthy sermons, Finney was exposed to a tradition which, while not eliminating the emotions, certainly sought to hold them in careful check. Although Starr usually preached his sermons in a style that the young Finney described as "monotonous" and "humdrum," Peter Starr was planting in Finney's mind the necessity of balancing heart with head.[6] Consequently, when Finney's remarkable religious conversion in 1821 and his subsequent ordination by the Presbyterian Church in 1824 launched him into a series of revivals that were to bring him the title "father of modern revivalism," he pursued his new responsibilities with a discipline of mind that could only make a New Englander proud.[7]

This is not to say, of course, that emotional outbreaks never occurred as a result of his preaching. Indeed, during his earliest revivals in 1824, held in the tiny villages of upstate New York while he was serving as a missionary for the Utica-based Female Missionary Society of the Western

---

[5]Charles Grandison Finney was born in Warren (a portion of Litchfield County first known as East Greenwich), Connecticut, 29 August 1792, and died in Oberlin, Ohio, 16 August 1875. The standard biography of Finney remains George F. Wright, *Charles Grandison Finney* (Boston and New York: Houghton Mifflin Co., 1891). See also James E. Johnson's helpful study, "The Life of Charles Grandison Finney" (Ph.D. diss., Syracuse University, 1959).

[6]For Starr's balance of heart and head, see his "Half-Century Sermon, Delivered at Warren, March 8, 1822" (Norwalk CT: S. W. Benedict, 1828) and "Nature and Importance of Covenanting with God, Illustrated in a Sermon by the Pastor of the Church in Warren, State of Connecticut, 1797" (Norwalk CT: S. W. Benedict, 1797).

[7]Most New England ministers were apparently aware of the dangers of excessive emotionalism. The cause celèbre, of course, had been the James Davenport incident in 1741, which many were convinced had brought down the curtain on the Great Awakening. See Alan Heimert and Perry Miller, eds., *The Great Awakening: Documents Illustrating the Crisis and its Consequences* (Indianapolis and New York: Bobbs Merrill Co., 1967) 201-304; and C. C. Goen's excellent introduction in Jonathan Edwards, *The Great Awakening* (New Haven: Yale University Press, 1972) 1-89.

District, Finney occasionally lost control of his audience.[8] Preaching a total of 154 times during those twenty-four weeks, as he noted in his detailed report to the Society, Finney's "plain and pointed" preaching had produced not only a "blessed work of reformation" in places like Evans Mills, Antwerp, Perch River, Brownville, Lerays Ville, Rutland, Gouverneur and DeKalb, but also a "deep anxiety" and "excitement."[9]

In Antwerp, for example, where Finney's ministry enlarged the Presbyterian membership rolls from sixteen to fifty-six adult communicants in three months, there were occasions on which his hearers would "fall from their seats in every direction," crying for mercy. "Nearly the whole congregation," Finney later reported, "were either on their knees or prostrate." The disorder became so great on some occasions that Finney found himself "obliged to stop preaching."[10]

Such occurrences—reflected also in accounts of the woman who fell unconscious, of the Universalist would-be assassin who found himself unable to pull the trigger, of those who dropped dead after opposing the revivals, or of the hundreds who toppled from their seats in anguish—so troubled the young minister that early in his career, in an area of the country where exhibitions of religious emotion were not uncommon, he set out to devise means of controlling them. So rigorously did Finney pursue his goal, in fact, that some of his own friends began to complain. "I fear that the peculiar circumstances in which you have been placed," wrote one in a letter to Finney, "have led you to a discussion . . . of abstract theological subjects" rather than to "those soul stirring appeals to the heart" which

---

[8]Finney, "Memoirs," 114-278; *Charles G. Finney: An Autobiography* (Westwood NJ: Fleming H. Revell, 1908) 61-143. Compare James E. Johnson, "Charles G. Finney and the Great 'Western' Revivals," *Fides et Historia* 20 (Spring 1974): 13-30; and William Charles Walzar, "Charles Grandison Finney and the Presbyterian Revivals of Northern and Western New York" (Ph.D. diss., University of Chicago, 1944) 49, 59-75.

[9]"Mr. Finney's Journal," in *The Eighth Annual Report of the Trustees of the Female Missionary Society of the Western District* (Utica NY: for the Society by Merrell and Colwell, 1824) 17-19. See also the letter from Sarah Kirkland to Charles Finney, 17 March 1824, in the Finney Papers, Oberlin College Library.

[10]Finney, "Memoirs," 184-209; *Autobiography*, 98-110. For additional information on the Antwerp revival see *Church Records of the First Presbyterian Church in Antwerp, 1819-1867* (handwritten congregational records, presently stored in the home of Mrs. Harriet Allen of Antwerp); and "Mr. Finney's Journal," 17-19.

we love to hear.[11] "Finney has got pretty rational," wrote another, fearing that his old friend was losing his "practical edge."[12] Their fears were not without foundation. Increasingly, as his fame spread and he began preaching in the larger centers, Finney was taking pains to draw "the emotions of his converts" under what historian Gilbert Barnes has called his "iron control."[13]

Naturally, Finney did not always succeed. Yet emotional outbreaks in his revival meetings became so infrequent as to raise serious question about any attempt to characterize his work as guided by a preoccupation with the passions. Nonetheless, contemporary commentators continued to press the charge of emotionalism against Finney and his colleagues. Not only did Dolphus Skinner, ubiquitous editor of one of Universalism's most potent periodicals, *The Evangelical Magazine*, like to typify Finney's meetings as "hubbub wild and sad confusion all,"[14] but Henry Ware, local Unitarian evangelist, published in the famous *Bunker Hill Contest* (1826) one of the most vicious attacks on Finney ever to appear in print, charging him among other sins with catering to the passions of his hearers.[15] Furthermore, William R. Weeks, minister from Paris Hill, New York, spoke for at least three New York Congregationalists when in his *Pastoral Letter* (1827) he charged that Finney's meetings were filled with "ostentation and noise," with much "profaneness," "familiarity with God," and "loud groaning, speaking out, or falling down in public worship." "Feelings," Weeks was convinced, were "controlling the judg-

---

[11]Letters from E. W. Clarke to Charles G. Finney, 23 May 1832 in Finney Papers, Oberlin College Library.

[12]Letter from Luther Myrick to Charles Finney, 3 September 1832, Finney Papers, Oberlin College Library.

[13]Gilbert H. Barnes, *The Antislavery Impulse, 1830-1844* (New York: Harcourt, Brace and World, 1964) 10. Compare Wright, *Finney*, 58.

[14]*The Evangelical Magazine* 3 (9 May 1829): 17.

[15]Ephraim Perkins, *A Bunker Hill Contest, A.D. 1826, Between the "Holy Alliance" For the Establishment of Hierarchy, and Ecclesiastical Domination Over the Human Mind, on the One Side; and the Asserters of Free Inquiry, Bible Religion, Christian Freedom and Civil Liberty on the Other. The Rev. Charles Finney, "Home Missionary," And High Priest of the Expeditions of the Alliance in the Interior of New York; Headquarters, County of Oneida* (Utica: for the author, 1826). It is my contention, argued elsewhere, that "Ephraim Perkins" was the pseudonym for Henry Ware.

ment."[16] Many Old School Presbyterians were ready to agree. When William B. Sprague, pastor of the Second Presbyterian Church in Albany, New York, dismissed Finney's revivals as mere animal excitements, he was voicing a common complaint of many in the denomination against their young colleague.[17]

Although Finney's friends preferred to describe his preaching as "plain" and "direct," it was increasingly apparent that there were plenty of others who thought it "better suited to a Bacchanalian row." Labeled "the madman of Oneida" as early as 1826, Finney was repeatedly accused of such errors as terrifying "weak-minded women and children half out of their senses" with his "appeals to their passions," his "descriptions of hell, and his imagery of the infernal regions," with which, it was added, he "seems to be very familiar."[18] Indeed, such reports became so widespread that one Berlin, New York man, concerned lest his nephew be taken in by Finney's emotional appeal, wrote in a letter, "William beware, beware . . . this noted Finney's character is said to be very bad (I know nothing personally). I have been informed that he was bred a lawyer and has had two wives without losing any (and) has had a child born to him by a third female since he was married . . . William," he pleaded, "look well at the foundation. Strip this man of his briefs and perseverance and what is he?"[19]

On the surface such reports seem overwhelming, pointing as they do to what many considered to be Finney's continued and flagrant appeal to the passions of his hearers. Such a conclusion, however, becomes less persuasive when one discovers that in virtually every instance, the reports were coming from individuals who had ample reason of their own for wishing to see Finney's work discredited. The Unitarians and Universalists like Skinner and Ware, for example, had long been engaged in a vigorous battle with Plan of Union ministers in the northeast. They were

---

[16]William R. Weeks, *A Pastoral Letter of the Ministers of the Oneida Association to the Churches Under Their Care on the Subject of Revivals of Religion* (Utica: Ariel Works, 1827).

[17]William B. Sprague, *Lectures on Revivals of Religion* (Glasgow: W. Collins, 1832).

[18]*The Evangelical Magazine* 3 (9 May 1829): 17. Compare the letter from Laura Fish to Lydia Finney, 6 August 1826, in the Finney Papers, Oberlin College Library.

[19]Letter from Stephen Hull to William Lapham, 2 October 1827, in the Finney Papers, Oberlin College Library.

guided, as John Ware phrased it, by an almost paranoid fear of the Presbyterian Establishment.[20] Furthermore, Old School Presbyterians like Sprague and some disenchanted Congregationalists like Weeks were locked in debate with New Divinity men—whose theological camp they considered Finney allied with—in an attempt to rescue the "faith once delivered" from what they thought to be the destructive work of innovators.[21] Even the misinformed, like Stephen Hull from Berlin, were little more than the unfortunate victims of a kind of whisper campaign launched by those who, out of vested interest, wanted Finney's demise. Such witnesses, as every historian knows, are notoriously unreliable.

Head

Finney's desire to curb excessive emotionalism becomes even more apparent when one notes, in addition to his Yankee concern with the life of the mind, that Finney's professional training was in law. During the four years preceding his conversion, from 1818-1821, he served as an apprentice-clerk to Judge Benjamin Wright in his law office in Adams, New York.[22] Although never admitted to the bar, Finney had read extensively in the legal literature of the day, from Latin and geometry to logic and Blackstone, and had even argued some minor cases before the Justices Court when it met in the village of Adams.[23] Consequently, when he entered the ministry, he did so as a trained lawyer, without benefit of any

---

[20]John Ware, *Memoirs of the Life of Henry Ware, Jr., by his Brother John Ware* (Boston: James Munroe, 1846) 1:177.

[21]Sydney E. Ahlstrom, "Theology in America: A Historical Survey," in *Religion in American Life*, ed. James W. Smith and A. Leland Jamison (Princeton: Princeton University Press, 1961) 1:251-71.

[22]Benjamin Wright (1784-1861), a prominent lawyer in Jefferson County, began to practice law in 1816 and was appointed judge in 1829. His law office was located near the main corner of Adams, New York. See "War of 1812 Pensioners" (handwritten MSS, Documents Room, Flower Memorial Library, Watertown, New York).

[23]"Docket Book of the Court of Common Pleas, Jefferson County" (MSS Records, Legal Files, County Clerk's Office, Watertown, New York); "Minutes of the Justices Court, Adams" (MSS Records, in attic of the Adams Center Town Hall, one end of the Town Barn); Luther J. Dorwin, "Bench and Bar of Jefferson County" in Hamilton Child, *Part First, Geographical Gazetteer of Jefferson County, New York, 1684-1890* (Syracuse: Syracuse Journal Co., 1890) 47-63. I know of no record indicating that Finney was ever formally admitted to the bar.

formal training in the theological disciplines.[24] Thus, law was the foundation of his religious understanding. His style of rhetoric was that of the courtroom, and his hermeneutic was derived from the study of legal briefs he made during his experiences as a lawyer in Adams. "I was bred a lawyer," Finney often remarked, "I came right forth from a law office to the pulpit, and talked to the people as I would have talked to a jury."[25]

"Religion," Finney insisted, "consists in the heart's obedience to the law of intelligence." It dare not be "influenced by emotion."[26] Adopting the faculty psychology common to his day, Finney saw the human personality as a combination of intellect, emotion, and will. Intellect and emotion, he believed, are by nature passive. Only will is voluntary. Therefore, a person is going to exhibit emotion involuntarily whether that person likes it or not. What he or she can control, however, are the elements that activate those emotions and keep them within proper limits. If a minister looked to stir the passions by rhetoric or any other artificial device, the effort would be not only unnatural but extremely dangerous—dangerous precisely because emotion tends to overpower one's reason. Preaching that appeals to feelings rather than the mind is bad preaching. Enthusiasm that is unintelligent is spurious. Authentic excitement comes only from an encounter with the truth.[27]

For Finney, then, the issue lay not in a choice between the head and the heart, but in discriminating between authentic and spurious passion. As early as 1827, in fact, Finney had drawn a line between "animal feeling" and "spiritual feeling."[28] Bad feeling, animal in nature, he argued, is "boisterous and unintelligent," whereas "spiritual feeling" is the "free

----

[24]Wright, *Finney*, 20. For Finney's attitude toward seminary training see his *Lectures of Revivals of Religion*, ed. William G. McLoughlin (Cambridge: Belknap Press, 1960) 186-88.

[25]Finney, "Memoirs," 158-83, quotation from 168; *Autobiography*, 85-97, quotation from 89.

[26]Charles G. Finney, *Revival Fire: Letters on Revivals* (Waukesha WI: Metropolitan Church Association, n.d.) 11.

[27]Charles G. Finney, *Lectures on Systematic Theology* (Oberlin: James M. Fitch, 1846) 1-66.

[28]Charles G. Finney, *A Sermon Preached in the Presbyterian Church at Troy, March 4, 1827* (Troy NY: Tuttle and Richards, 1827) 10-14.

and unembarrassed action of both the intelligence and the will."[29] "Read, study, think and read again," Finney repeatedly counseled his students, "you were made to think. It will do you good."[30]

Finney's attempts to translate into action his understanding of head and heart evidently met with success. Although some of his detractors continued to criticize him for what they alleged to be the excessive emotionalism of his revivals, the Presbyterian and Congregational ministers in whose churches he conducted them were uniformly consistent in their denial of the charges. Labeling the criticisms "misrepresentations" at best and outright "lies" at worst, pastors like John Frost, N. S. S. Beman, Noah Coe, and Samuel Aiken affirmed the order and solemnity of the meetings. The Oneida Presbytery's report of Finney's 1826 revivals, *A Narrative of the Revival of Religion in the County of Oneida*, concluded that there had been less "excitement of the passions" and more "wisdom and discretion" than any of them could recall having been exhibited in any prior revival within memory.[31] Indeed, the 1827 New Lebanon Convention—at which these matters were thoroughly aired—seemed to satisfy all but perhaps Asahel Nettleton that this was so.

"His language was based on the Bible, Shakespeare and Blackstone," wrote Alfred Vance Churchill, a member of Finney's Oberlin congregation and one who had himself been baptized by Finney. Although once in a while, Churchill admitted, "some sinner, feeling that he had outraged the laws of God and man, might be seized with convulsions," such cases were "rare" and "were by no means encouraged." Finney "hated excess. His religious services were marked by dignity and reserve." He spoke "like an inspired lawyer." He "based his discourse on reason." His words were "logic on fire," crashing through his listener's arguments "like cannonball through a basket of eggs . . . I have heard both Finney and the camp meeting revivalist," Churchill then concluded, "and I find no resemblance whatever" between them—except, he added with an apparent

---

[29]Finney, *Revival Fire*, 7-53, quotation from 35.

[30]Finney, *Lectures on Systematic Theology*, v.

[31]*A Narrative of the Revival of Religion in the County of Oneida, Particularly in the Bounds of the Presbytery of Oneida, In the Year 1826* (Utica NY: Hastings and Tracy, 1826) 35-39.

twinkle in his eye, "that Finney used a tent when the church was not big enough."[32]

Hands

The story cannot properly end with head and heart. While a genuine understanding of them both was central for Finney's ministry, of even greater importance to him was the role of human will. For Finney, it was simply not enough for one's mind to grasp the truth. One must also act upon it.[33] "Many professed Christians," Finney lamented, "hold that nothing is needful but simply faith and repentance, and that faith may exist without real benevolence, and consequently without good works." No "mistake" could "be greater than this." The "grand requisition which God makes upon man" is that he become "truly benevolent," that is, that he exhibit to others a "compassion like God's compassion."[34] As citizens of a moral government, Christians ought to be trained for usefulness, to produce in the world the "greatest amount of moral influence." They should "stand their ground and do their duty."[35] Personal piety is needful, but it is never enough. So let us "buckle on the harness and go forward," not "calculating so much to be happy as to be useful, not talking about comfort but duty, not desiring flights of joy and triumph, but hungering and thirsting after righteousness, not studying how to create new flights of rapture, but how to know the will of God, and do it." So "let us hear the cry" from all our pulpits, "*to the work* . . . let us have the United States converted to God." If the church will only do her duty, "the millennium may come in this country in three years."[36]

---

[32]Alfred Vance Churchill, "Midwestern: Early Oberlin Personalities," *Northwest Ohio Quarterly* Vol. 23, No. 4 (Autumn 1951): 228-32.

[33]I am greatly indebted to the members of The Hopkins-Harwichport Seminar in American Religious History who graciously read portions of the final section of this paper, originally presented under the title "Millennial Roots of Early Nineteenth-Century Reform." Their helpful comments aided me in reshaping the argument at several strategic points.

[34]Charles G. Finney, *Sermons on Gospel Themes* (New York: Fleming H. Revell, rpt. of the 1876 edition) 328.

[35]Finney, *Lectures on Revivals of Religion*, 242-43.

[36]Ibid., 305-306, 404-405.

Finney's appropriation of millennialist imagery and rhetoric is not surprising. For although the grand vision of a coming millennium has been a favorite theme of theologians throughout the history of the Christian church, seldom has the idea enjoyed a wider popularity than in the United States during the years following the War of Independence.[37] "America in the early nineteenth century," as Ernest Sandeen phrased it, "was drunk on the millennium."[38] Evangelical Christians across the new nation seemed to have been captivated by the vision of a genuinely Christian society, ruled by God and peopled by his saints.

They believed that Christ would return to earth to launch a thousand years of peace and prosperity. Indeed, hundreds of early nineteenth-century Christians prayed fervently for the coming of the Kingdom; they talked and wrote of it constantly; and they worked with enthusiasm for its achievement.

Few committed themselves more wholeheartedly to the millennial vision or worked more vigorously for its establishment than did Charles Finney. In the years between his first revival in Evans Mills, New York (1824), and his acceptance of a settled pastorate in New York City's Chatham Street Chapel (1832), the period of his most intensive evangelistic activity, Finney was able to enlist thousands of Northerners and New Yorkers in the cause of revivals and the work of reform.

The connection that Charles Finney established between his own revivals and the efforts for reform grew out of his literal interpretation of Revelation 20:4-6. Finney pictured America as the coming center of a divinely ordered universe, with God as its governor, the people as his obedient subjects, and the eternal "law of benevolence" as its guiding light. Christians, Finney believed, must engage the battlements of Satan and purge society of its sins. Business practices wanted reform; graft and

---

[37]On the nature and importance of the millennial theme see Nathan O. Hatch, *The Sacred Cause of Liberty: Republican Thought and The Millennium in Revolutionary New England* (New Haven: Yale University Press, 1977); James W. Davidson, *The Logic and Millennial Thought: Eighteenth Century New England* (New Haven: Yale University Press, 1977); and Robert T. Handy, *A Christian America: Protestant Hopes and Historical Realities* (London: Oxford University Press, 1971).

[38]Ernest R. Sandeen, *The Roots of Fundamentalism: British and American Millenarianism, 1800-1930* (Chicago: University of Chicago Press, 1970) 42-55, and his bibliographical essay, 285-89.

fraud must be overcome; and blacks in slavery should be set free. As soon as Christians are agreed on these matters, Finney argued, we shall "see what glorious things may be expected for Zion." When "ministers shall lay aside their prejudice and their misconstructions, and their jealousies, and shall see eye to eye, and when churches shall understand the Bible alike, and see their duty alike, and pray alike," then, Finney was convinced, "a nation shall be born in a day." With characteristic optimism, Finney predicted that this joyous new order, this glorious denouement, would be imminent. Only let Christians "feel as the heart of one man, and be agreed as to what ought to be done for the salvation of the world," Finney liked to say, and "the millennium will come at once."[39]

In contrast with Calvinism's emphasis upon human inability, Finney came increasingly to believe that human beings are active participants with God in both their own salvation and the affairs of this world. Operating under the unchanging "law of benevolence," which Finney defined simply as love to God and neighbor, both the Moral Governor and his faithful subjects were bound by covenant to join hands in common cause. Not only was the Kingdom about to arrive, but the faithful could actually hasten its coming by participating with God in bringing it about. "If the whole church as a body had gone to work ten years ago," Finney told his congregation, "the millennium would have fully come in the United States before this day."[40]

The vigor with which Finney himself pursued this grand vision seemed inexhaustible. Preaching often to the point of complete collapse, Finney sought not only to fill the Christian ranks with a great flood of new converts, but also to involve the faithful, old and new converts alike, in the great task of preparing society for the coming of the Kingdom. It should come as no surprise, consequently, to learn that great numbers of Finney's converts, seeking to realize his directives from the pulpit, were becoming active in reform causes. Furthermore, many of these were en-

---

[39]Finney, *Lectures on Revivals of Religion*, 328; see also xi-xvix, 277-309. Compare Barnes, *The Antislavery Impulse*, 3-28, and Donald Dayton, *Discovering an Evangelical Heritage* (New York: Harper and Row, 1976).

[40]Finney, *Lectures on Revivals of Religion*, 305-306.

listing as enthusiastic participants in one or more of the growing list of benevolent societies that were so popular in that day.[41]

Such societies were essentially nothing new. Since well before the American Revolution small groups of Christians had been gathering together in societies, voluntary in nature and free of denominational control, for the accomplishment of certain specific tasks. Although defensive in their earlier years, perhaps even a bit paranoid, they entered the new century with a growing sense of optimism. Originally a conservative movement geared to "resist change," as Bernard Weisberger put it, the societies fell increasingly "in step with the cadence of nineteenth-century American progressivism."[42] The dark jeremiads of revolutionary America became increasingly a thing of the past. Reflecting the hope of the new nation itself, the societies began to envision the establishment of the Kingdom of God on the shores of the Atlantic. As Donald Mathews has suggested, a "general social movement" seems to have been in progress during those years, organizing "thousands of people into small groups." Proposing to "change the moral character of America," the societies were the "Revolution at work in religion," mobilizing "Americans in unprecedented numbers."[43]

During the first three decades of the nineteenth century, working with intense zeal, evangelical Christians organized thousands of these societies, spent millions of dollars to run them, and set countless Americans to the task of working on their behalf.[44] "What a fertility of projects," exclaimed Ralph Waldo Emerson, "for the salvation of the world."[45]

----

[41]For an excellent treatment of the development of the voluntary societies, see Lefferts A. Loetscher, "The Problem of Christian Unity in Early 19th Century America," *Church History* 32 (March 1963): 3-16.

[42]Bernard A. Weisberger, *They Gathered at the River*, 78.

[43]Donald G. Mathews, "The Second Great Awakening as an Organizing Process, 1780-1830: An Hypothesis," *The American Quarterly* 22 (Spring 1969): 23-43; specific quotations from 27, 30-31, 35.

[44]Robert Hastings Nichols, *Presbyterianism in New York State: A History of the Synod and its Predecessors* (Philadelphia: Westminster Press, 1963) 103-110.

[45]Ralph Waldo Emerson, *Essays* (Boston: Ticknor and Fields, 1867) 243.

Charles Finney's relationship to the societies was largely unstruc-
tured during the early years of his ministry. He had, of course, heard
many of his friends argue that both "benevolent exertions" and "revivals
of religion" were "indispensible" [sic] to the "future prosperity and glory
of the church." Indeed, his Oneida Presbytery colleagues were convinced
that it was essential for the entire Christian community to unite in "promoting revivals of religion, and in diffusing the blessings of the gospel
among all nations." Only then, they believed, would the "shouts of victory . . . echo from continent to continent, and from the islands to the ends
of the earth."[46] Not until Finney's Rochester revival, however, did he
seem to forge a structural connection between his own revivals and the
societies. During those six months, in what Whitney R. Cross, Lyman
Beecher, and a host of others have described as one of the most impressive
revivals in American history, Finney's millennialism appeared to be more
concrete.[47] Literally hundreds of new Christians and old saints newly "revived" flowed out from the meetings to join one or more of Rochester's
benevolent societies, anxious to put their faith to work in hastening the
arrival of God's kingdom on earth.[48]

Like most other American cities, Rochester had its share of societies:
the Rochester Society for Prison Reform, the Monroe County Peace Society, the Rochester Female Charitable Society, the Society for Detecting
Thieves and Felons, the Monroe County Temperance Society, the Rochester Society for Sabbath Observance, the Monroe County Bible Society,
the Rochester Moral Reform Society, the Monroe County Foreign Missions Society, and a series of additional organizations all found zealous
promoters in the growing city. By the time Finney arrived, there could be

---

[46]*A Narrative of the Revival of Religion in the County of Oneida*, 84-87.

[47]Whitney R. Cross, *The Burned-Over District: The Social and Intellectual History of
Enthusiastic Religion in Western New York, 1800-1850* (New York: Harper Torchbooks,
1965) 155. For several contemporary reports on the revivals see the *Rochester Daily Advertiser and Telegraph*, 16 October 1830; *The Rochester Observer*, 15 October, 12 November, and 24 December 1830, and 13 January 1831; *The Gem and Ladies Amulet*, 16 October
1830. Compare Robert S. Fletcher, *A History of Oberlin College from its Foundations
Through the Civil War*, 2 vols. (Oberlin: for the College, 1943) 1:17-24.

[48]For a fascinating analysis of the Rochester revivals, see Paul E. Johnson, *A Shopkeeper's Millennium: Society and Revivals in Rochester, New York, 1815-1837* (New York:
Hill and Wang, 1978).

little question that the people of Rochester were deeply involved in such organizational efforts.[49]

Finney's meetings, however, brought new life to the societies, flooding them with enthusiastic recruits. The Rochester Female Charitable Society, for example, organized in February of 1822 for "the relief of indigent persons and families, in cases of sickness and distress," as the constitution put it, was greatly strengthened as a result of Finney's meetings.[50] When in 1831 they invited Finney to preach one of the sermons for their ninth anniversary celebration—at which occasion he helped to raise $78.03, one "gold ring and a penknife" in support of the tuition-free school for poor children that the society had established—it was their way of thanking him for what he had done on their behalf.[51] Moreover, an "association of gentlemen" was organized during the revivals themselves, for the purpose of inquiring weekly "into the situation of the poor and destitute" of the area so that their needs might be met and their difficulties "be relieved."[52]

Similar conclusions can be drawn concerning other benevolent societies. Efforts to hasten the emancipation of Negro slaves, to open new opportunities for women, to promote temperance, to widen educational opportunities, to provide better care for injured and disabled stage-line drivers, and to increase pressure upon the legislature to eliminate public transportation and the carrying of mails on Sunday, all received a tremendous boost in recruits and morale during the Rochester revivals.[53] One

[49]On Rochester's societies see *A Directory for the Village of Rochester* (Rochester: Elisha Ely, publisher, Everard Peck, printer, 1827) 104-109. Although news of the societies can be found throughout Rochester's newspapers, a helpful summary is provided by Whitney R. Cross, "Creating a City: Rochester, 1824-1830" (M.A. thesis, University of Rochester, 1936) 113-72. Compare William Charles Walzer, "Charles Grandison Finney and the Presbyterian Revivals of Northern and Western New York" (Ph.D. diss., University of Chicago, 1944) 160f., 206, 233-34.

[50]On the Rochester Female Charitable Society, see William F. Peck, *History of Rochester and Monroe County, New York* (New York: The Pioneer Publishing Company, 1908) 212-17.

[51]*Rochester Daily Advertiser*, 8 February 1831; and *The Rochester Observer*, 10 February 1831.

[52]*Rochester Daily Advertiser and Telegraph*, 8 October 1830.

[53]Of the many examples of Rochester's political activism, particularly with regard to travel and mail delivery on Sunday, see *Rochester Observer*, 1, 13, 29 January 1830.

association was formed with no other purpose than to pray for the success of all the other societies.[54] "In these revivals," as one Presbyterian report phrased it, "we have received testimony, that efforts to carry forward the great objects of benevolence, are the best cooperation the preaching of the Gospel can receive." Where "most has been done" for reform, the authors concluded, "the Revivals have been the most extensive." The Spirit of God has visited no place where these things have been neglected.[55]

Finney's contribution to reform in Rochester did not stem from the creation of new benevolent societies nor from his development of a new theology to sustain them. Clearly, others had pioneered in both these areas long before the young evangelist began his public ministry. Rather, Finney's contribution was to popularize a millennial ideology that helped to galvanize existing benevolent agencies into a broadly popular campaign both to convert sinners and involve them in the establishment of the Kingdom of God on the earth. To head and heart were added many hands and feet.

"The moral enterprises of the present day are novel," wrote Albert G. Hall, editor of *The Rochester Observer*, not so much "in their character and principle" as "in their combination and effect." Then, in a flight of fancy, he imagined hundreds of millions of Americans assembled in a vast amphitheater surrounding the young citizens of post-Revolutionary America. "Happy will it be for our country and the world," he mused, "if they can exclaim that

> these were the men of the nineteenth century, who came to the help of the Lord against the mighty;—these defenders of the sabbath and all its holy influences;—these friends and patrons of missionary and Bible institutions;—these supporters of a press truly free, which, by its salutary issues, emancipated the nation from the thraldom of sin;—these are the men who counted the cost of denying themselves and cheerfully made effort for the world's deliverance. God smiled upon their persevering and united labors, acknowledged them as his friends and servants, and we now hail them as benefactors of our happy millions, and thousands of millions yet unborn.

---

[54]*The Rochester Observer*, 12 March 1830.

[55]Minutes, "Synod of Geneva, 1812-1835," Union Theological Seminary, New York City.

"The time must arrive," the editor concluded, "when the full blaze of Millennial glory shall burst upon the world," when "love to God and love to man shall be the governing principle, and . . . not a discordant note shall disturb the perfect peace and harmony among the inhabitants of the earth."[56]

Nourished by the vision of a Christian America, its ranks swelled by the converts awakened in sweeping revivals, the evangelical movement looked to the grand possibilities of the future. Every step we take, Finney exclaimed, we "tread on cords that will vibrate to all eternity." Every time we move, we "touch keys whose sound will re-echo over all the hills and dales of heaven, and through the dark caverns and vaults of hell."[57] God has laid claim upon our hearts, our heads, and our hands. Each is essential to the fulfillment of the great Christian vision: the extension of benevolence throughout the earth and the longed-for arrival of the Kingdom of God in the world of women and men.

---

[56]*The Rochester Observer*, 17 December 1830.

[57]Finney, *Lectures on Revivals of Religion*, 153.

Chapter 5

Oberlin and Ojibwas:
An Evangelical Mission
to Native Americans

Henry W. Bowden

Sometime during the Revolutionary period a tornado swept across northern Ohio and in many places uprooted stands of timber. On 20 August 1794 a large force of Indian warriors faced American soldiers across some of those ruined trees to fight a showdown battle beside the Maumee River. For over a decade natives in the Midwest had been resisting white encroachment, with British officers encouraging their belligerency in order to retain strategic posts along the Great Lakes. An impressive alliance of Shawnee, Miami, Ottawa, Ojibwa, Potawatomi, Delaware, and Wyandot tribes led principally by Little Turtle and Blue Jacket had already defeated American armies twice. But this time they faced Anthony Wayne and well-disciplined troops that included several hundred mounted riflemen from Kentucky, "as hard-bitten a lot of troopers as ever swung steel."[1] The resulting Battle of Fallen Timbers lasted for only forty minutes, featuring a cavalry charge on the right flank and a frontal assault with bayonets that broke native resistance. As an example of military tactics the engagement was not impressive; as a catalyst for cultural change in the American heartland, it was an event of far-reaching consequences.

After the Battle of Fallen Timbers, Wayne's men destroyed native crops, food reserves, and villages over a broad area. This draconian policy did as much to discourage further resistance as did armed maneuvers. British agents found few groups willing to continue fighting, and the generally demoralized Indians sought peace the following year. On 3 August 1795 over ninety chieftains assembled at Fort Greenville to sign an agreement that ended the last phase of the Revolutionary War. The Treaty of Greenville ceded vast stretches of Indian territory, including two-thirds of Ohio, to the American government and effectively pacified the trans-Allegheny west. It opened the way for nineteenth-century settlement by farmers and craftsmen from New England and New York, many of whom embodied the moral piety that made Ohio part of the Yankee Belt.

One of these earnest pioneers was John J. Shipherd, a Presbyterian minister commissioned by the American Home Missionary Society in 1830 to help rescue "the Valley of the Mississippi" from hopeless degeneration. In 1832 he resigned a pastorate in Elyria, Ohio, to pursue a grander scheme in an unsettled section of Russia Township, Lorain County. His early associate was Philo P. Stewart, another evangelical-minded builder who had served as missionary to Choctaw Indians in Mississippi from 1821 to 1825 and 1827 to 1830.[2] Together these men planned to organize colonists into a special community, the western version of a city set on a hill, and implement with steady resolve the best of Christian ideals. They hoped to establish institutions for training students through manual labor and study, preparing by example and precept missionaries who would convert all who fell short of God's expectations. Their objective was nothing less than to bind Christians into a righteous community by

---

[1]Samuel E. Morison and Henry S. Commager, *The Growth of the American Republic* (New York: Oxford University Press, 1950) 1:358; see also Harry E. Wildes, *Anthony Wayne: Trouble Shooter of the American Revolution* (New York: Harcourt, Brace & Co., 1941) 414-26.

[2]William A. Love, "The Mayhew Mission to the Choctaws," *Publications of the Mississippi Historical Society* 11 (1910): 363-402.

solemn covenant, and have them provide a combination of industry, zeal, and self-denial that would enable them to concentrate their energies on spreading the Kingdom of God.

This example of Christian expansionism in northern Ohio, territory only recently pacified by American troops, was a microcosm of broader Protestant forces at work in the nineteenth century. In those decades aggressive evangelical influences manifested themselves in revivals plus innumerable voluntary societies that supported missionary work, Bible and tract distribution, religious education and Sunday schools, peace, temperance, and Sabbath observance. Citizens from all walks of life encouraged activities to reform physical health and moral habits. Sobriety and thrift, piety and practical virtues were the goals that lay behind everything from the Seaman's Friend Society to groups espousing an unpopular issue that eventually eclipsed all others, namely the abolition of slavery. These American activities were part of an international movement, coinciding with work championed by British Methodists and Quakers in the 1830s. Such endeavors to promote biblical reforms had actually begun a decade earlier in France and had received endorsement from such luminaries as Guizot, Lafayette, de Tocqueville, and an Alsatian minister named Jean Frederic Oberlin.[3] So it was fitting that Shipherd and Stewart chose to name their colony "Oberlin" in recognition of continental experiments to foster concrete patterns of human achievement and godly conduct. Their perception of salvation through evangelical experience and their solid, middle-class definition of morality embodied common traits that were assimilable on both sides of the Atlantic. Evangelical advocates shared a clear-cut and almost predictable set of attitudes as they sought to spread their gospel around the globe.

In its earliest years Oberlin was a small, struggling community whose goals and adjacent academy did not differ from many such enterprises afoot in Protestant activism. The decisive change came in 1835 when Charles G. Finney agreed to locate there as professor of theology. By that time Finney had emerged as the revivalist par excellence of his age, an evangelist whom many regarded as God's annointed. His own conversion experience had become legend, and the "new measures" that symbolized

---

[3]Robert S. Fletcher, *A History of Oberlin College: From its Foundation through the Civil War* (Oberlin: Oberlin College, 1943) 1:207.

modern revivalism had moved amid controversy to widespread acceptance. Finney had progressed from awakenings in small towns of New
York state, through the great 1830-1831 Rochester revival to a trying but
notable pastorate at the Second Free Presbyterian Church in New York
City. During all those years of preaching he emphasized both human responsibility in accepting divine grace and deliberate efforts to improve
upon forgiveness through righteous living. His move to Oberlin was
prompted by a need to train students recently arrived from Lane Seminary in Cincinnati. But from a more inclusive viewpoint, it was natural
for him to use the school as a base for launching evangelists in every direction who could spread revivals of the western New York type. At Oberlin, Finney found a home where he could prepare generations of workers
to convert sinners and thus fulfill an essential component of the expected
millennium.

Oberlin received a great boost when Finney agreed to align his future
with the institution. His passion for winning souls and affecting society
with the leaven of Christian reform fit well with the ideas of Shipherd and
Stewart. After 1835 their academy outstripped dozens of similar schools
and soon became a beacon for young men and women dedicated to vigorous gospel endeavors. Oberlin acquired a reputation for embracing issues on the cutting edge of cultural reform. Students and professors alike
advocated many radical and unpopular causes to further the twin goals of
salvation and social justice. Because of this, Oberlin was one of the earliest
educational institutions to support coeducation and social advancement
for women. It championed the rights of black Americans too and drew
national attention as a hotbed of abolitionist sentiment. These two issues
were perhaps the most publicly visible ones as Oberlin sought to further
both personal piety and cultural improvement in the 1840s.

But missions were also an important aspect of Oberlin outreach from
the beginning. Whether we consider missions to be a vocation in itself or
a general motivation underlying all forms of reformist zeal, Oberlin students manifested a desire to extend their views and affect the lives of others
wherever they felt summoned. Conceiving missionary activity in narrow
terms as an effort to convert those who had not heard the gospel before,
Oberlin sent hundreds of its emissaries to different fields during the nineteenth century. Many went to foreign lands such as Africa, Siam (Thai-
land), Jamaica, the Sandwich Islands (Hawaii), and China. In fact,
during the Boxer Rebellion of 1900 in China, two-thirds of the missionary

personnel killed in Shansi province were from Oberlin, and a memorial to them now stands on the campus. So missionary activity was recognized at the outset as an integral part of evangelical witness, and volunteers sustained that commitment throughout the century.

Missionary work among native Americans had its place in this larger scheme of Protestant cultural influence and worldwide evangelism, but it occupied a modest corner. In the early years most graduates concentrated on the abolition campaign or administered welfare agencies in midwestern states. Others volunteered to increase conversions abroad, but approximately fifteen percent carried out various evangelical efforts among Indian tribes.[4] In 1841 two Oberlin students and their wives went to serve as schoolteachers among the Cherokees, a southeastern tribe recently removed to Indian Territory that later became Oklahoma. Mr. Finney approved of such high-minded sacrifices and was once heard to remark that "a man was not fit for a missionary who could not take an ear of corn in his pocket and start for the Rocky Mountains."[5] One clergyman responding to that challenge was John S. Griffin (B.D., 1838) who tried to spread the Oberlin brand of Christian civilization to Oregon. Another Oberlin colonist, Asahel Munger, also volunteered to go west and witness as best he could, though Mr. Finney's church did not encourage him to do so. Munger came to a melancholy end at the Waiilatpu mission station in Oregon, but Griffin fared better. He stuck to the task of converting natives at Lapwai station and then made two unsuccessful overtures among the Snake Indians. Thereafter he served as chaplain for the Hudson's Bay Company's traders at Fort Vancouver and ended his days as editor of several northwestern newspapers.

Such sporadic and individualistic efforts did not have the numbers or continuity necessary for sustained missionary impact. But in one field, among Ojibwa Indians in northern Minnesota, Oberlin students provided everything essential to successful evangelical effort. Missions to the Ojibwas had started in 1830 under the auspices of the American Board of Commissioners for Foreign Missions (ABCFM) when it began support-

---

[4]Delavan L. Leonard, *The Story of Oberlin: The Institution, the Community, the Idea, the Movement* (Boston: Pilgrim Press, 1898) 333-34.

[5]James H. Fairchild, *Oberlin: The Colony and the College, 1833-1883* (Oberlin OH: E. J. Goodrich, 1883) 141.

ing Frederick Ayer, a Presbyterian already in the territory.[6] Ayer worked with ABCFM colleagues William T. Boutwell and Sherman Hall for a decade, but he decided that they needed more volunteers if they were to have a lasting influence on native residents. So in 1842 he traveled to Oberlin to recruit a fresh missionary contingent. That visit initiated a program wherein twenty Oberlin students devoted part of their lives to Ojibwa missions during the next sixteen years. The first volunteer was David Brainerd Spencer who accompanied Ayer back north in the winter of 1842-1843. They chose sites at Red Lake and Leech Lake because both areas were far away from white influence as well as a safe distance from marauding Sioux to the southwest. Territory around these lakes was the focal point of Oberlin's central contribution to Indian missions. Different stations lasted for varying periods of time, but other locations included Cass Lake, Winnibigosish, and St. Joseph mission on the Pembina River in Dakota Territory.

The new recruits applied for ABCFM funding, but none was forthcoming. Some have suggested that the school's reputation for abolitionist and perfectionist sentiments made the American Commissioners reluctant to subsidize Oberlin graduates. There is no evidence in ABCFM correspondence to substantiate this self-serving interpretation, though the official claim about inadequate funds has a slightly hollow ring to it. Still, the Oberlin people were undaunted and soon organized their own supporting organization, the Western Evangelical Missionary Society. This agency encouraged scores of missionaries to enter Ojibwa country; principal among those were Sela G. Wright, Alonzo Barnard, and John P. Bardwell. Bardwell soon left the mission grounds and traveled through northern states to raise money for his colleagues. In 1848 the American Missionary Association absorbed the more limited Western Evangelical Missionary Society, while Bardwell continued his publicity efforts and eventually collected over fifty thousand dollars for native evangelization.[7] This support provided no more than irregular salaries and meager sup-

---

[6]"Frederick Ayer, Teacher and Missionary to the Ojibway Indians 1829 to 1850," *Collections of the Minnesota Historical Society* 6 (1894): 429, 434-35; see also Frank H. Foster, "The Oberlin Ojibway Mission," *Papers of the Ohio Church History Society* 2 (1892): 1-25.

[7]William E. Bigglestone, "Oberlin College and the Beginning of the Red Lake Mission," *Minnesota History* 45 (1976): 27, 29-30.

plies, though, and local missionaries relied on their own energies to build dwellings and cultivate crops. Their efforts made Minnesota missions the showpiece of Oberlin's chapter in attempts to Christianize and civilize red Americans.

Before inquiring into the particulars of Oberlin's evangelical mission to Indians, we should know something about those people who received so much attention. The Ojibwas were a populous tribe of Algonquian-speaking Indians scattered through the upper Great Lakes region. They were one of the largest groups north of Mexico, but we know little about their size or location at the time of earliest contact. Though originally remote from white explorers, many of them began to locate along important trade routes, especially at Sault Sainte Marie where they were called Saulteur Indians. By the early decades of the eighteenth century Ojibwas began expanding southwestward into Minnesota and Wisconsin; despite Dakota opposition there, they added that section's woodland to their extensive domain. The natives who eventually experienced the impact of nineteenth-century Christian evangelism in Minnesota were relative latecomers to the territory and never passed beyond the line of timber that divides the state into two distinct parts. Overall population estimates for precontact Ojibwas suggest a figure well above 35,000. By the 1840s when Oberlin launched its mission, there were approximately 5,500 "Southwestern Ojibwas" in Minnesota.[8]

The tribal name, *Ojibwa*, means "to roast until puckered up." Some think this refers to the puckered seam on their distinctive moccasins, while others suggest that the word stems from their treatment of enemy captives.[9] Whatever gave rise to the term, Ojibwas were close cultural rel-

---

[8]Robert E. Ritzenthaler, "Southwestern Chippewa," in Bruce G. Trigger, ed., Northeast vol. 15 of the *Handbook of North American Indians*, genl. ed., William C. Sturtevant (Washington DC: Smithsonian Institute, 1978): 743; see also Harold Hickerson, "The Southwestern Chippewa: An Ethnohistorical Study," *Memoirs of the American Anthropological Association* 92 (1962): 12-13; Frances Densmore, *Chippewa Customs*, Bureau of American Ethnology Bulletin no. 86 (Washington DC: U.S. Government Printing Office, 1929) 7.

[9]George I. Quimby, *Indian Life in the Upper Great Lakes, 11,000 B.C. to 1800* (Chicago: University of Chicago Press, 1960) 122-23; see also Erminie Wheeler-Voeglin and Harold Hickerson, *Chippewa Indians I: The Red Lake and Pembina Chippewa* (New York: Garland Publishing Co., 1974) 21; Harold Hickerson, *Chippewa Indians II: Ethnohistory of Mississippi Bands and Pillager and Winnibigosish Bands of Chippewa* (New York: Garland Publishing Co., 1974) 21-26.

atives to Cree Indians in Ontario as well as to Potawatomis and Ottawas around Lakes Superior and Huron. In historic times they formed a loose confederacy with the latter two tribes and sometimes called themselves "The Three Fires" to indicate close affinities. After acquiring tenuous occupation of upper Minnesota, the Ojibwas spread through the territory between Red Lake and the Red River. Their life-style required approximately two square miles per person for adequate sustenance. Accordingly, scattered bands of no more than six hundred people (a maximum of thirty extended families averaging twenty persons each) considered the surrounding twelve hundred square miles theirs to exploit for survival.

Ojibwa territory lay on the periphery of European discovery and penetration, so local native response to successive white presence was relatively untroubled. Those located around the headwaters of the Mississippi River cooperated first with the French for trade goods. After 1763 British tradesmen monopolized the region until the nineteenth century. In 1805 Zebulon Pike's expedition up the Mississippi evidenced another shift of power among whites, and the erection of Fort Snelling in 1819 proved that United States military authority had come to stay. Ojibwas were not seriously affected by any of these events among outsiders.

Precontact life was seminomadic, dependent on an essentially hunting-gathering economy. Natives relied heavily on deer, moose, bear, beaver, and many smaller animals for subsistence. They fished a great deal too, taking principally whitefish and sturgeon with nets and spears during the summer months. In addition to these foodstuffs Ojibwas gathered wild rice that grew in the shallows of innumerable lakes. They also made use of maple sugar in springtime and foraged for berries and nuts in season. It was probably not until after contact times that Ojibwas adopted gardening as a supplement to their dietary mainstays, expanding their economy to include such Indian staples as corn, beans, and squash.[10] In a normal year each Ojibwa band hunted, fished, and gathered wild vegetable foods in an area fifty square miles in every direction from its summer base. During the fall, groups moved to rice shallows and harvested that essential grain and then scattered for the winter. During cold months small groups survived by hunting large furbearing animals. In the spring

---

[10]Ritzenthaler, "Southwestern Chippewa," 744, 746; Hickerson, "Southwestern Chippewa," 10; Densmore, *Chippewa Customs*, 39-40.

they reunited with relatives at sugar camps to take advantage of maple trees in their area. This cyclic activity began again at new summer villages where natives faced another round of feast and famine conditions that were inherent in such an economy.

Ojibwa housing suited a life-style that assumed periodic migration. Natives accustomed to following game and locating near seasonal food supplies had no use for permanent dwellings. They were content instead with wigwams, made from local materials and meant to last for only a few months. Wigwams were usually dome-shaped, built with a circular or oval framework of poles bent and tied at the top. These light frames were covered with strips of birchbark or cattail matting that kept out the elements. Large wigwams could accommodate several families, but the average size held about eight persons.[11] Housing and economy complemented each other, showing that natives had adapted well to their natural environment. The fact that they had no permanent village sites or perennial structures matched a way of living that accepted existence as transitory and uncertain.

Kinship and politics also corresponded to this native life-style. The most important social unit was the clan, an association inherited through one's father that united people across different bands and bestowed a sense of identity beyond the nuclear family. Each clan was thought to have been founded in mythic times by a *totem* (variation, *ototeman*), and these spiritual ancestors protected their blood relatives with special care. Ojibwas recognized about twenty clans that included the crane, loon, bear, marten, and wolf as some of their principal totems. Marriage within these patrilineal clans was strictly forbidden because it constituted incest and angered the totem. Marriage to a partner from any other clan was easily accomplished and normally followed a simple monogamous association. Sometimes a man married two women, usually sisters, and rarely three. Divorce was easy, however, and most natives entered a number of single marriages in series rather than several at once.[12]

---

[11]Ritzenthaler, "Southwestern Chippewa," 748-49; Quimby, *Indian Life*, 124; Densmore, *Chippewa Customs*, 22-28.

[12]Ritzenthaler, "Southwestern Chippewa," 753; Hickerson, "Southwestern Chippewa," 48-52, 88; Quimby, *Indian Life*, 125-26.

Social organization did not extend much beyond patrilineal, exogamous clans. There was no Ojibwa political system except at the village level, and even there it depended heavily on kinship ties. Ecological factors were largely responsible for this absence. Since settlement patterns created widely scattered, autonomous bands of people who shared a common language and culture, the concept of overarching authority hardly existed. Increased trade may have enhanced the stature of some headmen in local bands because whites wished to have one spokesman with whom they could deal all the time. But precontact Ojibwa life did not encourage political consolidation.[13] Even nineteenth-century Minnesota Indians did not substantially modify this particularism. There was rarely a camp circle under one headman, no council of chiefs, no regular military society, no universal law or extensive system for social control. Different bands were free to act as they saw fit, and there were no organizational mechanisms to encourage a wider horizon of consciousness or sense of interdependence.

In keeping with this rather classless egalitarian arrangement, social values laid great stress on individuality and self-reliance. People were not entirely atomistic, thrown simply on the temporary aid they could persuade others to give them.[14] But individuals were largely left to their own resources and such support as clan members might give them. Groups in autonomous bands cooperated for mutual benefit, but they acted expediently rather than from a desire to forge larger social or political interaction. The Ojibwa esteem for stoicism, emotional control, bravery, and resourcefulness outweighed any concern for higher authority or sense of obligation to communal standards. By historic times hunters, warriors, civil, and even religious leaders had learned to function in a cultural orientation that placed private initiative and personal choice over considerations of a wider consensus.

Congruent with this material culture and its social values, Ojibwa religious ceremonies emphasized individual relationships with the supernatural. As with peoples in many other parts of the continent, natives in this region made little distinction between sacred and profane realms. Na-

---

[13]Ritzenthaler, "Southwestern Chippewa," 743; Hickerson, "Southwestern Chippewa," 4.

[14]The prevailing argument, variant opinions, and pertinent bibliography can be found in Hickerson, "Southwestern Chippewa."

ture was permeated with supernatural presence, and each person experienced wills and powers for ill or good as those superior beings chose. Stars and trees, lakes and animals, stones and fish were potential sources of meaning for Ojibwas, who respected them as significant components of their universe. Since these "natural objects" were actually living beings alert to human conduct, natives treated them with ceremonial respect rather than indifference. They paid deference to higher powers in simple rituals associated with lighting fires, hunting animals, smoking pipes, and embarking on journeys. Ojibwas wanted to treat spirit-beings respectfully, and yet their rituals differed widely because personal experiences taught each one what constituted appropriate conduct. The only common denominator was universal agreement that the Indian world was alive with other-than-human persons who expected courteous treatment through appropriate ceremonial gestures.

One of the most effective media for interacting with spirit-beings was visions. People were encouraged throughout their lifetimes to communicate with spirits in this manner, but it was crucial at puberty. Upon entering adolescence especially boys of the tribe were urged to go in quest of a vision. The quester usually fasted in isolation for as many as four days in hope that a spirit-being would reveal itself to him and grant him special knowledge about his purpose in life. After successful contact with supernatural power, usually manifested in some animal form, the youth took a new name and thereafter revered his special animal as a guardian spirit.[15] For the rest of his life it was possible to reestablish contact with that individual spirit and seek protection from other powers or use it to exert a baneful influence on enemies.

Dreams were another widespread medium for communicating with the spirit world. Ojibwas considered sleeping experiences equal to waking events as an avenue to divine-human encounters. As with the more sporadic visionary moments, people could experience the larger world of reality through dreams and thereby learn more about what they should do for a rewarding life.[16] Spirit-beings spoke to humans in this way, and their

---

[15]Ritzenthaler, "Southwestern Chippewa," 751; Densmore, *Chippewa Customs*, 71-72, 78-83.

[16]A. Irving Hallowell, "Ojibwa Ontology, Behavior, and World View," in *Culture in History: Essays in Honor of Paul Radin*, ed. Stanley Diamond (New York: Columbia University Press, 1960) 24-25, 29-30, 40-45.

wishes affected decisions about hunting, warfare, village location, marriages, travel, and alliances. Fundamental aspects of native existence—everything from one's general purpose in life to daily activities—were affected by the messages of the spirit powers.

Individuals who had frequent visions or could interpret other people's dreams were thought to have a special gift, a capacity to move in and out of the spirit world easier than other humans. These persons were called shamans and provided the only institutionalized religious leadership in Ojibwa life. Shamans tried to enhance other people's contact with the spirit world; beyond that they were consulted for interpreting dreams, predicting the future, driving away malevolent powers who caused illness, and directing spiritual forces to afflict adversaries. All of one's life was permeated with divine persons, and each individual treated those beings as his experience led him to consider appropriate. The shamans simply provided an auxiliary means of following divine directives. They differed from normal tribesmen only in degree of religious capacity and by that quantitative margin helped others fulfill the duties all of them felt the spirit-beings required.

The most important religious ceremonies of this region were associated with the Midewiwin or Grand Medicine Lodge. There is a wealth of material related to Midé rituals because the Lodge constitutes the apex of sophisticated Ojibwa rituals. While the date of its origin is still in dispute, the weight of scholarly opinion now tends to view it as a postcontact phenomenon.[17] There is similar uncertainty over the status of Midé officials,[18] but whether shamans or priests, they provided the most exalted leadership and preserved the most esoteric religious lore in Ojibwa culture. On one level the Midé lodge kept alive mythological knowledge of Indian creation; in another frame of reference such tales are seen as a native Exodus story,

---

[17]Harold Hickerson, "Notes on the Post-Contact Origin of the Midewiwin," *Ethnohistory* 9 (1962):418, see also Ritzenthaler, "Southwestern Chippewa," 754-55; Selwyn H. Dewdney, *The Sacred Scrolls of the Southern Ojibway* (Toronto: University of Toronto Press, 1975) 167-74.

[18]There are some speculations that shamanism is associated with hunting-gathering culture while priesthoods develop in agricultural culture. This plausibility corresponds to many aboriginal situations in North America, but the Midewiwin is an anomaly in such schematic reasoning. For a review of these ideas, see H. W. Bowden, *American Indians and Christian Missions: Studies in Cultural Conflict* (Chicago: University of Chicago Press, 1981).

chronicling precontact Ojibwa migrations westward from the salt sea.[19] On a more immediate, behavioral level the semiannual Midé lodges provided an opportunity for shamans to progress through four or eight successive ranks and achieve greater power by learning specific ritual procedures.[20] The most practical expression of this acquired knowledge (recorded in pictographs on birchbark scrolls) was in healing. Midé initiates learned a great deal about herbs and poisons as well as helpful and harmful spirits to aid their religious ministrations. Secret ceremonies even included the practice of "shooting" a *megis* or white shell into other people's bodies and then removing it by mysterious means. Midé officials were thus thought to be able to cause death and bring their victims to life again.[21]

Through life Ojibwas sought to make their private covenants with divine beings. Their daily activities were filled with rituals they considered ceremonially appropriate to powers contacted through visions and dreams. Their individual efforts, aided by attendant shamans and enhanced through Midewiwin solemnities if need be, were enough to sustain native life over the passage of years. When death came, it held no lasting terror because people accepted it as passage to another form of existence. In a final religious ceremony the dead were usually interred in their finest clothes. After a four days' journey into the sky they were thought to join friends and relatives there in a new village. Just as life had been fraught with passing anxieties, this last transition had its dangers too. The recently dead had to cross a stream by means of a quaking log, which in reality was a water monster. However, giving it tobacco and addressing it politely were enough to appease the demon, and the departed could then continue his journey to final rest.[22] As with most native Amer-

---

[19]Walter Hoffman, "The Midewiwin or 'Grand Medicine Society' of the Ojibwa," *Seventh Annual Report of the Bureau of Ethnology, 1885-86* (1891): 165; William A. Warren, "History of the Ojibways, Based upon Traditions and Oral Statements," *Collections of the Minnesota Historical Society* 5 (1885): 78-81.

[20]See Hoffman, "Midewiwin," 189-274, for description of four degrees; see Densmore, *Chippewa Customs*, 86-94 for eight.

[21]Ruth Landes, *Ojibwa Religion and the Midewiwin* (Madison: University of Wisconsin Press, 1968) 116-29, 144-67; see also Densmore, *Chippewa Customs*, 86-94.

[22]Ritzenthaler, "Southwestern Chippewa," 752.

ican conceptions of the afterlife, Ojibwas thought that all their people would be reunited beyond the grave. They did not conceive of an unpleasant place where the wicked would be punished in contrast to another place of rewards for the good. Everyone was thought to thrive in the afterworld as all had contributed to cultural vitality on this level of existence.

Personal experience was the most fruitful source of religious ideas among the Ojibwas, just as it gave rise to the bulk of their ritual practices. Their world view included great numbers of spirit-beings who populated the universe, making it impossible to entertain any concept of impersonal natural forces.[23] Their general word for divine power was *manito* (local variation, *manido*), and the innumerable manito k who inhabited animals, birds, rocks, trees, earth, sky, and water made religious variation rich and deeply personal. But despite the fact that unseen powers and their physical manifestations dominated individual lives, Ojibwas also recognized a loose hierarchy of divine beings. The paramount spirit was called Kicci Manito (Kitshi Manido), who may owe some of his prominence to Christian influence. It is impossible to depict early Ojibwa religious ideas with any certainty because of the people's physical isolation. Their primary concern for practical ceremonial action also tended to de-emphasize any need for "systematic theology" as did their respect for individual preferences in religious expression.

However, it seems that Dzhe Manito ranked alongside or slightly beneath Kicci Manito. He too was benevolent to mankind and functioned as patron of the Midewiwin. These positive forces were matched by two fearful ones. Animiki was the Thunder God who exhibited his awesome power in storms and commanded respect as an overwhelming malevolent presence whom the Ojibwas had to placate. Dzhibai Manito was the Shadow or Ghost Spirit whose realm of the dead eventually influenced all natives and evoked dread among them.[24] In addition to these personalities, Ojibwas looked positively to the sun, moon, and four winds as helpful spirits who sustained their style of living. Conversely, they feared a

---

[23]Hallowell, "Ojibwa Ontology," 45, expresses it this way: "The central goal of life is . . . longevity, health and freedom from misfortune. This goal cannot be achieved without the effective help and cooperation of *both* human and other-than-human 'persons' as well as by one's own efforts."

[24]Hoffman, "Midewiwin," 163; Ritzenthaler, "Southwestern Chippewa," 754.

great number of malicious spirits who contrived to bring about native misfortune. Ghosts, witches, and water monsters lurked everywhere to wreak ruin if they could, especially the cannibalistic giant, Windigo, who stalked the winter woods to catch and devour victims. Ojibwas almost always attributed hunger, sickness, failure, bad weather, and insanity to these dark beings who affected life as much as the helpful gods.[25]

Coupled with this loose grouping of spiritual powers, Ojibwa religious thought also included a culture hero figure who had helped influence local living conditions. Apparently natives did not ask many questions about general creation, nor did they develop their ideas into elaborate creation myths. Most recorded stories of that sort have a recent, derivative flavor.[26] The culture hero, Nanabozho (local variation, Winabojo), was more important to them because he embodied down-to-earth qualities the people could understand, and he dealt with details of life as the Indians knew it. Nanabozho was thought to be responsible for practical gifts such as fire, edged weapons, hunting techniques, canoe design, and the like. Occasionally in a mischievous mood or by well-intentioned bungling, he also caused some of the difficult conditions natives had to endure.[27]

All in all, Ojibwa life constituted a workable blend of spirituality and practical skill in coping with the natural world. The people's ethos—their economy, housing, kinship relations, political organization, and social values—formed a congruent whole with their world view—those ideas and beliefs that explained reality in satisfactory fashion. Their chosen habits confirmed that their interpretation of the universe was true; their ideas about people and deities, nature and society, sanctioned practical behavior that proved realistic. Ojibwas had flourished for centuries with an integrated world view and ethos. Their successful adjustment to local conditions did not lead them to anticipate or prepare adequately for Christian missionaries when they came unbidden to Minnesota.

Ojibwas and Oberlinians embodied contrasting attitudes toward life and its opportunities. Indians accepted given conditions and adapted to

---

[25]Landes, *Ojibwa Religion*, 21-22.

[26]See, for example, a version recorded in 1930 in Landes, *Ojibwa Religion*, 89-95.

[27]Hoffman, "Midewiwin," 166-67, 175-77; Dewdney, *Sacred Scrolls*, 40-41.

them as best they could. Missionaries regarded present circumstances as a challenge to improve things according to traditional Christian ideals. To show how much Oberlin emphasized this ideal, in 1839 its college students vowed they would "prize nothing more highly than the elevation of humanity." The faculty endorsed that evangelical aspiration and to that end urged

> economy, frugality, industry, and self-denial . . . the hearty recognition of equal human rights as belonging to all whom God has made in his own image; a deep sympathy with the oppressed of every color . . . and finally this paramount principle, that the cultivation of the moral feelings is the first of all objects in education, Gospel love to God and man, the first of all acquisitions. . . .[28]

Fired with such lofty sentiments, Oberlin's missionary vanguard left Ohio in the summer of 1843, traveling by schooner to the head of Lake Superior. In addition to Ayer, Spencer, Barnard, and Wright mentioned above, the first contingent also included Peter O. Johnson and William Lewis, M.D., with enough wives to raise the total to ten persons.[29] After leaving the large trading post at La Pointe, they found travel so difficult it took them forty-two days to reach Red Lake. But on 7 October 1843 two missions began in earnest.

Four missionaries settled at Leech Lake while the other six resumed tasks already under way at Red Lake. Since winter was fast approaching, their first concern was to provide shelter and food. Cold weather ended construction of a log house when it was half-finished, and the Easterners had to be satisfied that first winter with a half-cabin joined to a frame covered with elm bark. They were able to purchase enough corn, potatoes, and fish from the Indians to survive until spring. Though spartan, the supplies were welcome:

> during the first six weeks of our being at Red Lake our diet and mode of cooking was after the most approved method of the Grahamites, not willingly, as we had not a particle of salt or grease of any kind. The vegetables

---

[28]Fletcher, *History of Oberlin College*, 1:231.

[29]Sela G. Wright, "Some Reminiscences of the Early Oberlin Missionaries and their Work in Northwestern Minnesota," 3. This was dictated by Rev. Wright at Oberlin, Ohio in 1890 and later typewritten from manuscript and stenographer's notes. The copy cited was loaned to the Minnesota Historical Society in 1920.

were boiled in clear water and we ate our fish without salt. During all this time not a word of complaint was heard; all were happy and content in the work. We had three condiments to make our homely fare relishable—a contented mind, earnest devotion to the work and a keen appetite.[30]

After these initial struggles at least ten more Oberlin evangelists arrived over the years to swell the missionary effort. Some of them stayed longer than others, but each gave himself to the work as needed. In trying to sum up their total contribution, the oldest and most experienced missionary recalled in a later decade that they contributed an aggregate of 135 years to evangelism. Women's work at the various stations counted as an additional sum.[31]

Missionary perceptions of the Ojibwas remained fairly constant over the years. Of course most generalizations about Indians reflected White Anglo-Saxon Protestant values, but their obvious disapproval of native preferences gave a somber undertone to red-white interaction. Even before the Oberlinians arrived, ABCFM missioner William Boutwell reported his negative appraisal: "At present there is among them nothing like personal rights, or individual property. . . ." Leaving no doubt as to his resolve in the matter, he noted, "It will require much patience, if not a long time, to break up and eradicate habits so inveterate."[32] The newcomers embodied similar cultural conditioning and echoed the same responses, mixing pity with disdain. As missionaries, by definition they arrived on the scene presuming that there was a need for their presence. As one evangelist put it, they had come "to commence an offensive war upon this citadel of the Prince of Darkness."[33] Since their attitude was so uniformly condemnatory, one wonders how much warmth occasionally leavened the missionaries' stern reaction to native customs.

---

[30]Ibid., 30.

[31]Letter from Sela Wright to Joseph Gilfillan, 20 October 1900; Joseph A. Gilfillan Papers, Minnesota Historical Society (hereafter cited as MHS). All italics, spelling, punctuation, and capitalization contained in the original manuscripts.

[32]Cited in Harold Hickerson, "William T. Boutwell of the American Board and the Pillager Chippewa: The History of a Failure," *Ethnohistory* 12 (1965): 5-6.

[33]Letter from William Lewis to Joshua Blanchard, 22 January 1845, William Lewis Papers, MHS.

When the Minnesota missionaries wrote to friends in Ohio, they included candid descriptions of prospective converts. One of the more articulate of them said:

> These Indians, it seems to me, are the perfection of Heathenism. The women are perfect slaves to the men, and are capable of enduring the greatest labor, almost the greatest imaginable. . . . The poverty of these people is beyond description, their clothing is oftentimes a mere shadow, and *many* of them are now without any [illegible] of food not even enough for a single meal; . . . They are noted for *thievery*, and no wonder if they are so poor, we expect much difficulty in consequence of their stealing. They are extremely filthy very few if any of them wash a shirt, after it is put on it stays there until worn out.[34]

The following year he had not softened his opinion; further acquaintance with their hunting-gathering economy only confirmed his view that the native way of living was unacceptable:

> The Indians here [Leech Lake] are called Pillagers and well they deserve the name. They seem to be all thieves of the worst stamp. The class is quite large, and one in greater need of missionary influence than any in the Territory. Although their Lake abounds with excellent fish and Rice is verry [*sic*] abundant throughout this whole region, still these Indians are starving one fourth of the year. They do very little in agriculture though they have excellent land around the Lake. . . . We shall make it our object to settle them down upon the soil as fast as we can have the means of doing it.[35]

The wife of a missionary expressed herself more gently, but the same abhorrence joined to compassion appears in her letters. She often referred to Indians as "miserable beings" who scarcely knew enough to understand their plight. Her sympathetic reports on people who were "indeed miserable looking objects" seemed all the more convincing because Indian culture lacked the comforts provided by white men's technology. Whether dire need made them steal, or their concept of sharing allowed them to take unwatched goods, they seemed altogether "a lazy thievish

---

[34]Letter from William Lewis to James R. Wright, 10 January 1844, William Lewis Papers, MHS.

[35]Letter from William Lewis to Joshua Blanchard, 22 January 1845, William Lewis Papers, MHS.

set."[36] This kindly lady believed that some improvement was possible, but in asking for support she left no doubt as to the difficulties they faced:

> let me earnestly request your sympathy and prayers for this poor degraded people. Would that I could set before you their wretchedness but language would fail to give an adequate description. I might say that from their indolence they often suffer from cold, hunger, nakedness; that they live in miserable huts, filthy & smoky. But the darkness of their minds remains untold the deep seated corruption, the entire selfishness, the utter indifference to all that relates to spiritual things. Such is their gross sensuality that it seems sometimes that an idea above eating was beyond their comprehension.[37]

On the other side of the coin, what did the Indians think of these intruders? Even though we have no direct evidence of their response, white observers recorded attitudes correspondingly negative. Just as whites considered natives to be squalid, shiftless, and degenerate, Indians generally harbored a bad opinion of whites too. One missionary looking back at his experience recalled that the Ojibwas "at first had not one particle of confidence in a white man. They believed that the whites were very wise, very strong, but very deceitful and dishonest, great liars, and ought not to be trusted by Indians." It was only through scrupulous fair-dealing that the missionaries slowly counteracted this general perception. Honest measures in trade as well as quiet self-control eventually demonstrated that Oberlinians were different from the average sort of white person whom Indians had encountered. Suspicions and a measure of distrust never entirely faded away, no matter how much kindness the evangelists manifested, but the Indians did relent a little. "They as readily comprehend character as a white man," the Red Lake preacher allowed, "and . . . gradually came to fully admit that while the white man in general was just what they supposed him to be, a finished rascal, . . . the missionaries were real exceptions."[38] After practical experience proved reliable, Ojibwas were willing to modify their overall impression and accept the evangelists' good intentions.

---

[36]Letter from Lucy Lewis to James R. Wright, 29 May 1844, William Lewis Papers, MHS.

[37]Ibid., 15 May 1846.

[38]Wright, "Reminiscences," 20-21.

Winning over natives with goodwill was an essential element in the missionary program. This benevolent spirit also extended to whites from other denominations engaged in the same work. Missionaries on the Minnesota frontier displayed an ecumenical acceptance of all persons who sought to spread the gospel. Oberlinians recorded several instances of receiving help and encouragement from other missionaries in the region. After mentioning favors from Baptists and Methodists who faced the same difficulties they did, one evangelist's wife reflected that "where heathenism presents its brazen front, other isms are, or should be, merged into one phalanx to oppose the common enemy."[39] Several years later this devout woman penned an appeal for ecumenical cooperation that has echoed through generations of missionaries around the world:

> When we see the heathen around us perishing for the bread of life and hear them calling from one little settlement & another, our souls cry out why cannot christians lay aside their little jealousies and enter heart and hand into this work. Were this the case, were the whole energy of the church thrown into this and the other great reforms of the day, how soon would the wilderness bud & blossom as the rose, and the car of salvation roll through the entire circumference of this sin ruined globe.[40]

This camaraderie in shared objectives did not extend to Catholics, however. The missionaries' references to them always singled out behavior that confirmed an inbred prejudice. Many traders, voyageurs, and half-breeds represented the lasting effects of French Catholicism in the area; Evangelicals noted that "there are many of this class . . . in this country and their influence is very bad." Catholics had "a withering effect" on mission work, refusing to allow wives or children to hear sermons or attend school. In fact, one Catholic at La Pointe had reportedly told Indians "to mind the [Oberlin] missionaries no more than they would the barking of dogs."[41] But this traditional enmity aside, Protestant missions on the frontier pooled their interests and enjoyed friendly acceptance among denominations to accomplish good in a common endeavor.

---

[39]Letter from Lucy Lewis to James R. Wright, 26 October 1843, William Lewis Papers, MHS.

[40]Ibid., 26 August 1847.

[41]Ibid., 15 May 1846.

How did these agents of the Second Great Awakening define their task and plan to accomplish it? What changes did they hope to foster and how discern the marks of salvation? Putting the whole enterprise in a nutshell, one evangelist explained, "We are missionaries living among the people only to do them good. We would love to teach you . . . how to be good and happy, and how to go to Heaven when you die."[42] Part of the difficulty from the start, of course, was to convince Ojibwas that they needed salvation. The traditional native world view did not distinguish between good and evil in an eternal sense, only between helpful and harmful acts in functional terms. So missionaries found it necessary to dwell on sin and to convince natives of their woeful state before saving them from it.[43] All preachers recognized the difficulty of persuading self-sufficient natives of their lost condition before offering Christ as their Savior. Persistence on this theme was a constant in their message, and not without appeals that grace might aid their effort:

> They know that they are ignorant, & for this reason [stay?] quite backward in expressing their ideas about God, a future state &c. We hope to yet see them an intelligent & happy people. We are aware, however, that increasing labor, accompanied by the blessing of the Lord must be bestowed on them before this will be accomplished. The church at home too, must lend a helping hand. We trust they will, and that their prayers also will ascend to God for us.[44]

But what was the best method of spreading this gospel and convincing Indians of their need? Oberlinians determined to exemplify the virtues of Christianity among natives and thus demonstrate by contrast how white values based on true religion were better than Indian beliefs and customs.

---

[42]Wright, "Reminiscences," 45.

[43]Robert F. Berkhofer, Jr., *Salvation and the Savage: An Analysis of Protestant Missions and American Indian Response, 1787-1862* (Lexington: University of Kentucky Press, 1965; New York: Atheneum, 1972), demonstrates how the Second Great Awakening atmosphere depended heavily on a sense of sinfulness to produce repentance and redemption. He cites Sherman Hall, an ABCFM missionary to the Ojibwas who arrived earlier than the Oberlinians. On page 54 Hall is quoted as reporting that even converted church members "have never manifested such pungent convictions of sin as I have desired to see, though I have taken much pains to instruct them correctly with regard to the nature of sin."

[44]Letter from Elizabeth Ayer to Mrs. Hemford, February 1844, William Lewis Papers, MHS.

To this end they threw themselves into construction work and farming. After clearing land, building houses, and plowing ground for their own needs, they offered to do the same for any Ojibwa who asked for help. One missionary said they were "anxious to give the indians an example of the benefits of labor," but on a practical level they also wanted to relieve their economic distress and discontinue their roving search for food.[45] Another pragmatic spokesman explained their combination of material aid and spiritual counseling in this manner:

> The people seem to have no desire for knowledge but would be very glad if we could feed them when hungry; and unless we can do this to some extent and improve their outward condition there is little hope I think of their being affected by the efforts we may make to convert them.[46]

Despite the altruistic tone of this approach, their policy retained a touch of Yankee shrewdness too. One commentator with long experience in the field acknowledged, "We do not wish to give to the Indians while they live in idleness." This would perpetuate bad habits. "But when an Indian expresses a desire to become industrious, & wants to work for some necessary article, we want to be able to encourage him . . . to see their wooden hoes exchanged for metal ones, and their tattered garments of rabbit skins for something comfortable & comely."[47] The Protestant work ethic seemed as compatible with Arminian theology as with Puritanism.

If natives responded favorably to the temporal and eternal benefits of Christian living, Oberlin missionaries did not welcome them prematurely into the church. They insisted that Indians accept both a new doctrinal point of view and a radically different life-style before they could be considered Christians. Instead of offering baptism to natives who embraced the new beliefs, then taking care to foster Christian conduct in subsequent years, Oberlinians insisted on proofs of full conversion before bestowing that ordinance. Only after an Ojibwa turned from the old

---

[45]Wright, "Reminiscences," 15, 18; see also letter from Sela Wright to Joseph Gilfillan, 28 October 1901, Joseph A. Gilfillan Papers, MHS.

[46]Letter from William Lewis to James R. Wright, 10 January 1844, William Lewis Papers, MHS.

[47]Letter from Elizabeth Ayer to Mrs. Hemford, February 1844, William Lewis Papers, MHS.

Adam and his wicked deeds and put on the new man through Christ, thus demonstrating that he truly lived the gospel, was he "considered a proper subject to be received into the Congregational Church."[48] So in the deliberate policy of these missionaries, understanding had to produce conviction and repentance; only unswerving moral reform could prove the efficacy of conversion. Many Ojibwas heard the plan of salvation and expressed interest in it, but only those who evidenced a sincere application of Christian ideas in their daily lives were acknowledged as new citizens in God's kingdom.

Oberlin missionaries delivered their brand of the gospel by more conventional methods too. A modest resident summarized the bulk of evangelical work this way: "Teaching, preaching & visiting are prominent means for endeavoring to elevate this degraded people. We trust some precious fruits of these labors will remain through eternity."[49] Four of the men learned to speak Ojibwa and preached quite often.[50] Looking back on the whole enterprise, evangelists agreed that Frederick Ayer set the pace for all of them, visiting wigwams and preaching at many firesides as well as in public meetings. There is no evidence to suggest that Oberlin missionaries used the full panoply of "new measures" popularized by Finney in nineteenth-century revivals, but we may confidently assume

---

[48]Wright, "Reminiscences," 32-33, 22-23.

[49]Letter from Lucy Wright to James R. Wright, 15 May 1846, William Lewis Papers, MHS.

[50]The four Oberlinians were S. G. Wright, A. Barnard, F. Spees, and J. S. Fisher; see letter from Sela Wright to Joseph Gilfillan, 20 October 1900, Joseph A. Gilfillan Papers, MHS. Since many missionaries complained that Indians were incapable of understanding Christian concepts because their language was inadequate, it is worth quoting Wright on this subject. In his "Reminiscences," 19-20, he observed that whites

had supposed that the indian conveyed his ideas partly by simple words and partly by signs. They had read this in books before they went into the country; but they found instead that the indian language is very copious, abounding in words and phrases wherewith they can communicate all their ideas and wherewith the missionary can preach the gospel completely, there being no lack of words to explain the Moral law in all its length and breadth. The language abounds in words whereby may be expressed the highest state of virtue or the lowest state of vice; the highest state of happiness or the lowest state of misery. The character of God as described in the bible may be fully set forth in this language. The missionary can discourse freely on all the ties of friendship, the duties of parents and children, husband and wife, neighbor or citizen.

that they emphasized individual responsibility in deciding to accept or reject the Christian message as well as its cultural packaging.

Besides preaching and personal counseling, setting a good example and expecting native conformity, the missionaries also established schools. The earliest classes met in a cedar-bark hut and then moved into a log house when completed. The original plan was to teach young Indians how to read and write in their native tongue, but that was modified in later years. In an attempt to prepare Indians for coping with an environment increasingly dominated by whites, the missionaries tried to help them master English, with Ojibwa surviving only in the New Testament and a hymnal.[51] As with most missions among different tribes across the country, preaching a strange gospel and using schools to inculcate unfamiliar habits did not result in widespread native enthusiasm. Though responses were mixed and converts in Minnesota few, one early mission report captured both its methods and hopes:

> The prospects of the Brethren at Red Lake are very encouraging; the Indians are beginning to build houses & settle down. Last year their crops of corn were larger and better than ever before, some families raised 100 bushels. They are sending their children to school, and the place of meeting is crowded with hearers on the sabbath. It is hardly two years since this mission commenced.[52]

With these methods and rigorous expectations the Oberlinians carried out their duties from year to year. But they never expressed any sense of urgency in their mission. This attitude may have been due to sober recognition of the fact that it would take a long time to wean natives away from a deeply entrenched life-style. It may be attributed to a conviction that missionaries were doing everything they could. If more conversions oc-

---

[51]Wright, "Reminiscences," 20. It is worth noting that the decision about changing to English instruction followed earlier policy laid down by the ABCFM. In 1816 the prudential board declared its intention of influencing native children to become "English in their language, civilized in their habits, and Christian in their religion. Assimilated in language, they will more readily become assimilated in habits and manners to their white neighbors; intercourse will be easy and the advantages to them incalculable." Cited in Clifton J. Phillips, *Protestant America and the Pagan World: The First Half Century of the American Board of Commissioners for Foreign Missions, 1810-1860* (Cambridge: Harvard University Press, 1969) 65.

[52]Letter from William Lewis to Joshua Blanchard, 22 January 1845, William Lewis Papers, MHS.

curred at a faster rate, it would have to be the Lord's doing. In all the letters written from Minnesota and in retrospectives of their efforts there, millennial expectancy is not mentioned a single time. There are not even indirect hints that Oberlinians accelerated their activities because Judgment Day was near or that they took heart in adding to God's new kingdom as it was gradually realized on earth. The millennialist theme is missing in this mission's surviving evidence. We find instead a rather trustful attitude regarding the outcome of evangelical witness. For example, one missionary's wife reported that an Indian child was sick at a nearby settlement. There the shamans were trying their best to restore health, to no avail. In an almost complacent mood the correspondent hoped that their failure would prove them frauds and thus turn Indians to the true Great Physician.[53] This lack of urgency resonates through many letters and reveals an almost fatalistic acquiescence in future developments. Not remiss in zeal, but patient until genuine reform occurred, another writer spoke of conversions: "The refreshing we have enjoyed here has been precious, though not a large number have come out from among the heathen, still there are fruits which we trust will be gathered into the garner of our Lord."[54]

Fruits of the mission ripened slowly, and when they appeared, evangelists were pleased by their quality rather than their number. In early 1846, after more than two years of effort, "the spirit was poured out and some souls we trust turned from the follow of heathenism." One male Ojibwa turned to Christianity after the death of his child. Refusing native burial rites, he requested a church funeral for his infant and thereafter led several kinsmen into the more settled ways of evangelical piety. By March of that year those shared experiences qualified ten natives for church membership.[55] Another notable example featured an old woman "who had been a notorious heathen and a drunkard." At the time of her spiritual crisis God seemed to be affecting many people, "sanctifying the truth to

[53]Letter from Cornelia Spencer to Diantha Leonard, 12 January 1849, James P. Schell Papers, MHS.

[54]Letter from Lucy Lewis to Lyman Burrell, 22 February 1844, William Lewis Papers, MHS.

[55]Letter from Lucy Lewis to James R. Wright, 15 May 1846, William Lewis Papers, MHS.

many hearts." Though most natives postponed a final decision, the old woman made a positive one. The personal transformation of her character and its happy consequences epitomized evangelical objectives:

> She came clear out renounced all that was heathenish and sought & found forgiveness . . . and great joy—she died a *triumphant* death about 4 years after. We received I believe 15 into the church and . . . I never saw any where such examples of *faith* and *Christian love* such *manifest* evidence as we saw in these converts of a radical change. . . .[56]

Considering Ojibwa population as a whole, the number of conversions was not large, but the fact that some natives embraced new standards encouraged missionaries to anticipate more as time went on.

Tangible evidence of conversions heartened missionaries too. They proudly noted that more and more natives were willing to accept a settled way of life. Instead of scorning labor as "women's work," men seemed increasingly interested in clearing land and cultivating it. Besides accommodating to manual labor, Ojibwas also adopted more sensible clothing and followed Oberlinian advice about "civilized methods of dress."[57] Natives showed themselves amenable to the missionaries' strong emphasis on Sabbath observance as well. Both red and white Christians took this aspect of proper behavior quite seriously, and the few violations that occurred were the cause of stern object lessons and tearful repentance.[58] Education was another sphere where evangelical efforts began to reap benefits. At the high point of this mild native revival, one report observed approvingly that:

> The school embraces most of the children near about twenty in winter. Several can read their own language well and write. They are now making good proficiency in english. They are fond of singing & learn hymns readily.[59]

So in addition to statements of belief and trimphant deaths, Ojibwa con-

---

[56]Letter from Sela Wright to Joseph Gilfillan, 28 October 1901, Joseph A. Gilfillan Papers, MHS.

[57]Wright, "Reminiscences," 16-17.

[58]Letter from Lucy Lewis to James R. Wright, 15 May 1856, William Lewis Papers, MHS.

[59]Ibid.

verts exhibited a change of heart by embracing agriculture, Western dress, Sabbath observance, and literacy. They seemed well on the way to exchanging their culture for white values and patterns—an end the missionaries had implicitly sought all along.

Skeptics might ask if natives, without relinquishing traditional beliefs, accepted white standards just for material advantage. In some instances this might have been the case, but in a few examples we can see that the extent of conversion was thorough indeed. Keep in mind that the traditional Ojibwa regard for personal experience made individual preferences the final arbiter in religious choices. Remember too that world view and ethos must form an integrated whole in most instances. So when changes occur in one area, it is not surprising to see adjustments in the other, forming at length a new congruence where beliefs and actions are consistent again.

Evangelists proudly recalled some outstanding fruits of their mission. One man named Kayzheash had turned from gambling and drinking to an earnest Christian life. After years of misguided habits he became a blacksmith and displayed exemplary signs of complete reformation. Kayzheash attended prayer meetings punctually, listened closely to instruction, raised his family under Christian precepts, and read his Ojibwa testament regularly.[60] In church, home, and work he showed other tribesmen that the new way of life had virtues unattainable through traditional means. Another native convert provided a briefer but more saintly example. This young woman, named Hannah at baptism, turned from village squalor to the well-scrubbed piety so highly prized among Oberlinians. But more important than outward appearances, "She was very prayerful, very earnest in her efforts for the spiritual good of others. From the day of her conversion to her death a few years afterwards no one supposed that she had ever backslidden at all, but rather seemed, from the start to grow in grace, daily." Hannah was the model convert in showing modest deportment and spiritual accomplishment. Her bright example was long remembered as "a burning light among the heathen and a joy to the missionaries."[61]

---

[60]Wright, "Reminiscences," 34-35.

[61]Ibid., 36; see also letter from Sela Wright to Joseph Gilfillan, 28 October 1901, Joseph A. Gilfillan Papers, MHS.

In less than two decades, though, Oberlin missionaries discontinued their collective effort. Some moved back east, others went to overseas posts, while a few remained in Minnesota as government agents or tradesmen and farmers. After 1859 the Episcopal church began missions among the Ojibwas and worked among them on a more sustained basis. Interestingly enough, Henry B. Whipple, first bishop of Minnesota who assumed his post that year, had studied at Oberlin in 1838 and 1839. His uncle, George Whipple, had moved from Lane Seminary to Oberlin in the early days to complete his education and then remained as professor of mathematics and natural philosophy. He also served as secretary of the American Missionary Association from 1846 to 1876. So in a tenuous and indirect sense Bishop Whipple can be said to have continued Oberlin's work among the Ojibwa, albeit in a less clearly evangelical vein.[62]

Oberlinians themselves mentioned causes for such disappointing results of their efforts. One obstacle cited was the wild country itself that forced whites to spend much time on secular pursuits for their own survival instead of concentrating exclusively on Indian needs. They found the Ojibwas prejudiced against them too, indisposed to trust whites in general or to believe that some wanted to help natives. Traders had unfortunately acquainted Indians with whiskey, and that debilitating item often thwarted gospel influence. Ojibwas were also distracted by warfare; quite often when mission hopes rose, rumors of a Dakota raid or an invitation to attack that traditional enemy would disrupt camps and divert people's attention from spiritual concerns. Finally, Oberlinians had to admit that they did not recieve enough support from the larger evangelical community back east. They realized that Indians did not rank high on the list of causes appealing for church support.[63] After sixteen years of labor with no salary and meager supplies, with a few conversions and no hope of establishing a native branch of the church, Oberlin missions disbanded with regrets and what must have amounted to feelings of abandonment.

---

[62]In retrospect the Oberlin missionaries resented Whipple's public reports that implied he started Ojibwa missions. Sela Wright criticized the bishop's ingratitude and poor historical sense several times; see, for example, his letters to Joseph Gilfillan, 10 October 1900 and 28 October 1901, Joseph A. Gilfillan Papers, MHS.

[63]Wright, "Reminiscences," 25-26, 42, 48. Fletcher, *History of Oberlin College* 1:219, reproduces a similar list of reasons in what appears to have been a shallow and derivative summary.

There were other factors at work besides those mentioned in the missionaries' own reflections. One was the rigorous demands Oberlinians made on natives. It was not easy to leave a roving life in forests inhabited by many gods and adopt instead agricultural patterns where a single deity expected hard work, literacy, and thrift. The missionaries made it no easier by just being there, exemplifying what Indians could accomplish. Whites saw conversion as an act of will which anyone could make, and hence available if Indians wanted salvation sincerely enough. And in expecting Ojibwas to accept such a manifestly superior religion with its beneficial life-style, evangelists did not compromise on what salvation included. Their exacting demands for thorough change made many natives hesitate to attempt living by impossibly high standards. Missionaries knew they could baptize Indians inclined toward Christianity, but they insisted that "credible evidence of a radical change of heart is always a prerequisite, is indispensible qualification, to entrance to the christian church."[64] Oberlinians went to Minnesota to acquaint Indians with what the gospel required; they did not build many bridges to facilitate change in native thinking or behavior. They reversed the Macedonian Call by standing on their own side of acculturated religion and inviting Indians to come over by their own efforts and help themselves to Christianity.

In a more general perspective, physical factors militated against the mission too. Land was always a problem because the Indians considered it theirs, and missionaries moved onto it without permission. Oberlinians may have thought their houses and farms were models of Christian civilization that would cause Indians to recognize inherent benefits. But Ojibwas more often resented the fact that whites settled on their land and used it for private purposes. They regarded missionaries as intruders and did not scruple to appropriate livestock and the produce growing on land that was theirs in the first place. White remonstrance at such "thievery" only exacerbated misunderstanding and made the concept of private property difficult to appreciate. This same resentment at uninvited whites also lay behind Ojibwa reluctance to attend church services and grammar schools.[65]

---

[64]Letter from Sela Wright to Joseph Gilfillan, 28 October 1901, Joseph A. Gilfillan Papers, MHS.

[65]Bigglestone, "Oberlin College and . . . Red Lake Missions," 36, where he also mentions isolation, cholera, floods, loneliness, travel hardships, mosquitoes, and brutal winters. See also Hickerson, "William T. Boutwell," 21.

Once begun, however, white immigration became overwhelming. In the last analysis Ojibwa missions were swept away by the tremendous wave of white population that flooded into the region. When Minnesota reached territorial status in 1849, whites numbered around 4,000. A year later 6,077 whites lived there according to United States census. But immigration rose dramatically after that, and within four years an estimated 140,000 whites had settled in Minnesota; another 10,000 arrived by 1857. Statehood was granted the following year, and the federal census of 1860 counted 172,023 whites on the land that Dakotas and Ojibwas had owned a scant three decades earlier.[66] But by that time the mission had been discontinued. The question of Ojibwa survival in face of white dominance was more insistent than ever, but Oberlinians were no longer there to guide their native friends.

In retrospect we cannot say that the Oberlin mission was successful by any empirical standard. Undoubtedly there were some natives who accepted Christian beliefs and adjusted their lives to its behavioral standards. In a strictly religious sense, souls might have been saved, and that is justification enough for years of missionary dedication. But deciding who is saved or not lies beyond the mundane capabilities of a historian, and leaving that significant question to higher authority, he must confine his judgment to lesser matters. Looking at this evangelical mission from the perspective of cultural interaction, it is fair to conclude that Oberlinians did not affect the lives of many Ojibwas. Their converts were not numerous, and there seems to have been no gathering momentum that could have promised more. Missionaries did not try to integrate Christian truths with native thought patterns, symbols, or customs. They did not organize an Indian church or develop native leadership to provide for it in later generations. Perhaps that might have come in time, but the effort was terminated before it could happen. Minnesota became a state, warranted by its huge white population, and the Oberlinians ended their work a year later because conditions had progressed to a point where they could no longer witness effectively.

----

[66]Theodore C. Blegen, *Minnesota: A History of the State* (Minneapolis: University of Minnesota Press, 1963) 153, 173, 175; see also Gardinal Goodwin, *The Trans-Mississippi West (1803-1853): A History of its Acquisition and Settlement* (New York: D. Appleton and Co., 1924) 273.

So the evangelical energy that affected national life in the early republic influenced native American missions to a minimal degree. It caused men and women to dedicate their lives to sharing with others the same religious joy they had acquired. But it did not lead to new approaches or attitudes vis à vis differing cultures nor did Evangelicalism create psychological conditions wherein conversions could occur more easily. In this example of missionary work derived from the Second Great Awakening, nothing was done better or with more zeal than similar activities fostered by Protestants and Catholics before revivalism became widespread in America. Evangelical enthusiasm was no detriment to native American missions, but all that can be said finally is that it added weight to procedures already in place rather than turning them in new directions.

Chapter 6

The Black Experience
in American Evangelicalism:
The Meaning of Slavery

Albert J. Raboteau

God is no respecter of persons, but in every nation, he that feareth God and worketh
righteousness is accepted of Him.
—Acts 10:34-35.

There is neither Jew nor Greek, there is neither slave nor free, there is neither male nor
female; for ye are all one in Christ Jesus.
—Galatians 3:28.

Princes shall come out of Egypt; Ethiopia shall soon stretch out her hands unto God.
—Psalms 68:31

Late in the eighteenth century, black Americans, slave and free, Southern and Northern, began to convert to Christianity in larger numbers than ever before. The type of Christianity that they joined and continued to join in mounting numbers during the next century was experiential, revivalistic, and biblically oriented. That is, it placed heavy stress upon the necessity of an inward conversion experience for Christian salvation; it institutionalized the revival as a means of converting sinners, extending church membership, and reforming society; and finally, it read the Bible literally and interpreted the destiny of America accordingly.

Black Evangelicals, no less than whites, sought conversion, attended revivals, and viewed their lives in biblical terms. There was a fundamental difference between the two, however. American slavery and the doctrine of white supremacy, which rationalized and outlived it, not only segregated evangelical congregations along racial lines, but also differentiated the black experience of evangelical Christianity from that of whites. The existence of chattel slavery in a nation that claimed to be Christian, and the use of Christianity to justify enslavement, confronted black Evangelicals with a basic dilemma, which may be most clearly formulated in two questions: what meaning did Christianity, if it were a white man's religion, as it seemed, have for blacks; and why did the Christian God, if he were just as claimed, permit blacks to suffer so? In struggling to answer these questions, a significant number of Afro-Americans developed a distinctive evangelical tradition in which they established meaning and identity for themselves as individuals and as a people. Simultaneously, they made an indispensable contribution to the development of American Evangelicalism. If evangelical Protestantism has formed a major part of the cultural history of Afro-Americans, from the beginning black Evangelicals have troubled the conscience of Christian Americans.

A White Man's Religion?

The fires of revival that initially swept most of the British North American colonies in the 1740s flared up intermittently during the 1780s and 1790s particularly in the Chesapeake region of the upper South, and broke out anew on the Kentucky and Tennessee frontier around the turn of the century. These successive "Awakenings" inaugurated a new religious movement in America. Whether viewed as a renewed Puritanism, an extension of Continental Pietism, or as the rise of popular denominations on the expanding frontier, Evangelicalism was by the early decades of the nineteenth century the predominant voice on the American religious scene. By the 1830s, revival had linked with reform to institute an energetic and influential evangelical front that intended nothing less than the purification of the nation from sin in order to prepare for the coming millennium, which undoubtedly would begin in America. During these same decades, 1780-1830, Evangelicalism had been planted and had taken hold among enslaved Africans and their descendants, some free, but most of them slaves.

Initially, blacks had heard the message of evangelical Christianity from whites, but rapidly a cadre of early black preachers, licensed and unlicensed, took it upon themselves to convert and to pastor their own people. By 1830, these "pioneers" had been succeeded by a second and more numerous generation of black clergymen, so that blacks were no longer exclusively dependent upon whites for the Christian gospel, though white missionaries might think so. Separate black churches, mainly Baptist due to the congregational independence of that denomination, sprang up—not only in the North, where emancipation gave blacks more leeway to organize institutionally, but in the South as well, where an increasingly entrenched slave system made any kind of black autonomy seem subversive. In the North and upper South, two black evangelical denominations formed and chose bishops of their own to lead them. Already, black American missionaries had established Baptist and Methodist congregations in Nova Scotia, Jamaica, and Sierra Leone. In short, blacks showed no reluctance in taking a leading role in the spread of evangelical religion.

The opportunity for black religious separatism was due to the egalitarian character of evangelical Protestantism; its necessity was due, in part, to the racism of white Evangelicals. The egalitarian tendency of evangelical revivals to level the souls of all men before God had been one of the major attractions to black converts in the first place. Early white Evangelicals in the South, where the majority of blacks were, appeared to the Anglican establishment as a revolutionary rabble, a disorderly, "outlandish, misshapen sort of people," in the words of one Virginian.[1] They threatened the established order, both in ecclesiastical and civil terms. The lower sort made up their church membership, and the unlettered, even including servants, spoke at their meetings. Racial and social status was overturned in the close communion of Baptist conventicles and Methodist societies in the 1780s and 1790s. Runaway slave advertisements in Virginia and Maryland newspapers complained that blacks were being ruined by the "leveling" doctrines of Baptist and Methodist sectarians. Not surprisingly, Anglican authorities in Virginia and North Carolina jailed evangelical preachers, and mobs frequently harassed or assaulted them. Some, but not all, eighteenth-century Methodists and Baptists concluded that holding slaves was sinful and encouraged converts either by legislation or admonition to emancipate their slaves.[2]

---

[1]David Benedict, *Fifty Years among the Baptists* (New York: Sheldon, 1860) 93-94.

[2]Rhys Isaac, "Evangelical Revolt," *William and Mary Quarterly* 3d Ser. 31 (July 1974): 348-53; Robert B. Semple, *A History of the Rise and Progress of the Baptists in Virginia*, revised and extended by the Rev. George W. Beale (Philadelphia: Pitt and Dickinson,

Blacks were impressed by this gospel of freedom; and after white Evangelicals retreated from their antislavery principles and became more respectable, they acknowledged that Christianity and slavery were contradictory. In the North, it was possible for blacks to criticize slaveholding Christianity publicly; in the South, the message had to be muted. Whether their critiques were open or secret, by 1800, black Evangelicals, slave and free, had already scored a significant victory in the war to assert their "manhood." By that date, the black church had begun.

Because they converted, churched, and pastored themselves, black Evangelicals were able to deny, in effect, that Christianity was a white religion. Even in the South, where whites were legally in control of black congregations, their control was nominal since black exhorters and deacons functioned in reality as the pastors of their people. At times black evangelical congregations challenged white authorities and in some cases succeeded in preserving their independence from white domination, as did the African Methodists of Mother Bethel in Philadelphia and the black Baptists of First African in Savannah. The astute leadership of men like Richard Allen and Andrew Marshall was tangible proof of black competence and skill in the affairs of men. Of even greater symbolic value was the power of black preachers in the affairs of God.[3]

Due to the emphasis on conversion, an awakened clergy was more important than a learned one, at least in the early days of American Evan-

---

1894) 30; Charles F. James, ed., *Documentary History of the Struggle for Religious Liberty in Virginia* (Lynchburg VA: J. P. Bell & Co., 1900) 84-85; *Virginia Gazette* (Purdie and Dixon) 1 October 1767; ibid., 27 February 1772; *The Maryland Journal and Baltimore Advertiser*, 14 June 1793; *The Maryland Gazette*, 3 January 1798; ibid., 4 September 1800; David Barrow, *Circular Letter*, 14 February 1798, 4-5; Wesley M. Gewehr, *The Great Awakening in Virginia, 1740-1790* (Durham NC: Duke University Press, 1930) 240-41; Nathan Bangs, *The Life of the Rev. Freeborn Garrettson* (New York: J. Emory & B. Waugh, 1832) 39; Donald G. Mathews, *Slavery and Methodism* (Princeton: Princeton University Press, 1965) 293-99.

[3]Robert E. Park, "The Conflict and Fusion of Cultures with Special Reference to the Negro," *Journal of Negro History* 4 (April 1919): 120; James M. Simms, *The First Colored Baptist Church in North America* (Philadelphia: J. B. Lippincott Co., 1888) 36-39; Walter H. Brooks, "The Priority of the Silver Bluff Church and Its Promoters," *Journal of Negro History* 7 (April 1922): 172-75, 182-90; John Rippon, *The Baptists Annual Register, 1790-1793* (ca. 1794), 263, 332-35, 340-42, 540-41; Simms, 46-78, 93-103; Rev. E. K. Love, *History of the First African Baptist Church* (Savannah GA: The Morning News Print, 1888) 10-24; Richard Allen, *The Life Experiences and Gospel Labors of the Rt. Rev. Richard Allen* (rpt. ed., New York and Nashville: Abingdon Press, 1959) 30-35.

gelicalism. Blacks seized the opportunity afforded by the willingness of Methodists and Baptists to license them to "exercise their gift." Whites as well as blacks fell under the powerful preaching of eloquent "brethren in black." The sight of whites humbled in the dust by blacks was a spectacular, if rare, demonstration of the lesson that "God is no respecter of persons."

More common was the day-to-day presence of the black minister in his community, slave or free, preaching funerals, weddings, prayer meetings, Sabbath sermons, with a force that uplifted blacks and proved the ability of black men. The point was not lost on defenders of the slave system who saw the existence of black churches and the activity of black clergymen as dangerous anomalies. Racists in the North and South found it necessary to denigrate black churches and black preachers by ridicule and restriction in order to be consistent with the doctrine of white supremacy. The racial hierarchy was threatened by any independent exercise of black authority, even though spiritual in nature. While whites had tried to limit Christian egalitarianism to the spiritual realm, the wall between spiritual and temporal equality was too frequently breached (most conspicuously by Denmark Vesey and Nat Turner). Yet, despite the threat to slave control that black religious independence posed, the evangelical tradition insured that suppression could only go so far. To deny blacks the possibility of preaching or gathering for religious meetings would have violated the tradition of gospel freedom as understood by evangelical Protestants (in contrast to a hierarchical tradition, like Catholicism, which had no such problem). When legislators took this step, evangelical objections led to amendment or evasion of the law.[4]

Thus black churches functioned as much more than asylums from the "spirit of slavery and the spirit of caste." As Bishop Daniel Alexander Payne of the A. M. E. Church put it, in the African Methodist and Baptist churches they "found freedom of thought, freedom of speech, freedom of action, freedom for the development of a true Christian manhood." Significantly, Payne and other black clergymen linked "true Christian manhood" with the exercise of freedoms that sound suspiciously like civil

---

[4]Whitemarsh B. Seabrook, *An Essay on the Management of Slaves* (Charleston SC: The Society, 1834) 14-22; Lewis G. Jordan, *Negro Baptist History, U.S.A., 1750-1930* (Nashville: The Sunday School Publishing Board, n.d.) 103-104.

and political rights. The ineluctable tendency of the black evangelical ethos was in the direction of asserting "manhood" rights, which were understood as a vital form of self-governance. In this sense, long before emancipation the black evangelical churches were political, though in the slave South they could be only incipiently so. In the North, the free black churches clearly functioned as a political institution, not simply because they were the only institutions that blacks were allowed to control, but because black Evangelicals connected the concept of "Christian manhood" with the exercise of political rights.[5]

Though Southern black Evangelicals had already experienced self-governance in separate congregations, they had to wait until emancipation to make the connection between church and political life clear and, for a short time during Reconstruction, viable. When they swarmed out of white-controlled churches to form independent congregations or to affiliate with Northern-based black denominations, the freedmen found immediate and tangible evidence of their manhood rights. Long after emancipation, William Heard, a former slave in Georgia, recalled that he had first learned the meaning of manhood from the example of William White, a black Baptist preacher from Augusta, who traveled to Heard's country town to give a political speech shortly after slavery. The seventeen-year-old Heard was so impressed by White's address that he determined "from that night to be a MAN, and to fill an important place in life's arena." He was even more impressed when White, despite threats from local white Democrats, went about his tasks as agent for the Freedman's Bureau, editor of the *Georgia Baptist*, and organizer for the Republican party, apparently without fear. He remained, according to Heard, "always outspoken for Orthodox Religion and for the Republican Party." White's example took, as Heard became a minister, a South Carolina state legislator, bishop in the A. M. E. Church, and minister to Liberia. The political activism of black evangelical preachers like Heard, Richard Cain, Henry McNeal Turner, James W. Hood, T. G. Campbell, Isaac S. Campbell, and others was not an aberration from the tradition of black Evangelicalism but its logical extension.[6]

-----

[5]Daniel A. Payne, "Thought about the Past, the Present and the Future of the African M. E. Church," *A. M. E. Church Review* 1 (July 1884): 1-3.

[6]William H. Heard, *From Slavery to the Bishopric in the A. M. E. Church* (Philadelphia: The A. M. E. Book Concern, 1924) 89-90.

Black Jeremiads

American blacks made evangelical Christianity their own by assuming, whenever possible, leadership of their own religious life. By doing so they denied that Christianity was a white religion. But the assertion of institutional autonomy was not enough. History affords many examples of oppressed people internalizing and institutionalizing the ideology of their oppressors in their own social organizations. Some critics of the black church have accused it of precisely this failure; however, black Evangelicals went beyond institutional separatism: they denied the doctrinal basis of "slaveholding Christianity" by refusing to believe that God had made them inferior to whites. Though whites might appeal to scriptural texts, such as "Cursed be Canaan; a servant of servants shall he be unto his brethren," or "Servants be obedient to them that are your masters," blacks rejected the notion that either the Bible or Christianity supported American slavery.

Among the first public protests by black "citizens" were pre-Revolutionary petitions from slaves in Massachusetts pointing out the contradictions between slavery and a "free and Christian land."[7] Over the next century, black condemnation of the sin of slavery ranged from the assignment of individual slaveholders to hell, to the castigation of American Christianity as hypocritical and false, to the prophecy that the nation itself was doomed to God's wrath unless it repented its crime.

By far the most affecting condemnation to emerge from the antebellum period was the pamphlet published by David Walker, a free black of Boston, in 1829. Known as Walker's *Appeal*, this amazing document has been read by some scholars as an early manifesto of black nationalism. Essentially it is a religious pamphlet, a black jeremiad urging the nation to turn from the sin of slavery before it was too late:

> Are. . . Americans innocent of the blood and groans of our fathers and us, their children? Every individual may plead innocence, if he pleases, but God will, before long, separate the innocent from the guilty unless something is speedily done—which I suppose will hardly be, so that their destruction may be sure. Oh Americans! let me tell you, in the name of the Lord, it will be good for you, if you listen to the voice of the Holy Ghost,

---

[7]*Collections of the Massachusetts Historical Society* 5th ser., no. 3 (1877) 432-33.

but if you do not; you are ruined!!! Some of you are good men; but the will of my God must be done. Those avaricious and ungodly tyrants among you, I am awfully afraid will drag down the vengeance of God upon you. When God almighty commences his battle on the continent of America for [because of] the oppression of his people, tyrants will wish they never were born.[8]

Besides issuing apocalyptic warnings, Walker attacked the claims of whites to superiority. Summarizing the evils of Greek, Roman, British, and European societies (American civilization's fictive pedigree), he concluded that "whites have always been an unjust, jealous, unmerciful avaricious and blood-thirsty set of beings, always seeking after power and authority." He questioned whether whites, given the record of the past, "are *as good by nature* as we are or not." Walker then raised a topic that would be discussed by black theologians for at least another century after his death: "It is my solemn belief, that if ever the world becomes Christianized (which must certainly take place before long) it will be through the means, under God of the *Blacks*, who are now held in wretchedness, and degradation, by the white *Christians* of the world. . . ."[9]

Walker contemplated a revolution, albeit couched in religious terms. He leaves the effecting of the revolution to God's designs, but has no doubt that it will happen in this world, not the next. His God is the biblical God of nations and wars "who rules in the armies of heaven and among the inhabitants of the earth, and who dethrones one earthly king and sits [*sic*] up another." Unless Americans speedily abandon slavery and oppression of blacks, "God Almighty," Walker warned, "will tear up the very face of the earth" and "you and your *Country are gone.*" Lest Walker's rhetoric make him seem like a religious eccentric, it should be remembered that the Psalms, prophets, and apocalyptic books of the Bible have fueled a long tradition of Christian protest against injustice. Walker's jeremiad was part of this tradition as well as an eloquent example of black American Christianity standing in prophetic judgment against the perversion of Christianity by whites.[10]

---

[8]*Walker's Appeal, in Four Articles Together with a Preamble, to the Colored Citizens of the World . . . (1830)*, in Sterling Stuckey, *The Ideological Origins of Black Nationalism* (Boston: Beacon Press, 1972) 83.

[9]Ibid., 55-57.

[10]Ibid., 76-77.

Though they could not declare it publicly, slaves in the South, like their Northern brethren, distinguished between true Christianity and false. They knew that holding a fellow Christian in bondage was a blatant violation of the fundamental spirit of Christianity and they saw that white Christians failed to understand this or else refused to acknowledge it. They scorned the doctrine of slavery's preachers, "don't steal, obey your masters," and held their own meetings when they wanted some "real preaching," even when it was forbidden. When their master's authority contradicted God's, some slaves risked severe punishment by choosing the latter. White claims of superiority and white norms of morality collapsed in the context of slavery. "They always tell us it am wrong to lie and steal," recalled Josephine Howard, "but why did the white folks steal my mammy and her mammy?" "That the sinfullest stealin' there is."[11]

Disdainful of the religious hypocrisy of whites, slaves protested in several ways. Some rejected Christianity outright as a sham. Others who were tired of the moralistic misuse of the gospel to make slaves better—that is, better slaves—focused on the experience of God's spirit in states of ecstatic possession as the essence of Christianity. When accused of immorality they defended their piety by denying that God was concerned about every little sin.

White (and Northern black) missionaries were shocked to find former slaves who valued the experience of God's power as the norm of Christian truth rather than the Bible. The Bible, for them, came *after* conversion. "They wanted to see their children and friends get religion as they did. They fell under the mighty power of God . . . after mourning many days, and then came out shouting, for an angel they said, told them their sins were forgiven. They said their masters and families were Bible Christians, and they did not want to be like them."[12] Undoubtedly the African heritage, which placed spirit possession at the center of religious worship, played a significant role in their interpretation of Christianity, but so did their reaction to the slaveowner's version of the Bible. At the other ex-

---

[11]George P. Rawick, ed., *The American Slave: A Composite Autobiography*, 17 vols. (Westport CT: Greenwood Publishing Co., 1972) 8 *Arkansas*, 1:35; 7 *Mississippi*, 24; 17 *Florida*, 166; 4 *Texas*, 2:163.

[12]*American Missionary* 12 (January 1868): 9; ibid., 14 (September 1870): 194, 221.

treme, some slaves cherished obedience to a strict moral code, in part at least because it assured their moral superiority over whites.

Despite their condemnations of white Christianity, black Evangelicals acknowledged that there were some good whites and offered them the hand of fellowship. Northern Evangelicals, black and white, cooperated in the antislavery movement, though blacks were irked at the paternalism and prejudice of the best-intentioned whites. In the South some slaves took to heart the hard saying, "Forgive your enemies, do good to those who persecute and spitefully use you," and tried, incredibly, to put the lesson into practice. Human relationships being as complex as they are, there were occasions of religious fellowship between blacks and whites, no matter how fixed in law and custom race relations were supposed to be. Particularly in the first years of the evangelical movement in the South, during the emotional tumult of the revivals and protracted meetings, blacks and whites influenced one another in the liminal experience of conversion.

Even as both races shared many of the same doctrines, beliefs, and rituals, they differed fundamentally about God's will for black people and about the meaning of the black presence in America.

The Meaning of Slavery

Blacks could accept Christianity because they rejected the white version with its trappings of slavery and caste for a purer and more authentic gospel. They were certain that God did not condone slavery and that he would end it: the problem was how and when. While black Evangelicals believed that the issue was ultimately in God's hands, they also believed that God used instruments. What were black people to do to end slavery? Vesey and Turner had offered one option: since God is on our side, we strike for freedom, confident in his protection. The Reverend Henry Highland Garnet offered a similar solution: "To such degradation it is sinful in the extreme for you to make voluntary submission . . . Brethren arise, arise! Strike for your lives and liberties. Now is the day and the hour. . . . *Rather die freemen than live to be slaves.*"[13]

---

[13]Henry Highland Garnet, *An Address to the Slaves of the United States of America* (1843), in Stuckey, 172.

Most blacks, slave and free, realized that revolt, even with God on one's side, was doomed to failure. Garnet's address, though stirring, was rejected by the National Negro Convention before which it was given. Black Evangelicals believed that the relationship between God's sovereignty and human action was more mysterious than Vesey, Turner, or Garnet appreciated. Still, it was their duty to act. Three movements formed the arenas for black organization and activism in the North—antislavery, anticolonization, and moral reform. Stressing solidarity with their slave brothers, Northern black clergymen, many of them refugees from the South, organized antislavery societies; agitated from pulpit, press, and platform against slavery and oppression; fostered boycotts of slave-produced goods; formed networks to assist fugitive slaves; and strenuously opposed the American Colonization Society's plan to repatriate Afro-Americans in Africa.

While they generally favored voluntary emigration of American blacks to civilize and Christianize Africans, most black clergymen decried the American Colonization Society as a hypocritical organization bent on pressuring Congress into deporting all free blacks in order to insure the permanent security of slavery. In freedom-day celebrations and annual sermons, the American identity of blacks, their contributions to the nation, and their sacrifices in its wars, were increasingly stressed by black ministers and other spokesmen to counter the threat of forced emigration. That descendants of Africans, forced to America against their wills, were now fighting against a forced return to Africa seemed a particularly galling irony.

Black Evangelicals in the North also viewed moral reform, self-help, and education as part of the campaign against slavery. Ignorance, poverty, crime, and disease not only enslaved nominally free blacks, they were also excuses employed by racists to argue that blacks were incapable of the responsibilities of freedom and citizenship. Thus for black Evangelicals, doing good and avoiding evil were proofs of racial equality as well as signs of justification or sanctification. In this context, bourgeois values of honesty, thrift, temperance, and hard work took on a social significance for free black communities in the North that they did not have for slave communities in the South. For slaves, dishonesty, theft, and malingering were moral acts if directed against whites but not fellow blacks.

Moreover, for slave Evangelicals the essence of Christian life was not ethics but liturgy. The ecstatic experience of God's powerful presence and the singing, dancing, and shouting that accompanied it were central, not rules, duties, and obligations. Although religious ecstasy was not absent from black evangelical churches in the North, increasing stress on education and moral reform (represented most firmly by men like Daniel Alexander Payne) led to discordance between the tone of black evangelical piety in the North and South. This discrepancy would become clear when Northern black missionaries, some originally from the South, began to work among the freedmen. Payne, for example, could not abide the former slaves' ring-shout, which he ridiculed as a "voodoo dance," heathenish, a disgrace to the race. He was shocked to find how resilient the custom was; the former slaves declared it to be "the essence of religion."[14]

Antislavery, anticolonization, and moral reform were three issues around which black Evangelicals organized in the North. In these causes they attempted to answer the question, "What must we do to end slavery?" Though they believed the final outcome was hidden in the providence of God, this belief did not lead them to fatalism or quietism but instead to activism.

In the South, slaves believed just as strongly that God would deliver them from bondage as He had the biblical children of Israel. Indeed, their situation seemed to be appropriately characterized in Moses' words to the Israelites at the Red Sea: "Stand still and see the salvation of God." According to testimony from former slaves, Christianity did foster quietism, just as it fostered acts of resistance, sometimes claiming both in the same slave. External acts must be distinguished from internal attitudes, especially in a situation like American slavery where coercion and effective police power made rebellion futile in the majority of cases.

External accommodation did not necessarily entail internal acceptance, however. Oppression may easily force outward acquiescence, but internal dissent is virtually impossible to control. The inner world of slaves was the fundamental battleground and there evangelical Christianity served as an important weapon in the slave's defense of his psychological, emotional, and moral freedom from white domination. In a brutal system, Evangelicalism helped slaves resist brutalization.

----

[14]Daniel Alexander Payne, *Recollections of Seventy Years* (1886) (rpt. ed., New York: Arno Press, 1969) 253-56.

In particular, conversion, a profound experience of personal acceptance and validation, reoriented the individual slave's view of himself and of the world. "The eyes of my mind were open, and I saw things as I never did before," recalled one, recounting his conversion experience. "Everything looked new," claimed another. The visionary experiences that occurred during the sometimes lengthy period of mourning and conversion moved the slave through a series of emotional transformations, from dread to security, from pressure to release, from depression to elation, from the danger of annihilation to the assurance of salvation. These "otherworldly" symbols clearly reflected "thisworldly" concerns.

In the *Narrative* of his life, Frederick Douglass articulated in romantic nature imagery that moment of internal transformation that convinced him that he was, though still enslaved, free. Many less famous former slaves described that same moment, but in the evangelical imagery of conversion. Contradicting a system that valued him like a beast for his labor, conversion *experientially* confirmed the slave's value as a human person, indeed attested to his ultimate worth as one of the chosen of God.

Like all "peak experiences" the intensity of conversion waned in the face of day-to-day drudgery and occasional brutality. Now and then the experience needed to be recaptured. Moreover, conversion was essentially an individualistic experience, though it certainly was influenced by and shared with others. It gave an invaluable sense of personal meaning and direction to the individual held captive in slavery, but it failed to explain why a just God allowed the innocent to be enslaved at all. In other words, evangelical conversion gave meaning *to* life in slavery; it did not explain the meaning *of* slavery. In the prayer meetings and worship services held in the quarters or the hush harbors of the plantation South, slaves sought a renewed vision of their worth and an answer to the riddle of slavery from the evangelical community.

Slaves did find tangible relief from the misery of slavery in the ecstatic worship of the praise meetings during which they literally "stood outside" their normal selves seized and refreshed by the spirit of God. One former slave vividly recreated the scene many years later: "They'd preach and pray and sing—shout too. I heard them git up with a powerful force of the spirit, clappin' they hands and walkin' round the place. They'd shout, 'I got the glory . . . in my soul.' I seen some powerful figurations of the spirit in them day."[15] The extemporaneous form of these meetings encouraged participants to include references to individual misfortunes and problems in their prayers and songs, so that they might be shared by all. This type of consolation, which has taken on the pejorative connotation of "compensatory," should be seen more positively as the answer to the crucial need of individuals for community.

The communal identity of slave Evangelicals was based upon the story of biblical Israel's enslavement and exodus from Egypt. Without doubt, the Exodus story was the most significant myth for American black identity whether slave or free. White Americans had always thought of themselves as Israel, of course, but as Israelites in Canaan, the Promised Land. Black Americans were Israelites in Egypt. And even after emancipation they found that Canaan was still a far way off. Even so, they were a chosen people, destined for some special task under the direct protection of God. Identification with Israel intensified during the emotional climaxes of the prayer meetings. As Lawrence Levine has suggested, slaves dramatically reenacted the events of the Bible in their worship, with the result that time and distance collapsed into the sacred time of ritual as the congregation imaginatively became the biblical heroes whom they sang, danced, and preached about.[16]

So strong was their identification with Israel that the slaves thought of Jesus, according to one missionary, as "a second Moses who would eventually lead *them* out of their prison-house of bondage." Though the longing was there, and sometimes expressed, no historical figure emerged around whom the Moses-Messiah figure could coalesce. Freedmen sometimes referred to Lincoln, Grant, and other Union figures as deliverers and saviors like Moses and Jesus, but it seems to have been an analogy and not a literal or symbolic identification. Others were quite clear that it was God who had freed them and left little credit to any man at all.

Nor did the slaves develop millenarian expectations around the long-hoped-for emancipation. Certainly they envisaged it as a glorious event,

[15]Rawick, 4 *Texas*, 2:170.

[16]Lawrence Levine, "Slave Songs and Slave Consciousness: An Exploration in Nineteenth-Century Social History," in *Anonymous Americans*, ed. Tamara K. Hareven (Englewood Cliffs NJ: Prentice-Hall, 1971) 114-15; see also Lawrence W. Levine, *Black Culture and Black Consciousness* (New York: Oxford University Press, 1977).

the day of "Jubilo," but perhaps they were too realistic about the ambiguities of freedom in a land that they did not control to forecast emancipation as the beginning of a thousand-year reign of peace and justice. As one former slave put it, "De preachers would exhort us dat us was de chillen o' Israel in de wilderness an' de Lord done sent us to take dis land o' milk and honey. But how us gwine-a take land what's already been took?"[17]

By thinking of themselves as Israelites in Egypt, the slaves assured themselves that the God who had delivered his people once would do so again. Understanding their destiny as a repetition of Exodus, slaves found hope and purpose, but at the same time deferred the underlying question: Why does God allow the innocent to suffer slavery? Similarly, free blacks in the North were preoccupied with the God of Israel who would someday soon overthrow the wicked and raise up the just as he had done in the past. However, they also were engaged in arguing for abolition and black manhood rights, intellectual tasks that forced them to face difficult questions about the past, present, and future destiny of the black race.

Emancipation proved that God was faithful to his people, that their trust had been justified, but it also sharpened the problem. As freedom turned out to be less than complete, as Reconstruction was overthrown, as civil rights legislation was declared unconstitutional, as terrorism and Jim Crow legislation mounted, the questions became all the more urgent: What was God's purpose in permitting Africans to be enslaved? What is his purpose for the colored race now? In the decades of the 1880s and 1890s black theologians and clergymen would confront these problems head-on. They would persist for the rest of the century and beyond.

During the last three decades of the nineteenth century, black Evangelicals (and other black Christians) articulated more fully than before systematic answers to the vexed problem of the destiny of black folk. Frequently their discussions revolved around the ubiquitous topic, "the Negro problem." Perhaps the most acceptable answer to the greatest

---

[17]W. G. Kiphant, Letter of 9 May 1864, Decatur AL, A. M. A. Archives, Amistad Research Center, Dillard University, New Orleans; Eugene D. Genovese, *Roll, Jordan, Roll: The World the Slaves Made* (New York: Pantheon Books, 1974) 273-79; Donald G. Mathews, *Religion in the Old South* (Chicago and London: University of Chicago Press, 1977) 222-25; Norman R. Yetman, ed., *Voices from Slavery* (New York: Holt, Rinehart & Winston, 1970) 75.

number of Evangelicals was that God had permitted but not condoned slavery, so that enslaved Africans might accept Christianity and civilization and then return one day to Africa to convert the fatherland. It was a disconcerting answer to some black Americans like T. Thomas Fortune, the radical editor of the New York *Age*, who dismissed the "talk about the black people being brought to this country to prepare themselves to evangelize Africa" as "so much religious nonsense boiled down to a sycophantic platitude." "The Lord, who is eminently just," insisted Fortune, "had no hand in their forcibly coming here, it was preeminently the work of the devil. Africa will have to be evangelized *from within*, not *from without*." Fortune's views did not convince many Evangelicals on this matter, but his voice—intellectual, rational, skeptical—did represent the development of a new force in black America with which Evangelicalism would have to cope.[18]

Some proponents of the evangelization of Africa linked it with the old theme of black manhood, most notably Henry McNeal Turner. For Turner and others, Africa was a challenge both to the missionary vocation of the black churches and to their full Christian manhood as formed by education and morality. Not all Afro-Americans would go to Africa, just as not all Israelites left Egypt, claimed Turner. However, it was clear in this schema that the colonization and evangelization of Africa was the destiny of Afro-Americans and the purpose of God in allowing slavery.[19]

Another not necessarily antithetical solution to the question of black destiny had been stated but not fully developed during the antebellum period. Actually, it had been implicit in all the critiques of white Christianity penned by blacks: American Christianity was corrupt and blacks

---

[18]T. Thomas Fortune, *Black and White: Land, Labor, and Politics in the South* (1884) (rpt. Chicago: Johnson Publishing Co., 1970) 86-87.

[19]H. M. Turner, "Essay: The American Negro and the Fatherland," in *Africa and the American Negro: Addresses and Proceedings of the Congress on Africa*, ed. J. W. E. Bowen (1896) (rpt., Miami: Mnemosyne Publication, Inc., 1969) 195-98; see also the collection of Turner's writings and speeches in Edwin S. Redkey, ed., *Respect Black* (New York: Arno Press, 1971), passim. For the opinions of other black clergymen on this issue, see "What Should Be the Policy of the Colored American toward Africa," a symposium published in the *A. M. E. Church Review* 2 (July 1885): 68-74; Bishop W. J. Gaines, *The Negro and the White Man* (1887) (rpt., New York: Negro Universities Press, 1969) 19-21; Alexander Walters, *My Life and Work* (London and Edinburgh: Fleming H. Revell Co., 1917) 173.

would reform it (or replace it with a pure Christianity). As early as 1837, the American Moral Reform Society had employed a striking image to state just this belief: the descendants of Africa should multiply and increase in virtue in America so "that our visages may be as so many Bibles, that shall warn this guilty nation of her injustice . . . until righteousness, justice, and truth shall rise in their might and majesty . . . and without distinction of nation or complexion, she disseminates alike her blessings of freedom to all mankind." Blacks, in this view, are the leaven that will save Christian America, whose noble ideals have been sadly betrayed by whites.[20]

A more radical version of this notion, explicated most fully by black theologians James Theodore Holly and Theophilus G. Steward in the late nineteenth century, declared that Euro-American Christianity and civilization were corrupt, violent, materialistic, and nearly at an end. Black Christianity, new and vital, would succeed white Christianity and usher in an age when religion would be practiced, not just preached.[21]

Black Evangelicals supported all these theological opinions by appealing to Psalms 68:31, probably the most widely quoted verse in Afro-American religious history, "Princes shall come out of Egypt; Ethiopia shall soon stretch out her hands unto God." Whether interpreted as a divine commission to evangelize Africa, as a prophecy of the black Christian role in restoring Christianity, or both of the above, it well represented the self-conscious identity of black Evangelicals as they struggled and suffered to build a separate tradition in search of the meaning of their distinct destiny in America. As the twentieth century approached, black Evangelicals like their forerunners for a century, would look to revival, conversion, and the Bible for the strength to endure and improve their lives.

---

[20]*Minutes and Proceedings of the First Annual Meeting of the American Moral Reform Society* (1937) in *Early Negro Writing, 1760-1837*, ed. Dorothy Porter (Boston: Beacon Press, 1971) 203.

[21]See James Theodore Holly, "The Divine Plan of Human Redemption, in Its Ethnological Development," *A. M. E. Church Review* 1 (October 1884): 79-85.

Chapter 7

Women and Religious Revivals: Anti-Ritualism, Liminality, and the Emergence of the American Bourgeoisie⋆

Carroll Smith-Rosenberg

During the Age of Finney, massive social change and ideological up-heaval simultaneously transformed American Protestantism and pro-vided the impetus for the first expression of American feminism. The denunciation of ritual and the rejection of traditional cosmologies accom-panied and intensified both events. While to the twentieth-century mind they seem unrelated, to contemporaries these phenomena appear as twin revolutions inaugurating a new order. Their linking was not coincidental. For a brief period at least, both activist women and clerical innovators self-consciously encouraged each other's revolt against formalism and tradition.

⋆This paper assumed its present form as a result of an ongoing intellectual exchange and the thoughtful criticisms of a group of scholars who meet regularly to discuss class and gender perspective on the analysis of culture. I am deeply indebted to the suggestions and criticisms of Judith Friedlander, Suzanne Hoover, Myra Jehlen, Esther Newton, and Judith Walkowitz.

Within the churches, "new men and new measures" struggled for dominance. Clerical radicals criticized any educated, traditionbound ministry. Time-honored liturgies no longer seemed relevant; individualism reigned. The immediate experience of the Holy Spirit, not the moral and ordered progress of the fathers, signified piety. Enthusiastic religion swept away Calvinist restraints. Youth criticized age. Perfectionism beckoned on to a boundless and unknown future. Experimental communities repudiated both social and sexual proprieties.[1]

Male clerics and reformers led this movement. Yet women were their most zealous adherents. Through sheer numbers, women dominated the Second Great Awakening's revivals and spiraling church membership.[2] They violated liturgical decorum by praying publicly and by prophesying. Setting Victorian proprieties and family needs to one side, they devoted whole days and nights to revival efforts. They rallied forth at dawn to countinghouses and city slums to shame male sinners and lead prayer meetings of men and women in their homes. The more radical ones left family, church, and community to flock to experimental communes and new religions.[3] Indeed, this new female elect became the voice and symbol of the men's theological revolt. Male evangelical leaders encouraged women to speak in church, to admonish individual sinners, to criticize ministers, and to question traditional theological positions. Baptists permitted women to assume the role of public preachers.[4] All evangelists urged their new female saints to cleanse the world of sin and injustice and

---

[1]For an overall discussion of the Second Great Awakening revivals, and especially of Charles G. Finney, see William G. McLoughlin, *Modern Revivalism: Charles Grandison Finney to Billy Graham* (New York: Ronald Press, 1959) and *Revivals, Awakenings and Reforms: An Essay on Religion and Social Change in America, 1607-1977* (Chicago: University of Chicago Press, 1978); T. Scott Miyakawa, *Protestants and Pioneers: Individualism and Conformity on the American Frontier* (Chicago: University of Chicago Press, 1964); Whitney R. Cross, *The Burned-Over District* (Ithaca NY: Cornell University Press, 1950); Donald G. Mathews, "The Second Great Awakening as an Organizing Process," *American Quarterly* 21 (1969): 23-43.

[2]Mary Ryan, *Cradle of the Middle Class: The Family in Oneida County, New York, 1790-1865* (Cambridge: Cambridge University Press, 1981). Chapter 2 presents a superb community study of women's participation in the revivals.

[3]Cross, *Burned-Over District*, chs. 3, 14, 16 and especially 176-78.

[4]Ryan, *Cradle*, 71-72; Cross, *Burned-Over District*, 177.

thus to call forth the promised millennium. Women's spiritual worlds expanded radically to incorporate a host of social problems—not only traditional religious concerns such as Sabbath-breaking, intemperance and sexual immorality, but increasingly as well, poverty, crime, and disease, problems associated with the new cities, with the new class structure, and with public space.[5]

Spiritually awakened women pioneered in the creation of a range of new roles for religious women. Inspired by revival enthusiasm, they founded national religious organizations, distributed Bibles and tracts, led Sunday schools, and raised money to send missionaries to the Sandwich Islands and to the new urban ghettos.[6] They founded female seminaries intent on both asserting women's right to education and preparing women as missionaries for the United States and abroad.[7] Those more worldly in their orientation followed their millennial enthusiasm into a host of reform movements: Garrisonian abolition, moral reform, temperance. These women wrote legislative petitions, edited national reform journals, and developed nondomestic skills and expertise as administrators, publicists, and lobbyists.[8] Others rejected all proprieties. Avowing Perfectionism, this minority of radical antistructuralists saw themselves as the handmaidens of the Lord. They abandoned traditional morality and the family to participate in the Oneida Community's sexual experimentations or the Mormons' polygamous families. Still others, rejecting organized religion, embraced Spiritualism. A few established new religions organized around a female godhead. Calling themselves Mother, the New Incarnation, or the Publick Universal Friend, they assumed di-

---

[5]For a discussion of the women's route from religious revival to the inner city, see Carroll Smith-Rosenberg, *Religion and the Rise of the City* (Ithaca NY: Cornell University Press, 1971).

[6]Ibid.; Cross, *Burned-Over District*, chs. 7 and 13; Nancy Cott, *The Bonds of Womanhood* (New Haven: Yale University Press, 1977).

[7]Kathryn Kish Sklar, "The Founding of Mount Holyoke College," in *Women of America: A History*, ed. Carol Berkin and Mary Beth Norton (Boston: Houghton Mifflin, 1979) 177-201.

[8]Blanche Glassman Hersh, *The Slavery of Sex: Feminist-Abolitionists in America* (Urbana: University of Illinois Press, 1978); Ryan, *Cradle*, ch. 3; Barbara Berg, *The Remembered Gate; Origins of American Feminism: The Woman and the City* (New York: Oxford University Press, 1978).

vine identities that transcended existing boundaries and epitomized the power of *communitas* and liminality.[9] Women responded enthusiastically to the call of their new saviors, becoming Shakers and Universal Friends. Thus for over thirty years, American women, rural and urban, embracing intense Pietism, threw liturgical and social standards to the winds and demonstrated a broad spectrum of unconventional beliefs and behavior.

Eventually the revolutionary thrust of religion ebbed, so that new men and new measures emerged as a new norm. Rituals and symbols once again offered religious inspiration and spiritual solace. Public morality took priority over private inspiration. Religious individualism and human ability, coupled with the insistence on rationalism and empiricism emerged as the new orthodoxy, increasingly in harmony with the economic individualism and self-reliance preached in more secular texts. It was at this point that male religious rebels began to disassociate themselves from iconoclastic and socially rebellious women. Repudiating their prophetesses, such men glorified a novel Victorian figure, the patient and homebound mother and a new institution, the bourgeois family, isolated and nuclear. Deemphasizing the intense piety of revivalistic conversions, clergymen now argued that salvation blossomed within the Christian nursery as a result of loving, maternal discipline.[10] Reinstating the time-honored boundaries encircling women's sphere, evangelical

---

[9]It is significant that so many of the new religions contained a critique of the traditional family and traditional sexuality. The Shakers, Mormons, the Oneida Community, the Universal Friends, all rejected the newly emerging bourgeois family, suggesting sexual and economic alternatives. All redefined the structure and nature of the family in the process of developing a religious utopian vision. See, for example, Sallie Teselle, ed., *The Family, Communes and Utopian Societies* (New York: Harper & Row, 1972); Maren Lockwood Carden, *Oneida: Utopian Community to Modern Corporation* (Baltimore: Johns Hopkins Press, 1969); Constance Noyes Robertson, *Oneida Community* (Syracuse: Syracuse University Press, 1972); Edward Andrews, *The People Called Shakers* (New York: Oxford University Press, 1953); Herbert A. Wisbey, Jr., *Pioneer Prophetess: Jemima Wilkinson, the Publick Universal Friend* (Ithaca NY: Cornell University Press, 1964); Cross, *Burned-Over District*, chs. 14 and 16; Thomas F. O'Dea, *The Mormons* (Chicago: University of Chicago Press, 1957).

[10]Horace Bushnell's *Christian Nurture* (New Haven: Yale University Press Reprint, 1967) epitomizes this position. Bushnell, significantly, is the leader of a new opposition to enthusiastic revivals. For the classic biography of Bushnell, see Barbara Cross, *Horace Bushnell: Minister to a Changing America* (Chicago: University of Chicago Press, 1958). For parallels among the Baptists, see William G. McLoughlin, "Evangelical Child-Rearing in the Age of Jackson: Francis Wayland's View on When and How to Subdue the Willfulness of Children," *Journal of Social History* 9:1 (Fall 1975): 21-34.

ministers shepherded their female adherents back towards the contained family and traditional femininity. The new woman who had embraced activism had either to renounce her expectations for radical new social and religious roles or reexamine her adherence to evangelical Protestantism.

What happened was that women did both. Many followed their ministers back into respectability.[11] They accepted the dictum of the newly appointed president of Oberlin College, Charles Finney, or the edict of the General Association of Congregational Ministers, which stated that women should abhor the public arena.[12] Female auxiliaries relinquished leadership to male societies. Formerly iconoclastic and radical women's organizations now began to glorify the home and act in ways that recognized and ultimately reinforced new class patterns. The history of specific institutions illustrates this pattern. At the height of Charles Finney's New York City revivals, the Female Moral Reform Society angrily denounced male sexual and economic hegemony and aggressively defended their right as a separatist female organization to wage a newspaper war against men's extradomestic sexuality. Its members violated virtually every social norm in the name of Christ's immediate demands and the coming millennium—even to the point of attacking men as economic, as well as sexual, exploiters of seamstresses and domestics. By the mid-1840s, this radical organization had merged with the Maternal Associations, its new goal being to save the world through the maternal manipulation of young children and the sexual supervision of working-class women, especially domestics.[13]

---

[11]Nancy Hewitt is especially adamant in arguing this position. See Nancy Hewitt, "An Ethnohistorical Approach to Women's Activism in Rochester," (unpublished paper, 1980). Ryan traces the gradual peaking of a radical perspective among the American Female Moral Reform Society members in "The Power of Female Networks: A Case Study of Female Moral Reform in Antebellum America," *Feminist Studies* 5 (1979): 66-86.

[12]Gerda Lerner, *The Grimké Sisters from South Carolina: Rebels against Slavery* (Boston: Houghton Mifflin, 1967) 188-92; Robert S. Fletcher, *A History of Oberlin College from Its Foundations through the Civil War*, 2 vols. (Oberlin: Oberlin College Press, 1943) see especially vol. 1, 377 ff. and vol. 2, 643 ff.; Jill Conway, "Perspectives on the History of Women's Education in the United States," *History of Education Quarterly* 14:1 (Spring 1974): 1-12.

[13]Carroll Smith-Rosenberg, "Beauty, the Beast and the Militant Woman," *American Quarterly* 23 (1971), and *Religion and the Rise of the City*; Ryan, "The Power of Female Networks."

Still other religiously inspired women reiterated their revolutionary religious and social vision. Unable to relinquish either their intense and individualistic religious commitment or their experience of a new unrestricted female role, they maintained their assault upon ritual and hierarchical order both within and without religious confines. A decade of religious and reform millennialism had led them to fuse religious antistructuralism and feminism. Indeed the 1830s, 1840s, and 1850s saw them engaged in an intense religious hegira. As evangelical Protestantism reasserted the necessity of hierarchical organization and of ritual, these women sought intellectual and spiritual purity in an increasingly antistructural religious and reform posture.

Quaker feminists such as the Grimkés, Susan B. Anthony, and Lucretia Mott repudiated orthodox Quakerism and its increasingly quietest and formal organization. Anthony, along with former Congregational minister, Antoinette Brown Blackwell, embraced Universalism. Congregationalist Sally Holley denounced Trinitarianism to become a Unitarian. Others, seeking religious affiliations that stressed personal revelation, nonhierarchical organization, and individual activism moved to the Hicksite Quakers and into other forms of similar religious activity. Elizabeth Cady Stanton, aided by Mary Livermore, constructed her own feminist Bible, which rejected both traditional Christianity and gender assumptions. The Grimké sisters, Abby Kelly Foster, and many other feminists turned their backs upon traditional Christianity completely. By espousing Spiritualism, they denied the boundary between the spiritual and the physical and rejected a structured male ministry and liturgy. The more assertive the feminist, the less easily she remained within the confines of traditional Christianity or hierarchically structured and socially acceptable reform organizations.[14]

While representing a broad spectrum of denominational and political alternatives, the religious protests of this persistently radical cadre shared a number of basic characteristics: a repudiation both of ritual and of formal organizational structures; a preference for intuitive or instinctive forms of knowledge and religious experience; a glorification of the indi-

---

[14]For an analysis of feminist religious transformations, see especially Hersh, *The Slavery of Sex*, chs. 1 and 4; Elizabeth Cady Stanton, *The Woman's Bible* (New York: European Publishing Co., 1972); Lerner, *The Grimké Sisters*, 176.

vidual; a rejection of punitive systems of punishment for violations of communal norms; a weakening—even denial—of boundaries between spirit and matter, time and eternity.[15]

During these years of radical economic and social dislocation and of ideological experimentation, American women's antistructuralism presented a complex pattern: an initial conflation of female and male religious iconoclasm; the reassertion of ritual and order by male religious radicals and by certain women; the sustained liminality of other women; the greater appeal of antistructuralism to women, as compared to men throughout this period—as measured in numbers of revival converts. Such a pattern was not unique to Jacksonian America or to evangelical Protestantism. We find strains of it within Albigensianism and similar popular medieval religious movements, within Reform Protestantism in France and Germany in the sixteenth century, in New England during the Antinomian controversy and in England during the Civil War.[16] Parallel patterns mark women's response to secular antistructuralism. A series of questions suggest themselves: What appeal does antiritual and antistructure hold for women? Why does this appeal wax and wane for some women but not for others? Can we relate persistent antistructuralism to social location? What ideational ties link religious antiritualism to women's demand for role expansion or political rights?

Women's espousal of antistructuralism occurs most frequently at times of rapid social upheaval. Yet female exponents of antistructuralism span class divisions as well as formal theological distinctions. They number not only the economically oppressed and socially marginal (displaced artisan women from the north of England during the Civil War, Mother Ann Lee's followers a century later) but members of the British aristocracy and the French royalty, and especially bourgeois women—Ann

---

[15]This list is informed by Mary Douglas's discussion of antiritualistic religion in *Natural Symbols* (New York: Pantheon Books, 1973) 40-41.

[16]Keith Thomas, "Women in the Civil War Sects," *Past and Present* 13 (1958): 42-62; Christopher Hill, *The World Turned Upside Down* (New York: Viking Press, 1972); Nancy L. Roelker, "The Appeal of Calvinism to French Noblewomen in the Sixteenth Century," *Journal of Interdisciplinary History* 2 (1972): 391-418; Lyle Koehler, "The Case of the American Jezebels: Anne Hutchinson and Female Agitation during the Antinomian Turmoil, 1636-1640," *William and Mary Quarterly* 31, Third Series, No. 1 (January 1974): 55-78; Mary Maples Dunn, "Saints and Sisters," in *Women in American Religion*, ed. Janet Wilson James (Philadelphia: University of Pennsylvania Press, 1980) 27-46.

Hutchinson as well as Mary Dyer.[17] Female antistructuralism, while thus apparently linked to economic discontinuity, confounds a simple economic explanation. It forces us to explore, with great precision, the interweaving of the processes of social change, social structural location, and the espousal of antiritualism. The problem has thus become not only one of understanding women's experiences, it now equally concerns the interplay of cultural forms and social structure. Women provide a particularly suggestive population for such an exploration.

The reasons why women's experiences are peculiarly suggestive are numerous. Women both belong to economic, ethnic, and religious groups and confound those classifications not only by differing from the men within their same social category but by sharing uniquely female experiences, language, and values with other women across classification lines. The pattern of cultural, institutional, and economic factors that shapes women's experiences and the language with which they give expression to those experiences is thus far more intricate than that affecting men's. Moreover, as already seen, antistructuralism held a peculiar attraction for women, far more so than it did for men. The complexity of this problem calls for correspondingly sophisticated analysis. One must carefully explore social change in terms of its differing affects upon *women* across class lines and at different stages in the process of change, and then one must correlate such economic and social-structural experiences with women's changing responses to iconoclasm and antistructure. One must, that is, determine what is specifically female in terms of both the experience of social-structural change and antiritualistic assertions. One must not, on the other hand, view women as a monolithic whole but rather as a complex layering of differing class and ethnic experiences, modified by marital status and regional traditions.

Change and difference are central to our analysis: change over time in relation to both economic and ideational factors; differences between women and men and among women across class boundaries. The key to the analytic problem is that women did not remain constant in their rela-

---

[17]Roelker, "The Appeal of Calvinism"; Thomas, "Women in the Civil War Sects"; Koehler, "American Jezebels"; Barbara Taylor, "Religious Heresy and Feminism in Early English Socialism," in Susan Lipshitz, *Tearing the Veil* (London and Boston: Routledge and Kegan Paul, 1978) 120-25.

tion to antistructure. The cultural forms they adopted changed, as did the world that surrounded them. It would be unfair to simplify the dilemma by freezing these women and their social setting at a single moment in time. One must be sensitive as well to ritual's competency as language and explore the possibility that antiritualism served as a language through which those in the midst of radical social change gave voice to their experiences.[18]

Two disciplines have traditionally addressed these issues: anthropology, whose realm is the study of cultural forms and their relation to social structure; and history, which among all the humanities and social sciences, is uniquely concerned with the dynamics of change and conflict. It does, in turn, focus on the complexity of social structures while asking what is unique to a given time and place. What is problematic, however, is that anthropologists and historians tend to ask radically different questions of the social structures they study. Their analyses tend to be predictably delimited, thus making interdisciplinary cooperation difficult. Anthropologists, especially British social anthropologists of the 1930s, 1940s, and 1950s, for instance, have frequently viewed social structures in artificially static terms. Traditionally focusing upon simple social structures, their analytic models have glossed over internal division and conflict. Concerned with continuity, they have ignored, or viewed as pathological, forces for change.[19] By contrast, while focusing on change, historians have at times lost view of the forces that support continuity and

---

[18]My use of the word "competency" is informed by Peter Worsley's discussion of antistructuralism in religion in his new introduction to *The Trumpet Shall Sound: A Study of 'Cargo' Calls in Melanasia* (New York: Schocken Press, 1968).

[19]This is criticism frequently leveled at Radeleppe-Brown, but from the perspective of contemporary social and cultural history, even some of Clifford Geertz's work fails to address issues of diversity when analyzing ritual and other cultural forms. Thus while Geertz makes diversity and change key to his analysis of conflict during a Javanese funeral in his essay, "Ritual and Social Change: A Javanese Example," we are also left without an explanation for the marginal inclusion of certain participants at a Balinese Cockfight. Women and poor men stay literally at the periphery of the circle that surrounds the cock fight. In what ways do their understandings of Balinese culture differ from the biggest cocks? What separate rituals do they engage in? See Clifford Geertz, *Interpretation of Cultures* (New York: Basic Books, 1973); ch. 6, "Ritual and Social Change: A Javanese Example," 142-69; and ch. 15, "Deep Play: Notes on the Balinese Cockfight," 412-53.

social consensus; so often we have settled for description rather than analysis.[20] Merging the strengths and perspectives of both disciplines would do much to enrich the analysis of each. Such a goal lies behind this study of antistructuralism and women.

Two conceptual models seem particularly useful in this effort. Both are borrowed from symbolic anthropology. Mary Douglas offered the first in *Natural Symbols*, Victor Turner the second with his theories of liminality, *communitas*, and the rite of passage.[21] Both are concerned with the relation of ritual and language to social structure and social location. Further, each is involved with movement—between types of social structure, between stages of life or social positions. They are sympathetic to the application of anthropological insights to contemporary Western societies. Yet neither asks the questions the historian must answer: did economic and gender differences affect these revival meetings, influencing who attended or what their actions (rituals, language) meant to themselves, to others there, to members of the society who chose not to be there? Will an economic and gender analysis help us to better understand the quintessential historical question: why this particular cultural form at this particular time? It thus remains for the historian to adopt these highly suggestive anthropological models to an analysis of the role antiritualism plays during periods of massive social transformation.

Mary Douglas, in *Natural Symbols*, suggests that an intrinsic harmony exists between degrees of institutional and economic structure and degrees of ideological or cosmological structure. Systems of classification, values, and beliefs reflect and articulate a society's underlying economic and institutional arrangements. Imagery and ritual both shape and reinforce existing social structures. For Douglas, religion serves as a particularly sensitive reflector of such correspondence. "Cosmology, based

---

[20]These descriptions are decreasingly valid. Philip Greven, while ignoring women in a study of family patterns in seventeenth-century Andover, does address the issues of cohesion and fragmentation among male family members. Philip G. Greven, *Four Generations: Population, Land, and Family in Andover, Massachusetts* (Ithaca NY: Cornell University Press, 1976). Ryan's study focuses upon the tension among families to preserve traditional structures and norms and resist the pressures of social-structural change. Ryan, *Cradle*, ch. 1.

[21]See especially Victor Turner, *Ritual Process: Structure and Antistructure* (Ithaca NY: Cornell University Press, 1977) chs. 3, 4, and 5.

on its particular hierarchy of values and upholding a particular pattern of behavior, is derived from society," Douglas argues. "As the grip of his immediate society on the individual tightens or slakens something happens to his religious attitudes. Religious forms as well as social forms are generated by experiences in the same dimension."[22] Douglas argues that elaborately and hierarchically structured organizations—those characterized by social and economic stability, a strong sense of social pattern and tight community bonds, clearly defined and ascribed roles, and the subjugation of the individual to community and family—will conceive and espouse highly structured cosmologies. Within such societies, Douglas argues, "The principal use of language is to affirm and embellish the social structure which rests upon unchallengeable metaphysical assumptions." Douglas continues:

> In such a system . . . the admired virtues are those which unquestionably uphold the social structure and the hated signs are transgressions against it. . . . Such a culture will tend to produce a ritualistic religion concerned with the correct orientation of the individual within elaborate cosmic categories.

The self will be perceived as passive and ineffectual, Douglas argues, as an arena in which external forces war for control. God will be anthropomorphized, and so defined by attributes rooted in the social structure. He will be the Father-creator, the judge, the ruler, powerful, distant, unreceptive to human manipulation. In such cultures and religions, sin is concerned primarily with external behavior, not with internal motivation or inner consciousness. Such societies encourage a deep respect for constituted authority and its symbols: punitive systems of magical control reinforce the structured system. The most hated sins will be those that attack social order. Sharply drawn categories will mark social and spiritual outcasts.[23]

In sharp contrast, societies characterized by economic and political diversity and competitiveness, by geographic mobility, by a loose sense of social affiliation, by impersonal systems of economic organization and social control, and by short-term loyalties will value the individual over

---

[22]Douglas, *Natural Symbols*, 57 and 32; see also 12, 16.

[23]Ibid., 34, 49, 51, 54-55, 87-88, 91, 102, 111, 176 and chs. 2, 4, 6 passim.

the community and family, youth over age, inner experience rather than conformity to social norms. In such cultures, "God has turned against ritual," Douglas tells us. "He does not apply fixed rules automatically but pierces behind the symbolic facade to judge the inner heart of men." We will, consequently, find a preference for intuitive and instinctive forms of knowledge. Language exists to challenge received ideas, to encourage autonomy, to question or deny boundaries, to reject authoritarian control and symbols of hierarchical power. Here Douglas predicts we will find "the literature of revolt."[24]

While loosely organized societies espouse religious antiritualism, Douglas continues, so do societies caught in the process of radical social and economic transformation. The experience of social change itself, she argues, leads to the denunciation of ritual, the praise of disorder, and the affirmation of individualism. Radical or prolonged social change destroys old institutional and hierarchical arrangements. Contemporary issues no longer elicit cultural consensus or reinforcement. Members of societies in the process of change face contradictory demands and rewards. Subgroups in that society experiment with altering definitions of the social outcast. In doing so they redefine social spheres, boundaries, and divisions of power. The individual, detached from a complex web of social interactions and agreed-upon values, is outside known order, loose, unconnected. Cosmology, reflecting movement and detachment, will be flexible, open, and likely to reject rituals and structure.[25]

The destruction of one form of social organization, however, does not lead to permanent disorder but ultimately to the reconstitution of order. As economic and demographic change progresses, a new social equilibrium evolves, which is satisfactory to some of these protesters. Form, pattern, ritual, and classification return, reflecting, reinforcing, and embellishing new economic and institutional arrangements.[26] But for those still dissatisfied with the new order, or marginal to it, disorder and fluidity may maintain their attraction: these groups may continue to use religious antiritualism to resist the new social structure and power dy-

---

[24]Ibid., 33, 44, 52, 104, 109-10, 195.

[25]Ibid., 34-35, 40, 91, 179-81.

[26]Ibid., 19-36.

namic or simply to give voice to their marginality. Their cosmology may prove anachronistic, pointing only to the promise of change already belied, or it may be a harbinger of further discontinuities. Much revolves around the nature of the social change, the socioeconomic location of the social dissidents, and the amount of actual power they can mobilize.[27] Do social and religious developments in America substantiate Douglas's overall analytic model? If so, what light does her insistence that antiritualism is the language of social change throw on its appeal for nineteenth-century American women?

There is little question that Douglas's conceptual framework provides a remarkably accurate overview of the essential congruence between degrees of social and ideational structure in both eighteenth- and early nineteenth-century America. Certainly strong parallels exist between Douglas's tightly structured type of social organization with its ritualized religious systems, and eighteenth-century New England society with its orthodox Congregationalism. Throughout much of the eighteenth century, New England remained an economically static and hierarchically structured society—a world of tightly organized agricultural communities, each jealously guarding their borders against incursions from neighboring villages and against disaffection from within. This was a world as well of patriarchal and patrilocal families and of densely interwoven kin networks. A corporate village structure bound families together, monitored public order, and punished deviant behavior. Rigid rules delimited class, gender and age—rules that were ritualistically strengthened by precise dress codes, differentiated levels of literacy, educational and career options, the location of family pews in village churches, and even the rank sons held in college. Insubordination by the young, by servants, by the poor, or by females was physically punished and reinforced through public shaming rituals.[28]

---

[27]Ibid., 40, 114, 182-88.

[28]See, among other studies, Greven, *Four Generations*; John Demos, *A Little Commonwealth; Family Life in Plymouth Colony* (New York: Oxford University Press, 1970); Demos, "Old Age in Early New England," in Michael Gordon, *The American Family in Social Historical Perspective*, 2d ed. (New York: St. Martin's Press, 1978) 220-56; Michael Zuckerman, *The Peaceable Kingdoms: New England Towns in the Eighteenth Century* (New York: Norton, 1970); Kenneth Lockridge, *New England Town: The First Hundred Years* (New York: Norton, 1970).

Not surprisingly, we also find a hierarchically organized religion that both paralleled and helped reinforce social and economic structures. Seventeenth- and eighteenth-century Congregationalism made the tribal family sacred. The promise of heaven was traced back to God's covenant with a founding male ancestor, just as possession of land stretched back to this same ancestor. The Half-Way Covenant perpetuated a family-centered mentality.[29] An educated clergy, constituting virtually a hereditary caste, dominated this church.[30] Except at the height of revival enthusiasm in the 1730s and 1740s, ritualized services turned the community's attention towards external moral behavior and conformity to community norms. Throughout the seventeenth and much of the eighteenth centuries, predestination defined an elaborate and socially recognized category of spiritual outcasts. The self was passive, without ability to understand God and secure salvation. Its fate was determined by divine fiat, mitigated only by God's promise to the founding male ancestor. In virtually all respects, then, the individual, saint or sinner, assumed the role of dependent child, or behaved as wife to the powerful Godhead. Inability and limited atonement reaffirmed this childlike or womanlike dependence.

As the eighteenth century progressed, the early commercial revolution introduced some variables to family-based agriculture: land scarcity and commercialization of agriculture interacted to encourage geographic mobility and also led to an increase in economic dislocation.[31] Economic options and autonomy increased. These social patterns paralleled Douglas's description of the gradual loosening of social structure as one moves from quadrant A to quadrant B of Douglas's grid model. American Protestantism in the closing decades of the eighteenth century demonstrated a predictable movement away from earlier orthodoxy. Hopkinsianism

---

[29]Perry Miller, *The New England Mind: From Colony to Province* (Cambridge: Harvard University Press, 1954) and *Errand into the Wilderness* (Cambridge: Harvard University Press, 1956).

[30]David Hall, *The Faithful Shepherd: A History of the New England Ministry in the Seventeenth Century* (New York: Norton, 1974); Joseph Haroutunian, *Piety vs. Moralism* (New York: Holt, 1932).

[31]Charles S. Grant, *Democracy in the Connecticut Frontier Town of Kent*, Studies in the Social Sciences, No. 601 (New York: Columbia University Press, 1972); Kenneth Lockridge, "Land, Population and the Evolution of the New York Society, 1630-1790," *Past and Present* 39 (April 1968): 62-80.

with its greater (though still limited) acceptance of human reason and ability reflected the loosening of the static and patriarchal village order. The growing cosmopolitanism of the cities and the movement of the mercantile elite away from a family-centered business world provide a background for understanding the growing appeal of Unitarianism and Deism among that population.[32]

Change, gradual in the eighteenth century, became overwhelming in the early nineteenth century. Radical and pervasive social upheaval destroyed the traditional agrarian world of eighteenth-century New England, uprooting and transplanting entire geographic regions, undermining old modes of social cohesion, creating new institutions and new systems of social organization. Mercantilism died; the bourgeoisie established its hegemony; industrial capitalism emerged. Thousands of young men and women fled New England's worn-out lands to populate the rich farm lands that stretched across New York, Ohio, Indiana, and the Great Lake plains—or to enter the ranks of the new urban bourgeoisie as clerks and professionals.[33]

As historians, we can see how slow and hesitant the process of commercialization and industrialization really was. As late as mid-century, the society and economy of the North resembled a patchwork quilt of modernized communities and households that remained traditional and unchanged. Contemporaries, however, experienced these years as cataclysmic. For them, the institutional and social arrangements that had maintained social order and contained the individual had fragmented. New economic arrangements now warred against time-honored norms and values.

The economic, demographic, and structural revolution seemed to affect the young and women especially. Momentarily at least, the young and women appeared to float beyond structure. Definitions of women's roles

---

[32]Peter Dobkin Hall, "Marital Selection and Business in Massachusetts Merchant Families, 1700-1900," in Gordon, *The American Family*, 101-14; James A. Henretta, *Evolution of American Society, 1700-1815* (Lexington MA: Heath, 1973).

[33]David Allmendinger, *Paupers and Scholars: The Transformation of Student Life in New England* (New York: St. Martin's Press, 1975); Paul E. Johnson, *A Shopkeeper's Millennium: Society and Revivals in Rochester, New York* (New York: Hill and Wang, 1978); Allan S. Horlick, *Country Boys and Merchant Princes* (Louisburg PA: Bucknell University Press, 1975).

were in flux. New alternatives beckoned them to an unknown and frightening future. Contradictions and conflict characterized this new world. The 1820s, 1830s, and 1840s thus saw the confluence of massive social change with a newly emerged economic and institutional order that valued individualism and christened progress. Not surprisingly, this was a culture that questioned traditional authority and denigrated religious ritual. It was during these years that the last vestiges of orthodox eighteenth-century Congregationalism, the insistence on an all-powerful Father-God, and an eternity patterned after agrarian patriarchy, predestination, and a spiritual economy of scarcity were challenged and ultimately abandoned: God became a loving brother, indeed, a loving and concerned mother. Man was responsible for his own salvation.[34] Reform groups insisted on new notions of the social outcast, thus underscoring changing social patterns and the growing social and cultural diversity. This was called the Era of the Common Man. In another sense, it was the Age of Finney.

Just at this time, male religious rebels turned to women as a receptive population and as a group whose activism symbolized a more general rejection of traditional rituals and boundaries. Using religion to develop extradomestic roles, they created powerful local and nationwide single-sex organizations expressive of women's particular angers, anxieties, and demands. Momentarily the needs of male religious spokesmen and of women coincided.

It is important to understand the roots of women's antistructuralist enthusiasm. Clearly, it reflected the general social fragmentation and movement that women and men experienced together. But women's sense of change differed perceptibly from that of men. Eighteenth-century New England's hierarchical and structured order had subjected women to elaborate social, economic, and religious restraints. Despite their economic productivity, they moved in an orbit of dependency. Their status was always that of daughter or wife. Even widowhood held few benefits. Most New England women died the dependents of their

---

[34]For shifts in theology, see McLoughlin, *Revivals, Awakenings and Reform*, ch. 4, and McLoughlin's Introduction to Charles G. Finney, *Revivals of Religion* (Cambridge: Harvard University Press, 1960). Private correspondence and diary entries in collections of women's papers support the conclusion that women at least emphasized God's maternal and nurturing qualities.

sons and boarders in a home that had never legally been theirs.[35] Their enforced silence in religion had ritually underscored accompanying institutional and legal insistence upon their inferiority.

America's emergence as a commercial and early industrial state seemed, momentarily, to open the possibility of new roles and power for women. It increased the number of single women, delayed marriage for many others, and reduced the birth rate.[36] Multiplying the number of nondomestic institutions, especially in the new urban centers (schools, publishing houses and journals, orphanages, shelters for the homeless), it created novel employment opportunities for women and thus made it possible for the new bourgeois women to aspire to economic autonomy.[37] By proletarianizing the artisan family and destroying the economic base of the New England farming family, industrialization forced growing numbers of working-class women to assume that autonomy.[38]

The process of urbanization and commercialization opened to that new entity, the bourgeois matron, a host of new opportunities for extra-domestic roles and power vis-à-vis males of the same class. Furthermore, changes in church governance and ritual benefited women specifically. From having been ritually and repeatedly silenced within sacred confines, women were now offered a central role in the religious revolution. In addition, the denigration of hierarchical structure, the assertion of individual autonomy against the primacy of community and familial norms mirrored their particularly female experience of suppression under the patriarchy. Thus women across class, married and unmarried, briefly experienced revolutionary and somewhat frightening changes. A vision of

---

[35]Marylynn Salmon, "Equality or Submersion? Female Covert Status in Early Pennsylvania," in Berkin & Norton, *Women of America*, 92-113; Mary Beth Norton, "The Myth of the Golden Age," in Berkin & Norton, *Women of America*, 37-47; Ryan, *Cradle*, ch. 1; Greven, *Four Generations*.

[36]Robert Wells, "Women's Lives Transformed: Demographic and Family Patterns in America, 1600-1970," in Berkin & Norton, *Women of America*, 16-33.

[37]See, for example, Kathryn K. Sklar, *Catharine Beecher: A Study in American Domesticity* (New York: Norton, 1976).

[38]Susan Hirsch, *Roots of the American Working Class: The Industrialization of Crafts in Newark* (Philadelphia: University of Pennsylvania Press, 1978).

new power and autonomy danced before them, held out and authorized, if only momentarily, by their male spiritual leaders.

But in the end, both social disorder and an open social structure proved to be temporary. The unattached youth of this transitional period were not social protesters but rather loose young men and women cast off by a declining agrarian economy, at sea in a new commercial and urban environment. Their one desire was to establish themselves securely within the new bourgeois hierarchy. Nor did institutional and economic change appear to bring greater upward mobility or a true democratization of decision-making processes. Impersonal modes of economic organization and social control developed to deal more efficiently with problems of scale and with rapid population turnover. Economic hegemony only narrowed and intensified;[39] a new theology and new religious institutions developed to enforce that hegemony, as did new values and rituals.

Thus the revolutionary thrust of evangelical Protestantism ebbed before women were able to use religion to permanently restructure female-male power relations. As male religious leaders had used women's activism and public presence to symbolize their male revolt against an older Congregational world order and the experience of a new and changing social order, women's silence became equally symbolic to male religious leaders who sought to restore order and ritual to the social and religious world.[40] By the 1840s, the Victorian woman, economically impotent and religiously demure, had emerged as the symbol and personification of male bourgeois hegemony. Clearly some women, sensitive to the loss of their new power and centrality, fought male clerics' desire to silence them once again. Religious and social antistructuralism expressed their continued social discontent, which surfaced finally as feminism.

---

[39]For this argument see, among others, Edward Pessen, *Jacksonian American: Society, Personality and Politics*, rev. ed. (New York: Dorsey, 1978); Stuart Blumin, "Residential Mobility with the Nineteenth Century City," in Allen F. Davis and Mark H. Haller, *The Peoples of Philadelphia: A History of Ethnic Groups and Lower-Class Life* (Philadelphia: Temple University Press, 1974); James A. Henretta, "Economic Development and Social Structure in Colonial Boston," *William and Mary Quarterly* 22:1 (January 1965): 75-92, shows the beginnings of this trend towards increasing economic inequality in the eighteenth century.

[40]See, for example, Barbara Welter, "The Cult of True Womanhood, 1820-1860," reprinted in Gordon, *The American Family*, 313-33.

But while the macrocosmic congruence of social and cosmological structure seems clear, questions remain. Why did the vast majority of evangelical women shed their recently acquired autonomy so promptly to follow male ministers back into respectability and order? Which women, resisting the pressures of religion and society, persisted in their new deviance?

It is here that issues of diversity as well as change emerge; and it is at this point that Douglas's model falters. For while Douglas sees antiritualism as the language of sociostructural change, her model does not explain which voices within highly complex social structures will speak that language and which voices will be hushed. It is at this point that one must append a class and gender analysis in order to determine specifically which groups of women persisted in the language of revolt and which internalized the language of acquiescence. Further, informed by Douglas's insistence upon the relation between cosmology and social structure, one must attempt to answer the most difficult question of all: why?

For the purpose of more precise analysis, let us focus for the moment only on religious revivalism, holding in abeyance the lesser structured options that stretched beyond evangelical enthusiasm into a utopian or formless world. When we have accounted for the waxing and waning of women's response to revival enthusiasm, we can then proceed to an explanation of even more discordant female voices.

Mary Ryan, in her analysis of the social structure and religious revivals of Utica, Oneida County, New York, during the first half of the nineteenth century, offers us an ideal case study with which to explore a series of new hypotheses. Utica is a crucial community for our analysis. The first major port on the Erie Canal, Utica epitomizes the rapid transformation of a traditional agrarian community and the emergence of a commercial and industrializing entrepôt. Between 1810 and the 1840s, Ryan argues, the class and family structure of Utica changed utterly. Utica as a commercial and industrial center grew at the expense of its agricultural base. Wealthy families and landless farming youth moved together into Utica, the former as a new bourgeois elite, the latter as a newly proletarianized working class. The amorphous mercantile social and economic categories of farmer and artisan that had structured eighteenth-century Utica became obsolete. A stratified bourgeoisie, comprised of merchants, industrial entrepreneurs, professionals, and shopkeepers emerged as did the new working class. Household size and structure changed as the family lost most of its economic production functions, making work and residence separate spheres. These transformations, beginning with a pre-Canal boom in 1810 and essentially in place by the late 1830s, paralleled Utica's revival enthusiasm, which itself began in 1813-1814 and continued through the late 1830s.[41]

Ryan presents us with a careful analysis of the socioeconomic and familial characteristics of the revival converts. Their most salient characteristics, at all times and in all of Utica's revival churches, were youth, transience, and being female. Though their percentage of revival conversions did vary by church per year, women always constituted a majority of revival converts during each of Utica's revivals. The lowest percentage of female converts occurred during Utica's first revival, 1813-1814, when women constituted fifty-two percent of the converts (a figure well above their representation in the general population of this still frontier village). In Utica's last major revival, in 1838, women comprised seventy-two percent of the converts.

Geographic rootlessness was the second major characteristic of the revival convert. Most converts, both men and women, could not be found in any of Utica's censuses or city directories. Of male converts, for instance, more easily traced by historical demographers than women, Ryan could trace only one-fourth of any given revival in any of the city directories. Among those male converts who could be located in subsequent church records, thirty percent requested letters of dismissal within five years of their conversion so that they could depart Utica and join churches in other communities. Presumably many others left with far less formality, especially women.

Of those who remained in Utica long enough for Ryan to trace, youth was a significant characteristic. Sixty-five percent of the traceable male converts (presumably the most stable and oldest of those converts) listed themselves as boarders. In terms of the social structure of early industrial America, this meant young men, divorced from their families and not yet married, moved to the city, where they most likely found employment as clerks in Utica's growing mercantile houses, as semiskilled laborers for wholesale merchants, or in Utica's new factories. Sixty percent of Utica's female revival converts appear to have been neither mothers nor married

---

[41]Ryan, *Cradle*, ch. 2.

and thus formed a group comparable to the youthful male boarder. "It is safe to make this single conclusion about this silent majority of converts," Ryan tells us. "They were largely young and, in the short term at least, a peripatetic lot with fragile roots in church and community. Thus far it would seem that the Second Great Awakening expressed the waxing religious enthusiasm of a second generation, recently uprooted from their frontier families."[42]

Thus far then, Douglas's hypotheses, when tested against a close demographic study of revival converts, hold true. Revival enthusiasm—the rejection of orthodox dogmas and the repudiation of traditional rituals—appealed primarily to the uprooted and potentially dispossessed of the new economic order, and chief among these, of course, were young women. The comments of contemporaries underscore the relationship between youth, rootlessness, and antiritual. In a pastoral letter, the ministers of the Oneida Association, one of the Presbyterian pillars of communal propriety, complained in 1827 that revival enthusiasm "allow[ed] anybody and everybody to speak and pray . . . as they pleased." Young men, the letter reported, had harshly criticized established ministers and church elders, saying " 'you old grey headed sinner, you deserved to have been in hell long ago,' 'This old hypocrite,' 'That old apostate' . . . 'That old veteran servant of the devil.' . . ."[43] Clearly revivals permitted those marginal to Utica's new social structure to express tension and discontent. As we saw earlier, revivalists also encouraged women to criticize antirevival ministers and church elders.

While these overall characteristics remained constant over the twenty-five-year period, significant changes also marked the pattern of Utica's revival conversions, changes crucial to an understanding of the precise function of antiritualism within a rapidly changing society, and thus to an understanding of women's diverse patterns. The percentage of male revival conversions was greatest during Utica's 1813-1814 revival— the revival that coincided with the first major impact of the commercial

---

[42]Ibid., 75-83. See Johnson, *A Shopkeeper's Millennium*, ch. 2; Horleck, *Country Boys*, and Allmendinger, *Paupers*, for corroborative information about youthful male rootlessness.

[43]Ryan, *Cradle*, 78. Cross, *Burned-Over District*, 239-40, give similar examples among Methodists in other New York State communities.

and transportation revolutions on Utica's traditional agrarian social structure. Women, as fifty-two percent of the converts of this revival, while in excess of their percentage of the population, were significantly below their percentage of prerevival church membership, which had been seventy-two percent.[44] Thus, for this one period, when the full force of the commercial revolution hit Utica initially, male religious enthusiasm peaked and came as close to paralleling women's as it ever would. Significantly, from the perspective of later revival patterns, the men involved were highly unusual in their own right, coming in significant numbers from Utica's economic elite. Merchants and lawyers—and their wives—were, Ryan tells us, "conspicuously present" among the converts, as were Utica's leading landholders and industrialists. The Van Rensselaers, for example, converted en masse.

During Utica's second revival, in 1819, when the first touches of the Canal boom had begun to spread through agrarian Oneida County, a significant change in the social and economic composition of the convert group occurred. During this revival, men from the lower rather than the upper echelon of Utica's emerging bourgeoisie—artisans and small shopkeepers—joined in the enthusiasm and embraced the new ways.[45] Utica's upper middle class, on the other hand, no longer responded to the appeal of antistructuralism; their enthusiasm had already been restructured. (We must remember that in discussing male merchants and petty shopkeepers, we are analyzing only a small, albeit significant, minority of all converts. Both of these economic groups were more often represented by their female than by their male members. A class without a simultaneous gender analysis is deceiving. But let us hold that level of analysis in abeyance for the moment.)

These shifting economic patterns suggest an addition to Douglas's model: revival enthusiasm reflected not only social marginality but the very act of social movement itself. As change flows through the social structure, different groups will embrace antiritualism as they themselves are embraced by structural transformation. Thus, within our particular case study, as different social groups or families were swept up by the commercial and industrial revolutions and literally moved from the tradi-

---

[44]Ryan, *Cradle*, 78.

[45]Ibid., 82-83.

tional agrarian world into Utica's new class structure (for example, when the Van Rensselaers shifted their economic base within Oneida County from agriculture to commerce, or when less affluent families left their farms and moved into Utica as shopkeepers and artisans) the antiritualism and revival enthusiasm became a language through which they gave voice to their experience of social-structural relocation.

Those closest to social and economic power responded first, joining the course of the 1813-1814 revival. Smaller shopkeepers and artisans, recruited into the bourgeoisie at later stages of commercial and industrial development (themselves more responders than shapers), converted as the new economic ways began to incorporate them—generally during the 1819 revival or during the revivals of the 1820s. Once a group had been successfully incorporated into the new bourgeoisie, its response to revivalism then slackened significantly, especially with regard to men of that group. Individuals within the group would maintain their allegiance to key evangelical doctrines, but they gradually renounced antiritual and antistructural enthusiasm.

The changing Utica revival profile thus points out the dynamic interaction between forces of social and ideological change and forces of stabilization. Antistructure, Utica's revivals demonstrate, will appeal to powerful socioeconomic groups—groups clearly committed to the perpetuation of social cohesion—at the moment those groups actively participate in the formation of a new economic and institutional order. Once the new system has become operative and the elite has established its centrality within the new system, such groups will resume their customary role as spokesmen for cohesion and stasis. Significantly, from the point of view of changing cosmologies, such elites will continue their opposition to the ideology that supported the old social order (as orthodox Congregationalism supported the old mercantile-agrarian structures), but now they will espouse not antistructure but a newly evolved counterstructure. And this counterstructure will gradually accumulate an increasingly restrictive cultural overlay in keeping with its function to affirm and reinforce the new class order. As more and more groups become incorporated within the new structure, the acceptance and elaboration of conservative cultural forms and rituals will grow.

It is important, however, not to artificially compress and simplify this process. Social change is never sudden. The birth pangs of the American bourgeoisie encompassed half a century or longer. During these years—

roughly the 1790s to the 1850s—no clear-cut cultural hegemony emerged. Rather, many voices experimented with degrees of antistructure and variant forms of counterstructure. The debris resulting from this babel of contentious builders still marks the political, reform, and religious history of America during the first half of the nineteenth century. Only at mid-century, perhaps only after the Civil War, did a Victorian consensus emerge. But by then, of course, new heresies had already gathered in the wings.

If we are now certain that antiritualism accompanies social movement, we are still left with the question, why? In what conceptual, structural, or psychological way does the wild assertion of disorder become a language through which individuals in the throes of social relocation express the emotional qualities of their experience? Victor Turner's analysis of liminality and rites of passage is particularly suggestive in terms of explaining the precise role antiritualism and antistructure play in the movement of individuals and groups between social locations. Within Turner's conceptual framework the successive waves of evangelical revivals that swept the North during the opening decades of the nineteenth century take on the characteristics of a massive rite of passage marking the emergence of the new social structure.

Rites of passage, Turner argues, accompany major changes in social position, status, or role, and are the processes by which an individual leaves one set of known and recognized rights and responsibilities and adapts to a new social position and public persona. Traditionally, cultures have elaborated rituals that both articulate a sense of personal upheaval, of being outside of form, and simultaneously seek to contain the potential threat of social disarray.[46] These rituals are particularly charged when the society itself, as well as key groups within the society, are in movement.

Rites of passage classically contain three specific stages. The first, *Separation*, involves "symbolic behavior signifying the detachment of the individual or group . . . from an earlier fixed point in the social structure." The individual then passes through a second phase, *Liminality*, where she is "betwixt and between the positions assigned and arrayed by law, custom, convention and ceremonial." Liminal individuals are felt to be outside of social restraints and norms; they embody the limitless power

---

[46]Turner, *Ritual Process*, 44-45.

of disorder. In the final stage of the rite of passage, *Reaggregation*, society attempts to reintegrate the liminal person back into society, albeit through a new role or social position.[47] Ritual and antiritual demarcate these different stages.

While recognizing, indeed giving expression to, the power of disorder involved in the process of social change, the rite of passage functions essentially as a conservative or restorative social instrument. Through the rite, social movement and change—and the elation and fear that accompany such movement—by being ritualized, become formalized and controlled. Indeed, Turner argues, societies use liminal rituals not only to contain the fragmenting and explosive emotions involved, but also to socialize the unformed individual, to train her to accept her new roles and responsibilities. "Neophytes in many *rites du passage*," Turner tells us, "have to submit to an authority that is nothing less than that of the total community."[48]

Specific parallels exist between the rituals and imagery associated with the liminal passage and those of the revival conversion. Liminal rites blend characteristics of lowliness and sacredness. The liminal person experiences the process as one of death and rebirth, feeling that she has been "reduced or ground down . . . to be fashioned anew." The liminal person is often removed from ordinary communal space, stripped of her normal clothing, and left naked or in rags. At the same time she is frequently encouraged or allowed to engage in unrestrained behavior and to experience new and heady spiritual powers. It is a time when all the old restraints are dead and new ones are as yet unforged. The world appears upside down. Disorder rules, momentarily unchallenged.[49]

This description epitomizes early nineteenth-century evangelical revivals. Revivals violated the normative confines of sacred space, for they could be held in fields and forest clearings. In cities, profane theaters were transformed into new churches as religious enthusiasm spilled out into the secular world. Revivals disregarded as well conventional allocations of sacred time; they converted working days into God's time, laid claim

---

[47]Ibid., 94, 106-11.

[48]Ibid., 103.

[49]Ibid., 100, 102.

on the night, and continued for weeks. No liturgical traditions constrained the new enthusiasm as form was cast to the winds and souls cried out in fear or joy. The individual sinner, in the throes of conversion, assumed many of the characteristics Turner found among liminal Africans. She would feel herself cast down, the lowest of the lowly. No social or economic attributes from the secular world seemed relevant or offered consolation. Her naked soul was engaged in a Promethean struggle with God. Overthrown at last, renouncing the world and its temptations, the saved Christian emerged a new person, invested with inner light, an agent of the Lord.

While tolerating temporary disorder and role expansion, however, the revivals also functioned as resocializing or reaggregating devices. They were especially effective mechanisms for containing the protests of women and defining the new roles of the Victorian Lady or bourgeois male. Much in the message disseminated by Finney, Lyman Beecher, and other established evangelical revivalists was directly supportive of a new capitalist mentality.[50] While Charles Finney was overtly critical of an unrestrained drive for material advancement, suspicious of banks, and opposed to credit and debt financing, the two pillars of his religious beliefs proved to be the pillars of a new commercial order: optimism and self-help. Renouncing a spiritual economy of scarcity, Finney proclaimed unlimited atonement. Grace and redemption were available to anyone who, with her free will, would assert her belief in God and her determination to do good. Salvation was now the "business" of men.

The greatest spiritual rewards would go to those who worked the hardest. Finney's new saint was the self-reliant individual, not the helpless brand plucked up by an omnipotent father-god. To this doctrine of optimism, goal orientation, and self-reliance, Finney added a psychology of delayed satisfaction and control. Frugality lay at the heart of Finney's creed. These beliefs, combined with Finney's insistence upon personal loyalty, honesty, and the acceptance of economic stratification—which he had inherited from his eighteenth-century New England forebears—made an ideal belief system for the emerging bourgeoisie. No wonder Finney's staunchest supporters numbered the mercantile elite of the revival

---

[50]See, for example, McLoughlin's Introduction to Finney's *Revivals*, xxxvi-xxxviii, and McLoughlin, *Revivals, Awakenings and Reform*, 123-27.

towns (be they Utica, Rochester, even New York City) or that the Tappan brothers required that their clerks regularly attend church services at Finney's Broadway Tabernacle.[51]

This analysis has briefly slipped away from its focus on women. Women, far more frequently than men, represented the bourgeoisie at revival meetings. How did the doctrines of evangelical Protestantism and of revivalism relate to and affect women as female members of the new bourgeoisie?

Women, of course, heard and internalized the religious doctrines that so closely dovetailed with the economic world into which their brothers, husbands, and sons had moved. Since these women—as employers of domestics and as urban residents—participated along with their male kin in the new bourgeois social and economic order, the spiritual economy preached by Finney and other evangelists helped rationalize their new world.

Other aspects of the evangelical message, however, appeared particularly appropriate for women and were so emphasized by male evangelists. Within rites of passage, Turner argues, the liminal figure is taught to be submissive and humble, to temper pride and individuality. Sexual continence and the subordination of self to a spiritual leader and the demands of the community are encouraged. (These aspects most often accompany rites of passage marking upward social movement.[52]) Certainly these points played a key role in the evangelical revival messages which, as we have seen, encourage the soul seeking Christ to see herself as the lowest of the low. Women, moreover, tended especially to glorify the service and sacrificial aspects of Christian imagery—often with the encouragement of male ministers. These characteristics, ideal goals for the evangelical elect, were central to the new role of bourgeois housewife. Thus, while revivalism had freed the new bourgeois woman from eighteenth-century forms of religious subordination, promised her new powers and access to a public sphere, the new theology contained a highly restrictive message. While sanctioning women's acts of religious self-as-

---

[51]McLoughlin, *Modern Revivalism*, 113-20; Johnson, *A Shopkeeper's Millennium*, ch. 5.

[52]Turner, *Ritual Process*.

sertion (in themselves incidents of liturgical disorder) revivals simultaneously inculcated a self-image of effacement and dependence.

Nancy Hewitt, in her study of revival enthusiasm in Rochester, found
that this was the experience of a number of evangelical women who were
members of Rochester's emerging bourgeoisie. Rochester revival convert Mary Mathews, for example, prayed publicly, denounced nonrevi-
val ministers, and served as an officer in one of the women's new voluntary
reform associations. Her religious experiences, however, led her at the
same time "to see more and more [my] utter weakness" and "utter dependence on Christ." Nineteenth-century revivals, Hewitt believes, had
carefully instilled in these women a heightened sense of spiritual inferiority that could then be translated into subordination to men and to the
new bourgeois family structure.[53] By the 1840s, the Victorian woman,
economically impotent and religiously demure, as we've noted, emerged
as the symbol and personification of male bourgeois hegemony.

The Second Great Awakening's revivals thus accompanied and ritualized an extremely complex pattern of social-structural relocation for
women. The changes these female saints experienced encompassed both
those which they shared with their fathers, brothers, and husbands as
members of the new bourgeoisie, and those related to the rapid and extreme redefinitions of woman's role that accompanied the rise of the
bourgeoisie. Woman's movement into her new social position was stormy
and traumatic. As a result, religious antiritualism spoke to her more forcefully than it did to the men in her life whose experience of social movement
had, after all, been relatively straightforward. On one level, the intensity
of woman's liminal disorderliness, her bitter confrontations with conservative male spiritual and social leaders, bespoke the attraction that spiritual autonomy, powerful new roles, and the very right to speak held for
her. On a second level, the liminal phase of her rite of passage, marked by
radical liturgical inversions and the denial of social and spiritual hierarchies, reflected the contradictory social processes that took her from an
eighteenth-century wife, through momentary role expansion, to the new
constraints placed upon the bourgeois housewife. It is not surprising that
society secured her reaggregation with the elaborate rituals of the Victo-

---

[53]Hewitt, essay in this collection, 233-56.

rian Era. Her new silence, so hard to secure, had been chosen, after all, as symbol for the new hegemony.

But a word of caution. We deny the complexity of this process— and of the women's responses—if we see women at the end of the revivals returned to society shorn of all power, passive spokeswomen for class and husband. Women emerged from the revivals cloaked with new skills that they had acquired in their own right as members of the bourgeoisie. They headed regional and national women's organizations (which never could have existed half a century earlier) and held such male-sounding titles as president, treasurer, or trustee. They lobbied city councils and state legislatures for women's causes, drew up constitutions, raised and spent money. Their publications and their calls for financial support all followed the lines laid down by the commercial and transportation revolutions that had first transformed these women into bourgeois urban dwellers. While these new women's organizations in the end supported rather than undermined the new economic order, they still served to alter the power balance within the bourgeois home. Through these reform organizations, bourgeois women escaped the home and familiarized themselves with recent economic and institutional realities. A conservative (perhaps) but not a powerless or an ignorant woman emerged from the process of religious reaggregation. Women used, as well as were used by, the new bourgeois class structure.[54]

We now have some understanding of the attraction great revival conversions and antistructuralism held for bourgeois women, as distinct from bourgeois men. But what of those women who were not successfully incorporated into the new Victorian proprieties and economic order, the women who clung to antiritualism and to religious and social radicalism? Victor Turner, while concentrating on the ritualized and socially contained aspects of liminality, suggests two other sources of liminality— sources that reflect social-structural stratification and potential conflict. These are the liminality of the socially inferior and the liminality of the socially marginal.[55] Here lies the final clue to the disparate religious and reform experiences of those women.

----

[54]Ryan, *Cradle*, ch. 3.

[55]Turner, *Ritual Process*, 110, 125.

To the complexity of their movement into the new bourgeois social order, women added a second experience uniquely their own—that of social and economic inferiority. Ironically, as the Jacksonian Era progressed and the new bourgeoisie became more economically and institutionally entrenched, the insistence on female inferiority became an unquestioned cultural assumption. Eighteenth-century women had, of course, been seen as inferior to the men in their lives. The wills of America's yeoman farmers, the contracts drawn up for indentured servants, the refusal to provide public education for women, all demonstrate women's inferior status. But in the hierarchically structured eighteenth century, this inferiority was always limited to men of like class. Farming and artisan women, merchants' wives and daughters also shared in the ascribed status of their class and family.

As equalitarian rhetoric came increasingly to characterize the political world and educational principles of this Era of the Common Man, women became inferior not only to men of their class, but to all white men. Moreover, while the traditional world of the eighteenth century assumed inequality as man's natural lot, the nineteenth century denied and condemned it—for all white men, that is. Definitions of female inferiority thus became more widespread; they were now legitimated in the new language of medicine and biology. Pietism and ecstatic religion offered one escape from this definition of female inferiority, as did political and reformist attacks upon the new economic hegemony, and specifically upon its exclusion of women from the new promises of equality.

Presumably these aspects of religious and secular reforms appealed to a number of women. But again—to which women? Since men defined all women as potentially inferior to all white men, the inferiority argument becomes circular when we try to use it to explain why some women resisted their second-class status and others acquiesced. Let us look at Turner's third source of liminality, social marginality.

Social marginality affected the newly emerging bourgeois woman in two ways. As the industrial revolution slowly but irrevocably took work out of the home, married women especially, but all bourgeois women, lost their role as socially recognized economic producers, and thus their right to move freely within the *agra*.[56] Business and politics—the world of men

---

[56]Hirsch, *Roots*, 40, discusses the effect of industrialization on limiting the availability of work for all women and especially for married women. For a general discussion of this phenomenon, see Louise Tilley and Joan W. Scott, *Women, Work and Family* (New York: Holt, Rinehart & Winston, 1978).

and of power—were acted out in spaces now forbidden to women. (Hence, of course, the added appeal religion held since sacred space was both newly opened to women and the only public space in which they could assert their right to be present and, at times, to be heard).

All bourgeois women and all married women were defined as economically and institutionally marginal. To their experiences certain bourgeois women added other forms of marginality. This was especially true of single women who were institutionally marginal to the increasingly nuclear family of the bourgeoisie and ideologically marginal to Victorian social beliefs that insisted that biology marked all women as wives and mothers. Yet during these very years, the numbers of single women, especially along the eastern seaboard and among the bourgeoisie, increased significantly. Women experienced another form of social marginality through their families rather than outside of them. The commercial and industrial revolutions, while irresistible, swept unevenly across the American landscape. As late as the 1850s, pockets of traditional communities remained. Furthermore, individual families might still cling to a preindustrial economic and institutional order, and maintain extended households where apprentices and journeymen lived with master craftsmen or farmers who still honored the old values. These families structurally and economically were marginal to the bourgeois revolution. At times they remained geographically or residentially marginal as well. Their social-structural marginality might have an ideational component, such as membership in a Quaker meeting in an area where the Presbyterian Church dominated the social and political structure.

Nancy Hewitt's study of the social mobilization of women in Rochester pinpoints such a group of structurally marginal families who in the 1840s and early 1850s maintained an extended household structure. They remained outside the center of Rochester's economic and political power base and lived on the residential fringes of the city. They were frequently Quakers or had reform connections with Rochester's Quaker families. The women from these families tended to be the most extreme in both their religious and their reform antistructuralism. It was these women who engaged in a restless spiritual hegira, moving ever in the direction of religious antistructure; who shocked society with the extremes of their reform demands (everything from Garrisonian abolitionism to women's rights); whose reform organizations were themselves loosely structured; and whose vision was universalist (with regional, national, and international religious and reform ties) rather than parochial.[57] These women combined in their own lives all three of Turner's forms of liminality: social-structural movement, inferiority, and marginality.

Out of this exploration of the differing religious responses of Jacksonian women, an explanatory model suggests itself—one that utilizes Turner's three sources of liminality. Consider the following hypothesis. Women's enthusiastic response to religious antiritualism and to antistructuralism and their numerical superiority among revival converts reflects the greater complexity of women's class relocation, as did the elaborate rituals with which Victorian society hedged in women's reaggregation. But within the social category *woman*, we find a number of social structural differences that influenced women's differing responses to antiritualism and antistructuralism.

Women whose families occupied a central position within the social order, whose emergence into the bourgeoisie was unmarred by economic uncertainty, experienced only the mildest sense of social discontinuity. Their liminal phase was fleeting, since their sense of social inferiority as women had been cushioned by their family's economic security and by the new Victorian ideology concerning women's proper place. Disorder, or the need to turn the world upside down, would hold little appeal for them. Alternatively, women whose movement into the bourgeoisie was less certain, demonstrated more intense liminal behavior. Their consciousness of social inferiority was less cushioned by class confidence. Their liminal phase ended only after a husband or father finally had established a secure place within the new order. Finally, women who never married or whose families remained marginal to the new social structure, merged women's peculiar political and economic inferiority and marginality with the economic and institutional marginality of their families. They appear to be those women who never really terminated their liminal religious phase, just as they were never really integrated into the emerging bourgeois social structure. They were the perennial rebels—both religious and political—and, in their discontent, the harbingers of future upheavals.

On still another level, the implications of women's attraction to, and rejection of, antistructuralism are more far-reaching than this class anal-

---

[57]Hewitt, essay in this collection, 233-56.

ysis suggests. While we have pinpointed social movement and social marginality as the crucial variables, we have ignored the liminality and disorder that surround the socially and ideologically inferior. We have done so because the question asked— why did some women return to social respectability and structure?— pointed ultimately to the power of social cohesion as opposed to the power of disorder. But to narrow our perspective exclusively to that question is to ignore a fundamental aspect of the repeated appeal that antistructuralism held for women, not just at this point of capitalist development, but over time and across cultures: women abhor a synthesis.[58] They are, in fact, the quintessential symbol of diversity and opposition, the eternal Other. Rigid categorization and clearly defined status systems, historically, are ascribed male qualities and thus illegitimate and frightening female attributes. Power in women must always be an androgenous characteristic, praised only at moments in time when liminality, the crossing of categories, and the rejection of rigidity are embraced, just as women secure actual power and autonomy only at those moments when rigid economic and institutional structures are broken open. Then a few women (who they are may indeed be predictable in social-structural terms) will seize upon both literal and symbolic disorder and attempt to transform it into both a tool for power and a symbol of freedom. The reinstitution of order, ritual, and form is experienced by men and women alike as a struggle to contain that almost universal symbol of disorder and of the world turned upside down—the powerful woman. At such times, within the human imagination, two symbols of women's elevation war against each other—one the affirmation of order, the other the threat of social disorder. They are the Woman on the Pedestal and The Woman on Top.

---

[58]Myra Jehlen, "Marxism and Feminism" (unpublished paper, 1981). Jehlen argues that ultimately Marxists and feminists fall apart because Marxism, which focuses on differences and conflict, assumes an ultimate synthesis and a unitary experience. Women, she argues, not only have been historically excluded from this synthesis, but because their experiences will always differ from men's, always will be excluded. I am indebted to this fine paper.

Chapter 8

The Perimeters of Women's Power in American Religion

Nancy A. Hewitt

Both Charles Grandison Finney and Rochester were relatively young when the former shed his light on the latter in 1830. The village had been founded in 1812 by a group of Maryland land speculators who were soon joined in the settlement by Yankee shopkeepers, artisans, and millers. The opening of the Erie Canal in 1822 changed the village to a boom town; and by the 1830s Rochester was a burgeoning commercial center, the hub of an increasingly specialized agricultural hinterland, and one of the fastest growing cities in the nation. The economic and social changes in the region nurtured a varied and vital community of religious enthusiasts and political activists who carved out a profusion of pathways to social reform. Women were prominent, often dominant, on those paths. Virtually every activist woman tied her social concerns to her religious commitments, but those religious commitments were not necessarily evangelical in origin, nor were the social concerns necessarily perfectionist in aim.[1] These women, with their different understandings of the relationships between women's religious and social roles, provide an excellent opportunity to evaluate Smith-Rosenberg's interpretive framework by lending historical specificity to the anthropological theories she employs.

Three groups of women were active in the reformation of social values and social order in early nineteenth-century Rochester. Of these, two were not deeply involved in the revival enthusiasm of the Second Great Awakening. The one group—affluent Episcopalians and Presbyterians from well-to-do families of Maryland and New England—had made the transition from agrarian to commercial and from rural to town life previous to their migration to Rochester. They and their families migrated to Rochester as part of elaborate kin groupings in the first years of settlement and forged the village's first circles of economic, political, and social leadership. Women in these families experienced little economic uncertainty and, by the 1810s, looked back rather than forward to the major changes in their lives. The churches of which they were members were affected by the doctrinal changes accompanying the Second Great Awakening, but they were only briefly touched by the revivals themselves. In their religious and voluntary associations, such as the Female Missionary Society and the Female Charitable Society, these benevolent women replicated the hierarchical organization and the orientation to social control found in the eighteenth-century towns from which they emerged.

A second group, including women who participated most actively in Finney's revivals, experienced far more traumatic economic and social transformations. They bore the brunt of the transition from agrarian to commercial society at the same time that they were migrating to new homes in western New York. They moved to Rochester in smaller family units and endured a significantly longer period of economic uncertainty than the women who preceded them to the city. Both men and women of these later settlers were active revival enthusiasts and key Finney supporters. The women embraced not only revival enthusiasm but also, in

---

[1] The perfection of society and the pursuit of the millennium were aims specifically of the Finneyite revivals of the 1830s. Earlier evangelical campaigns had encouraged renewed commitment by individuals to the church without expecting to achieve the perfection of society as a whole. The perfectionist aims of the Finney-led revivals were a product, in part, of Charles Grandison Finney's extension of the concept of human agency.

its wake, a variety of potentially radical causes: moral reform, temperance, and antislavery. Moreover, they claimed for themselves the most extreme positions of the day in each case: to wit, the immediate and total eradication of slavery, drink, and vice. These perfectionist women sharply criticized those, including men and ministers, who failed to meet their standards.

While the process of geographical and economic mobility was fraught with great anxiety for these families, most emerged over two decades as solid members of Rochester's newly established bourgeoisie. Many of the men involved in the early period of revivalism soon turned their attention back to more worldly affairs, gradually gaining economic status and political connections that translated anxiety into affluence. By the 1840s evangelical women's spiritual journeys and the radical social critiques they fostered began to conflict with evangelical men's economic journeys and the stable social position they offered. Simultaneously, as Smith-Rosenberg has noted, evangelical ministers began to withdraw their support from women's activism. By the late 1840s economic stability and ministerial censure convinced most evangelical women to relinquish their radical critiques of the social and sexual order and to accept the boundaries of a new religious and cultural norm of womanhood.

A few Finney converts rejected this reaggregation, however. They moved from revivalism to Spiritualism, antislavery to disunionism, community life to communitarianism, temperance to teetotalism, and moral reform to women's rights. The lives of the few women who followed such a path are not as well documented as those of their sisters who submitted to the new urban, commercial order. We do know that they left or were dismissed from the evangelical churches from which they emerged and joined forces instead with ultraist Quakers. The latter group had migrated to Rochester in the 1830s from downstate Quaker farming villages and broke with the local Quaker meeting in the late 1840s. These Progressive Quakers and spiritualists rejected rituals and the boundaries between sacred and secular space and advocated the power of personal inspiration along with equality of the sexes. Their associational efforts—antislavery, protesting capital punishment, dress and health reform, Spiritualism and women's rights—were based on strictly democratic and egalitarian principles: individual liberty and fulfillment rather than social control or perfection were their watchwords.

The radical Evangelicals and the radical Quakers, labeled ultraists by their contemporaries, shared several economic and social characteristics. They and their families remained distant from Rochester's commercial and cosmopolitan developments. They lived on the periphery of the city and remained outside local circles of economic and political power. The narrowing economic opportunities of the mid-nineteenth century and the sedimentation of Rochester's economic and social structure left these groups permanently marginal to the city's primary institutions. In turn, men and women in these families maintained their antiritualistic and antistructural stance and articulated ever more radical demands for religious, economic, and sexual equality. Moreover, it was the women of these families more often than the men who led the public campaigns for social change.

In general, then, female Finneyites followed the pattern of separation, liminality, and reaggregation set forth by Smith-Rosenberg à la Turner. Yet while Victor Turner and Mary Douglas attempted to include an element of process or change in their analyses, their models appear static compared to the deep and widespread changes experienced by even the most stable nineteenth-century women. According to Turner, for instance, a rite of passage occurs within a relatively stable society as a self-consciously created aid to individuals passing from one stage or position to another. The revivalism of the early nineteenth century occurred *amidst* widespread change: reaggregation could not have been the initial aim of revivalists because revivalism began as an open-ended process that sought further change rather than as a self-conscious aid to maintaining the traditional social order. When bourgeois men, evangelical ministers, and eventually evangelical women chose reaggregation, they did so partly because they had successfully altered the social and economic order from which they had emerged. Moreover, the social meaning of evangelical women's experience of religious liminality can only be fully understood in the context of a larger community of women who, considering themselves equally committed to religious values, chose different paths in mid-nineteenth-century society. A combination of economic location and religious experience serves as the best indicator of the forms of social activism chosen by any particular woman. Yet personal experiences, kin connections, the models offered by other women, and the needs of the community for women's labor complicated the translation of religious and economic experience into social roles. Let us trace that translation in detail to illuminate the points where human experience diverged from anthropological models.

Generally, benevolent women experienced little economic or social instability and, therefore, should have experienced little enthusiasm for revivalism or the new social roles it offered. Still, these women did seek to employ new social circumstances and religious doctrines to justify a wider social role for women. The transition to commercial agriculture and a market economy was gradual before 1820 and was accompanied by a shift toward a more rationalistic religious tone. Rather than disrupting a community's order, these economic and theological changes often solidified the position of leading families in New England villages and encouraged individual efforts to order and control society.

The New Haven theology was the theological outgrowth of economic change. As preached by Asahel Nettleton, Lyman Beecher, and Nathaniel Taylor, it emphasized man's active role in his spiritual and social well-being, asserting that man was "a free, rational, moral creative cause." Taylor insisted that "no man becomes depraved but by his own act. . . ."[2] Beecher, focusing on the positive side of this theology, linked man's moral agency to his duty to promote charity, temperance, and virtue. Women formed a majority of the congregations in which powerful preaching and inquiry meetings fostered small-scale revivals and brought the message of free moral agency to man. Yet the New Haven theologists did not actually offer women the wider roles that the New Haven theology suggested. Nettleton, for instance, considered the "praying of females in the presence of males as the greatest evil to be apprehended" while Beecher sought to channel women's religious enthusiasm into maternal associations and child nurture.[3]

Women did not always immediately recognize the restraints on moral agency assumed by their ministers. In Guilford, Connecticut, a group of Presbyterian women were inspired to organize a female charitable society in 1806, only to discover that their major opponent was their spiritual leader, the Reverend Mr. Elliott. One of the women, Mary Stone, wrote to

---

[2]Sydney E. Ahlstrom, *A Religious History of the American People*, 2 vols. (Garden City NY: Doubleday & Co., 1975) 1:509 and ch. 26, passim.

[3]John Frost to Charles G. Finney, 21 April 1827, Charles Grandison Finney Papers, Oberlin College Library, Oberlin College, Oberlin, Ohio.

her friend and neighbor, Mrs. Levi Ward, that the Reverend's "opinion would bear great weight with many." He believed such "S[ocietie]s to be ostentatious" and thought women could "find sufficient objects upon which to bestow their mite, within their own limits."[4] Though Mary Stone did not entirely agree with the Reverend, she and her concerned sisters decided to "omit meeting" and "to gather what money we can, . . . and send it enclosed in a letter with as little noise and ostentation as possible. . . ."[5]

The Levi Wards moved to western New York the following year, settled in Rochester in 1818, and joined the First Presbyterian Church. In 1822 Mrs. Levi Ward helped to found the Rochester Female Charitable Society and served as its first president. In the society's meetings, the women of First Church, which "number[ed] among its members a large portion of the wealth, talent, and influence of the village," gathered in meetings with their equally affluent sisters from St. Luke's Episcopal Church.[6] The Reverends Comfort Williams and Francis Cuming, of First Presbyterian and St. Luke's Episcopal respectively, preached fund-raising sermons for the society in its founding year. A local editor applauded the clergy's support, claiming that it "would be an offense against God and humanity to withhold from these almoners of Heaven who are carrying education, nourishment, and consolation into the retreats of ignorance, sickness and misery, the means of continuing their divine administrations."[7] Shortly thereafter, Mary Stone, now Mrs. John Bush, joined Mrs. Ward at the First Presbyterian Church and in the offices of the Charitable Society.

The Wards and the Bushes were economic and religious leaders in the new community, as they had been in the New England villages they left. The new community contained only the most basic institutions, however; founding families had to create, with the resources of frontier life, the social order they left behind. It was the "educational wants of the poor, to-

---

[4]Mary Stone to Mabel Hand Ward, 20 August 1806, Presbyterian Historical Society, Philadelphia, Pennsylvania. I wish to thank Lori Ginzburg for this citation.

[5]Ibid.

[6]James K. Livingston to Charles G. Finney, 7 December 1832, Finney Papers.

[7]*Rochester Telegraph*, 4 March 1823, quoted in Amy Hanmer-Croughton, "The Rochester Female Charitable Society," *Rochester Historical Society Publication Fund Series* 9 (1930): 71.

gether with other destitutions consequent upon sickness in a new country," that "prompted, for the purpose of more efficient action, the formation of [the] Society." These factors also encouraged local men, including ministers, to hope that "the benevolent ladies" would "be sustained and strengthened" in their efforts.[8]

The sense of social duty rooted in deep religious commitment fostered women's charitable efforts in Guilford and Rochester. In the latter community, however, with its primitive institutions, women's duties were more easily acknowledged as an important component in the establishment of a new paternalistic order. Both men and women of the founding families believed in "our Savior's admonition 'the poor ye have always with you.' "[9] Now they also accepted women's role in publicly and collectively "softening the pangs of grief, soothing the despair of affliction, assuaging the pains of sickness, wiping the widow's eyes and warming and educating her orphans" so long as women worked "noiselessly, economically, and efficiently."[10]

During the late 1820s, economic change and geographical mobility intensified and increasing numbers of families moved to Rochester in an attempt to enter rather than to reestablish economic and social leadership. Signs of change, expressing both growth and disorder, proliferated. The Erie Canal was the most notable of these. In 1827 the city directory noted that the Canal, "together with the vast waterpower, conspire to give the village its commanding position for trade . . . as well as for manufactures."[11] It also conspired to give the village several hundred itinerant laborers, a vast influx of immigrants, and a sprawling dockside community of groceries, taverns, shacks, and brothels. Change was irreversible, open-ended, and highly visible.

---

[8]Ibid.; Rochester Female Charitable Society, *Charter, Constitution, By-Laws and Officers of the Rochester Female Charitable Society . . . together with its History and Annual Reports for the Year 1860* (Rochester NY: C. D. Tracy & Co., 1860) 3.

[9]Rochester Female Charitable Society, *Annual Reports for the Year 1860*, 5.

[10]Hanmer-Croughton, "Rochester Female Charitable Society," 71; Rochester Female Charitable Society Minute Book, 1 March 1859, Papers of the Rochester Female Charitable Society, University of Rochester, Rochester, New York.

[11]*A Directory for the Village of Rochester* (Rochester NY: Elisha Ely and Everard Peck, 1827).

It was the rapidity and extent of change that led Third Presbyterian Church Elder Josiah Bissell to write Charles Finney of " 'the large budget of evils rolling through our land and among us,' dwelling on the moral dangers of canal life." At the same time he invited Finney to preach in the village.[12] Evangelical ministers, such as Finney, joined the battle against these evils with men and women who were concerned with their own salvation and with establishing a moral order that would assure the community's salvation. After Finney's arrival in Rochester, women became increasingly active in pursuing this personal and community salvation. As Paul Johnson noted in *A Shopkeeper's Millennium*, "Revival enthusiasm began with the rededication of church members and spread to the people closest to them. Inevitably much of it flowed through family channels."[13] It was predominantly "pious women" and "Christian wives" who directed that flow.[14] Melania Smith, Mrs. Everard Peck, Artemissia Perkins, Mrs. David Scoville, Mrs. Hobart Ford, and many other female Finneyites "retain[ed] hope" for the conversion of family members and "laid the foundation for moral community among persons who had been strangers. . . ."[15]

Finney's departure from the city did not diminish women's spiritual or social activity. Rather, female Finneyites seem to have become increasingly self-conscious of their special role in achieving the millennium. At first, some of these women wrote to Finney and his wife that "coldness" had already set in: your "children," wrote Mrs. Mary Mathews, "are starving here."[16] Mrs. Mathews considered herself and her husband "the greatest *Finneyites* in this village"; yet she asked to be remembered in Mrs. Finney's "daily prayers" that she might "be kept from di[shaming]

---

[12]Quoted in Paul Johnson, *A Shopkeeper's Millennium: Society and Revivals in Rochester, New York, 1815-1837* (New York: Hill and Wang, 1978) 94.

[13]Ibid., 99.

[14]Ibid., 98.

[15]Mrs. Mary Mathews to Mrs. Charles Finney, 1 August 1831, Finney Papers; Johnson, *A Shopkeeper's Millennium*, 101. I have used the forms of women's names employed by the women themselves.

[16]Mrs. Mary Mathews to Mrs. Charles Finney, 24 April 1831, Finney Papers.

religion and be made," instead, "an instrument of promoting the cause of Christ."[17]

Mrs. Mathews and her evangelical sisters served as such instruments within their circle of family and friends. They repeatedly expressed their "hopes" for their "husbands' conversions" and denounced women who married "infidels" and then expected "the Lord to smile upon their union."[18] Mrs. Scoville visited New York City "for no other object but to endeavor to be useful to the souls of her friends there who [were] unconverted."[19] Mrs. Mathews wrote to Mrs. Finney frequently, listing the saved and the unregenerate within neighboring households.[20]

Concern for family and friends soon extended into wider circles. In the fall of 1832, Mrs. Mathews reported to the Finneys that her husband Selah was thinking of becoming a missionary: "I feel it would be delightful to spend my life teaching the heathen," she wrote. When her husband turned his attention instead to local political and business ventures, Mrs. Mathews sought missions closer to home. As a member of the Charitable Society, she "visit[ed] the poor to converse with them and watch by their sick bed. . . ."[21] She and her evangelical sisters joined in prayer circles and maternal associations; they established Sunday schools, collected funds to send teachers to the West, and fostered conversions among the scholars of local female seminaries.[22] A seminary principal, Sarah T. Seward,

---

[17]Mrs. Mary Mathews to Mrs. Charles Finney, 19 December 1831, 24 April 1831, Finney Papers.

[18]Mrs. Mary Mathews to Mrs. Charles Finney, 1 August 1831, Finney Papers.

[19]Mrs. Mary Mathews to Mrs. Charles Finney, 1 August 1831, 24 April 1831, Finney Papers.

[20]Mrs. Mary Mathews to Mrs. Charles Finney, 24 April 1831, 16 May 1831, 1 August 1831, 19 December 1831, 25 February 1832, 15 September 1832, and 22 June 1836, Finney Papers.

[21]Mrs. Mary Mathews to Mrs. Charles Finney, 16 May 1831, Finney Papers.

[22]Elizabeth Selden Eaton to Amos B. Eaton, 16 April 1833, 27 October 1839, in Blake McKelvey, comp., "Letters Postmarked Rochester," *Rochester Historical Society Publications* 21 (1943): 45, 65; Susan W. Selden to Mrs. Charles Finney, 11 June 1834; Sarah T. Seward to Mrs. Charles Finney, 4 December 1833, Finney Papers.

voiced the feelings of many such women when she wrote the Finneys, "I have long since sacrificed myself *soul & body* to the cause of my Master."[23]

Many female Finneyites came to view the criticism of unregenerate men, especially elders and ministers, justified by their soul-and-body sacrifice, as part of their mission. As early as May of 1831, Mary Mathews claimed that only two of the male church elders at Third Presbyterian Church "retain[ed] interest" in the community's spiritual state. She also noted that Josiah W. Bissell, whose father called Finney to Rochester, was as "hardened as ever."[24] She condemned the husband of an evangelical sister as "entirely thoughtless," that is, without any religious feeling, and blasted the "blasphemous theater," which encouraged such thoughtlessness.[25] The theater also contributed to licentiousness among men, another of Mary Mathews's primary concerns. In 1836 she inquired of Mrs. Finney whether the local Female Moral Reform Society should debate the question, "Ought licentious [men] be exposed. . . ."[26] Whatever Mrs. Finney replied, the results of just such a debate appeared in a future issue of *The Advocate of Moral Reform*, the editorial voice of the American Moral Reform Society.[27] Nor did Mary Mathews shy away from criticizing ministers. She bemoaned the "deplorable state" of religion in the village and described a minister being considered for the Third Church pulpit as "a lovely spirit," but one who "lacks energy."[28] She frequently wrote of the divisions within the Third Church and claimed that it was only with the removal of the Reverend Mr. Lyons that the Third Church gained a true minister.[29] Simultaneously, she condemned the Reverend Hastings of Brick Presbyterian Church who "meant to make all the converts . . . *Anti*-Abolitionists."[30]

---

[23]Sarah T. Seward to Mrs. Charles Finney, 9 March 1835, Finney Papers.

[24]Mrs. Mary Mathews to Mrs. Charles Finney, 16 May 1831, Finney Papers.

[25]Mrs. Mary Mathews to Mrs. Charles Finney, 1 August 1831, Finney Papers.

[26]Mrs. Mary Mathews to Mrs. Charles Finney, 22 June 1836, Finney Papers.

[27]*Advocate of Moral Reform* (New York City), 15 October 1837.

[28]Mrs. Mary Mathews to Mrs. Charles Finney, 16 May 1831, 1 August 1831, Finney Papers.

[29]Mrs. Mary Mathews to Mrs. Charles Finney, 19 December 1831, Finney Papers.

[30]Mrs. Mary Mathews to Mrs. Charles Finney, 22 June 1831, Finney Papers.

Mrs. Mathews's voice was joined by that of Mrs. Elizabeth Eaton. In 1833 Mrs. Eaton complained to her husband Amos that Judge Ashley Sampson, chosen as a church elder, "*never* had the holy ghost, instead of being filled with it as the deacons of the primitive church were."[31] She was particularly concerned about his and others' rejection of Finney's ideas of sanctification and devised "a way of getting at the subject among old stupid professors," especially ministers and elders. By taking "them on their own ground & *language* with *their own terms*," she argued, they could be shown "the necessity of striving for a *deeper work of grace*." By 1834 Mrs. Eaton believed that "the Lord [had] begun the refining process; those things that *can be shaken* I think will soon be, & whatsever [*sic*] is not founded upon the *rock* will fall."[32] In the same letter, she spoke of a new religious "circle" about which there were "many falsehoods afloat . . . & much misunderstanding," but through which she found her "own faith strengthened & confirmed. . . ."[33] "As yet," she wrote, "I see nothing, rightly understood, unscriptural in them."[34] At least in letters to her husband, Mrs. Eaton was willing to pass judgment on new clergy, provide commentaries on theological debates, and abstract Finney's sermons, restating his position on sanctification. On this last topic, she claimed that the city's "Clergymen know next to nothing of [Finney's] views & have no idea of the popularity & strength they are gaining."[35]

Still, the mission of female Finneyites was to serve not only as critics of the unregenerate but also as "harbinger[s] of the millennium."[36] Beginning with prayer circles and maternal associations, evangelical women soon founded antislavery, moral reform, and temperance associations. These associations advocated more controversial positions in more strident tones than did the earlier charitable societies founded by village elites. Believing, for instance, "that the slavery existing in our land is a gross violation of the law of God" and that God "has made it the duty of all . . . to do what they can to remove this sin," female Finneyites formed

---

[31] Elizabeth Selden Eaton to Amos Eaton, 20 April 1833, in McKelvey, "Letters," 46.

[32] Ibid., 45

[33] Ibid., 47.

[34] Ibid., 47.

[35] Ibid., 48, 66, 70-71.

[36] Ibid., 74-75.

themselves "into a Society" in 1834 to arouse the Christian community to action.[37] Two years later Mary Mathews reported on the successes of this society to Mrs. Finney and announced the organization of "a Moral Reform Society" of "about 60 members."[38] Through the Moral Reform Society, evangelical women sought to "*restrain licentiousness and criminal indulgence*"; to aid "such of the unfortunate as are disposed to return to habits of rectitude and virtue"; and to impose a single, woman-defined moral code.[39] Elizabeth Eaton believed that "christians cannot expect the blessing of God in these times, who do not do whatsoever their hands find to do to rid the world of [the] vice" of intemperance.[40] By the early 1840s she rejoiced that local women's "temperance enterprize [*sic*]" seemed to have "prospered & [been] blessed." "I have no doubt," she wrote Amos, "that the great & universal disposition & effort to forsake this vice . . . is a preparing of the way of the Lord. . . ."[41] As part of this preparation, the women's temperance society collected some 1,000 signers to the pledge in four weeks in December 1841, and the following month Elizabeth Eaton reported "1350 names of females" recorded on temperance pledges.[42]

In pursuit of the millennium, evangelical women condemned unregenerate men, took upon themselves the role of theological interpreters, and launched a three-pronged attack on vice that attracted the attention and participation of several thousand local women. Yet neither the condemnations nor the attacks were sustained. The women who founded the Female Anti-Slavery Society in 1835 retreated from public abolitionist efforts in the early 1840s and reemerged a decade later as an auxiliary to a local male society. The Female Moral Reform Society, founded by these same women, dropped its overt critique of male licentiousness in the mid-

---

[37]Rochester Female Anti-Slavery Society Constitution [1835], Samuel Drummond Porter Family Papers, University of Rochester, Rochester, New York.

[38]Mrs. Mary Mathews to Mrs. Charles Finney, 22 June 1836, Finney Papers.

[39]*Daily Sun* (Rochester NY), 27 June 1839; *Canfield and Warren's Directory of the City of Rochester, for 1845-46* (Rochester NY: John Canfield and Ansel Warren, 1845) 9.

[40]Elizabeth Selden Eaton to Amos Eaton, 11 January 1842, in McKelvey, "Letters," 73.

[41]Elizabeth Selden Eaton to Amos Eaton, 31 December 1841, in ibid.

[42]Elizabeth Selden Eaton to Amos Eaton, 25 January 1842, in ibid., 74-75.

1840s and concentrated instead on providing a temporary home and an employment agency for "friendless" women in Rochester. Simultaneously, women's "temperance enterprize [sic]" shifted away from door-to-door canvassing and public demonstrations to the establishment of soup kitchens in conjunction with the Charitable Society and the distribution of alms to reformed drunkards.[43]

Women's retreat from radical perfectionist activities occurred as the "new men and new measures" became, as Smith-Rosenberg claims, the new norm. Evangelical men and women acknowledged the waning of activist enthusiasm that accompanied this transition. In May 1836, Mary Mathews complained of the ill-treatment accorded antislavery lecturer Theodore Weld at Third Presbyterian Church: "If it had been any other lecturer—and in any other house—I could have borne it—but to see a crowd in that house—where every association is sacred, hissing and insulting Mr. Weld . . . it was more than I could endure."[44] Rather than try to resurrect Third Church's sacred and abolitionist tone, several evangelical families banded together in the formation of the Bethel Free Church in the year of Weld's visit. One of the founders, Samuel D. Porter, wrote that the church had its origins in the "spirit of christian progress and reform. . . . Active Christianity in the varied walks of life was the standard of religion and the publically recognized motto of the church." He wrote these words in 1845 when he and his wife Susan resigned their membership. In explaining their action, the Porters pointed to the "spiritual bareness of the church" and "its striking and retrograde movement . . . upon the subject of slavery" in the decade since the church's founding.[45] Yet before these words were even written, the Female Anti-Slavery Society, of which Susan Porter was a founder, had dispersed. Before its echo died on the ears of Bethel Church elders, Susan Porter had also retreated

---

[43]On the reemergence of evangelical activists in the late 1840s and the 1850s, see Rochester Ladies' Anti-Slavery Sewing Society, "Circular, the First Report of the Rochester Ladies' Anti-Slavery Sewing Society, 1852," (Rochester NY: n.p., 1852); Rochester Friendly Home [Home for Friendless Women] Papers, University of Rochester, Rochester, New York; Rochester Female Charitable Society Minute Book, 3 January 1853, Rochester Female Charitable Society Papers.

[44]Mrs. Mary Mathews to Mrs. Charles Finney, 22 June 1836, Finney Papers.

[45]Samuel D. Porter to Pastor and Sessions of the Washington Street [Bethel Free] Presbyterian Church, 29 September 1845, Porter Family Papers.

from perfectionist and moral-reform efforts. She, like Mary Mathews and other female Finneyites, did not withdraw entirely from public works but instead retreated to more respectable benevolent associations and activities.

After more than a decade of activity to perfect society, why did these women abandon those associations that promised them such widely expanded roles in the salvation of their community? They have left few direct statements as to their motives, but Smith-Rosenberg's analysis suggests two areas of inquiry: the structural movement of evangelical women into a stable and secure, if subordinate, role in the emerging urban bourgeoisie, and the ideological preparation for that role in the humiliation and subjugation women experienced during the conversion process. Indeed, it appears that these forces did converge in the lives of many female evangelical leaders.

Between 1830 when Finney aroused Rochesterians to evangelical commitment and the mid-1840s when revivalism and female activism waned, the families of many female Finneyites secured their location in Rochester's emerging bourgeoisie. Elizabeth Eaton entered Rochester as a member of the well-to-do Selden family, married attorney Joseph Spencer, and joined the Female Charitable Society in its founding year. However, her husband's death in 1823 placed her in a more precarious financial position, which her marriage to Amos Eaton in 1831 did not entirely relieve. As an Army supply officer, Amos Eaton traveled extensively to maintain an adequate income for his family. About the time of her marriage, Elizabeth joined the Finney-led Third Presbyterian Church and soon thereafter participated in temperance, moral reform, and antislavery causes. Meanwhile, Amos Eaton was rising in Army ranks and accumulating a comfortable savings. By mid-century, Elizabeth Eaton was returned to the financially secure position in which she had been raised. At that point, she joined her husband in a more permanent residence in New York City and there turned her attention to more privatized and institutionalized forms of moral salvation. The Home for Friendless Women, which she helped to establish in New York City, served as a model for Rochester's evangelical women as they too traveled the path from evangelical Perfectionism to bourgeois reform.

Most of Rochester's female Finneyites followed a less circuitous path to economic stability, social position, and circumscribed social roles than did Elizabeth Eaton. Mary and Selah Mathews moved into the ranks of middle-class comfort and security between the mid-1830s and the mid-1840s. Selah developed a lucrative law practice and, simultaneously, gained political clout as a city recorder in 1841 and a federal judge by 1847. He combined these successes with seats on the Commercial Bank's Board of Directors and the Third Presbyterian Church's Committee of Elders. Moreover, he directed these manifold activities from his residence in the Third, or "Ruffled Shirt," Ward in the city's center. Thus Selah brought his family to the forefront of Rochester's new wealth. Similarly, Samuel D. Porter rose from store clerk to printer to successful land agent between 1827 and 1850. He served as a Presbyterian Church elder as well, and though his abolitionist stances kept him out of local political office, he was a leader in statewide third-party efforts. While less affluent and politically powerful than Selah Mathews, Samuel Porter had successes that were sufficient to establish his family in a Third Ward home and provide them with the economic and social signifiers that attended such residence.

Sarah Seward, who had sacrificed herself to Christ's cause "body and soul" in the 1830s, married Jacob Gould in 1841. A shoemaker by trade, Jacob Gould had established the successful Rochester Boot and Shoe Factory in the early 1820s. The first Mrs. Gould was a Charitable Society charter member, an appropriate role for the wife of a prosperous merchant, a First Church elder, bank director, and local political official. When Sarah Seward became Jacob's second wife, she too joined First Presbyterian Church, the offices of the Charitable Society, and the affluent circles of the Third Ward. She could look about her and feel justified in her new life as she saw Mary Mathews, Elizabeth Eaton, Susan Porter, and other evangelical sisters also settling into more comfortable circumstances and more circumscribed social roles.

The transition to bourgeois womanhood based on economic stability and social subordination was eased not only by the collective character of the transition but also by the individual subjugation experienced by these women during the height of revival enthusiasm. Women who condemned unregenerate men and organized activist campaigns simultaneously expressed their subjection to and humiliation before God. Sarah Seward, for instance, nurtured numerous conversions among her seminary students yet believed her successes depended on her "body & soul" sacrifice to her heavenly "Master."[46] Susan Porter expressed the same depend-

---

[46]Sarah T. Seward to Mr. and Mrs. Charles Finney, 9 March 1835, Finney Papers.

ency in starker terms when a friend and fellow activist, Mrs. Lester, lost her baby girl "after only one or two breaths." The "ways of Providence," she claimed, "sometime seem mysterious to us who are but shortsighted worms of the dust. . . . 'We have but to bow the head in silence when God calls back the things we love,'" she concluded.[47]

Elizabeth Eaton wrote to her husband in 1833, begging him "to be much in prayer. What the Lord will have us do . . . I do not know—but everywhere to do his work we must be wholly his."[48] Mrs. Mathews found so "many unholy motives and such unsanctified feelings rise up," even while performing "external christian duties," that her "only hope" was "Jesus Christ." Her "own wicked heart" was her gravest concern, and she applauded those women who could accept the burdens of financial failure or a child's death "as a true christian." She too wished to be "an instrument" in Christ's hands: "I have been led to see more and more my utter weakness—and my utter dependence on Christ."[49] Self-doubt that could be relieved only by total subjection to God or Christ must have made women vulnerable to ministerial censure and increased their willingness to subject themselves to the new dictates of a post-revival bourgeois order.

Many evangelical women who had emphasized the liberating aspects of revivalism for a decade finally chose to retreat from further social dislocation in the face of male censure and economic rewards. The experience of humiliation before God, which conformed to women's earlier socialization into subordinate and privatized roles, eased women's retreat into new forms of submission. It was apparently essential, however, that this ritual humiliation be complemented by economic security, since the few women who refused submission and instead pursued increasingly radical social critiques and wider roles for women are distinctive in their failure to achieve such security.[50]

---

[47]Mrs. Samuel D. Porter to Mrs. Charles Finney, 20 September 1845, Finney Papers.

[48]Elizabeth Selden Eaton to Amos Eaton, 16 April 1833, in McKelvey, "Letters," 45.

[49]Mrs. Mary Mathews to Mrs. Charles Finney, 16 May 1831, 19 December 1831, 20 October 1832, 24 April 1833, Finney Papers.

[50]Unfortunately, we can only examine those few women from Presbyterian congregations who fell into this category due to the absence of records for the major Methodist and Baptist congregations in Rochester. No doubt these churches contained a high proportion of economically marginal families.

Sarah C. Owen was an evangelical convert who joined Brick Presbyterian Church and local moral reform and antislavery efforts in the 1830s. In 1839, at the Semi-Annual Meeting of the American Female Moral Reform Association, evangelical women unanimously adopted a resolution offered by Sarah Owen:

> That in uniting together for the purpose of concentrating our influence in behalf of humanity, morality, and religion, we are not leaving our own proper sphere . . . but acting strictly in accordance with the dictates of reason and the word of God.[51]

Yet the evangelical sisters who supported her so fully then were no doubt hesitant when she criticized "all Churches of different Sects" as "corrupt" for their acceptance of slavery. In 1842 when Brick Church elders accused her of "unchristian conduct" for these words, most of her former allies had retreated from public antislavery efforts. By 1845 church elders were asking her to provide "evidence of repentance or reformation" or face excommunication. Sarah Owen responded by proclaiming her intention to follow "the direction of the Apostle 'to withdraw from those that walk disorderly.' "[52] When she next stood on a public platform, at the 1848 Rochester Woman's Rights Convention, it was to declare that in the future "woman shall stand where God designed she should, on an even platform with man himself."[53] The only evangelical sisters who are known to have stood by her side then were also *former* Brick Church perfectionists or Third Church converts.

These women, such as Abigail Bush, shared more than excommunication with Sarah Owen; they also shared economic uncertainty. Throughout her years in Rochester, Sarah Owen supported herself through nursing and needlework. She traveled to Michigan periodically to help care for the family of her sister and appears to have moved there permanently sometime in the early 1850s. Abigail Bush, born Abigail

---

[51]*Advocate of Moral Reform*, 15 October 1839.

[52]Second [Brick] Presbyterian Church Session Minutes, vol. 3 (1841-1863), 31 October 1842, 8 December 1845, Presbyterian Historical Society, Philadelphia, Pennsylvania.

[53]Rochester Woman's Rights Convention, "Proceedings," in *The Concise History of Woman Suffrage*, ed. Mari Jo Buhle and Paul Buhle (Chicago: University of Illinois Press, 1978) 102.

Norton, was raised in a relatively affluent household in Rochester and attended First Presbyterian Church and the Female Charitable Society.

In 1833 she married Henry Bush, a stove manufacturer and radical abolitionist, and her life changed drastically. Within five years her name was missing from both Brick Church and Charitable Society ranks. By the mid-1840s she was a leader, along with Henry, in the Quaker-led Western New York Anti-Slavery Society. Throughout this period, Henry Bush's financial fortunes seem to have fallen as he devoted increasing amounts of time to antislavery politics. Abigail sought to maintain her public activities while also maintaining her household and giving birth to six children, two of whom died in 1846. Abigail Bush presided at the woman's rights convention at which Sarah Owen spoke, but her activist career in Rochester was cut short when Henry decided to invest his family's economic future in the California Gold Rush. In 1850 he left his wife, once again pregnant, behind and headed west. She followed, with a new baby, the following year. On her departure, she bemoaned the fact that so many young men and women were "leaving Home, its Comforts and Endearments" when most would be "Doomed to Disappointment, Sorrow, & a Grave. . . ." As to her own future, she wrote glowingly of her Rochester "Home, & Home's Loved Ones," never expecting to find others "to stand side by side with me, Heart to Heart, in our Labours of Love & Good will, to our Afflicted and Downtrodden Fellow Ones." In leaving behind her Progressive Quaker friends, Abigail Bush clearly believed she was also leaving behind her efforts to change the world.[54]

The network of women acknowledged by Abigail Bush provided more than personal support. Many women, in other years and other cities, had found in evangelical religion a possible vehicle for the expansion and redefinition of women's roles. Yet without a supportive network of women with similar views on women's roles, they retreated under pressures of male censure or remained isolated and ostracized. In Rochester, the circle of Progressive Quakers who advocated an antiritualistic and spiritualist religion and a variety of social critiques provided a haven and a platform for evangelical women who pursued the radical implications of Finneyite revivalism beyond the pale of bourgeois order.

---

[54]Abigail Bush to Amy Post, [185-], Amy and Isaac Post Family Papers, University of Rochester, Rochester, New York.

For Progressive Quakers, antiritualism was rooted in a centuries-old tradition of religious dissent. This dissent was forged into radical social criticisms when geographical mobility and sustained social and economic marginality fired reevaluations of class, race, and gender relations. Quakers believed in the Inner Light, which revealed to each individual unmediated truths, and supported Quaker women's absolute right to speak out as equals of men on theological and social issues. Moreover, Quaker women lacked a conversion experience and the ritual humiliation and subjugation such a rite of passage entailed. Having started on the path of antiritualism, social criticism, and public activism, Progressive Quakers felt far fewer pressures than their evangelical counterparts to accept subordination within a new bourgeois order. Reaggregation was impossible for Quaker women, who had never been integrated into the social order from which female Finneyites emerged, and Progressive Quakers in particular came from decidedly different types of communities: downstate farming communities populated almost exclusively by Quakers and relatively untouched by the commercial or industrial developments that reshaped New England in the 1810s and 1820s. Those Quakers who did gain the economic status necessary to move into Rochester's emerging bourgeoisie, or who became enmeshed in the commercial nexus of the city's economy, retreated from the more radical implications of Quaker theology, thus paralleling evangelical women's retreat from radical Evangelicalism.

Progressive Quakers were always a small minority within local Quaker ranks. They were more agrarian-oriented, economically marginal, and geographically mobile than their Orthodox Quaker peers, and at least somewhat distinct in these same features from their Hicksite Quaker counterparts.[55] They were part of dense, kin-connected groups with stronger ties to Quaker farming communities in downstate New York, southern Pennsylvania, and the Midwest than to Rochester. In each community where Progressive Quakerism emerged, abolitionism, Spiritualism, and women's rights also appeared and attracted the support

---

[55]For discussions of the divisions within the Society of Friends and the social and economic characteristics of the various Quaker groups, see Robert J. Doherty, *The Hicksite Separation: A Sociological Analysis of Religious Schism in Early Nineteenth-Century America* (New Brunswick NJ: Rutgers University Press, 1967) and A. Day Bradley, "Progressive Friends in Michigan and New York," *Quaker History* 52 (1963): 95-103.

of a few women who emerged from and then rejected Finneyite Evangelicalism. These ex-Evangelicals joined Progressive Quakers in believing that woman had "too long rested satisfied in the circumscribed limits which corrupt customs and a perverted application of the Scriptures [had] marked out for her." They also sought to "move in the enlarged sphere" that woman's "greater Creator" had truly "assigned her."[56] Those who followed antiritualism and unmediated revelation into the realms of Spiritualism even came to accept that "a fond mother" was "better qualified to direct the spiritual life of her own sex than any belov'd disciple or even Jesus himself as a man. . . ."[57] The religious and social implications of these statements were far more radical than anything voiced by those who stayed within the evangelical fold, and Progressive Quakers and their allies refused to retreat.

By mid-century, then, three groups of women with distinctive senses of their spiritual and social state lived side by side in Rochester: pre-Finneyite benevolent women, evangelical perfectionists in retreat, and Progressive Quaker egalitarians. In many respects, the experiences of these women confirm the patterns suggested by Douglas's and Turner's anthropological models. The polar culture-types described by Douglas—the one, rigid, hierarchical, and highly ritualized and the other fluid, egalitarian, and antiritualistic—are visible in the benevolent women and the Progressive Quakers, respectively. The movement between such poles as individuals shift from one social position to another in a society is schematized by Turner, and the rites of passage he describes clearly resonate with the experiences of evangelical women. The divergence from these models is evident when we consider that these three groups of women coexist in one society. Models provide pure types against which we can test reality; history provides overlapping and discontinuous processes that can be schematized by, but not contained in, such models.

Early nineteenth-century Rochester, as a frontier and boom town village, does not fit easily on Douglas's grid of a rigid and hierarchical society, even in the years when the affluent families of benevolent women predominated. Nor, despite the existence of Progressive Quakers within Rochester, does the city replicate the open-ended, loosely structured, and mobile society offered as Douglas's alternative grid point. Rather, by

---

[56]Rochester Woman's Rights Convention, "Proceedings," in Buhle and Buhle, 102.

[57][Sarah Thayer] to Amy Post, 9 March 1853, Post Family Papers.

mid-century, rigidly bound and loosely affiliated, hierarchical and egalitarian, ritualistic and antiritualistic groups coexisted in Rochester. Various sectors of the city's population advocated different models of social and cosmological order simultaneously, and they fought throughout the first half of the nineteenth century for the dominant voice in the community.

A new urbane, bourgeois order eventually won out—one that, not surprisingly perhaps, lay somewhere between the ordered elitism of the founding families and the leveling egalitarianism of the Progressive Quakers. From the perspective of revivalism's seeming potential for liberation, that bourgeois society appears as a reaggregation to older hierarchies and boundaries. Thus it does seem to reflect the pattern suggested by Turner, in which antistructuralism is a contained social process only temporarily altering social and cosmological configurations. Yet revivalism's seeming potential for liberation, when combined with the vast economic changes of the 1820s and 1830s, was not wholly lost in women's retreat from radicalism. Evangelical women expanded their public roles in the 1830s and retreated in the 1840s, but they reemerged in the 1850s to institutionalize at least a limited range of new roles for women.

Susan Porter, for instance, whose career was traced above into the 1840s, was not idle during her retreat from radicalism. She turned her energies to the work of the Orphan Asylum and the Home for Friendless Women, both joint benevolent-evangelical efforts. In the Orphan Association, moreover, she fought for the equal treatment of black and white children, and in the Home advocated vocational as well as domestic education for working-class women. In 1851, when abolitionist Frederick Douglass's editorial assistant, Julia Griffiths, called for the organization of a new Rochester Ladies' Anti-Slavery Society, Susan Porter joined and was elected the society's first president. In this society, she and several of her evangelical sisters raised funds, aided fugitive slaves, and supported the education of Southern blacks. Susan Porter died in September 1880, having just returned from a meeting of the Board of Directors of the Home Association. She was eulogized in the city's papers as "a woman peculiarly sympathetic in her nature and charitable in the best application of the term. . . . Her loss is felt like that of a mother, by many more than her own children."[58] As an abolitionist and an activist, Susan Porter was not

---

[58] *Union and Advertiser* (Rochester NY), 25 September 1880.

only recognized but praised. Clearly her post-revival "reaggregation" was as incomplete as her revival-inspired radicalization.

The particular balance between reaggregation and radicalism chosen by any particular evangelical woman in the 1850s depended on a number of factors, including relative affluence and kin connections. Susan Porter's in-laws were less well-to-do than her own family and were more involved in antislavery activities and antiritualistic religious worship than many Evangelicals. Susan and Samuel Porter's integration into the city's emerging bourgeoisie may have kept their poorer relatives from pursuing more radical ventures at the same time that Susan herself was encouraged to continue her abolitionist activism by those kin.

Mary Mathews, whose husband and in-laws were more prosperous and politically powerful than the Porters, retreated further from her evangelical origins. In the 1850s and 1860s she joined her sister, Mrs. Frederick Whittlesey, in the Home Association and Charitable Society. Mrs. Whittlesey, married to one of Rochester's earliest and most successful attorneys, only strayed outside of benevolent circles in the 1850s, perhaps at the behest of Mary Mathews. In the following decade, Mrs. Whittlesey's daughter, Mary Mathews Whittlesey, began her activist career in the Home Association. Clearly, family members, drawing on slightly different economic and religious experiences, could influence the forms of activism undertaken by sisters, daughters, and in-laws.

By the 1860s the question was no longer should women be publicly active but rather what form that activism would take. When Mary Mathews Whittlesey entered the offices of the Home Association in 1866, she replaced Mrs. John Bush, the former Mary Stone, as treasurer. In 1806 Mary Stone had submitted to Reverend Elliott's request that the ladies "omit meeting" for charitable purposes. By 1866 no evangelical reverend was likely to make such a request, nor was an evangelical woman likely to submit should he do so. The economic and theological changes of sixty years did not create equal roles for women, but they did assure women's roles in "S[ocietie]s" that were once considered "ostentatious."[59]

Perhaps ministers and the public no longer saw women's charitable ventures as ostentatious because that term was now reserved for spiritualist circles and women's rights conventions. A new and far broader spec-

---

[59]Mary Stone to Mabel Hand Ward, 20 August 1806, Presbyterian Historical Society.

trum of activist roles was open to women, redefining public perceptions of radicalism and women's perceptions of subordination. In light of women's restrictions to home and church in 1806, the formation of a charitable society appeared as an unwarranted departure from women's proper sphere. In light of Progressive Quakers' rejections of any human authority and their demands for complete equality for women, Susan Porter's extensive activism and outspoken abolitionism were viewed as "charitable in the best application of the term."[60]

While Turner and Douglas's models are insufficient to capture the complex and manifold transitions experienced by women in the first half of the nineteenth century, they do help us envision and investigate the relations between women's religious and economic circumstances. Douglas encourages us to look for the meaning of cosmological shifts in structural relations, while Turner provides a way of understanding women's differential responses to those shifts. Returning to Turner's analysis of liminality one last time, we see that he notes three sources of liminality: falling in the interstices of the social structure, marginality, and social inferiority. All women of the period could be defined as socially inferior; yet those of Finney's female converts who returned to respectability did so within families that were socially and economically central to the emergence of Rochester's bourgeoisie. All women also fell, at least temporarily, into the interstices of the social structure; however, only a minority of Finney's converts joined their Quaker neighbors as permanent members of a marginal class. Thus for most female Finneyites, revivalism and the rejection of existing authority and structure were only a temporary phase marking the parameters of socioeconomic movement.

Only those evangelical women in whose lives all three forms of liminality converged maintained their liminal, antistructural phase. Moreover, they were able to translate personal liminality into social activism by joining with a larger group of Progressive Quakers who rejected revivalism from the beginning, basing their religious and social critiques on a heritage of marginality, antiritualism, antistructuralism, and egalitarianism.

Finally, if we remember that the Finney-led revivals affected women's lives over a lengthy period of extensive change, we can redefine Turn-

---

[60]*Union and Advertiser* (Rochester NY), 25 September 1880.

er's stage of reaggregation to incorporate that change. Revivalism eased and contained many women's transitions from one social, economic, and familial position to another. It also helped to transform social, economic, and familial orders. Revivals inculcated values and behaviors that ultimately encouraged women's retreat to respectability, as that was redefined in the emerging bourgeois order. This respectability embraced a wide range of public roles for women.

To foster both transitions in women's positions and redefinitions of social order, revivals had to momentarily free women from all restraints. Having experienced such freedom, women could never be returned to earlier and more rigid boundaries on their "sphere." Religious enthusiasm thus served as a powerful force in many women's lives and, for a few, provided the impetus to demand fundamental social change. That impetus, in conjunction with the existence of Quaker allies well versed in antiritualism and feminism, enabled these few evangelical women—in the face of male censure and social restrictions—to formulate and maintain a female-oriented social critique and a feminist politics.

Chapter 9

The Fundamentalist Leaven and the Rise of an Evangelical United Front

Joel Carpenter

On 7 April 1942, J. Elwin Wright, director of the New England Fellowship and a national fundamentalist leader, stood to speak before a modest crowd of about two hundred at the Coronado Hotel in St. Louis, Missouri. He had spoken to more people, no doubt, on snowy Sunday evenings in New England, but he must have felt a special thrill as he addressed these delegates and observers at the National Conference for United Action Among Evangelicals.[1] They had come from all over the country and from thirty-four denominations, many at Wright's personal invitation, to make decisions that, according to another speaker, might "affect the whole future course of evangelical Christianity in America.[2]

---

[1]Wright's speech and a full report of the proceedings are found in *Evangelical Action! A Report of the Organization of the National Association of Evangelicals for United Action* (Boston: United Action Press, 1942).

[2]Harold John Ockenga, "The Unvoiced Multitudes," in ibid., 19.

Thus began the National Association of Evangelicals, a fellowship organized to present a united voice for conservative Protestants. Some of the delegates were members of denominations already represented by the Federal Council of the Churches of Christ. Others were from denominations that were neither represented by the Federal Council nor wished to be. Together, they comprised a major segment of the American evangelical mosaic. Among them were Baptist, Presbyterian and independent fundamentalists, holiness Wesleyan Methodists and Free Methodists, Assemblies of God pentecostals, Southern Baptists and Southern Presbyterians, a Missouri Synod Lutheran, Mennonite Brethren, and Scandinavians from Evangelical Free and Evangelical Covenant churches.[3] This meeting fulfilled one of Wright's most cherished visions. He had brought hundreds of evangelical pastors and congregations of varied traditions into fellowship and cooperation in New England.[4] Now, after several years of travel, correspondence, and conferences, he and other leaders such as Ralph T. Davis, secretary of the Africa Inland Mission, and Harold J. Ockenga, pastor of Park Street Church, Boston, had assembled Evangelicals of all kinds to plan for a national organization.[5]

The National Association of Evangelicals was called together largely by fundamentalists. This does not sound very surprising, since it has usually been labeled a fundamentalist organization.[6] In fact, the NAE was inclusively evangelical, and American Evangelicalism comprises a vast

---

[3]A roster of delegates is included in *Evangelical Action!*, 92-100.

[4]The only published account of Wright's work in the New England Fellowship is Muriel Wright Evans and Elizabeth M. Evans, *Incidents and Information of the First 48 Years: Rumney Conference's 75th Anniversary* (Rumney NH: n.p., 1978).

[5]Wright's opening speech to the St. Louis conference, "An Historical Statement of Events Leading Up to the National Conference at S. Louis," in *Evangelical Action!*, 3-16, summarized the developments leading up to that point; but for a more detailed record of the discussion, meetings, and correspondence involved, see the letters, memos, and committee minutes in Ralph T. Davis's correspondence, located in the Records of the Africa Inland Mission, collection 81, box 14, folder 27, Billy Graham Center Archives, Wheaton, Illinois. This collection is cited hereafter as AIM Records.

[6]William G. McLoughlin, *Modern Revivalism: Charles Grandison Finney to Billy Graham* (New York: Ronald Press, 1959); Winthrop S. Hudson, *Religion in America* (New York: Scribner's, 1973) 383; Martin E. Marty, *Righteous Empire: The Protestant Experience in America* (New York: Dial Press, 1970) 246-49.

and varied mosaic of which Fundamentalism is but one segment. Thus to claim that fundamentalists initiated the call for the NAE points to some significant developments among Evangelicals at large and within the fundamentalist movement in particular.

"Fundamentalism" is indeed an elusive term, which begs definition in order to avoid confusion. In journalistic circles it has become such common and debased coinage as to lose its usefulness, but in American religious history it has recently gained new precision. Ernest Sandeen defined it as a historic millenarian movement that joined with conservative Calvinism to defend Protestant orthodoxy from theological liberalism and secularization.[7] George Marsden's new study shows the movement's roots in D. L. Moody's revivalism, Common Sense philosophy, and the Keswick holiness movement, as well as premillennialism and biblical inerrancy.[8] Thus it has become easier to say who the fundamentalists were and who they were not. Fundamentalism was an interdenominational, evangelical movement that grew up around the Bible schools, magazines, missions, and conferences founded by Dwight L. Moody and his protégés, such as Adoniram J. Gordon, Cyrus I. Scofield, and Reuben A. Torrey in the 1880s and 1890s. Its denominational roots were in the generally Reformed wing of North American Evangelicalism: the Baptists, Presbyterians, and Congregationalists. The movement became known as "fundamentalist" when it took the offensive after World War I. America was turning its back on God, fundamentalists thought, and only a return to the fundamentals of the faith and evangelical mores would set things right.[9]

---

[7]Ernest R. Sandeen, "Toward a Historical Interpretation of the Roots of Fundamentalism," *Church History* 36 (March 1967) 66-83; and Sandeen, *The Roots of Fundamentalism: British and American Millenarianism, 1800-1930* (Chicago: University of Chicago Press, 1970).

[8]George M. Marsden, *Fundamentalism and American Culture: The Shaping of Twentieth Century Evangelicalism, 1870-1925* (New York: Oxford University Press, 1980).

[9]The problem of defining Fundamentalism is discussed ably in Sandeen, *The Roots of Fundamentalism*, xiii-xxiii; George M. Marsden, "Defining Fundamentalism," *Christian Scholar's Review* 1 (Winter 1971): 141-51; Sandeen, "Defining Fundamentalism: A Reply to Professor Marsden," *Christian Scholar's Review* 1 (Spring 1971): 227-32; and Marsden, *Fundamentalism and American Culture*, 3-8, 199-205.

Fundamentalists are Evangelicals, but not all Evangelicals were fundamentalists. Missouri Synod Lutherans, for example, made the proclamation of the gospel and opposition to Modernism central concerns, but they abhorred the fundamentalists' low view of the sacraments.[10] The Assemblies of God and other Pentecostals considered themselves to be "fundamental," but they insisted that the infilling of the Holy Spirit was accompanied by speaking in tongues, which alienated them from fundamentalists.[11] Many Church of the Nazarene people militantly opposed Modernism; however, as part of the Wesleyan holiness movement, they believed grace could wholly cleanse the believer's heart of the inward moral propensity to sin, while fundamentalists denied it could happen this side of heaven.[12] Southern Baptists were heartily evangelistic and theologically conservative, but they resented Northern fundamentalists' making premillennialism a test of orthodoxy while downplaying Baptist fundamentals such as restricted communion and believer's baptism.[13]

Why is it significant, then, that a group of fundamentalists initiated the call for a National Association of Evangelicals? It indicates, first, a ferment within Fundamentalism. The movement had not faded but had thrived during the 1930s, when old-line Protestantism suffered a depression.[14] By the 1940s a contingent of leaders was trying to bring revival to

---

[10]Milton L. Rudnick, *Fundamentalism and the Missouri Synod: A Historical Study of Their Interaction and Mutual Influence* (St. Louis: Concordia Publishing House, 1966) 84-90, details these Lutheran confessionalists' criticisms of Fundamentalism. See Theodore Graebner, *The Problem of Lutheran Union and Other Essays* (St. Louis: Concordia Publishing House, 1935) 50-52, 62-66, 70-72, on their aversion to unionism and "chiliasm" in particular. See also F. E. Mayer, *The Religious Bodies of America* (St. Louis: Concordia Publishing House, 1954) 419-26, 480-81, for critical articles on premillennialism and Fundamentalism.

[11]William W. Menzies, *Anointed to Serve: The Story of the Assemblies of God* (Springfield MO: Gospel Publishing House, 1971) 24-28, 180-81.

[12]Timothy L. Smith, *Called unto Holiness, The Story of the Nazarenes: The Formative Years* (Kansas City: Nazarene Publishing House, 1962) 315-21.

[13]Kenneth C. Hubbard, "Anti-Conventionism in the Southern Baptist Convention, 1940-1962," (Ph.D. diss., Southwestern Baptist Theological Seminary, 1968) 83-94.

[14]The author discusses fundamentalist growth after 1930 in "Fundamentalist Institutions and the Rise of Evangelical Protestantism, 1929-1942," *Church History* 49 (March 1980): 62-75.

America. They criticized the doctrinal exclusiveness and aggressive tactics of the older Fundamentalism and sought the cooperation of all other Evangelicals.[15] The formation of the NAE and a militant fundamentalist rival, the American Council of Christian Churches, helped produce a split in the movement.

Fundamentalist initiative in forming the National Association of Evangelicals also helps us understand some of the complex relationships within the evangelical network. Fundamentalist ideas and emphases permeated many non-fundamentalist traditions and helped the NAE founders call together a new evangelical coalition. It was easy, then, for the chastened fundamentalists who first conceived of this "new Evangelicalism" to presume that its theology would mirror their own. In the 1940s and 1950s, many other Evangelicals accepted the NAE invitations on those terms. Still other Evangelicals, then and since, have interpreted their faith differently. The NAE encouraged new levels of evangelical fellowship and cooperative evangelism, but it failed to provide a common ground for all of America's Evangelicals. Thus the fundamentalist leaven both helped to make evangelical cooperation possible and to limit its range.

Elwin Wright began his quest for a national evangelical association in 1937. As he and his radio ensemble toured national fundamentalist centers such as the Church of the Open Door in Los Angeles, leading pastors and institutional heads heard about the New England Fellowship. Its hundreds of evangelistic meetings, Bible conferences, and radio broadcasts each year were supported not only by fundamentalists, but also by Evangelicals from the Protestant Episcopal, Nazarene, Assemblies of God, Christian Reformed, Advent Christian, and Methodist churches. Many asked Wright whether he thought evangelical cooperation could happen nationally. Not one to refuse a challenge, he began to promote the idea in 1939.[16]

---

[15]See, for example, a pointed expression of Wright's intentions and criticisms of older Fundamentalism in a letter he proposed to send to the *Sunday School Times*, enclosed in J. E. Wright to Herbert J. Taylor, 2 July 1942, Herbert J. Taylor Papers, collection 20, box 65, folder 16, Archives of the Billy Graham Center, Wheaton, Illinois; cited hereafter as H. J. Taylor Papers.

[16]Evans and Evans, *Incidents and Information*, 22-24.

The same idea had occurred to others. Ralph T. Davis, associate secretary of the Africa Inland Mission, wrote to several Bible school presidents in December of 1940 to propose a national committee to represent evangelical groups. His most immediate concern was the effect the military draft might have on missionary candidates. He also worried, though, about evangelical representation in general, fearing that the government would rely exclusively on the Federal Council of Churches to voice Protestant concerns. Will H. Houghton of Moody Bible Institute, J. Davis Adams of the Philadelphia School of the Bible, and Howard W. Ferrin of the Providence Bible Institute responded favorably, sharing Davis's concerns and offering their support.[17]

Throughout early 1941 Davis and Wright promoted the idea among fundamentalist and other evangelical leaders. In September they heard some disconcerting news. Fundamentalist separatists H. McAllister Griffiths, Harold Laird, and Carl McIntire of the Bible Presbyterian Church were forming the American Council of Christian Churches and offering membership to anyone else who wished to militantly oppose the Federal Council. These men were not nationally recognized leaders, and did not want to let others help shape the council's purpose, leadership, and mission.[18] As Wright later explained it, his group now faced a dilemma: should they join forces with the McIntire organization or continue their own plans, even if it meant a damaging rivalry?[19]

He and Davis assembled nationally known evangelical leaders at the Moody Bible Institute in Chicago on Monday evening, 27 October 1941 to discuss this matter.[20] The group included William Ward Ayer, pastor of Calvary Baptist Church, New York City; T. J. Bach, secretary of the

---

[17]R. T. Davis to Will H. Houghton, J. Davis Adams, Howard W. Ferrin, and Louis T. Talbot, 11 December 1940; Will H. Houghton to Ralph T. Davis, 23 December 1940; J. Davis Adams to Ralph T. Davis, 13 December 1940; Howard W. Ferrin to Ralph T. Davis, 13 December 1940, Davis correspondence, AIM Records.

[18]Wright, "An Historical Statement," 5-7; form letter from Temporary Committee for United Action Among Evangelicals per R. T. Davis, secretary, 2 March 1942, received by Herbert J. Taylor, H. J. Taylor Papers.

[19]Wright to Herbert J. Taylor, 2 July 1942, H. J. Taylor Papers.

[20]Wright, "An Historical Statement;" Minutes of the Committee for United Action among Evangelicals, 27-28 October 1941, Chicago IL, AIM Records.

Scandinavian Alliance Mission; Horace F. Dean, vice-president of the Philadelphia School of the Bible; V. Raymond Edman, president of Wheaton College; Charles E. Fuller, of the Old Fashioned Revival Hour; Will H. Houghton, president of Moody Bible Institute; Harry A. Ironside, pastor of Moody Church, Chicago; and Steven W. Paine, president of Houghton College. Only Paine represented a tradition other than Fundamentalism, coming from the holiness-oriented Wesleyan Methodist Church. Griffiths, Laird, and McIntire also came to state their case.[21] After lengthy discussion, the group decided that it could not unite with the American Council because of differing objectives. Any new association, they believed, should be organized on a positive basis, and not primarily to attack the Federal Council.[22] This group wanted all Evangelicals to help found the organization, so they believed that no small, unrepresentative group had the moral right to start a national organization.[23]

Wright and his colleagues agreed to proceed with their plans. They decided to invite representatives from every evangelical sector to a national conference in St. Louis, 7-8 April 1942. They would ask for no detailed doctrinal statement, and would avoid a belligerent tone and volatile labels like "modernist" or "fundamentalist." Their call would state an agenda in only the most general terms. They then formed a committee to decide whom to invite, make contacts, issue the call, and plan the April meeting. All on the new committee except Paine were fundamentalists.[24]

The new committee met several times in New York City during the winter of 1941-1942 to prepare for the St. Louis conference. The first item of business was to gain the support of a great cross section of evangelical leaders. Eventually Wright would cover thirty-four states in this task while Davis followed up with a letter drafted by the committee. Those

---

[21]Ibid., 5-6, lists those attending; rounding out the list were Henry C. Crowell, a vice-president at MBI; Charles A. Porter, associate pastor at Moody Church; and Ernest M. Wadsworth, secretary of the Great Commission Prayer League.

[22]Minutes of the Committee, 27-28 October 1941.

[23]Wright, "An Historical Statement," 13-14.

[24]Minutes of the Committee, 27-28 October 1941; the new committee is listed in Wright, "An Historical Statement," 7.

who responded positively would be asked to sign the call to St. Louis.[25] The letter simply stated the need for evangelical cohesion, for a "front" to represent Evangelicals before the government, a "clearing house" for evangelism, benevolence, and education, along with a unified public witness against "the forces of unbelief and apostasy which threaten our liberties and our civilization." It disclaimed any connection with any other group, alluding of course to the American Council, and asked that all who believed that "a united effort of evangelical Christians is a necessity in our country today" reply.[26] Based on response to this letter and Wright's promotion, the call was signed by 147 evangelical leaders from all regions and a wide variety of denominations and agencies. The organizers, though mostly fundamentalists, were genuinely inclusive in their invitation.[27]

Why did the conveners seek evangelical cooperation? First, they desired protection from "insidious forces"[28] that they believed were working against them. They had in mind the possible implications of growing governmental regulatory power for missionaries' travel clearance, the draft, chaplain supply for the armed services, church planting, and religious radio. Another "insidious force," especially if it became recognized as the only Protestant voice, was the liberal-oriented Federal Council of Churches. The Federal Council had already helped persuade two major radio networks, CBS and NBC, to deny paid broadcast time to religious programs and to offer free time instead to the major faiths. The Federal Council, of course, had been awarded the Protestant share of air time. Now an interfaith coalition, including the Federal Council, was persuading the Mutual Broadcasting System to stop selling time for religion, and urging the National Association of Broadcasters to adopt the same policy.

-----

[25]Minutes of the Committee, 10 November 1941, New York NY; Minutes of the Committee, 22 December 1941; Minutes of the Committee, 19 January 1942—all in AIM Records.

[26]The text of the letter is in the Minutes of the Committee, 10 November 1941, AIM Records.

[27]Wright includes the text of the call and the list of signers in "An Historical Statement," 8-13. A copy is also in the Davis Correspondence, AIM Records.

[28]Davis to Houghton, Adams, Ferrin, and Talbot, 11 December 1940, Davis Correspondence, AIM Records.

Fundamentalists and other Evangelicals who bought time for their programs feared that the airways would be closed to them.[29] In the dark, early days of World War II, and in the light of fundamentalists' belief that a great world religious and political dictator would soon arise, fears of religious monopoly pervaded the NAE conveners' rhetoric. At the St. Louis conference, William Ward Ayer issued a grim warning. "Evangelical religion has suffered much in totalitarian countries," he said, "and it takes no great prophetic vision to see that in our own nation tendencies are developing which in due time will work considerable hardship upon unorganized Christianity." The only recourse, he urged them, was to organize.[30]

One might expect fundamentalists to inject such fears, but the NAE initiators had immense hopes as well. Said Harold J. Ockenga in his presidential address at the second NAE convention, "We . . . are standing at the crossroads and . . . there are only two ways that lie open to us. One is the road of the rescue of western civilization by a . . . revival of evangelical Christianity. The other is a return to the Dark Ages of heathendom, which . . . is emerging in every phase of world life today."[31] But Ockenga was hopeful; he thought that the tide was turning back to "common sense, faith, vision and the Christian outlook." He believed that the NAE would "spearhead . . . the invasion of the Christian consciousness of this nation. . . ."[32]

---

[29]Ibid.; Houghton to Davis, 23 December 1940; J. D. Adams to Davis, 13 December 1940; H. W. Ferrin to Davis, 13 December 1940; Davis Correspondence, AIM Records. William Ward Ayer, "Evangelical Christianity Endangered by Its Fragmentized Condition," *Evangelical Action!*, 41-46; Daniel P. Fuller, *Give the Winds A Mighty Voice: The Story of Charles E. Fuller* (Waco TX: Word Books, 1972) 151-56; circular letter, "To All Sponsors of Religious Radio Broadcasts," 16 April 1942, signed by Louis Minsky, National Conference of Christians and Jews; Edward J. Heffron, National Council of Catholic Men; Henrietta Harrison, National Council of the Y.M.C.A.; Rabbi Saul B. Appelbaum, Union of American Hebrew Congregations; Frank C. Goodman, The Federal Council of Churches; John G. Becker, Bible Magazines, Inc.; AIM Records.

[30]Ayer, "Evangelical Christianity Endangered," 41.

[31]Harold J. Ockenga, "Christ for America," United We Stand, A Report of the Constitutional Convention of the National Association of Evangelicals, Chicago IL (3-6 May 1943) 11.

[32]Ibid., 15.

Those thoughts might seem odd, coming from Ockenga and echoed by other fundamentalists, whose movement seemed thoroughly defeated fifteen years earlier. But by 1942 a vigorous, evangelistically aggressive wing of Fundamentalism now believed that it stood on the threshold of a revival. In its eagerness to bring renewal, this progressive wing was willing to chasten and even alienate colleagues in order to make new friends. Wright implored the NAE to "heal the wounded spirits of our brethren in Christ who have been cold-shouldered . . . by a narrow and bigoted leadership."[33]

This irenic, cooperative spirit prevailed at the St. Louis meeting and the constitutional convention the following year in Chicago. Delegates and observers from some fifty denominations at the Chicago conference received balanced representation among the officers and committees.[34] The NAE, then, would not be another World's Christian Fundamentals Association, which welcomed only those who would jump on the fundamentalist bandwagon. It tried to be genuinely inclusive.

The NAE soon developed into a major symbol and power center of the new evangelical resurgence. By 1947 it represented thirty denominations totaling 1,300,000 members, and a service constituency of another 3,000,000 whose denominations were not members.[35] These Evangelicals now saw that they were not so weak and isolated as they had supposed. Encouraged by the prospects of revival through united efforts, they would make the Youth for Christ movement and the Billy Graham crusades more successful than their fundamentalist founders could have by themselves. By early 1952, it looked as though the revival the early NAE leaders had envisioned was breaking at last.

The moderate, chastened fundamentalists who led in founding the NAE freely offered participation and leadership to other Evangelicals, but the most visible and vocal of the new evangelical leaders—Billy Gra-

---

[33]J. Elwin Wright, "Report of the Promotional Director," *United We Stand*, 8.

[34]*Evangelical Action!*, 63-71, 92-125, includes delegate and committee rosters, business sessions, and committee reports from the St. Louis conference; James DeForest Murch, *Cooperation without Compromise: A History of the National Association of Evangelicals* (Grand Rapids MI: Eerdmans, 1950) 62-71, likewise documents the Chicago conference.

[35]Murch, *Cooperation without Compromise*, 196, 202-203.

ham, Torrey Johnson, and Percy Crawford of the new Youth for Christ movement, Charles E. Fuller of radio fame, and NAE spokesmen Wright and Ockenga—were all of fundamentalist background. Their informal domination of the new evangelical movement has led interpreters to label the varied traditions involved as "fundamentalist." This is a distortion, as we have seen, but for every stereotype there is a measure of truth; and the truth here is that Fundamentalism had become a catalyst, a leavening agent among some of the other traditions. This is not to say that other Evangelicals lost their distinctiveness. In fact, fundamentalists who joined the NAE withheld one of their own tests of fellowship, premillennialism, in order to establish common cause with the others. Nevertheless, these postfundamentalists remained prominent, and the NAE's fundamentalist-shaped image both attracted and repelled other Evangelicals. For what reasons did the new evangelical movement develop along such lines? Briefly stated, the fundamentalists had the presumption, position, and penetration necessary to herald a call that many other Evangelicals would hear and accept.

Fundamentalism, according to George M. Marsden, has a paradoxical tension in its character. Sometimes it identifies with the "establishment" and sometimes with the "outsiders."[36] At times it presumes to speak for the "main stream" of American evangelical Christianity, seeing itself as the central guardian of the "faith once delivered to the saints." This view adds the great Wesleyan-Arminian, Disciples-Christian, and Lutheran traditions only as afterthoughts and virtually ignores many others. It considers what Timothy L. Smith called the "evangelical Calvinist" wing of American Protestantism the normative mainline. Fundamentalist evangelist and Bible teacher Reuben A. Torrey presumed that he spoke for the "main line" when he once told an inquirer that he was an "Episcopaleopresbygationalaptist."[37] By choosing the label "fundamentalist," the movement conferred nonsectarian centrality and normativeness on itself.

---

[36]Marsden, *Fundamentalism and American Culture*, 6-7, 11-21. See also Marty, *Righteous Empire*, 133-76. Timothy L. Smith comments on this lingering presumption in his review of *The Evangelicals: What They Believe, Who They Are, Where They Are Changing*, eds. David F. Wells and John D. Woodbridge, in *Christian Century* 93 (4-11 February 1976): 125-27.

[37]Robert A. Harkness, *Reuben Archer Torrey: The Man and His Message* (Chicago: Bible Institute Colportage Association, 1929) 68.

On the other hand, fundamentalists, like holiness groups, Pentecostals, peace churches, and immigrant-based denominations, often acted like isolated, embattled sectarians. During the fundamentalist-modernist controversies some fundamentalists either formed their own denominations such as the General Association of Regular Baptist Churches and the Bible Presbyterian Church, or withdrew their congregations in the interest of total independence.[38] This separatist wing of the movement in particular became increasingly isolated and despaired of ever bringing reform.

The majority of fundamentalists remained in the larger denominations, especially the Northern Baptists and Northern Presbyterians, but felt ambivalent toward them. They gave increasing support to an interdenominational network of institutions such as the Moody Bible Institute, Dallas Theological Seminary, *The Sunday School Times*, and Africa Inland Mission. They had failed to purge their own denominations, but they still hoped that evangelical orthodoxy would again prevail.[39]

This nonseparatist wing believed that American culture had lost its spiritual moorings, but that they could be restored. America was following the same moral decline that led to the rise of dictators, the persecution of the Jews, and the senseless war now raging. Ultimately, they believed, only the Second Coming would bring a stop to it all, but their sense of responsibility toward American Protestantism and American culture led most of them to hope for one last revival.[40] Indeed, God had raised *them* up, entrusting *them* with the best grasp of evangelical truth, and had given *them* the task of forming a new evangelical coalition to save America. As presumptive as this vision was, it encouraged them to try to fulfill it.

Other Evangelicals had similar hopes and fears for America, and similar beliefs in their own strategic importance; but outside of the South,

---

[38] Marsden, *Fundamentalism and American Culture*, 124-31, 180-84, 192-93.

[39] Ibid., 192-95; Carpenter, "Fundamentalist Institutions."

[40] See, for examples, "Again America Hears," *Moody Monthly* 40 (September 1939): 2-3; "Preliminaries to a Great Revival," *Watchman-Examiner* 29 (18 September 1941): 976-77; George Dewey Blomgren, "Our First Line of Defense," *The Standard* 31 (15 November 1941): 3; "May We Hope for Revival Today?" *Sunday School Times* 83 (22 March 1941): 225; J. Elwin Wright, "Revival," *New England Fellowship Monthly* 41 (April 1943): 8.

where evangelical Protestantism still dominated, none had as salient a position, nor as well-developed interdenominational networks as the fundamentalists. They were all vigorous and growing, and some denominations had vast institutional empires. On the other side, fundamentalist institutions had a broader, interdenominational influence that turned the Moody Bible Institute and the *Sunday School Times*, to give two examples, into evangelical ecumenical centers, attracting supporters from many traditions.[41] Thus fundamentalists believed that they offered the common ground on which to unite Evangelicals.

By the late 1930s the mood among the less radical, nonseparatist wing of Fundamentalism was swinging back toward a desire for fellowship and cooperation, and an urge to be positive and culturally responsible. The best way to do that, they thought, was to begin a new evangelistic thrust. Fundamentalists' outlook had taken a dark, apocalyptic cast during the decade's crises. Their millenarian belief in inevitable cultural decay, the enormity of current problems, and their powerlessness and alienation made them disparage social and political reform efforts. Still, they believed that revival, which they thought was God's means of reforming society, would work.[42] Fundamentalist spokesmen repeatedly appropriated a promise made to the Hebrews. "If my people, which are called by my name, shall humble themselves, and pray, and seek my face, and turn from their wicked ways; then will I hear from heaven, and will forgive their sin, and will heal their land."[43]

The prospects for a fundamentalist-led revival looked rather grim in the mid-1930s. In 1935 Billy Sunday died. He had been the nation's lead-

---

[41]In 1940, for example, the Moody Bible Institute reported fifty-eight denominations and forty-four states represented in its student body. W. H. Houghton, "Educational Number," *Moody Bible Institute Bulletin* 19 (February 1940): 3.

[42]James S. Pemberton, "Revival or Revolution," *Moody Monthly* 40 (September 1939): 63. See also the Farm Mother [pseud.], "A Crop Survey," *Sunday School Times* 76 (28 July 1934): 481-82; "Rapture, Revolution, Revival," *Revelation* 2 (May 1932): 205; Paul H. Rood, "On the Threshold of a New Year," *King's Business* 28 (January 1937): 4.

[43]2 Chronicles 7:14, King James Version; see "How to Bring Back Prosperity," *Moody Monthly* 32 (October 1931): 64-65; J. D. Williams, "God's Cure for Depression," *Alliance Weekly* 67 (29 October 1932): 693; S. Paul Weaver, "Pray for Revival!" *Sunday School Times* 76 (March 1934): 209-10; "The Year Closes," *Moody Monthly* 39 (December 1938): 171.

ing evangelist in the pre-World War I heyday of mass evangelism, but since the war his career and revivalism itself had taken a downturn.[44] Billy Sunday "was the last of his line," *The Christian Century* smugly announced. "Revivalism reached in him its final expression." His frenetic, vulgar style, according to the *Century*, marked "the desperate and hopeless condition of the evangelical type of piety."[45] Fundamentalists paid no heed;[46] they were finding new ways to attract interest and organize support for revivalism.

J. Elwin Wright, a real estate developer from New England, became one of the movement's most successful evangelistic impresarios. His New England Fellowship would show Evangelicals nationwide how to cooperatively sponsor evangelism. In 1930 Wright told his supporters what he considered to be preconditions for revival. Revival demanded more prayer, a desire to win converts, a nonsectarian spirit, patience, courage, and new methods. If revival were to come, said this businessman, people must "cut the red tape of precedent and explore new fields."[47]

Wright started out boldly. He invited over 6,000 pastors and church workers from nearly every denomination with churches in New England to a five-day conference featuring the nationally famous Baptist fundamentalist, William Bell Riley. Hundreds attended and received a new vision for cooperative evangelical work. The New England Fellowship grew rapidly, adding over five hundred pastors in 1930-1931 alone.[48] By 1935 the NEF was sponsoring over fifty small evangelistic campaigns a year; seven hundred special services and short conferences; three summer conferences at its Rummey, New Hampshire, conference grounds; a guest Bible teacher circuit with 240 services in thirty-five cities; several

---

[44]William G. McLoughlin, *Billy Sunday Was His Real Name* (Chicago: University of Chicago Press, 1955) 260-72, 286-88; Robert S. and Helen M. Lynd, *Middletown in Transition: A Study in Cultural Conflicts* (New York: Harcourt, Brace & Co., 1937) 302-307.

[45]"Billy Sunday, the Last of His Line," *The Christian Century* 52 (20 November 1935): 1,476.

[46]"Are Revivals Over?" *Sunday School Times* 79 (15 May 1937): 347.

[47]J. Elwin Wright, "The 1931 Program," *The Sheaf of the First Fruits* 28 (October 1930): 12.

[48]Evans and Evans, *Incidents and Information*, 9; Minutes of the Annual Meeting of the Advisory Council, 30 September 1931.

laymen's and young people's gospel teams; and a Radio Ensemble that had broadcast 420 programs over forty stations that year.[49] The New England Fellowship helped sponsor two mass meetings in Mechanics Hall, Boston, with Charles E. Fuller drawing a total of 16,000 people.[50]

Of all the activities that the New England Fellowship supported, radio broadcasting was the newest and one of the most attractive. Whenever Wright went on tour, he brought along his pride and joy, the Radio Ensemble.[51] Indeed, while radio listening was becoming the nation's favorite pastime, the fundamentalists were making radio broadcasting a major fixture in their network.[52] In May of 1931, a *Sunday School Times* reader-contributed list of radio ministries included over one hundred different programs by seventy broadcasters, including Philadelphia Presbyterian Donald Grey Barnhouse's CBS network program on Sunday afternoons. An update in 1932 showed over four hundred programs on eighty stations.[53] Some of these attracted large and loyal audiences. A *Kansas City Star* poll in 1932 named the "Morning Bible Hour," taught by Dr. Walter L. Wilson of the city's Central Bible Church, the area's most popular radio program.[54]

Radio proved a potent aid to fundamentalist outreach and institutional growth. Broadcasts brought the movement's adherents together and helped make new friends among nonfundamentalist Evangelicals. The programs gave their sponsors broad publicity and increased the "personal" intimacy that printed publicity or periodicals did not have. Radio made preachers and gospel musicians public figures once again.

[49]*New England Fellowship Official Report for 1935* (Boston: n.d.) 3.

[50]*Annual Report of the New England Fellowship for 1939* (Boston: n.d.).

[51]Evans and Evans, *Incidents and Information*, 20-24; "The N.E.F. Radio Ensemble," *New England Fellowship Monthly* 32 (August 1934): 6; "Coming Events of Interest," *New England Fellowship Monthly* 33 (January 1935): 10; "Coming Events of Interest," *New England Fellowship Monthly* 33 (June 1936): 14-15.

[52]"Fortune Survey: Radio Favorites," *Fortune* (January 1938): 88.

[53]"The Sunday School Times Radio Directory," *Sunday School Times* 73 (30 May 1931): 313; "A Directory of Evangelical Radio Broadcasts," *Sunday School Times* 74 (23 January 1932): 44-45.

[54]"Notes on Open Letters: Do People Want Gospel Radio Broadcasts?" *Sunday School Times* 74 (23 January 1932): 42.

No other fundamentalist radio venture illustrates this potential better than station WMBI of the Moody Bible Institute. Station WMBI, inaugurated in 1926, aired a variety of programs, including a weekly Radio School of the Bible, devotionals, the "Know Your Bible," or "KYB Club" for children, MBI campus activities, guest preachers, and plenty of gospel music.[55] By 1930 the station had become a fixture in Chicago and Midwestern Fundamentalism generally; it received over 20,000 letters annually.[56] By 1940 the KYB Club had over 17,500 members, and the Radio School of the Bible had added 11,500 members.[57]

The radio station aided the Moody Bible Institute measurably. Over one hundred new students each year said WMBI led them to the school, while the radio brought the *Moody Monthly* several hundred subscribers each year, and the Development Office added thousands of donors from the station's 50,000 letters received annually by 1939.[58] Meanwhile, WMBI groups such as the Announcer's Trio, which now recorded on Victor Records, had held meetings in nearly three hundred different churches by the early 1940s.[59]

The evangelistic potential of radio was not lost on MBI President Will Houghton, who was a convert-winning preacher himself.[60] In the pages of the *Moody Monthly* he called for a revival to cure the nation's ills.[61] While preaching in Toronto during the D. L. Moody Centenary celebrations of 1937, he predicted that a revival would soon break over the land.

---

[55]"Salvation by Radio," *Moody Bible Institute Bulletin* 10 (November 1930): 41.

[56]*Annual Report of the Broadcasting Station of the Moody Bible Institute of Chicago for the year ending April 30, 1930*, 6-7, 13, 15, 21. This and other annual reports are on file at station WMBI, Chicago.

[57]Ibid., 6; *Annual Report . . . March 31, 1940*, 8-12.

[58]*Annual Report . . . April 30, 1931*, 28; *Annual Report . . . April 30, 1933*, 26; *Annual Report . . . March 31, 1937*, 30; *Annual Report . . . March 31, 1938*, 27-29; *Annual Report . . . March 31, 1939*, 30-31.

[59]Figures compiled from WMBI *Annual Reports* from 1929-1942.

[60]Houghton's earlier career is covered in Wilbur M. Smith, *A Watchman on the Wall: The Life Story of Will H. Houghton* (Grand Rapids MI: Eerdmans, 1951) 28-100.

[61]See, for example, "Social Reform and Revival," *Moody Monthly* 38 (February 1938): 296-97; "The Hope of the Church," *Moody Monthly* 30 (August 1938): 607.

The next year he launched a new evangelistic chain broadcast, "Let's Go Back to the Bible," for which he preached twenty-six sermons over Mutual System stations in eleven major cities.[62] Houghton's theme was the need for national repentance. He believed: "God has a stake in the nation, and He is concerned that his word of warning and invitation shall be given forth."[63] A book of the messages was published with copies sent to major dignitaries and congressmen. All told, the institute received 40,000 letters in response, and Houghton initiated a second broadcast the following fall, hoping once again that the broadcast would help spur revival.[64] Another venture began in 1940, a transcribed weekly program, "Miracles and Melodies," that featured WMBI's baritone soloist, George Beverly Shea. By early 1942 the program was heard on 197 stations in forty-three states.[65]

These new measures had not yet revived the mass revivalism of earlier days, but fundamentalists' new evangelistic thrust was gaining momentum and morale. Charles E. Fuller's "Old Fashioned Revival Hour" reached a national audience on the Mutual Network by 1938, and crowds filled great public arenas wherever and whenever he spoke. He was invited back to Boston by the New England Fellowship in the fall of 1941, and in two evangelistic meetings at the Boston Garden, he spoke to a total of 32,000 people.[66] The Founder's Week Conference at the Bible Institute in February of 1942 featured Houghton, Fuller, and Ockenga. Its theme was devoted to the subject that had the movement humming with activity and anticipation: "America's God-Given Opportunity for Revival To-

---

[62]"Great Revival Due Soon, Moody Successor Certain," *Toronto Daily Star*, 13 February 1937, noted in Smith, *Watchman on the Wall*, 191; Ibid., 128-30; "Report of the President for the Business Division," *Moody Bible Institute Bulletin* 19 (31 March 1939): 3, 8.

[63]Smith, *Watchman on the Wall*, 130-31.

[64]"The Year Closes," *Moody Monthly* 39 (December 1938): 171; "Again America Hears," 2-3; Smith, *Watchman on the Wall*, 130-31.

[65]"Report of the Business Division for the Fiscal Year 1939-1940," *Moody Bible Institute Bulletin* 20 (October 1940): 7; *Annual Report . . . March 31, 1940*, 2; "Hear WMBI Favorites over Your Station," *Moody Monthly* 41 (September 1940): 31; *Annual Report . . . March 31, 1942*, 13; "Miracles and Melodies," *Moody Monthly* 42 (April 1942): 497.

[66]Fuller, *Give the Winds*, 115-27, 133-37, 143-44; *A Quick Glance Back over the 1941 Trail* (Boston: N.E.F., n.d.) 3.

day."[67] The St. Louis conferees two months later had high hopes that their new association would help bring a national revival.

This evangelistic quickening encouraged many fundamentalists to reassess their place in American Christianity. In reaction to their defeats in the denominational battles and the antievolution crusade, fundamentalists became increasingly insular and defensive, drawing sharp doctrinal and associational boundaries to separate themselves from "the apostasy." Their impetus was to form more pure fellowships, whether or not they actually left their old denominations. They often lashed out at even nonfundamentalist Evangelicals whose beliefs did not meet their standards. Louis A. Bauman, noted Bible teacher from southern California, called the Pentecostal movement a "demonic imitation" of the apostolic gifts.[68] Fundamentalism was not totally hypercritical and exclusive by nature, however. Its roots were in the irenic, common-denominator evangelism of D. L. Moody as well as in B. B. Warfield's argumentative orthodoxy. Their desire for revival was now forcing many fundamentalists to reconsider the basis for fellowship and cooperation with other Evangelicals.

By the late 1930s a number of leaders were openly criticizing fellow fundamentalists' censorious, sectarian spirit. Donald Barnhouse, editor of *Revelation* magazine, mourned that "born again men . . . are bitterly quarrelling with each other over secondary matters," and raiding other churches to fill their own pews. Will Houghton chided fundamentalists for forgetting the difference between "contending for the faith and contending with the faithful." J. Elwin Wright complained that radical fundamentalists were "hyper-critical and intolerant of all others who differ with them on even the finer points of doctrine."[69] When Wright toured

---

[67]Advertisement, *Moody Monthly* 42 (January 1942): 307.

[68]Louis Bauman, *The Modern Tongues Movement Examined and Judged in the Light of the Scriptures and in the Light of Its Fruits* (Long Beach CA: n.p., 1941) 1, quoted in Horace S. Ward, "The Anti-Pentecostal Argument," in *Aspects of Pentecostal-Charismatic Origins*, ed. Vinson Synan (Plainfield NJ: Logos International, 1975) 8.

[69]"Personal Feelings," *Revelation* 7 (October 1937): 420; "How to 'Contend,' " *Moody Monthly* 39 (February 1939): 307; J. E. Wright, "A Few Observations," *New England Fellowship Monthly* 35 (April 1937): 8.

the country in 1937, however, he found another strong group that he said consisted of "fundamentalists *plus* believers in . . . the graces of the spirit," who had rejected a "merely militant fundamentalism." He predicted that an association of these people would arise in the next decade.[70] Apparently, he was already preparing to help make that happen.

Not only were fundamentalists experiencing internal ferment, but at the same time they were penetrating and influencing other traditions. During different eras, popular religious movements have swept through traditions other than the ones in which they began. The holiness movement, for example, captured popular interest and commitment across denominational lines in the mid-to-late nineteenth century.[71] In similar fashion Fundamentalism was a leavening agent in many sectors of evangelical Protestantism during the 1930s and 1940s. Both the attraction and the misgivings other Evangelicals felt in considering the NAE's call were often conditioned by their experience with Fundamentalism in the preceding years.

One of the great and relatively unexplored ironies of American religious history is that many people in immigrant-based denominations found in Fundamentalism an attractive, modern American Christianity. Especially in Protestant denominations with Northern European roots, Fundamentalism offered an appealing way to sing Zion's songs in a strange land. This shouldn't be too surprising; for in its formative years the movement provided vital faith communities for native Americans who felt like strangers in modern industrial cities. The fundamentalist tension between a popularly responsive idiom and a sense that "this world is not my home" appealed to many immigrant people who were torn between making good here and preserving the faith of their parents.[72] The holiness movement had a similar accommodating influence in the 1880s

---

[70]Wright, "A Few Observations," 8-9.

[71]Timothy L. Smith, *Revivalism and Social Reform in Mid-Nineteenth Century America* (Nashville: Abingdon Press, 1957) 63-79, 135-47, 225-37; Smith, *Called unto Holiness*, 21-26; Marsden, *Fundamentalism and American Culture*, 72-85.

[72]Marsden deals suggestively with this theme in *Fundamentalism and American Culture*, 202-205, and in "From Fundamentalism to Evangelicalism: A Historical Analysis," in *The Evangelicals*, ed. Wells and Woodbridge, 130-31.

and 1890s,[73] but now Fundamentalism was the most visible evangelical representative of American religion.

Fundamentalist beliefs and emphases penetrated these varied traditions with uneven success. Some communions with close previous affinity to American churches, such as the Swedish Baptists, became thoroughly part of the fundamentalist movement.[74] Others, such as the Swedish Evangelical Mission Covenant, the Mennonite Church, and the Dutch Christian Reformed Church,[75] had both affinities and strong antagonisms toward aspects of Fundamentalism. They had been penetrated by the movement while struggling to assert a unique and substantially different identity. The Christian Reformed Church, for example, was highly ambivalent toward Fundamentalism. These conservative Dutch Calvinists contributed several of their best scholars to J. G. Machen's Westminster Seminary, but denominational leaders criticized fundamentalists. They saw them as culture-denying, anti-intellectual, individualistic, and too shallow theologically to provide a satisfactory defense of orthodoxy.[76] On the popular level, however, members of the Christian Reformed Church often took secret delight in attending gospel tabernacle

---

[73]Walter H. Lugibihl and Jared F. Gerig, *The Missionary Church Association* (Berne IN: Economy Printing Concern, 1951) 19-33; and Martin H. Schrag, "Societies Influencing the Brethren in Christ toward a Missionary Program," *Mennonite Quarterly Review* 42 (April 1968): 117-31. Both provide examples of holiness permeation in two small communions of Anabaptist heritage.

[74]Carpenter, "Fundamentalism and the Swedish Baptists' Search for Identity," a paper presented at the Trinity College conference on "The Shaping of American Christianity," 19 April 1980. Other groups that entered fundamentalist circles by the 1930s include both the Swedish and Norwegian Evangelical Free Churches. Hints of this transition appear in H. Wilbert Norton, et al., *The Diamond Jubilee Story* (Minneapolis: Free Church Publications, 1959).

[75]Karl A. Olsson, *By One Spirit* (Chicago: Covenant Press, 1962) 526-46, 618-20, discusses struggles with Fundamentalism in the Evangelical Covenant Church; Rodney J. Sawatsky, "History and Ideology, Mennonite Identity Definition through History" (Ph.D. diss., Princeton University, 1977) chs. 6-8, traces the heavy influence of Fundamentalism on the Mennonite and Mennonite General Conference churches; Joseph H. Hall, "The Controversy over Fundamentalism in the Christian Reformed Church, 1915-1966" (Th.D. diss., Concordia Seminary, 1974) shows the tensions over Fundamentalism in that communion.

[76]James D. Bratt, "Dutch Calvinism in Modern America: The History of a Conservative Subculture" (Ph.D. diss., Yale University, 1978) 269-74, 278-80.

services and listening to fundamentalist radio programs. A letter written by two Dutch children from Holland, Michigan, to WMBI's KYB Club shows the competing loyalties many felt: "We listen to your Bible class every Saturday morning," they reported. "Sometimes we have to hurry home from catechism. We try to answer your questions as best we can."[77] Strict Lutheran confessionalists such as the Lutheran Church-Missouri Synod proved much less permeable. Missourians considered fundamentalists' dispensational premillennialism to be nearly as heretical as Modernism, and shunned any fellowship with what they called the "Reformed sects."[78]

Fundamentalism also attracted people out of their former denominations into independent, tabernacle-like churches. For example, Jacob Stam, a delegate at the 1942 St. Louis NAE conference, was director of the Star of Hope Mission, which had been founded as a home mission for the Christian Reformed Church in Paterson, New Jersey. The Stam family's revivalistic tactics, premillennialism, and independence estranged them from the Christian Reformed Church, however, and led them into nondenominational Fundamentalism.[79] Fundamentalism produced rifts among ethnic churches as well, most notably the "Grace" Brethren, which conducted a premillennial, revivalistic, and missions-minded schism in 1939 from the Brethren Church, a peace church of German origin.[80]

In addition to influencing immigrants, Fundamentalism penetrated Anglo-American denominations other than those in which it was rooted. Fundamentalists' highly publicized struggles in the 1920s paralleled and often prompted conservative protest movements elsewhere. The funda-

---

[77]*Annual Report . . . March 31, 1936*, 22.

[78]Graebner's *The Problem of Lutheran Union*, best captures the Missouri Synod's exclusivism in the 1930s. On their assessment of premillennialism, see "Premillennialism and Dispensationalism" in F. E. Mayer, *Religious Bodies of America*, 419-26; and Theodore Engelder, "Dispensationalism Disparaging the Gospel," *Concordia Theological Monthly* 8 (September 1937): 649-66.

[79]"One Dutch Immigrant Plus One New Testament," *Revelation* 1 (December 1931): 405, 428-30.

[80]Dennis Martin, "Law and Grace: The Progressive Brethren and Fundamentalism," independent study, Wheaton College, 1973.

mentalist-modernist controversies, generically speaking, extended far beyond the self-consciously fundamentalist movement. They occurred in the Northern and Southern Methodist, Protestant Episcopal, Southern Baptist, and Disciples of Christ denominations, as well as among Northern Baptists and Northern Presbyterians, where true fundamentalists were most numerous.[81] Remember Ernest Sandeen's caution, however, that one should not confuse the controversies with the movement, which both preceded and survived the 1920s conflicts.[82] Most of these other conservative protests did not establish any direct or lasting connections with Fundamentalism. Protestant Episcopal conservative bishops, for example, may have instituted heresy proceedings against liberal clergy; but they neither held to the verbal inerrancy of the Bible nor developed any major contact with, say, the fundamentalist Bible schools.[83]

The movement's role as a public champion of orthodoxy did introduce it as trustworthy ally to other conservative organizations such as the Southern Baptists and the Southern Presbyterians. In later decades, these contacts provided openings for genuinely fundamentalist penetration. Both the Southern Baptist Convention and the Presbyterian Church in the U. S. have often been labeled fundamentalist. Although they showed close affinity to the movement's doctrinal standards and views on evolution and prohibition, their leaders reacted anxiously to fundamentalist influences in their ranks. Both communions expected intense denominational loyalty to the virtual exclusion of support for other endeavors. They felt threatened and compromised by the common Northern pattern of interdenominational cooperation upon which both the Federal Council of Churches and the fundamentalist movement were based.[84]

---

[81]Norman F. Furniss, *The Fundamentalist Controversy, 1918-1931* (New Haven: Yale University Press, 1954) 119-26, 142-76 and Stewart G. Cole, *The History of Fundamentalism* (New York: Richard R. Smith, 1931) 132-92, describe these other conflicts.

[82]Sandeen, *Roots of Fundamentalism*, 247-49.

[83]Marsden, *Fundamentalism and American Culture*, 178.

[84]Ernest Trice Thompson, *Presbyterians in the South, Volume 3: 1890-1972* (Richmond: John Knox Press, 1973) 266-73, 486-90, 552-53; Walter B. Shurden, *Not A Silent People: Controversies that Have Shaped Southern Baptists* (Nashville: Broadman Press, 1972) 65-81; "Southern Baptists Concerned about Fundamentalist Invasion," *The Baptist* 3 (7 October 1922): 1,111; "Essentials and Non-Essentials," *Baptist and Reflector* 106 (9 May 1940): 2.

Fundamentalist influence was especially widespread and disruptive among the Southern Baptists, whose denominational centralization and increased support for colleges, seminaries, and hospitals angered many fiercely independent constituents.[85] Fundamentalism became a means of expressing discontent with the Southern Baptist Convention's program, since it offered a conspiratorial theory of the growth of churches' power and an alternate support network. J. Frank Norris, pastor of First Baptist Church, Fort Worth, Texas, became the godfather of independent Baptist Fundamentalism in the South, by means of thirty years of agitation against the Southern Baptist Convention.[86] Fundamentalist teachings infiltrated the Convention through the widespread use of the Scofield Reference Bible and the influence of independent evangelists such as John R. Rice and Bob Jones. Young "preacher boys" like Billy Graham were attracted to a growing number of independent Southern fundamentalist Bible schools such as Bob Jones College in Cleveland, Tennessee, and the Florida Bible Institute near Tampa.[87] These influences made Southern Baptist leaders nervous about potential division in the ranks and stand-offish toward overtures from Northern fundamentalists.[88]

---

[85]Patsy S. Ledbetter, "Crusade for the Faith: The Protestant Fundamentalist Movement in Texas" (Ph.D. diss., North Texas State, 1975) 70-91, 200-204; Kenneth C. Hubbard, "Anti-Conventionism in the Southern Baptist Convention, 1940-1960 " (Th.D. diss., Southwestern Baptist Theological Seminary, 1968) 83, 88. Hubbard's work proved a valuable reference to Southern Baptist sources, notably the *Baptist and Reflector*. Most of the references to that paper were first found in his footnotes.

[86]Ledbetter, "Crusade for the Faith," 90-92, 204-209, 228-36, 257-60; Hubbard, "Anti-Conventionism," 83-86, 103-11; C. Allyn Russell, "J. Frank Norris, Violent Fundamentalist," in Russell, *Voices of American Fundamentalism: Seven Biographical Studies* (Philadelphia: Westminster Press, 1976) 20-46.

[87]Hubbard, "Anti-Conventionism," 86, 89, 96, 98, 101; James M. Morton, "The Millennarian Movement in America and Its Effect upon the Faith and Fellowship of the Southern Baptist Convention" (M.Th. thesis, Golden Gate Baptist Theological Seminary, 1962) 47, 62-66, 87-89; Robert A. Baker, "Premillennial Baptist Groups," *Encyclopedia of Southern Baptists* 2 (Nashville: Broadman Press, 1958) 1,111; John C. Pollock, *Billy Graham, the Authorized Biography* (New York: McGraw-Hill, 1965) 9-24.

[88]"Fundamentalist Invasion"; William Owen Carver, *Out of His Treasure* (Nashville: Broadman Press, 1956) 76-81, 96-97; "Preying on the Southern Baptist Convention," *Baptist and Reflector* 106 (25 April 1940): 2-3; "The Brother Is Exactly Right," *Baptist and Reflector* 106 (7 March 1940): 2; "We Like the Bryant Blend," *Baptist and Reflector* 110 (3 August 1944): 5; "Meeting of Evangelicals in St. Louis," *Baptist and Reflector* 108 (7 May 1942): 3.

Southern Presbyterians had been almost unanimously conservative and Calvinistic during the 1920s, but during the 1930s and 1940s the denomination diversified. Those whose theology had been shaped by critical biblical scholarship and neo-orthodox thought entered the official leadership, while Fundamentalism made popular inroads.[89] Columbia Bible College of Columbia, South Carolina, and Evangelical Theological College (later known as Dallas Theological Seminary) of Dallas, Texas, had been founded by Northern fundamentalists in the 1920s[90] and since then had drawn support from Southern Presbyterians.[91] During the 1940s a coalition of Bible school millenarians and Old Calvinist conservatives led by L. Nelson Bell, a retired China missionary doctor, and Tom Glasgow, an elder from Charlotte, North Carolina, formed the *Southern Presbyterian Journal*.[92] Dispensational millenarian theology was officially judged contrary to Presbyterian doctrine in the 1940s, and Columbia Bible College and Dallas Seminary gradually shifted to other constituencies.[93] Yet the fundamentalist-influenced "Concerned Presbyterians" movement grew stronger. It delayed reunion with the Northern Presbyterians and continually opposed ecumenicalism, theological liberalization, and social activism among Southern Presbyterians.[94]

---

[89]Thompson, *Presbyterians in the South, Volume Three*, 302-39, 486-503.

[90]R. Arthur Mathews, *Towers Pointing Upward* (Columbia SC: n.p., 1973) 10-22; Rudolf A. Renfer, "A History of Dallas Theological Seminary" (Ph.D. diss., University of Texas, 1959) 56-57, 97-100, 134-38.

[91]Thompson, *Presbyterians in the South*, 3:487-88; Renfer, "Dallas Theological Seminary," 189, 215, 219, 264 (see his Table C); Marguerite C. McQuilkin, *Always in Triumph: The Life of Robert C. McQuilkin* (Columbia SC: n.p., 1956) 103-104, 114-15, 176, 215-17.

[92]Thompson, *Presbyterians in the South*, 3:335-39, 488-90; John C. Pollack, *A Foreign Devil in China: The Story of Dr. L. Nelson Bell, An American Surgeon* (Grand Rapids MI: Zondervan, 1971) 227-29.

[93]Thompson, *Presbyterians in the South*, 3:488; Renfer, "Dallas Theological Seminary," 264-66; McQuilkin, *Always in Triumph*, 215-17.

[94]Pollack, *A Foreign Devil*, 229-34, 242-46; Thompson, *Presbyterians in the South*, 3:539-40, 550, 555, 566-82; L. Nelson Bell, "Why the Journal at This Time?" *Southern Presbyterian Journal* 1 (May 1942): 2-3.

The holiness, Pentecostal, and fundamentalist movements shared roots in the revivals that swept American Protestantism in the 1880s and 1890s. In many respects the Wesleyan holiness movement had preeminence then, prompting others to seek the sanctifying power of the Holy Spirit. As Wesleyan holiness people consolidated into denominations, however, their need to define a distinctive identity overrode their earlier friendships with other holiness advocates.[95] Wesleyan spokesmen attacked the Reformed-oriented Keswick holiness members for not believing in the Holy Spirit's eradication of man's sinful nature. The American Keswick people, under pressure from Calvinist critics, attacked radical Wesleyan sanctification doctrines. When Pentecostalism arose after 1900, both the Keswick-oriented early fundamentalists and the holiness Wesleyans denied any affinity to the tongues-and-healing movement although it obviously had roots in both of them. Thus by 1920 these three evangelical families had virtually curtailed fellowship with one another.[96]

Nevertheless, fundamentalist perspectives and emphases had entered the holiness movement. The Church of the Nazarene, for instance, absorbed independents and former Methodists who combined radical Wesleyanism with premillennialism and militant anti-Modernism.[97] Although they distanced themselves from both fundamentalists and Pentecostals, Nazarenes favored fundamentalist, inerrantist doctrines for a time.[98]

Holiness-oriented denominations not of Wesleyan origin, such as the Evangelical Friends, began to shade their emphases more toward premillennialism and antiliberal protest than they had before World War I.[99]

---

[95]Marsden, *Fundamentalism and American Culture*, 94, 95.

[96]Ibid., 93-99; Smith, *Called unto Holiness*, 315-21, details this trend among the Nazarenes.

[97]Smith, *Called unto Holiness*, 298-315.

[98]Paul Merritt Bassett, "The Fundamentalist Leavening of the Holiness Movement, 1914-1940; The Church of the Nazarene: A Case Study," *Wesleyan Theological Journal* 13 (Spring 1978): 65-91.

[99]Stanley Nussbaum, "Ye Must Be Born Again," study of the Evangelical Mennonite Church, 1976, 32-33, 36-38, 47-48; Lugibihl and Gerig, *The Missionary Church Association*, 122-30, 138; Arthur O. Roberts, *The Association of Evangelical Friends: The Story of Quaker Renewal in the Twentieth Century* (Newberg OR: Barclay Press, 1975) 4-5; Rob-

Several leading holiness educational institutions provided contacts with fundamentalists. Stephen Paine, the Wheaton-College-trained president of Houghton College, established ties with J. Elwin Wright and others in the New England Fellowship and drew fundamentalist students to his school. Taylor University in Upland, Indiana, made increasing contacts with fundamentalists while remaining Methodist-related and holiness in emphasis.[100] By the early 1940s the time was ripe for rapprochement and cooperation between holiness and fundamentalist Evangelicals.

Pentecostals, especially those with roots in the Keswick branch of the holiness movement, considered themselves to be "fundamental," and held their own variety of dispensational premillennialism.[101] They were separated from the fundamentalists not so much by choice as by the fundamentalists' abhorrence of their tongues-speaking, atonement-based healing doctrines, and their reputation for emotional extravagance.[102] When the World's Christian Fundamentals Association condemned Pentecostals for these reasons in 1928, an Assemblies of God editor asked his readers to "love these fundamentalists and pray, 'Lord, bless them all.' "[103] Not all fundamentalists shunned Pentecostals. Robert C. McQuilkin, Keswick holiness teacher and president of Columbia Bible College, kept an open mind toward Pentecostalism.[104] J. Elwin Wright

erts, "Significant Trends Affecting Friends," *Report of the Fourth Triennial Conference of Evangelical Friends*, 11-15 July 1956, Denver, Colorado, 10-11; Edward Mott, *The Friends Church in the Light of Its Recent History* (Portland OR: n.p., ca. 1936) a fundamentalist exposé by a Friends Bible teacher.

[100]*Annual Report of the New England Fellowship for 1939* (Boston: n.p.) lists Paine as a featured conference speaker, while major fundamentalist journals carried regular advertisements for Houghton College. See *Revelation 7* (May 1937): 217; *Sunday School Times* 81 (16 September 1939): 632. On Taylor University, see William C. Ringenberg, *Taylor University: The First 125 Years* (Grand Rapids MI: Eerdmans, 1973) 96-97, 101, 138-39.

[101]Robert Mapes Anderson, *Vision of the Disinherited: The Making of American Pentecostalism* (New York: Oxford University Press, 1979) 5, 149; William W. Menzies, "Non-Wesleyan Origins of the Pentecostal Movement," in Synan, *Aspects of Pentecostal-Charismatic Origins*, 84-85.

[102]Anderson, *Vision of the Disinherited*, 147-52.

[103]Menzies, *Anointed to Serve*, 180-81.

[104]McQuilkin, *Always in Triumph*, 232.

encouraged Pentecostal participation in the New England Fellowship;[105] and when he proposed a national evangelical convention, he insisted that Pentecostals be invited. This surprised Assemblies of God leaders, but they were glad to be recognized as orthodox and evangelical.[106]

The new evangelical coalition represented by the National Association of Evangelicals came from all these sources and more. These other traditions did not simply become fundamentalist; they had reasons of their own for joining or not joining the NAE. Each tradition's story reveals unique considerations, and deserves extensive treatment not possible here. Nevertheless, fundamentalists' presumption of national evangelical leadership, their position as an interdenominational movement, and their penetration of other traditions led them to envision and successfully call together this broad, cooperative alliance. Evangelical cooperation under the NAE banner would have its limits, though, to a great extent because of the fundamentalist conveners' peculiar problems and attitudes.

Several denominations refused to join the NAE because they thought the fundamentalist influence was too strong. The Southern Baptists, who would have instantly dominated the NAE membership with their five million members, backed away after initial interest.[107] Their leaders blamed Northern fundamentalists for the millenarianism, independence, and separatism that was disturbing them with new intensity in the 1940s.[108] Since then, they have avoided contact with the new evangelical coalition. "We are *not* evangelicals; that's a Yankee word," huffed South-

---

[105]J. E. Wright, "Is the Day of Miracles Past?" 29 (August 1931): 12-13; "Dispensationalism," 27 (December 1929): 10; Cornelius Vlot, "Allentown (Pa.) Thanksgiving Convention," 28 (January 1930): 20; "New England News," 28 (January 1930): 21; *The Sheaf of the First Fruits.*

[106]Menzies, *Anointed to Serve*, 184-89; "Basic Unity of Evangelical Christianity," *Pentecostal Evangel*, (19 June 1943): 8.

[107]Southern Baptist eminences, such as Robert G. Lee and R. J. Bateman, played prominent roles in the St. Louis conference, but did not return in 1943. O. W. Taylor, who was also there, gives a cool, critical perspective on the proceedings, "Meeting of Evangelicals in St. Louis," *Baptist and Reflector* 108 (7 May 1942): 3.

[108]Carver, *Out of His Treasure*, 76-81, 96-97; "We Like the Bryant Blend"; " 'Essentials' and 'Non-Essentials'"; "An Unfair Test of Fellowship," *Baptist and Reflector* 106 (8 February 1940): 2-3.

ern Baptist executive Foy Valentine in 1976. "We don't share their . . . fussy fundamentalism."[109] The Christian Reformed Church joined the NAE in 1943, but it withdrew after eight uneasy years. Church leaders feared that NAE contacts were planting "fundamentalistic" tendencies among their people and compromising their Reformed distinctiveness.[110] The Evangelical Covenant Church considered joining the NAE on several occasions, but did not do so. The Covenant Church's anticreedalism, one of its major differing points with Fundamentalism, made its members object to the NAE's statement of faith. Church politics also dictated that neither the fundamentalistic conservatives' petitions to join the NAE nor the more liberal Evangelicals' desires for National Council of Churches affiliation would prevail.[111]

While some Evangelicals rejected the NAE for being too fundamentalistic, others would find it not fundamental enough. When the conveners of the NAE decided to reject the merger offer of the American Council of Christian Churches, they knew they were risking controversy. In fact, they were renewing a debate that would split the fundamentalist movement. The issues were not new; they had been smoldering for a long time. Since the 1920s fundamentalists had differed on strategy, tactics, and the basis for fellowship. Militants from the Northern Baptist Convention and the Northern Presbyterian denomination, tired of patient tactics, decided to either purge their denominations or leave. From their ranks came the General Association of Regular Baptist Churches in 1932,[112] and the Orthodox Presbyterian and Bible Presbyterian Churches in 1936 and

----

[109]Valentine quoted in Kenneth L. Woodward, "Born Again!" *Newsweek*, 25 October 1976, 76; see also Russell Bradley Jones, "A Digest of Religious Thought: Interdenominational Schools," *Baptist and Reflector* 115 (2 June 1949): 5; Duke K. McCall, "Northern Fundamentalism," *Baptist and Reflector* 119 (3 September 1953): 12; John Scott Trent, "Pastors Beware!" *Baptist and Reflector* 123 (26 July 1957): 6.

[110]Hall, "The Controversy over Fundamentalism," 94-118.

[111]Olsson, *By One Spirit*, 641-42; *Covenant Yearbook*, Annual Conference of the Evangelical Covenant Church of America, Rockford, Illinois, 16-20 June 1943, 180-81; Murch, *Cooperation without Compromise*, 199-200.

[112]Robert G. Delnay, "A History of the Baptist Bible Union" (Th.D. diss., Dallas Theological Seminary, 1963); Joseph M. Stowell, *Background and History of the General Association of Regular Baptist Churches* (Hayward CA: Gospel Tracts Unlimited, 1949).

1937.[113] These groups, J. Frank Norris's movement among Southern Baptists, and thousands of independent congregations comprised the separatists.[114] They sought doctrinally pure churches that would be separated from all worldliness, especially from Modernism, which they believed now permeated the major denominations. They believed that they should attack and expose this alleged apostasy whenever they found it, and they urged conservatives to "come out and be separate" as well.[115] McIntire's American Council clearly spoke for this position.

The separatists who joined the American Council accused the NAE of compromising with liberalism. The NAE did not expressly condemn the Federal Council of Churches as apostate and allowed members to join without renouncing all ties to the "near-communist" Federal Council. Furthermore, NAE leaders advocated evangelism and infiltration of old-line denominations instead of separation. Because appealing to old prejudices was not yet forgotten, the separatists also accused the NAE of being infested with Pentecostalism.[116]

The NAE leaders responded with some polemics of their own. Harold J. Ockenga, for example, ripped into Fundamentalism as though it were an alien faith, not his own heritage. Fundamentalism was divisive, he charged. It was plagued by "an utter incapacity for cooperative groups."

---

[113]George Hutchinson, *The History behind the Reformed Presbyterian Church Evangelical Synod* (Cherry Hill NJ: Mack Publishing Co., 1974) 215-70; George M. Marsden, "Perspectives on the Division of 1937," four-part series in *Presbyterian Guardian* 28 (January-April 1964): 5-8, 21-23, 27-29, 43-46, 54-56.

[114]George W. Dollar, *A History of Fundamentalism in America* (Greenville SC: Bob Jones University Press, 1973) 187-289, gives a helpful survey of the separatist wing of Fundamentalism and a separatist perspective on postwar development.

[115]R. T. Ketcham, *Facts for Baptists to Face* (Gary IN: n.p., 1936) is a classic separatist polemic. For a clear exposition of the separatist position, see Carl McIntire, "Separation from Unbelief," *Christian Life* 1 (March 1948): 23-26, 82-84.

[116]Carl McIntire, *Twentieth Century Reformation* (Collingswood NJ: Christian Beacon Press, 1944) 186-98; R. T. Ketcham, "J. Elwin Wright on Separation," *Baptist Bulletin* 11 (October 1945): 10-12; Carl McIntire and associates kept a running debate with NAE's statements and actions in the weekly *Christian Beacon*. For representative pieces through the early years of the controversy, see McIntire, "The NAE and 'Separation,'" *Christian Beacon* 13 (7 October 1948): 4-5; "NAE Leader Defends Communist-Front Preachers," *Christian Beacon* 14 (7 April 1949): 5; Carl McIntire, "Cooperation without Compromise," *Christian Beacon* 14 (26 May 1949): 1-2, 4-5, 8.

One example was the American Council, which slandered its brethren as compromisers and cowards for not submitting to "a new hierarchy of intolerant bigots."[117] The result was a long, protracted battle that divided the old fundamentalist movement. Various fundamentalist fellowships and agencies were pressured to choose between the militant separatist and evangelical inclusivist positions.[118] As Billy Graham became the nation's most prominent evangelist and evangelical spokesman, his ministry became the center of debate. Separatists charged that Graham diluted the gospel and undermined the standing of fundamental churches by cooperating with liberals.[119] Post-fundamentalist leaders criticized separatists for their hypercritical attitudes and anti-intellectualism while leading a new wave of conservative evangelical scholarship. They eschewed the fundamentalist label altogether in favor of "evangelical."[120]

This controversy provoked the separatists to an even more anti-worldly and conspiratorial outlook. The liberal poison, they believed, had invaded the fundamentalist camp and the most dangerous enemy was now "neo-evangelicalism," not liberalism. Separatists became militantly

---

[117]Ockenga, "Can Fundamentalism Win America?" *Christian Life and Times* 2 (June 1947): 13-15; see also, Elwin Wright, "Separation Is Not Scriptural," *United Evangelical Action* (15 August 1947); Stephen W. Paine, "The NAE and 'Separation,'" *United Evangelical Action* (15 September 1948); Carl F. H. Henry, *The Uneasy Conscience of Modern Fundamentalism* (Grand Rapids MI: Eerdmans, 1947).

[118]Just after the NAE's first convention, Mr. Hobart S. Geer, a deacon at the Calvary Baptist Church of New York and active in the Gideons and Christian Business Men's Committee, refused to give Davis mailing lists for those groups. He said that he was "in hot water" for cooperating with the NAE. Ralph T. Davis to Hobart S. Geer, 26 May 1942, AIM Records.

[119]William A. Ashbrook, "Evangelicalism: The New Neutralism," *The Voice* (October 1956): 6-7, 13; part two (November 1956): 6-7, 11; Carl McIntire, "The Bible, Christ's Commands, and Separation," *Christian Beacon* 22 (30 January 1957): 1-2, 4-5; Alva J. McClain, "Is Theology Changing in the Conservative Camp?" *The Sword of the Lord* 28 (5 April 1957): 1, 12; Robert L. Sumner, *Man Sent from God: A Biography of Dr. John R. Rice* (Grand Rapids MI: Eerdmans, 1959) 199-220, explains Rice's critical position toward Graham.

[120]Edward John Carnell, "Post-Fundamentalist Faith," *The Christian Century* 76 (26 August 1959): 971; "Theology, Evangelism, Ecumenism," *Christianity Today* 2 (20 January 1958): 20-23; "Is Evangelical Theology Changing?" *Christian Life* 9 (March 1956): 16-19. See also, Edward John Carnell, *The Case for Orthodox Theology* (Philadelphia: Westminster Press, 1959) where he castigates Fundamentalism as "orthodoxy gone cultic," 120-212.

opposed to any trend in doctrine and practice that could ever be thought to denote softness toward liberalism. They retreated into their own religious communities, especially in the Sunbelt states where political conservatism and Protestant hegemony better suited their outlook.[121] They were split by continued internal rivalry, but are rapidly growing today, with vigorous new spokesmen such as Jerry Falwell and Bob Jones III.

The issues separatists raised disturbed other fundamentalists. Several independent Bible schools and seminaries that the NAE hoped would support it backed away. Some feared that postfundamentalists such as Ockenga and Wright were going too far, were compromising fundamentalist testimony by fellowshipping with liberal denominations and Pentecostals. Others, fearing a loss of support throughout the movement, held a noncontroversial, nonaligned position between the separatists and the NAE.[122]

The separation debate also made the postfundamentalists overly defensive. Their orthodoxy and spiritual health had been questioned, and they struggled to convince other fundamentalists that their theology was still "fundamental," but that they were calling for reform in attitudes and practices.[123] This defensive stance has hampered the development of a

---

[121]This feeling is portrayed poignantly in Carl McIntire, "N.A.E., Fuller Seminary, Championed by Ockenga," *Christian Beacon* 16 (10 May 1951): 1, 4, 5, 8, in which McIntire accuses Ockenga and other nonseparating Presbyterians, such as Wilbur M. Smith, of having sold out to the modernists. Robert T. Ketcham expresses the same sense of having "counted the cost," while others compromised themselves to gain security, in his taped correspondence with Virgil Bopp (undated) on file at the Ketcham Library, Grand Rapids Baptist College. Robert T. Ketcham, "A New Peril in our Last Days," *Christian Beacon* 21 (17 May 1956): 2, 6-7; Charles J. Woodbridge, *The New Evangelicalism* (Greenville SC: Bob Jones University, 1969); William E. Ashbrook, *The New Neutralism* (Columbus OH: Calvary Bible Church, 1969).

[122]Moody Bible Institute and Dallas Theological Seminary, for instance, two major fundamentalist centers, stayed nonaligned although their presidents gave the NAE early encouragement. *United Action!*, 144-45; Houghton to R. T. Davis, 23 December 1940, AIM Records. William Bell Riley shows the less than positive response of this nonaligned group, "National Association of Evangelicals for United Action," *The Pilot* 23 (November 1942): 53-54; and Dollar, *A History of Fundamentalism*, 282-89, delineates the new, tripartite configuration of the movement.

[123]Stephen W. Paine, "Cooperation without Compromise," *United Evangelical Action* (May 1949); Vernon Grounds, "The Nature of Evangelicalism," *Eternity* (February 1956): 12-13, 42-43; Harold John Ockenga, "Resurgent Evangelical Leadership," *Christianity Today* 4 (10 October 1960): 13, states "The evangelical and the fundamentalist could sign the same creed."

genuinely unitive evangelical theology and has perpetuated postfundamentalist presumptions of centrality. Spokesmen such as Ockenga and Harold Lindsell were still defining "evangelicalism" in the 1960s as if it were exclusively Reformed in theology.[124] Only in very recent years has the self-proclaimed evangelical establishment, centered around *Christianity Today*, acknowledged that something might be learned from the peace churches, the Wesleyans, and the Pentecostals.

No wonder, then, that these traditions and others, especially black Evangelicals, who have been almost entirely left out, emphasized their unique heritages in the 1960s and 1970s. The fundamentalist leaven may have invaded many of these groups, but now they recognize it has a tradition other than their own.[125] Evangelicals' common identity has not faded as a result, but has blossomed into a divergent, pluralistic unity. Diversity and decentralization make the postfundamentalists uneasy; however, these are signs of vitality, not weakness.

---

[124]Ockenga, "Resurgent Evangelical Leadership," 11-15; Harold Lindsell, "Who Are the Evangelicals?" *Christianity Today* 9 (18 June 1965): 3-6.

[125]Richard Quebedeaux traces these developments in a highly subjective study, *The Young Evangelicals: Revolution in Orthodoxy* (New York: Harper & Row, 1974); John Howard Yoder, *The Politics of Jesus* (Grand Rapids MI: Eerdmans, 1977); and C. Norman Kraus, ed., *Evangelicalism and Anabaptism* (Scottsdale PA: Herald Press, 1979) represent Anabaptistic renewal; Richard J. Mouw, *Politics and the Biblical Drama* (Grand Rapids: Eerdmans, 1976) and Nicholas Wolterstorff, *Reason within the Bounds of Religion* (Grand Rapids: Eerdmans, 1977) present Reformed critiques of evangelical traits; Donald Dayton's *Discovering an Evangelical Heritage* (New York: Harper & Row, 1976) and Howard Snyder's *The Radical Wesley* (Downers Grove IL: Inter-Varsity Press, 1979) display resurgent Wesleyanism; Vinson Synan, ed., *Aspects of Pentecostal-Charismatic Origins*, and Quebedeaux's *The New Charismatics: The Origins, Development and Significance of Neo-Pentecostalism* (Garden City NY: Doubleday & Co., 1976) examine the new Pentecostalism; William E. Pannell, *My Friend, The Enemy* (Waco TX: Word Books, 1968); Columbus Salley and Ronald Behm, *Your God Is Too White* (Downers Grove IL: Inter-Varsity Press, 1970) and John Perkins, *Let Justice Roll Down* (Glendale CA: Regal Books, 1976) describe the travail and self-discovery of those black Evangelicals closely related to white Evangelicalism. Robert Webber and Donald Bloesch, eds., *The Orthodox Evangelicals* (Nashville: Thomas Nelson, 1978) calls for a new appreciation of the historic church and sacramental theology.

Chapter 10

Searching for Norman Rockwell: Popular Evangelicalism in Contemporary America

Grant Wacker

> *America, America—until about fifteen years ago the name by itself would evoke a feeling of warmth. Whether it was pride or gratitude or hope, the response of the majority of people on earth was deeply positive. . . . The American Dream was about to come true. And then, with a suddenness that is still bewildering, everything went out of balance.*
> —Peter Marshall and David Manuel
> *The Light and the Glory*(1977)

> *But man's primary problems aren't political; they're philosophical. Until humans can solve their philosophical problems, they're condemned to solve their political problems over and over again. It's a cruel, repetitious bore.*
> —Tom Robbins
> *Even Cowgirls Get the Blues*(1976)

In the dusk of the nineteenth century, Scottish churchman Marcus Dods remarked that he did not envy those who would carry the banner of Christianity in the twentieth century. "Yes, perhaps I do," he conceded, "but it will be a stiff fight." As it turned out, Dods's apprehensions were well founded, for one can scarcely doubt that throughout the Western world

and in much of the non-Western world as well, the drumroll of secularization has set the cadence of twentieth-century history.[1]

The cultural diversity of the United States makes it difficult to know
exactly when the old orthodoxies were displaced by the crippling doubts
of modern life. Many historians believe that the scale started to wobble
during the 1890s, then tipped decisively between the First and Second
World Wars. By 1980, in any event, polls showed that sixty-one million
were unchurched and that conventional belief was in disarray. And for
some that was hardly the worst of the news. In the preceding twenty years
the Protestant Establishment—the American Baptist Church, the Christian Church (Disciples), the Lutheran Church in America, the Protestant
Episcopal Church, the United Church of Christ, the United Methodist
Church, and the United Presbyterian Church—had lost nearly four million members. Roman Catholics had effectively lost hundreds of thousands and Jews had long since quit counting. As they neared the end of
the century, the major religious groups necessarily entertained few illusions that in the foreseeable future they would grow at all, much less out-
pace the population. Hoping only to stop the decline, they seemed
resigned—in words David Ignatow used in a different context—to "feel
along the edges of life/for a way/that will lead to open land."[2]

---

[1]Dods quoted without citation in Charles W. Gilkey, "Preaching: The Recovery of
the Word," in *Protestant Thought in the Twentieth Century: Whence and Whither?* ed. Ar-
nold S. Nash (New York: Macmillan, 1951) 220. I owe this reference to Roberts Moats
Miller, *Harry Emerson Fosdick*, forthcoming. For secularization see Peter L. Berger et al.,
The Homeless Mind: Modernization and Consciousness (New York: Random House, 1973).
At the beginning of this essay the first epigraph is taken from Peter Marshall and David
Manuel, *The Light and the Glory* (Old Tappan NJ: Revell, 1977) 13. The second is quoted
in Daniel Yankelovich, *New Rules: Searching for Self-Fulfillment in a World Turned Upside
Down* (New York: Random House, 1981) frontispiece.

[2]Old orthodoxies displaced: Henry F. May, *The End of American Innocence: A Study
of the First Years of Our Own Time* (Chicago: Quadrangle Paperbacks, rpt. 1964 [1959]).
Unchurched: George Gallup, Jr. and David Polling, *The Search for America's Faith* (Nashville: Abingdon, 1980) 80. Polls: "The Christianity Today-Gallup Poll: An Overview,"
Christianity Today, 21 December 1979, 1668. Protestant Establishment: *Yearbook of
American and Canadian Churches* 1981 (Nashville: Abingdon, 1981), cited in Harold
Lindsell, "The Major Denominations Are Jumping Ship," *Christianity Today*, 18 September 1981, 1189-90; see also David A. Roozen and Jackson W. Carroll, "Recent Trends
in Church Membership and Participation," in *Understanding Church Growth and Decline:
1950-1978*, eds. Dean R. Hoge and David A. Roozen (New York: Pilgrim Press, 1979) 22-
28. Catholic decline: James Hennesey, S. J., *American Catholics: A History of the Roman
Catholic Community in the United States* (New York: Oxford, 1981) ch. 21. Jewish decline:

Nonetheless, as the curtain opened on the 1980s the religious situation was not as grim as the media suggested and intellectuals hoped. In all parts of the nation churches were, in fact, buzzing with a powerful resurgence of evangelical fervor. Theologically this new Evangelicalism, as it was often called, looked like a dapper version of the frowzy Fundamentalism of the 1920s. But sociologically there was a big difference: it was almost fashionable.[3]

Actually, the movement had been flourishing just beneath the surface—or more precisely, just outside the view of the press—for at least twenty years. But in 1976—dubbed by *Time* and *Newsweek* as the Year of the Evangelical—the general public seemed suddenly to become aware of its existence. Little wonder. In that one year Black Panther Eldridge Cleaver announced that he had had an old-fashioned religious conversion; Charles Colson's autobiography, *Born Again*, shot to the top of the book charts; and a strongly evangelical Southern Baptist became president.[4] Soon it was no longer clear who the mainstream Protestants really were. In 1980 the annual circulation of Billy Graham's newspaper *Decision* topped twenty-four million, while the thoughtful and ever-so-sober

Nathan Glazer, "Jewish Loyalties," *Wilson Quarterly* 5 (1981): 134-45. Ignatow: epigraph to his *Rescue the Dead*, quoted in *New World Metaphysics: Readings on the Religious Meaning of the American Experience*, ed. Giles Gunn (New York: Oxford, 1981) 405.

[3]For a succinct survey, see Winthrop S. Hudson, *Religion in America* (New York: Scribner's, 3rd rev. ed., 1981 [1965]) ch. 17. For general news accounts see Kenneth L. Woodward, "Born Again!" *Newsweek*, 25 October 1976, 68-78; "Back to that Oldtime Religion," *Time*, 26 December 1977, 52-58; James Mann, "A Global Surge of Old-Time Religion," *U. S. News & World Report*, 27 April 1981, 38-40. More extensive treatments include Donald G. Bloesch, *The Evangelical Renaissance* (Grand Rapids MI: Eerdmans, 1973) chs. 1-2; Richard Quebedeaux, *The Worldly Evangelicals* (San Francisco: Harper & Row, 1978); John D. Woodbridge et al., *The Gospel in America: Themes in the Story of America's Evangelicals* (Grand Rapids MI: Zondervan, 1979) esp. ch. 3; Ed Dobson et al., *The Fundamentalist Phenomenon: The Resurgence of Conservative Christianity* (Garden City NY: Doubleday, 1981) chs. 5-6.

[4]Evangelical background: George M. Marsden, *Fundamentalism and American Culture: The Shaping of Twentieth-Century Evangelicalism: 1870-1925* (New York: Oxford, 1980), and Joel Carpenter, "A Shelter in the Time of Storm: Fundamentalist Institutions and the Rise of Evangelical Protestants, 1929-1942," *Church History* 49 (1980): 62-75. Woodward, "Born Again!" *Newsweek*, 25 October 1976, 68-78; "Back to that Oldtime Religion," *Time*, 26 December 1977, 52-58. Cleaver: *Time*, 26 December 1977. Colson: Gary C. Wharton, "The Continuing Phenomenon of the Religious Best Seller," *Publisher's Weekly*, 14 March 1977, 82-83.

Christianity Today outstripped its jaunty liberal rival, *Christian Century*, five subscribers to one. Evangelical publishers were given access to a score of spectacularly successful titles. (Of course they were accustomed to success: each year between 1971 and 1974 they had marketed the best seller of the year—not to mention Hal Lindsay's 1970 blockbuster, *The Late Great Planet Earth*, which, next to the Bible, may have been the nonfiction best seller of all time.) Bill Bright's Campus Crusade for Christ, funded by high rollers like Nelson Bunker Hunt and T. Cullen Davis, rapidly moved toward its goal of raising a billion dollars to take the gospel to every person on the globe. Sixteen thousand Christian academies, proliferating at the rate of one a day, comprised a two-billion-dollar-a-year private education industry. At staunchly evangelical Wheaton College (IL), the number of National Merit Scholars and alumni with earned Ph.D.'s rivaled the most prestigious colleges in the nation. Radio and television evangelists attracted millions. No one knows exactly how many millions, and it is clear that the number was smaller than commonly believed, but there is reliable evidence that the prime-time preachers drew a weekly audience of at least twenty million and garnered annual contributions exceeding a half-billion dollars. Every index of membership and participation showed that most evangelical denominations were bursting at the doors. The Southern Baptist Convention lumbered past the thirteen million mark while numerous smaller groups like the Assemblies of God posted decennial growth rates of thirty percent or more. Perhaps most astonishing were the numerous polls showing that by 1980 at least thirty million Americans considered themselves reborn evangelical Christians, and another twenty million styled themselves evangelical in belief and sympathy.[5]

---

[5]*Decision: Christianity Today*, 5 February 1982, 69. *Christianity Today v. Christian Century*: P. J. Schemenaur, *1981 Writer's Market* (Cincinnati: Writer's Digest Books, 1980) 489-90. Best sellers: Wharton, "Continuing Phenomenon," and John B. Breslin, "Religious Best Sellers," *Theology Today* 34 (1977): 311-17. Campus Crusade: "Big Bucks for Evangelism," *Christian Century*, 3-10 June 1981, 632-33, and Quebedeaux, *Worldly Evangelicals*, 55-59. Academies: Frances FitzGerald, "A Disciplined, Charging Army," *New Yorker*, 18 May 1981, 63, and Kenneth Pierce, "A Care for Moral Absolutes," *Time*, 8 June 1981, 54-56. Wheaton: Richard N. Ostling, "All That and Billy Graham Too," *Time*, 22 September 1980, 83. Radio and television: William Martin, "Television: The Birth of a Media Myth," *Atlantic Monthly*, June 1981, 7-16, and Jeffrey K. Hadden and Charles E. Swann, *Prime Time Preachers: The Rising Power of Televangelism* (Reading MA: Addison-Wesley, 1981) 47-57. Evangelical denominational growth statistics overviewed in Harold Lindsell, "The Decline of a Church and Its Culture,"

After decades of relative quiet, why did Evangelicalism mushroom like this in the 1960s? Several scholars have suggested that external structural changes were a relevant factor. Reginald Bibby has shown, for example, that the birth rate rose faster among evangelical than among nonevangelical Protestants. Taking a very different line, Jeffrey Hadden has argued that the surge was powered by the movement's willingness to exploit the microelectronics revolution. Evangelicals, he has noted, quickly adopted advanced computer technology that enabled them to target likely contributors and thus move into the satellite and cable television market. At the same time, Frances FitzGerald has pointed out that policy changes by networks and local radio and television stations enabled religious groups to buy air time. This particularly helped Evangelicals, who seem to have had fewer inhibitions about raising money through high-powered public appeals. Dean Hoge has discerned that the movement's growth may have been a by-product of demographic shifts. Although the evidence is murky, the tilt of the population into the Sunbelt, where evangelical churches already predominated, may have especially benefited Evangelicals, simply because migrants tend to join more accessible churches.[6]

More commonly, though, evangelical strength has been interpreted as a symptom of broad cultural changes. For example, Dean Kelley has argued that churches that made strict demands and presented a distinctive theology flourished because they met an enduring need for ethical challenge and ultimate meaning. Mainstream churches asked little and gave little, and so watched their members walk away. Daniel Yankelovich

---

Christianity Today, 17 July 1981, 931-34, and Bruce L. Shelley, "Sampling the Spirit of the Smaller Denominations," *Christianity Today*, 11 December 1981, 1665-67. General polls summarized in "Overview," *Christianity Today*. For an overview of evangelical insurgence in popular culture, see Richard Quebedeaux, *By What Authority: The Rise of Personality Cults in American Christianity* (San Francisco: Harper & Row, 1982) 46-69.

[6]Reginald W. Bibby, "Why Conservative Churches *Really* Are Growing: Kelley Revisited," *Journal for the Scientific Study of Religion* 17 (1978): 134, 136. Jeffrey K. Hadden, "Soul Saving via Video," *Christian Century*, 28 May 1980, 609-10. FitzGerald, "A Disciplined, Charging Army," 54, 59. Dean Hoge, "A Test of Theories of Denominational Growth and Decline," in Hoge and Roozen, *Church Growth*, 186-90. Compare with Robert Wuthnow and Kevin Christiano, "The Effects of Residential Migration on Church Attendance," in *The Religious Dimension: New Directions in Quantitative Research*, ed. Wuthnow (New York: Academic Press/Harcourt Brace, 1979) 268-74.

has offered a variant of this argument, claiming that the heightened visibility of evangelical religion was a direct reaction to the heightened visibility of hedonistic life-styles in the 1960s and 1970s. Virginia Stem Owens, on the other hand, has insisted that Evangelicalism flourished precisely because it did not impose serious demands. She has suggested that the tension between evangelical ethics and the ethics of middle America may have been great enough to give the appearance of separation, but it was not sufficient to prevent substantial enjoyment of the material good life. Others, like J. Lawrence Burkholder, have charged that evangelical success is partly the result of a willingness to give easy answers to difficult questions; to sanctify mundane aspirations by telling people exactly what they wanted to hear. For Theodore Roszak, evangelical growth has been the result of a "hunger for wonders"—a reaction that quite predictably erupted in a culture devoted to an exclusively "science-based reality principle." More grandly, Jeremy Rifkin has proposed that just as the sixteenth century disclosed an elective affinity between Protestantism and capitalism, the 1970s may have disclosed the beginnings of an elective affinity between evangelical asceticism and postindustrial scarcity. In the end, though, Evangelicals themselves will be most persuaded by Martin E. Marty's judgment that they thrived because they clearly understood what the Puritans did not: that Godliness does not pass through the loins of Godly parents, but must be actively rekindled in the minds and hearts of each generation.[7]

Scholars have offered other explanations, but this is enough to indicate that the explanations are extremely diverse and, to some extent, off target. The problem is that the premise has not been adequately examined. These and other thoughtful observers have invested considerable energy trying to account for evangelical growth on the assumption that Evangelicalism is, in fact, growing. I propose, rather, that what is grow-

---

[7]Dean M. Kelley, *Why Conservative Churches Are Growing: A Study in the Sociology of Religion* (New York: Harper & Row, 1972) 39-42, 52-53, 84, 131. Yankelovich, *New Rules*, 5-6. Virginia Stem Owens, *The Total Image: Or Selling Jesus in the Modern Age* (Grand Rapids MI: Eerdmans, 1980) esp. ch. 3. J. Lawrence Burkholder, "Popular Evangelicalism: An Appraisal," in *Evangelicalism and Anabaptism*, ed. C. Norman Kraus (Scottdale PA: Herald Press, 1979) 30-33. Theodore Roszak, "In Search of the Miraculous," *Harper's*, January 1981, 54-62. Jeremy Rifkin, with Ted Howard, *The Emerging Order: God in the Age of Scarcity* (New York: Putnam's, 1979) xii. Martin E. Marty, "The Marks and Misses of a Magazine," *Christianity Today*, 17 July 1981, 947.

ing is not Evangelicalism, conceived as a religious and theological move-ment, but rather a segment within Evangelicalism defined by its allegiance to a cluster of values derived from Victorian middle-class so-ciety. More precisely, it is defined by its identification with that part of Victorian society whose ideals were represented in 120,000,000 copies of the *McGuffey Reader*, and in later years sentimentally remembered in Norman Rockwell magazine covers. I shall call this smaller, more overtly politicized segment the Evangelical Right, and the consensus it seeks (borrowing a term from George M. Marsden) Christian Civilization.[8]

By now there is nothing startling about the suggestion that there is a distinction between Evangelicalism in America and Evangelicalism for America. Scarcely anyone—that is, anyone outside the evangelical camp—would doubt that the evangelical label truly belongs to theologi-ans like John Howard Yoder and Clark Pinnock; scholars like David O. Moberg and Timothy L. Smith; activists like Jim Wallis and Jon Alex-ander; public figures like Mark Hatfield and John Anderson; organiza-tions like the Berkeley Christian Coalition and Koininia Farm; magazines like the *Wittenburg Door* and *Daughters of Sarah*; or denominations like the Christian Reformed Church and the Brethren in Christ. Yet for one reason or another, all have distanced themselves from the Christian Civ-ilization clamor. When we assess the growth of this wing of Evangelical-ism—which for lack of a better term we might call the Evangelical non-Right (it would be too much to call it the Evangelical Left)—it is clear that this wing is not measurably stronger now than it was ten or twenty or even fifty years ago.[9]

---

[8]For the nature of Victorian culture in America, see the articles in *Victorian Culture in America*, ed. Daniel Walker Howe, special issue of *American Quarterly* 27 (1975). For *McGuffey* see Robert Wood Lynn, "Civil Catechetics in Mid-Victorian America," *Religious Education* 68 (1973): 5-27. For the concept of Christian Civilization, see Marsden, *Fundamentalism*, passim, and Mark Thomas Connelly, *The Response to Prostitution in the Progressive Era* (Chapel Hill: University of North Carolina Press, 1980) 8-10.

[9]For the social, cultural, and especially political diversity within contemporary Evan-gelicalism, see Robert D. Linder, "The Resurgence of Evangelical Social Concern (1925-75)," in *The Evangelicals*, ed. David F. Wells and John D. Woodbridge (Nashville: Abingdon, 1975) 189-210; Timothy L. Smith, "Protestants Falwell Does Not Repre-sent," New York *Times*, 22 October 1980, Op Ed page; Cullen Murphy, "Protestantism and the Evangelicals," *Wilson Quarterly* 5 (1981): 105-16; Richard Quebedeaux, *The Young Evangelicals* (New York: Harper & Row, 1974); Robert E. Webber, *The Moral Ma-*

It is important to stress that the distinction between the Evangelical non-Right and the Evangelical Right is not invidious. Neither side has forged a pure theology free of ideological agendas, and neither has lived a pure faith free of cultural entanglements. It is just as important to stress that the distinction ignores the kaleidoscopic complexity of the movement. Nonetheless, the concept of an Evangelical Right, functionally defined by its commitment to the rebirth of Christian Civilization in America, is analytically useful. It illumines the fact that we have witnessed in the late 1970s and 1980s the rise of a particular kind of Evangelicalism with a particularly explicit set of social and cultural commitments. Beyond this, the distinction helps to unravel the knot in which clearly evangelical, sort-of-evangelical, and clearly nonevangelical groups— such as the Independent Fundamentalist Baptist Fellowship, the Coalition for Better Television, and the National Congressional Caucus—are entangled.[10]

---

jority: Right or Wrong? (Westchester IL: Cornerstone Books, 1981) 119-82. For a contrasting view, see Martin E. Marty, *A Nation of Behavers* (Chicago: University of Chicago Press, 1976) ch. 4.

For evidence that the Evangelical non-Right is not growing, see Norris Magnusson, *Salvation in the Slums: Evangelical Social Work, 1865-1920* (Metuchen NJ: Scarecrow Press, 1977) x, 25, 168; Leo P. Ribuffo, "Fundamentalism Revisited: Liberals and That Old-Time Religion," *Nation*, 29 November 1980, 570-73; Lawrence W. Levine, *Defender of the Faith: William Jennings Bryan: The Last Decade 1915-1925* (New York: Oxford, 1965) esp. chs. 1-2. For CRC and BIC statistics, see *Yearbook of American and Canadian Churches* for 1951, 1961, 1971, and 1981. For works that address the question of whether theological conservatism (or strictness) per se enhances growth, see the summary in Hoge, "Denominational Growth," 182, and Dean R. Hoge and David P. Roozen, "Some Sociological Conclusions about Church Trends," in Hoge and Roozen, *Church Growth*, 325-27, 329; Jackson W. Carroll, "Understanding Church Growth Decline," *Theology Today* 35 (1978): 80; Robert R. Monaghan, "Three Faces of the True Believer: Motivations for Attending a Fundamentalist Church," *Journal for the Scientific Study of Religion* 6 (1967): 236-45.

[10]The secondary literature on the Evangelical Right is already extensive. For succinct overviews, see Erling Jorstad, "The New Christian Right," *Theology Today* 38 (1981): 193-200, and James E. Wood, Jr., "Religious Fundamentalism and the New Right," *Journal of Church and State* 23 (1981): 409-21. By far the best book-length account to date is Samuel S. Hill and Dennis E. Owen, *The New Religious Political Right in America* (Nashville: Abingdon, 1982). Others include Hadden and Swann, *Prime Time Preachers*; Erling Jorstad, *The Politics of Moralism: The New Christian Right in American Life* (Minneapolis MN: Augsburg, 1981); Peggy L. Shriver, *The Bible Vote: Religion and the New Right* (New York: Pilgrim Press, 1981). For Jerry Falwell and the Moral Majority, see esp. FitzGerald, "A Disciplined Charging Army." For Pat Robertson and the CBN empire, see esp. Dick Dabney, "God's Own Network," *Harper's*, August 1980, 33-52. For a com-

A Christian Civilization is not so much a list of discrete ideals as a co-herent world view, a way of seeing reality. But in order to understand this world view, we first have to do what no partisan would do: dismantle it, block by block, piece by piece. It becomes evident, then, that there are several cornerstones. Fundamental, and buttressing all else, is the con-viction that there are numerous moral absolutes human beings do not cre-ate but discover. In this case the problem is, of course, that modern culture is deceived by the opposite notion: that moral standards are forged within specific historical settings and thus wobble from one context to an-other. Despite this, Christian Civilization is grounded upon the sure rec-ognition that some things never change.[11]

This outlook certainly is not restricted to the Evangelical Right. Even so modern a man as Harry Emerson Fosdick could make a trademark out of the phrase, "astronomies change while stars abide." But the Evangel-ical Right is distinguished by the range and diversity of cultural forms it considers absolute. Homer Duncan's widely circulated booklet, *Secular Humanism: The Most Dangerous Religion in America*, is unusually stri-dent, but his point of view is typical.

> When we discard the Bible as our standard of absolute truth . . . we have no standard for determing moral values. The Bible says that murder is wrong, but nowadays many murderers are set free to kill again simply because the judge thinks they are mentally sick. Rapists are not account-able for their actions, so they are set free to ravish sweet little girls. . . . The Bible says that adultery and fornication are wrong, but since we have thrown away the Bible, college students and thousands of others live to-gether with no restraint. The Bible pronounces the death penalty for ho-mosexuality, but if the Equal Rights Amendment passes we will be compelled by law to send our children to homosexual teachers.[12]

---

parative persepctive, see Martin E. Marty, "Fundamentalism Reborn," *Saturday Review*, May 1980, 37, passim. For an astute critique of the phenomenon, see George M. Marsden, "The New Fundamentalism," *Reform Journal*, February 1982, 7-11.

[11]Examples are endless. See any issue of the biweekly *Moral Majority Report*, or: Jerry Falwell, "Future-Word: An Agenda for the Eighties," appended to Ed Dobson et al., *Fundamentalist Phenomenon*, 186-223; Falwell, *America Can Be Saved* (Murfreesboro TN: Sword of the Lord Publishers, 1979) ch. 3; Falwell, *Listen, America!* (New York: Bantam/Doubleday, rpt. 1981 [1980]) 101-103.

[12]Harry Emerson Fosdick, *The Living of These Days: An Autobiography* (New York: Harper & Bros., 1956) 230. For the widespread belief in moral absolutes in America, see Yankelovich, *New Rules*, 87-88, 91, and Jackson W. Carroll et al., *Religion in America:*

The temper of Duncan's remarks suggests another difference between conventional notions of moral absolutes and those common within
the Evangelical Right. Erling Jorstad has called it moral*ism*: the assumption that for every moral question there is one and only one morally correct
answer. Jorstad's analysis is accurate as far as it goes, but moralism stems
from an underlying presupposition that moral absolutes can be discerned
with absolute clarity and certainty. Consider Paul Weyrich's admonition
to campaign workers: "Ultimately everything can be reduced to right and
wrong. Everything." Moralism also assumes that reality can be sliced
down the middle. Thus Tim LaHaye characteristically asserts that everywhere in life there are "two basic lines of reasoning . . . atheistic humanism
or Christianity. What this life is all about is *the battle for your mind*: whether
you will live your life guided by man's wisdom (humanism) or God's wisdom (Christianity)." The world of the Evangelical Right is, in essence, a
realm in which moral absolutes are strewn about like boulders on a desert.
Yet they cast no shadows, making disagreements about their size and
shape not legitimate differences of perception but deliberate distortions
of moral judgment. [13]

The second cornerstone of Christian Civilization is the conviction that
moral absolutes ought to form the visible foundation of the laws that govern society. This means, quite simply, that norms and sanctions that regulate private conduct ought to regulate public conduct too. On significant
questions like abortion, public legal determinations ought to be no different than private moral judgments. Here again the Evangelical Right is
hardly unique. Many thoughtful persons agree that morality—or what
Richard John Neuhaus aptly terms "sacred points of reference"—ought
to inform all aspects of public policy. But the Evangelical Right is distinguished by its insistence that the real question is not *whether* society's laws
will express a particular moral code, but whose. The point is that laws,

---

1950 to the Present (San Francisco: Harper & Row, 1979) 29-33. Homer Duncan, *Secular
Humanism: The Most Dangerous Religion in America* (Lubbock TX: Missionary Crusade,
1979) 46-47.

[13]Jorstad, *Politics of Moralism*, 8-10. Weyrich quoted in Bill Keller, "Lobbying for
Christ: Evangelical Conservatives Move from Pews to Polls," *Congressional Quarterly
Weekly*, 6 September 1980, 2630. Tim LaHaye, *The Battle for the Mind* (Old Tappan NJ:
Revell, 1980) 9. The epistemology of the Evangelical Right is well analyzed in Hill and
Owen, *Religious Political Right*, 18, 36-38, 119, 150-54.

and for that matter public policies, always reflect a society's ultimate values. Thus law is "inescapably religious," argues R. J. Rushdoony, a leading architect of the Christian Civilization ideal, because law "establishes in practical fashion the ultimate concerns of a culture." We shall return to this point, but here it is important to recognize that in the world view of the Evangelical Right, no law or public policy is morally neutral—and to claim otherwise is naive if not deliberately dishonest.[14]

The third cornerstone of Christian Civilization is the conviction that the moral absolutes that undergird—or that ought to undergird—society's laws are commonly revealed in nature and explicitly revealed in the Bible. Moreover, the moral values disclosed in nature and the Bible are precisely the values that until recently have been highly esteemed in Judeo-Christian culture. That this is true is obvious in the Declaration of Independence and Constitution of the United States. "Our Founding Fathers were not all Christians," Jerry Falwell admits, "but they were guided by biblical principles. They developed a nation predicated on Holy Writ."[15]

Not surprisingly, this perceived identity of natural, biblical, Western, and republican values bristles with ramifications for contemporary society. Most consequential is, perhaps, a severe narrowing of the American tradition of religious pluralism. Although partisans of the Evangelical Right often assert that Christian Civilization can embrace healthy diversity, thoughtful spokesmen like Harold O. J. Brown acknowledge

---

[14]Richard J. Neuhaus quoted without citation in Shriver, *Bible Vote*, 45. R. J. Rushdoony, *The Institutes of Biblical Law* (1973) 4, quoted in John W. Whitehead and John Conlan, "The Establishment of the Religion of Secular Humanism and Its First Amendment Implications," *Texas Tech Law Review* 10 (1978): 20, n. 111. See also Howard Phillips, "How to Clean Up America by 'Defunding the Left,'" in *How You Can Help Clean Up America*, ed. Jerry Falwell (Washington DC: Moral Majority, Inc., 1981) 30-40. For expressions of the same point of view by nonpartisans of the Evangelical Right, see Harold J. Berman, "Law, Religion, and the Present Danger," *Worldview*, September 1979, 46-52, and Terry Eastland, "In Defense of Religious America," *Commentary*, June 1981, 39-45. The most sophisticated version of this argument is Whitehead and Conlan, "Establishment . . . of Secular Humanism." The notion is pervasive in the literature of the Evangelical Right. For a summary and perceptive critique, see George M. Marsden, "America's 'Christian' Origins: Puritan New England as a Case Study," in *John Calvin: His Influence in the Western World*, ed. W. Stanford Reid (Grand Rapids MI: Zondervan, 1982) 241-60, 386-87.

[15]Falwell, *Listen, America!*, 25; see also 8, 15, 45. LaHaye, *Battle for the Mind*, 36-38.

that pluralism is feasible only within a consensus of biblically grounded, traditional values. Recent attempts by the Evangelical Right to ban *Ms.* magazine from public libraries, or to press for laws prohibiting unmarried couples from renting motel rooms, or to push for federal funding of programs to promote teenage chastity, are powerful reminders that in a Christian Civilization the boundaries of permissible behavior are tightly drawn. Donald Howard, founder of the influential Accelerated Christian Education program, puts it plainly: "Legislation against apparent and obvious evil . . . [is] what will happen when Jesus Christ reigns."[16]

The confluence of natural, biblical, Western, and republican values means also that in a Christian Civilization, government's role is to foster conventional virtues, such as the preservation of unborn life, and to restrain vices like homosexuality, which decent men and women have always shunned. Government's role is not to tinker with the operations of a free market economy. The Evangelical Right has never developed a systematic rationale for the latter position—which political scientist Michael Lienesch aptly calls a "supply-side theory of salvation"—but that is beside the point just now. The fact is that in a Christian Civilization government, no less than church or family, is squarely responsible for the cultivation of moral fiber.[17] Yet it scarcely needs to be said that this has not been the reigning political philosophy during the past half-century. In this period, as columnist George F. Will has phrased it, an influential

---

[16]For typical (and typically ambivalent) assertions of the value of pluralism, see Jerry Falwell, as interviewed in *Christianity Today*, 4 September 1981, 1097, and in *Nutshell*, October 1981, 34, 41. See also Reo Christenson, "It's Time to Excise the Pornographic Cancer," in Falwell, *Clean Up America*, 94-95. Harold O. J. Brown, "The Road to Theocracy?," *National Review*, 31 October 1980, 1328-29. Ban *Ms.* and motel rooms: William Scobie, "Unholy Crusade on Sexual Battlefront," *Macleans*, 4 May 1981, 13-15. Teenage chastity: Michael Posner, "The Might of the Righteous," *Macleans*, 4 January 1982, 23. Donald Howard quoted in Michael Disend, "Have You Whipped Your Child Today?," *Penthouse*, February 1982, 186. The ambiguities embedded in the Evangelical Right's views on pluralism and religious freedom are analyzed in Hill and Owen, *Religious Political Right*, 44-45, 114-16.

[17]For the moral role of government, see any issue of *Moral Majority Report*, but one particularly pointed example is William A. Rusher, "Goldwater and the Religious Right," *Moral Majority Report*, 19 October 1981, 7. The economic theories of the Evangelical Right are assayed in Michael Lienesch, "The Paradoxical Politics of the Religious Right," *Soundings* 66 (1983): 70-99. See also Falwell, *Listen, America!*, 11, and LaHaye, *Battle for the Mind*, 39.

minority of Americans have come to believe that government is to be "ubiquitous and omniprovident regarding material things, but . . . neutral regarding values. It can concern itself with nurturing soybeans, but not virtue." To the Evangelical Right, the result is literal craziness—an incomprehensible inversion of values. Philosopher Michael Novak is not necessarily a partisan, but he makes the point well: "Children in our public schools are to be allowed sex education but not prayer. Can it be true that prayer is more dangerous to the schools than sex?" This abdication of responsibility for moral nurture by government at all levels is perceived to be as much a cause as a symptom of the nation's deterioration. Indeed, it is just this notion—that government has a pastoral role—that explains why many conservatives like William Safire and Barry Goldwater have distanced themselves from the Evangelical Right; for they have perceived, quite correctly, that the movement is fired by an interventionist rather than libertarian vision of society.[18]

These, then, are the cornerstones of Christian Civilization: recognition that there are moral absolutes any honest person can rightly discern; that these moral absolutes ought to be reflected not only in a Christian's private life but also in a society's fundamental laws; and finally, that the preservation of moral absolutes is the proper task of government.

Perched atop these cornerstones, the Evangelical Right believes it is easy to see how the arbiters of contemporary culture have led America astray. First, the media. In the eyes of the Evangelical Right newspapers, magazines, radio, and television undermine Christian Civilization not so much by direct attack as by unintentional distortion and intentional snideness and caricature. Journalists who spend more time in New York than in Peoria, and who rarely know what it means to earn a living with

---

[18]George F. Will, "Who Put Morality in Politics?" *Newsweek*, 15 September 1980, 108. Michael Novak, "Prayer, Education," *National Review*, 17 October 1980, 1270. "Goldwater Blasts New Right," *Time*, 28 September 1981, 27. William Safire, "Line Forms Right," New York *Times* News Service, reprinted in Chapel Hill *Newspaper*, 18 November 1980. Alan Crawford sharply distinguishes what he calls traditional, New Right, and hearth-and-home styles of conservatism in America in *Thunder on the Right: The "New Right" and the Politics of Resentment* (New York: Pantheon Books, 1980) 7, 34-39, 148-62. Models of political organization and behavior within the Evangelical Right are astutely analyzed in Michael Lienesch, "Right-Wing Religion: Christian Conservatism as a Political Movement," *Political Science Quarterly* 97 (1982): 403-25. See also John C. Bennett, "Assessing the Concerns of the Religious Right," *Christian Century*, 14 October 1981, 1018-22.

callused hands, or meet a payroll, or run a business in a maze of entangling government regulations, persistently skew the news toward the interests of a liberal welfare state. More insidious is television entertainment. In the world of the soap opera and sitcom, the mores of Hollywood parade as the mores of middle America. Sex, as columnist Dick Dabney has noted, usually is extramarital and God frequently is an epithet or an anthropological reference to a being still believed in through some parts of the South. Religious conviction emerges as fanaticism, self-discipline as prudery, and sharing one's faith as zealotry. Conservative Christians end up as hayseeds who think Bach is a beer and Haydn a quarterback for the Rams.[19]

The Evangelical Right has a point. Donald E. Wildmon, leader of the Coalition for Better Television, justifiably complains that millions of Americans profess Christianity, pray before meals, and every Sunday morning pack up the kids for church, but never are these scenes enacted on television. According to one study, in a given testing period ninety-four percent of the references to sexual intercourse on daytime soap operas involved unmarried partners. Indeed, many so-called secularists would agree with television critic Ben Stein's judgment that TV "lowers educational achievement, encourages violence, generates lassitude, and paints a wildly untrue and distorted picture of American life."[20]

Still more serious, in the mind of the Evangelical Right, is the fact that America's educational institutions are harming the souls of its youth. Several issues are involved here. Most obvious is the growing commitment in high schools and colleges—including church colleges—to the use of critical, historical, and empirical methods in the humanities and behavioral sciences. The result, inevitably, has been a greater willingness by students as well as teachers to reexamine inherited traditions. Incompe-

---

[19]The Evangelical Right's perceptions of the media: Falwell, *Listen, America!*, 104, 117, 164-70; LaHaye, *Battle for the Mind*, 147-48; Nick Thimmesch, "Lear," *Moral Majority Report*, 20 July 1981, 7; William A. Henry III, "Another Kind of Ratings War," *Time*, 6 July 1981, 17-20. See Hadden, "Soul Saving via Video," 610, for a case in point. Dabney, "Network," 35-36.

[20]Donald E. Wildmon, "Let's Get Religion in the Picture," *Christianity Today*, 19 February 1982, 11. University study: Eliot Kaplan, "The Dirt on Soaps," *Family Weekly*, 11 October 1981, 30. Ben Stein, "The War to Clean Up TV," *Saturday Review*, February 1981, 23-27.

tent teachers, classroom crime, and peer domination are not new. What is new is the assumption that nothing is assumable. And this is the heart of what the Evangelical Right means by secular humanism: a determination to question moral truths that the Bible and great men of all ages have never dreamed of doubting. But secular humanism does not stop there. A series of pamphlets published by Bob Jones University on Christian scholarship (*The Christian Teaching of English, The Christian Teaching of History*, and so forth) accordingly charges that "modern unbelief in the possibility of being sure about anything produces an attitude of relativism in interpreting and evaluating literature." The final product of this "irresponsible and pernicious" tendency is the notion that "all interpretations are equally valid, that there are no right or wrong interpretations." Thus what secular humanism boils down to, argues Francis Schaeffer, who probably qualifies as the official intellectual of the Evangelical Right, is "the absolute insistence that there is no absolute."[21]

Less obvious but equally nettlesome to the Evangelical Right is what it perceives as the fraudulence of public education. One of the clearest manifestations is the perennial mediocrity of the public schools, a mediocrity perpetuated by intellectual laziness in professional schools of education. Within the movement is a deep suspicion that its children are being shortchanged with the jargon of "interpersonal dynamics" and "self-image enhancement" rather than, as one partisan bitterly put it, the "substance of scholarship . . . history, long division, and Spanish." Closely related is a perception that social science textbooks and supplementary reading texts in history and English make extraordinary efforts to legitimate the values of urban Jews, alienated intellectuals, militant blacks, radical feminists—everyone, in short, except the millions of lower middle-class whites whose taxes support the schools. The Evangelical Right is acutely aware that in these books, as elsewhere, the only ethnic

---

[21]Bob Jones University pamphlets quoted in Wray Herbert, "Fundamentalism vs. Humanism," *Humanities Report*, September 1981, 8. Francis Schaeffer, *How Should We Then Live?* (1976), 217, quoted in Whitehead and Conlan, "Establishment . . . of Secular Humanism," 61. For secular humanism as the denial of moral absolutes in the schools, see Falwell, *Listen, America!*, 15; LaHaye, *Battle for the Mind*, 57; Onalee McGraw, *Secular Humanism and the Schools* (Washington DC: Heritage Foundation, 1976) 4-7; David Cook, *Christianity Confronts Communism, Humanism, Materialism, Existentialism* (Wheaton IL: Tyndale House, rpt. 1981 [1979]) ch. 4; Kenneth L. Woodward, "The Right's New Bogeyman," *Newsweek*, 6 July 1981, 48-50.

stereotype one can freely use as a slur is WASP or redneck. "In all their exoduses and liberation plots," complained one such WASP, "I'm the Pharaoh."[22]

To partisans of the Evangelical Right a still more pernicious deception is the claim that modern education is value-free when it is perfectly clear to them that it is not. Sex education is a good example. The movement is not, as a rule, opposed to human reproduction education in a biology class. What it resists is sex education in a health or ethics class where behavior traditionally considered immoral is portrayed in ostensibly value-free terms as normal or, at worst, unusual. Seventh-grade textbooks, which suggest that from a cross-cultural perspective conventional Christian sexual ethics are "irregular," or textbooks that describe homosexuality, incest, masochism, and nymphomania with the clinical impartiality of a survey of table manners, are constant reminders to the Evangelical Right that public education is anything but value-free. Another irritant is the omnipresence of the evolutionary hypothesis in high school and college textbooks. Although leaders of the Evangelical Right bravely maintain that creation is scientifically credible, the real thrust of their argument is the contention that evolution, no less than creation, presupposes a particular metaphysical position. It is simply disingenuous, they insist, to purport that methodological agnosticism has no relation to substantive agnosticism. They admit that there may be an analytic distinction between the how and the why, between process and meaning; but for actual human beings, and especially for honest adolescents, these issues are not easily separated. In this regard, the honest outsider can hardly disagree. When leading scientists like Carl Sagan and Theodosius Dobzhansky boast on television and in popular magazines that evolutionary

---

[22]Mediocrity of schools: quotation from Falwell, *Listen, America!*, 184; Walter E. Williams, "Public Schools Promote Mediocrity," *Moral Majority Report*, 21 September 1981, 14; Curtis Seltzer, "West Virginia Book War: A Confusion of Goals," *Nation*, 2 November 1974, 432. For a similar critique by a nonpartisan, see Joseph Adelson, "What Happened to the Schools," *Commentary*, March 1981, 36-41. WASP values excluded: quotation from Martin E. Marty, *Context*, 15 July 1980, excerpted in Shriver, *Bible Vote*, 39-40; Seltzer, "Book War"; Cal Thomas, "California Tries for Traditional Values," *Moral Majority Report*, 20 July 1981, 11; Blair Adams and Joel Stein, advertising prospectus for *Education as Religious War: A Historical Perspective of the Role of Education in the Paganizing of America* (Grand Junction CO: Truth Forum, 1981) 5. I am indebted to Jim W. Jones of the Fort Worth *Star Telegram* for leading me to these materials and for discussion of this issue.

cosmology *is* the metaphysics of the modern world, we are reminded that science and religion mix all too well.[23]

So in the eyes of the Evangelical Right the nation's schools grievously threaten Christian Civilization. Secular humanism permeates instructional content and fraudulence twists instructional method. However, that is not the worst of it. The schools are infected by a disease more difficult to extirpate because it is more difficult to pin down. It afflicts the nation as a whole but shows up most clearly in the educational system. This disease is America's inability to produce great men and great leaders of men. Thus Jerry Falwell characteristically warns that the United States is facing a "vacuum of leadership," especially by men. The lack of "male leadership in our families is affecting male leadership in our churches, and it is affecting male leadership in our society." To persons like Falwell it is clear that, along with drugs that cloud the mind and secular humanism that rots the soul, America's youth have been saturated with social attitudes that soften the backbone. They have grown up in a society "void of discipline and character-building," an environment that teaches them "to believe that the world owes them a living whether they work or not."[24]

This deep-running fear of moral weakness is the key to understanding the rapid growth of the manliness syndrome in the academies and colleges of the Evangelical Right—the high premium placed upon "hard-hitting"

------

[23]For deceptions in sex education, see Duncan, *Secular Humanism*, 21-24; Falwell, *Listen, America!*, 122-27, 179; LaHaye, *Battle for the Mind*, 212; Reo M. Christenson, "Clarifying 'Values Clarification' for the Innocent," *Christianity Today*, 10 April 1981, 501-504; James Robison, *Attack on the Family* (Wheaton IL: Tyndale House, 1980) 87-97; and the series of articles in *Moral Majority Report*, 18 May 1981, 7. For teaching of evolution, see Whitehead and Conlan, "Establishment . . . of Secular Humanism," 47-57; LaHaye, *Battle for the Mind*, 60-68; transcript of nationally televised debate between Duane Gish, Institute for Creation Research, and Russell F. Doolittle, Department of Chemistry, UC San Diego, at Liberty Baptist College, Lynchburg VA, 13 October 1981. Theodosius Dobzhansky, "Changing Man," *Science*, 27 January 1967, 409-15. For the cultural significance of creationism, see the excellent analyses by Dorothy Nelkin, "The Science-Textbook Controversies," *Scientific American*, April 1976, 39, and Ronald L. Numbers, "Creationism in 20th-Century America," *Science* 218 (1982): 538-44. More generally, see Charles S. Blinderman, "Unnatural Selection: Creationism and Evolutionism," *Journal of Church and State* 24 (1982): 73-86.

[24]Falwell, *Listen, America!*, 15-16. See also Robison, *Attack on the Family*, 21-32. For a larger perspective on the underlying issue, see Leonard I. Sweet, "The Epic of Billy Graham," *Theology Today* 37 (1980): 90-92.

sermons, short haircuts, cold showers, and winning (not just competing) in rigorous contact sports. In a milieu in which born-again generals and professional athletes are not so much admired as venerated, it is understandable that Falwell would assure his hearers that Jesus was "not a sissy"; that the monthly *Christian Athlete* would headline "Jesus the Competitor"; or that Concerned Women for America would excoriate gender-integrated gym classes where boys, who formerly played basketball and football, "are now having dancing, instead."[25]

The symbols are ludicrous but the underlying concerns are not. The literature of the Evangelical Right often resembles the old-fashioned jeremiad. Some of it, such as the materials published by Rus Walton's Plymouth Rock Foundation, is fiercely ideological. Yet books like Francis Schaeffer's *A Christian Manifesto*, John W. Whitehead's *The Second American Revolution*, or Peter Marshall and David Manuel's *The Light and the Glory*, all of which try to prove that America has strayed from its Protestant origins, reflect deep bewilderment about the reasons for the faltering of the American dream. They convey the hurt of disillusioned love for America as much as they expose the naiveté of the movement's understanding of early American history. But once again, the Evangelical Right is not alone. Critics who are not naive have discerned similar shadows: for social historian Christopher Lasch, it is the culture of narcissism; for intellectual historian Robert Nisbet, it is the twilight of authority; for cultural historian Giles Gunn, it is the myth of historical entitlement; for sociologist Daniel Bell, it is the presumption of economic entitlement; for journalist Lance Morrow, it is the illusion of the discontinuous self. For all of these writers, something has gone terribly wrong. An earthquake seems to have buckled the spiritual landscape so that moral accountability has shifted from the individual to society in every part of modern life.[26]

---

[25]For the manliness syndrome, see FitzGerald, "A Disciplined, Charging Army," 78, 96; Quebedeaux, *Worldly Evangelicals*, 74-76, and *By What Authority*, 8-9; Jerry Sholes, *Give Me that Prime-Time Religion: An Insider's Report on the Oral Roberts Evangelistic Association* (New York: Hawthorn Books, 1979). Falwell quoted in "Politicizing the Word," *Time*, 1 October 1979, 68. *Christian Athlete* quoted in James R. Goff, Jr., "The Role of Sports in Evangelical Religion," (senior seminar paper, Duke University Divinity School, April 1981). Concerned women quoted in LaHaye, *Battle for the Mind*, 151.

[26]Plymouth Rock Foundation book lists, "FAC-Sheets," cassettes, etc., Marlborough NH 03455. Best known is Rus Walton's *One Nation Under God*. Francis Schaeffer, *A Christian Manifesto* (Westchester IL: Crossway Books, 1981). John W. Whitehead, *The Second American Revolution* (Elgin IL: David C. Cook, 1982). Marshall and Manuel, *The Light and the Glory*. For a thoughtful critique of this outlook, see Ronald A. Wells, "Fran-

In the perspective of the Evangelical Right, though, the arbiters of contemporary culture who pose the most deadly threat to Christian Civilization are not media folk, nor educators, but the enemies of the traditional, patriarchal, nuclear family. What the historian sees as a cluster of closely related cultural changes, the Evangelical Right experiences as a finely tuned conspiracy, coordinated by a master blueprint of international scope. To the members of the Evangelical Right, the *Attack on the Family*, as James Robison describes it, or *The Battle for the Family*, as Tim LaHaye describes it, is so perfectly orchestrated it could not be anything except the handiwork of the Antichrist.[27] The leaders of the movement consider the general loosening of sexual restraints the most conspicuous manifestation of the Antichrist's determination to destroy the family. And it has been conspicuously successful too. No-fault divorce, abortion-on-demand, civil rights for homosexuals, and sexual freedom for teenagers seem to them to have become staples of American life. They point to polls that show a million couples living together and two-thirds of the population cheerfully winking at such arrangements. Across the land, Tim LaHaye grouses, secular humanists have opened the floodgates to "adultery, fornication, perversion, abomination, and just plain *sin.*" When it is clear that humanists are determined to crush "every vestige of the responsible, moral behavior that distinguished man from animals," he asks, is it surprising that a movement like the Evangelical Right has come into existence to take a stand for old-fashioned family values?[28]

---

cis Schaeffer's Jeremiad," *Reform Journal*, May 1982, 16-20. Christopher Lasch, *The Culture of Narcissism: American Life in an Age of Diminishing Expectations* (New York: W. W. Norton, 1978); Robert A. Nisbet, *The Twilight of Authority* (New York: Oxford, 1975); Giles Gunn, *New World Metaphysics*, 405; Daniel Bell discussed without citation in Martin E. Marty, *The Public Church: Mainline-Evangelical-Catholic* (New York: Crossroad, 1981) 29; Lance Morrow, "What Does an Oath Mean?" *Time*, 24 August 1981, 70. More generally, see Godfrey Hodgson, *America in Our Time: From World War II to Nixon* (New York: Random House, 1976).

[27]Perception of international antifamily conspiracy: LaHaye, *Battle for the Mind*, 110, 143-44; Robison, *Attack on the Family*, 7; Falwell, *Listen, America!*, 112-16; David A. Noebel, *Rock 'n Roll: A Prerevolutionary Form of Cultural Subversion* (Manitou Springs CO: Summit Ministries, 1980). Virtually every concern of the Evangelical Right is exhibited in Tim LaHaye's *The Battle for the Family* (Old Tappan NJ: Revell, 1982). The vituperativeness of this volume is reminiscent of the publications of Gerald L. K. Smith and Gerald Winrod in the 1930s.

[28]For changing sexual mores, see Yankelovich, *New Rules*, 93-96, and "Black and White, Unwed All Over," *Time*, 9 November 1981, 67. LaHaye, *Battle for the Mind*, 64-65.

Perhaps not, but many observers do find it surprising that the Evangelical Right should exhibit such fascination with the sexual revolution. Its fear of homosexuals, its preoccupation with the dangers of pornography, its misperception of rape as an act of lust rather than violence, its racially tinged opposition to birth-control clinics and over-the-counter sales of birth-control devices, and above all, its appetite for sex manuals for Christian couples, suggest that the new liberation stirs a murky well of libidinous fears and passions within the movement as much as it violates the rules of comportment in Christian Civilization.[29]

In addition to the so-called sexual revolution, the Evangelical Right sees a general threat to the family in feminism, and a very particular threat in the inevitable rebirth of the Equal Rights Amendment. Feminism arouses a storm of fear within the Evangelical Right, which outsiders find difficult to understand, much less take seriously. Although the causes of the fear are complex, historians Donald G. and Jane DeHart Mathews have persuasively argued that much of it grows from distrust of the deregulated adult male. In its heart of hearts, they note, the Evangelical Right believes that feminism will liberate men rather than women from conventional expectations. Under all the noisy rhetoric about states' rights and unisex toilets runs a silent but desperately serious question: If the adult male is no longer compelled by law to protect and provide for his family, is there any reason to believe that he will corral his marauding impulses?[30] Thus evangelical antifeminists like James Robison firmly believe that the feminist movement will inevitably turn women into "objects for exploi-

---

[29]The Evangelical Right's preoccupation with sexual issues is particularly evident in LaHaye's *Battle for the Family* and Robison's *Attack on the Family*. See also any issue of *Moral Majority Report*, particularly the issue of 20 July 1981. For analysis of homosexuality and the Evangelical Right, see Quebedeaux, *Worldly Evangelicals*, 128-31; Robert K. Johnston, *Evangelicals at an Impasse: Biblical Authority in Practice* (Atlanta: John Knox Press, 1979) ch. 5; Tom Minnery, "Homosexuals Can Change," *Christianity Today*, 6 February 1981, 172-77. More broadly, see Quebedeaux, *Worldly Evangelicals*, 77-78, 126-28; Robert M. Price, "Ye Must Be Porn Again (Some Trends in Evangelical Books on Sex)," *Wittenburg Door*, April-May 1981, 28-30.

[30]Donald G. Mathews and Jane DeHart Mathews, "The Cultural Politics of ERA's Defeat," *OAH Newsletter*, November 1982, 13-15. See also George Gilder, interview, *Playboy*, August 1981, 94.

tation or . . . resources to be 'used.'" Nowhere are their fears and frustrations more revealingly focused than in a provision of the proposed Family Protection Act of 1981 that *requires* overseas military personnel to send a prescribed portion of their paychecks home to their spouses each month. Indeed, journalist Frances FitzGerald concluded, after an extended visit to Jerry Falwell's Thomas Road Baptist Church in Lynchburg, Virginia, that women might well have invented the church.

> The prohibitions [mainly] fall on traditional male vices such as drinking, smoking, running around, and paying no heed to the children. To tell "Dad" that he made all the decisions would be a small price to pay to get the father of your children to become a respectable middle class citizen.[31]

Even so, the most lethal threat to the family, in the judgment of the Evangelical Right, is neither the sexual revolution nor feminism, but the awful truth that the established institutions of American society have determined to keep parents from controlling the values of their adolescent children. Although the television evangelists are usually too upbeat to say it explicitly, the literature of the movement leaves a haunting impression that the rawest nerve of all is parents' fear that their kids will grow up to scorn them. A prospectus advertising Blair Adams and Joel Stein's three-volume history of American education—significantly entitled *Education as Religious War: A Historical Perspective on the Paganizing of America*—articulates the brokenheartedness that shadows countless articles and letters-to-the-editor.

> Millions of parents know the sadness and despair of rejection by the offspring of their own loins. Their children either openly or secretly hold their ideas in contempt. . . . Parents . . . see their children drawn into a whole culture, or rather anticulture, which the parents recognize to be destructive and harmful. Yet there seems to be nothing that they can do.[32]

---

[31]Robison, *Attack on the Family*, 23. Family Protection Act discussed in Deryl M. Edwards, "Jepsen, Laxalt, Smith Say Americans Want to Strengthen Family," *Moral Majority Report*, 20 July 1981, 10. FitzGerald, "A Disciplined, Charging Army," 74. See also Phyllis Shlafly, "How to Clean Up America," in Falwell, *Clean Up America*, 24.

[32]Falwell, *Listen, America!*, 78; LaHaye, *Battle for the Mind*, 64; Robison, *Attack on the Family*, 133; Adams and Stein, *Education as Religious War*, 1, 3. Discussions of sexual permissiveness are almost always framed in terms of teenage, not adult, deviance from traditional norms. For one of countless examples, see Glen C. Griffin, "Children . . . Being Rocked by Audio Pornography," *Moral Majority Report*, 20 April 1981, 15.

Ironically, the Evangelical Right has no qualms about using these same established institutions—notably schools and government—to reinforce the authority of the family. One of the principal aims of the Family Protection Act, for example, is to buttress by force of civil law parents' ability to oversee the lives and values of their adolescent children. Nonetheless, for countless parents desperate measures are needed in desperate times. In the final analysis, the force that really propels the Evangelical Right is not the preachers, not the bankrollers, and certainly not the hucksters. Rather, it is the ordinary mothers and fathers who believe, as columnist Dick Dabney has phrased it, that America is gripped by a disease that has "undermined the character of the young" by teaching children that they are animals and thus "justified in living as amorally as animals." In the minds of these angry, bewildered parents, it is an "inward philosophical disease . . . that [has] gone down so deep into the nation's bones that it would take some kind of miracle to cure it."[33]

Intergenerational conflict is not new. But two factors do seem to have made the current situation peculiar, if not unique, in American history. One is the ambivalence Americans have come to feel toward some of their most basic values. Polls show that on some issues, such as premarital celibacy, attitudes fundamentally changed in the 1960s and 1970s, while on others, such as marital chastity and the normativeness of the traditional family unit, there was little alteration. Thus the apparent tension between generations is to some extent a tension within generations and, undoubtedly, within individuals as well. The other factor is that there is a large measure of truth in the Evangelical Right's charge that the "reality-defining agencies" of contemporary society are committed to a scientific and historical—or what they call a secular humanistic—view of life. The grip of the scientific and historical world view is symbolized by *United States v. Seeger*. In this 1965 decision the United States Supreme Court ruled that even though a person may be an atheist in the ordinary meaning of the term, a belief held by that person may be considered religious, and thus constitutionally protected, if it "occupies a place in the life of its pos-

---

[33]Dabney, "God's . . . Network," 35. See also James M. Wall, "What Future for the New Right?" *Christian Century*, 25 November 1981, 1219-20, and more broadly, Christopher Lasch, *Haven in a Heartless World: The Family Besieged* (New York: Basic Books, 1979).

sessor parallel to that filled by the orthodox belief in God." One need not be a partisan of the Evangelical Right in order to see that when one of the main "reality-defining agencies" of modern life finds it more useful to write about religion in functional rather than in substantive terms, something akin to a cultural continental divide has been crossed within our lifetime.[34]

These, then, are the forces which, in the eyes of the Evangelical Right, have conspired to destroy Christian Civilization: the media, the schools, the foes of the family. Still, an important question remains. Why are Evangelicals so powerfully attracted to the Christian Civilization ideal in the first place? Although many Catholics, Mormons, Jews, and others are sympathetic, the real loyalists are the Evangelicals. Yet if Evangelicalism is essentially a religious and theological system, why are Evangelicals so prone to identify their faith with a social ideal so firmly rooted in Victorian middle-class culture?

Historical reasons first come to mind. The simplest and in some ways most compelling answer is that Victorian culture is ineradicably encoded in the genes of evangelical religion. Since the late 1950s, when professional historians started seriously to explore the evangelical tradition, it has been increasingly evident that Evangelicals perennially have felt an irresistible attraction to the early-to-mid-nineteenth-century milieu in which they were born. Of course, American Protestants have always been inclined to identify God's purposes with American destiny. But scholars like Ernest Lee Tuveson and Robert Handy have convincingly shown that Evangelicals have often gone much further, identifying God's purposes with *evangelical* destiny, and both of these with a particular stage in the development of American culture.[35] Beyond this, from the 1830s (if not earlier) through the 1930s, Evangelicals were strongly disposed to

---

[34]For value ambivalences, see Yankelovich, *New Rules*, 93-96, 103, and Gallup and Polling, *America's Faith*, 43-44. For "reality defining agencies" and the Seeger decision, see Whitehead and Conlan, "Establishment . . . of Secular Humanism," 1, n. 5, 13-14.

[35]Ernest Lee Tuveson, *Redeemer Nation: The Idea of America's Millennial Role* (Chicago: University of Chicago Press, 1968) ch. 5. Robert T. Handy, *A Christian America: Protestant Hopes and Historical Realities* (New York: Oxford, 1971) chs. 3-4. See also Marsden, *Fundamentalism*, ch. 3 and 204-205; and, for cross-cultural perspective, Hartmut Lehmann, "Piety and Nationalism: The Relationship of Protestant Revivalism and National Renewal in Nineteenth Century Germany," *Church History* 51 (1982): 39-53.

consider themselves the moral custodians of the culture. The antislavery and temperance crusades on both sides of the Atlantic are proof enough of that. But the more important point, as major studies like Paul Boyer's examination of urban reform or George Marsden's exploration of fundamentalist origins amply demonstrate, is that Evangelicals considered themselves the moral custodians of the culture in direct proportion to the degree that they felt alienated from it. As they felt less and less at home, they struggled with greater determination to make America safe for Christian Civilization. In the long perspective of nineteenth- and twentieth-century history, the spectacle of contemporary Evangelicals leaping into the public arena is not a bit curious. What is curious is the relative quiet of the 1940s and 1950s.[36]

There are also sociological reasons why Evangelicals have been eager to lead the crusade for Christian Civilization. Here we have to be unusually careful. There is no question that Evangelicals *tend* to fall into the lower middle class and *tend* to vote as WASPS ordinarily vote. Despite the general accuracy of this categorization, there are many exceptions. The large bloc of black Evangelicals, the relatively rapid vertical mobility of blue-collar Evangelicals, the liberal-to-radical politics of "new" or "young" Evangelicals and old-line pacifist Evangelicals are only a few of the problems that defy the conventional sociological categorizations.[37]

---

[36]Marsden, *Fundamentalism*, and Paul Boyer, *Urban Masses and Moral Order in America, 1820-1920* (Cambridge MA: Harvard University Press, 1978). See also Richard V. Pierard, *The Unequal Yoke: Evangelical Christianity and Political Conservatism* (Philadelphia: Lippincott, 1970), and James Fulton Maclear, " 'The True American Union' of Church and State: The Reconstruction of the Theocratic Tradition," *Church History* 28 (1959): 53-59.

[37]For the social position, cultural attitudes, and political habits of Evangelicals in general, see the summary of the literature in John Wilson, *Religion in American Society: The Effective Presence* (Englewood Cliffs NJ: Prentice-Hall, 1978) 349-53. For the extraordinary complications involved in constructing a social-cultural-political profile of the typical Evangelical, see John Stephen Hendricks, "Religious and Political Fundamentalism: The Links between Alienation and Ideology," (Ph.D. diss., University of Michigan, 1977) summarized in ch. 7. For a close-grained profile of evangelical voting behavior in the 1980 general election that also underscores the risk of sociological generalizations, see Seymour Martin Lipset and Earl Raab, "The Election and the Evangelicals," *Commentary*, March 1981, 25-31, and George Gallup, "Evangelicals Not Monolithic in Views on Key Issues," reprinted in Chapel Hill *Newspaper*, 8 September 1980, 2B. See also Gallup, "Overview," *Christianity Today*, 1671-72.

However, scholars as diverse as Peter Berger, Daniel Patrick Moynihan, and Martin E. Marty have discerned in American society the outline of a group that goes by various names, but is often called the New Class. The New Class, they argue, is composed of persons who procure information, exchange ideas, and manipulate the organs of communication—in short, writers, artists, intellectuals, teachers, professors, bureaucrats, advertisers, and so forth. The New Class is, in other words, the class that generates the symbols that define social reality. The Old Class, in contrast, is composed of persons who produce, market, and maintain goods and services—farmers, blue-collar workers, technicians, business people, sales people, and many in the service professions. Clearly the New Class, which pretty much coincides with the ascribed enemies of Christian Civilization, has a vested interest in the preservation of what might be called modern civilization: a strong welfare state and absence of restraint in matters of thought, communication, and life-style. The Old Class, which embraces most Evangelicals, just as clearly has a vested interest in the preservation of Christian Civilization: a strong concern for the cultivation of morality and absence of restraint in matters of economic exchange.[38]

Finally, there are cultural reasons why Evangelicals are so powerfully attracted to the Victorian values embodied in the Christian Civilization ideal. Nostalgia is a big part of it. Norman Rockwell's America probably never existed, but until the 1960s it was reasonable to suppose that it might have. Then everything went wrong. Small towns, summer nights, and stable values became not so much an elusive memory as a bitter hoax. By 1970 a leading historian of American religion could plausibly assert that the nation had passed into a "post-Puritan, post-Protestant, post-Christian, post-modern and even post-historical" era. And for many thoughtful Americans, he later judged, the dominant feeling had come to be, in Yeats's words, "all coherence gone."[39]

---

[38]See the articles (esp. that by Peter Berger) in *The New Class?*, ed. B. Bruce-Briggs (New Brunswick NJ: Transaction Books, 1979). See also Martin E. Marty, "Interpreting American Pluralism," in Carroll et al., *Religion in America*, 89; James Davison Hunter, "The New Class and the Young Evangelicals," *Review of Religious Research* 22 (1980): 155-69; Robert Wuthnow, "The Current Moral Climate," *Theology Today* 36 (1979): 249-50.

[39]See, for example, Richard L. McCormick, "Ethno-Cultural Interpretations of Nineteenth-Century Voting Behavior," *Political Science Quarterly* 89 (1974): 351-77. Quotations from Sydney E. Ahlstrom, "The Radical Turn in Theology and Ethics: Why

Still, the arteries that link Evangelicalism and the Victorian Christian Civilization ideal run deeper than nostalgia. Here Donald G. and Jane DeHart Mathews's analysis of the continuities between religious and cultural Fundamentalism (which closely correspond to what I have termed theological Evangelicalism on one side and the Evangelical Right on the other) is particularly illuminating. They argue that religious and cultural fundamentalists tend to think in the same way. For both, historical process and cultural pluralism are ignored or denied; social reality is fractured by a Manichean faultline that divides absolute good from absolute evil; and public discourse is structured to avoid moral discriminations, so that abortion and genocide, or nudity and pornography, or honest doubt and destructive criticism, all come out very much the same. Further, what is most important for both, holiness is defined as purity: the maintenance of time-hallowed boundaries. Thus holiness is "keeping distinct the categories of creation." To attack the "anomalies of women-who-want-to-be-men and men-who-refuse-to-be-men, therefore, is part of the process that purges society of its impurities."[40]

Yet having said all this, it is important to remember that the forces that prod Evangelicals to identify with a particular cultural outlook are also the forces that keep Evangelicalism from lapsing into irrelevance. The Evangelical Right represents, in other words, cultural captivity, but it also represents cultural awareness, a genuinely pastoral concern that tradition should still have a place in the modern world. Still more pertinently, it represents an awareness that this age, like all ages, "is standing in the need

---

It Occurred in the 1960s," *Annals of the American Academy of Political and Social Science* 387 (1970): 1-13, reprinted in *Religion in America: Interpretive Essays*, ed. John M. Mulder and John F. Wilson (Englewood Cliffs NJ: Prentice-Hall, 1978) 445, and Ahlstrom, "The Traumatic Years: American Religion and Culture in the '60s and '70s," *Theology Today* 36 (1979): 522.

[40]Mathews, "Cultural Politics." For the interpenetration of religious and cultural symbols, see Joseph Gusfield, *Symbolic Crusade: Status Politics and the American Temperance Movement* (Urbana: University of Illinois Press, rpt. 1969 [1963]), and Giles Gunn, editor's introduction, *New World Metaphysics*. For splitting the world into absolute good or evil, see Marsden, *Fundamentalism*, 223-24, and Luther P. Gerlach and Virginia H. Hine, *People, Power, Change: Movements of Social Transformation* (Indianapolis: Bobbs-Merrill, 1972) ch. 6. For the integral relation between religion and boundaries, see Catherine L. Albanese, *America: Religions and Religion* (Belmont CA: Wadsworth, 1981) 3-5, 12-13. See also Fredrik Barth, *Ethnic Groups and Boundaries: The Social Organization of Culture Difference* (Boston: Little, Brown and Co., 1969).

of prayer.'' The question is whether a message that owes more to the old-fashioned gospel of the nineteenth century than it does to the transforming gospel of the first century will do much good. But grace has always been amazing.

List of Contributors

Henry Warner Bowden is professor of religion at Rutgers University, an editor of two volumes and author of *Church History in the Age of Science*, (1971), *Dictionary of American Religious Biography* (1977), and *Native Americans and Christian Missions: Studies in Cultural Conflicts* (1981), as well as many other essays and reviews.

Jon Butler, associate professor of history at the University of Illinois at Chicago, has contributed articles on early American religious and social history to the *William and Mary Quarterly*, the *Journal of American History*, the *American Historical Review*, and other journals. His most recent book is *The Huguenots in America: A Refugee People in New World Society* (1983).

Joel Carpenter is assistant professor of history at Wheaton College, Wheaton, Illinois. He has published "Fundamentalist Institutions and the Growth of Evangelical Protestantism, 1929-1942," *Church History* (1980).

Nathan O. Hatch is associate professor of history at Notre Dame University. Noted for his publications in *Church History*, *William and Mary Quarterly*, and the *Journal of American History*, as well as for his expertise in organizing successful historical conferences, he is the author of *The Sacred Cause of Liberty: Republican Thought and the Millennium in Revolutionary New England* (1977) and co-editor with Mark A. Noll of *The Bible in American Culture* (1982). He has recently edited with four other historians *Eerdmans' Handbook to Christianity in America* (1983).

Nancy Hewitt is assistant professor of history at the University of South Florida. She currently is under a contract with Cornell University Press for a book entitled *Women's Activism and Social Change: The Case of Rochester, New York, 1822-1872*.

Albert J. Raboteau is the author of the award-winning *Slave Religion: The "Invisible Institution" in the Antebellum South* (1978). A former associate dean at the College of Letters and Sciences at the University of California at Berkeley, he is presently professor of religion at Princeton University.

Garth M. Rosell is vice president for Academic Affairs, Dean of the Faculty and professor of history at Gordon-Conwell Theological Seminary. Focusing attention principally in the field of American religious history, he has published a variety of books, articles, and case studies in that area. He is presently working with Richard A. G. Dupuis on *The Memoirs of Charles Finney: The Complete, Original and Unedited Edition* due to be published during the coming year.

Carroll Smith-Rosenberg is associate professor of history and psychiatry at the University of Pennsylvania. She is the author of *Religion and the Rise of the American City: The New York City Mission Movement, 1812-1870* (1971) as well as some of the most widely quoted articles in the past decade on women's history and sexual ideology.

Leonard I. Sweet is provost and professor of church history at Colgate Rochester Divinity School/Bexley Hall/Crozer Theological Seminary. His books include *Black Images of America, 1784-1870* (1976), and *The Minister's Wife: Her Role in Nineteenth-Century Evangelicalism* (1983). He also serves as pastor of the United Methodist Church of the Resurrection in Rochester, New York, and publishes in the area of ministry and theology, most recently *New Life in the Spirit* (1982) and *A Four-Dimensional Faith* (forthcoming).

Grant Wacker, assistant professor of religion at the University of North Carolina, Chapel Hill, is most widely known for his studies of contemporary American religion. One of his recent articles is "The Dilemmas of Historical Consciousness: The Case of Augustus Hopkins Strong" in Joseph D. Ban and Paul R. Dekar, eds., *In the Great Tradition: In Honor of Winthrop S. Hudson* (1982).

MUP *The Evangelical Tradition in America*

Binding designed by Alesa Jones

Interior typography design by Margaret Jordan Brown

Composition by MUP Composition Department

Production specifications:
    text paper—60 pound Warren's Olde Style
    endpapers—80 pound Caress text printed PMS 100
    cover—(on .088 boards) Holliston Crown Linen 13453
    dust jacket—100 pound enamel printed two colors PMS 518 (purple) and
    PMS 100 (yellow). Varnished.

Printing (offset lithography) by Omnipress of Macon, Inc., Macon, Georgia

Binding by John H. Dekker and Sons, Inc., Grand Rapids, Michigan